Natural Law and Contemporary Public Policy

Natural Law and Contemporary Public Policy

EDITED BY
David F. Forte

GEORGETOWN UNIVERSITY PRESS / WASHINGTON, D.C.

An earlier version of the article *Privacy* by David Novak appeared in the August/September 1997 issue of *First Things*, a monthly journal published in New York City by the Institute on Religion and Public Life.

The opinions expressed in the article *Just War and Defense Policy* by John Hittinger are those of the author and do not represent the view of the United States Air Force or of the United States government.

The article, *Family, Nurture, and Liberty*, by David Forte originally appeared under the title, *Nurture and Natural Law*, in 26 U.C. DAVIS L. REV 691(1993) Copyright 1993 by The Regents of the University of California. Reprinted with permission.

Georgetown University Press, Washington, D.C.

Printed in the United States of America

10 9 8 7 6 5 4 3 2 1 1998

THIS VOLUME IS PRINTED ON ACID-FREE OFFSET BOOK PAPER

Library of Congress Cataloging-in-Publication Data

Natural law and contemporary public policy / edited by David F. Forte.
p. cm.
"The essays in this volume grew out of a conference held at Cleveland–Marshall College of Law, Cleveland State University in April 1996"—P. x.
Includes index.
1. Natural law. 2. Public policy (Law) I. Forte, David F.
K460.N347 1998
340'.112—dc21
ISBN 0-87840-692-1 (cloth) 98-13260

For our children,
and theirs

Contents

Introduction

Ideas have consequences and practice follows theory. There are reasons why government is so paramount in today's American society, and why, at the same time, the social structure is increasingly fractured. These political facts are the fruits of ideas that began in the academy, that were learned by generations of students, and that are applied today by those in power who were so educated.

In the past few decades, a "new" movement has appeared. It is a movement rooted in the ancient classical and medieval philosophies of the West. In dozens of books and hundreds of articles by a new generation of philosophers and political and legal theorists, a renewed voice for the study of the permanent things in life, for the fundamentals in morals, is now heard. Natural law theorists have called upon the deepest traditions of Western civilization to contest the enlightenment and relativistic philosophies that have long been dominant in the academy and in politics. Especially in America, young philosophers have advanced the study of natural law to the point where it is now commonplace to hear of it not only in ordinary philosophy and political science courses in colleges, but also in jurisprudence and constitutional law courses in law schools.

It even pops into legislative consciousness through the now-famous statement of Senator Joseph Biden that there is "good natural law and bad natural law." Political and legal theory has not seen such a flowering of vital natural law philosophy for centuries.

The time is now ripe to take the richness of contemporary natural law theory and apply it to the specific social, political, and constitutional problems of America today. By what standards should government reform welfare? What role should the United States play in securing fundamental rights of peoples not under our jurisdiction? Does progressive taxation violate moral norms, or is it required under the rules of justice? Does the state have any role in securing the integrity of the family, and if so, what kind of family? What is the ultimate purpose of education?

Policy analysts, legislators, teachers, and community leaders need to know what a philosophy that reaches back into the fundamentals of life and existence can illuminate as they search for solutions to problems such as racial discrimination and affirmative action, to questions of medical technology, to issues of tolerance, to the structure of the family, and to the justice of schemes of taxation. In short, many are searching for a principled basis for political reform, one rooted in the verities of one of the most noble traditions of Western civilization.

What follows is not a mere collection of essays around a unifying theme. Rather, the authors of this volume apply natural law principles to specific social problems of today. Its authors include many of the most well-known and well-regarded thinkers of that tradition. Each essay is a refined argument, yet each is an approachable analysis of a current social issue from the perspective of natural law theory.

The reader will notice that the discipline of natural law carries many variants. Some authors can envision an activist role of the government in instantiating natural law norms within society. Others find that the moral flourishing of the individual under the norms of natural law can only occur in a society where private and voluntary associations are the major methods of social organization. In no case does any author provide a "recipe." Instead, each seeks to explore in a practical manner how a respectful concern for the norms of natural law could translate into practical public policy. And being philosophers and commentators of a tradition that holds that there are indeed objective truths obtainable by reason, each contributor invites and expects responses and even disputes from all those who seek the right answers to our common human quest. And that is why this volume includes such a response.

This volume does not fill a niche. It is but an initial attempt to fill a chasm. It begins to satisfy a demand that all philosophies ought to satisfy: how will its principles change people's lives?

Acknowledgments

The essays in this volume grew out of a conference held at Cleveland–Marshall College of Law, Cleveland State University, in April 1996. Generous support was provided by the Earhart Foundation, the Intercollegiate Studies Institute, the Potomac Foundation, and the Cleveland–Marshall Fund. The American Public Philosophy Institute cosponsored the conference.

The professionalism, dedication, and sacrifice by a number of persons made the conference and this volume a reality. They include Sandra Natran, Joan Shirokey, Leon Boyd, Paul Carrington, and Laverne Carter; Financial Officer Victoria Plata; Dean Steven Smith; Director of the Law Library, Professor Michael Slinger; Reference Librarians Ellen Quinn, Laura Ray, and Marie Rehmer; as well as staff librarians Wayne Hogue and Mark Gooch. The completed volume is also due to the research assistance of Joseph Rodgers and the stamina, care, and intelligence of Rita Pawlik.

PART ONE

Natural Law Today

The Natural Law Moment

DAVID F. FORTE

On the day when humanity was first gifted with reason, the natural law moment truly began. On the day that man first felt the ego-tug of his passions, the natural law moment was in danger of passing. The ambivalence of that first day is with us still.

Natural law's metaphysical moment will be with humanity until it passes from the earth. But we live in time and within cultures. Within that essential and permanent identity between natural law and human nature, there are times and places when natural law is consciously part of the human enterprise and others when it is not. Natural lawyers who reflect upon history will judge that where the principles of natural law are rejected, human society and the individuals within it suffer and decline. The degradation of human beings by one another in the twentieth century has been unparalleled. The question natural lawyers ponder is whether a new natural law moment may be upon us. Can we be drawn away from the ideologies that brought the terrors of the recent past and the continued present? Will humans in the West and in the world flourish under a new and conscious acknowledgment of the force of the natural law?

Beginnings

As a philosophical discipline, natural law has been with us since the times of the Greeks, Aristotle in particular. Natural law was made universal by the Stoics, incorporated into the law by the Romans, allied with Christianity, and finally raised to its highest exposition by Aquinas in his scholastic philosophy. But Aquinas did not operate alone. With the revival of Roman law and its systematization by the schools, and the growing influence of the papacy, natural law achieved its dominant cultural moment in the high middle ages. Classical philosophy and Christian doctrine allied in a powerful synthesis, but that synthesis was shattered in the Reformation and with the development of independent scientific inquiry. Protestant theologians found the good solely through the will of God as revealed in His Word, while rationalists forsook natural law thinking as being too close to religion. The

Reformation disparaged Scholasticism. It feared the idolatry of reason and relegated reason to its instrumental uses in accomplishing God's will, but not in its capability of discovering the good. God's law was divine positive law, and no natural law could independently find the good, or worse, could limit God Himself.

The age of Reformation and Rationalism was launched. Faith sought to undo the shackles of reason, while reason tried to free itself of the shackles of religion.

Not that natural law was extinguished at the end of the high middle ages. On the contrary, the cultural force that the alliance of faith and reason had created lasted for centuries. Even though Protestant theology rejected Scholasticism, biblical values paralleled the norms of natural law. Magnanimity was charity, courage was fortitude, fidelity was faithfulness, and community was congregation. For their part, scientific philosophers in their own way tracked the system of the scholastics by discerning a clearer order to nature. They did not relegate the visible world to the flux and chaos of the Sophists.

Thus, although few philosophers "did" natural law from the fourteenth century on, most traded on its fundamental norms. Sir Edward Coke found natural justice to be "right reason," which was the basis of the common law. John Locke presumed those norms to be in the law of nature which both limited and gave legitimacy to individual liberty. When international politics degenerated into self-interested discord, Grotius, Pufendorf, and Vattel sought to revive a modified natural law to restore some moral order to the relations between states.

It is true that on the purely rationalist level, Descartes seemed to try to leave nature and reality behind. But then came Emmanuel Kant, who, in the realm of reason alone, erected a fortress which neither solipsism nor skepticism has been able to breach.

But on the ground, so to speak, natural law norms continued to provide a basis for all kinds of philosophical and political enterprises. In the most astounding synthesis of all, the framers of the American constitutional experiment melded classical political theory, natural law moral norms, liberal conceptions of individual rights, the pragmatic lessons of the eighteenth-century utilitarians, a Protestant belief in a providential God, and the normative values of the common law into a polity that was complex, balanced, and elegant.

By the end of the eighteenth century, however, the cultural heritage of the natural law was becoming more and more attenuated. A new synthesis arose, drawn from the estrangement of faith and reason of centuries before.

In its own way, the conceit of Catholic scholasticism had let loose rationalism, and the obeisance to the will of God by the Protestants had let loose positivism. And in the nineteenth century, when rationalism and positivism each became unconstrained by religion or revelation, they merged. Extraordinary philosophical constructs arose, the wages of whose experiments we have paid in body count in the twentieth century. It is not much of an exaggeration to say that the problems of politics since the nineteenth century lay in the contest between the supposedly self-sufficient power of the state on the one hand and the supposedly self-sufficient power of the individual on the other. The higher law that tames both was absent.

But what of natural law in all of this? For the most part, natural law had ceased to be a philosophical discipline. There were some exceptions, Duguit in France, for example. But they are names hardly any of us know, or need to know (save for academic specialists), for they did not constitute an ongoing conversation within a philosophical discipline. Natural law devolved to become a part of the intellectual life of the Catholic Church, sounding warnings of approaching disaster, but not achieving a momentum of its own.

Its continuing association with the Catholic Church, of course, only brought it to even greater disdain. A character in Stendahl declares, "There's no such thing as natural law. This expression is nothing but old nonsense." (This paralleled Holmes's view of the common law as a "brooding omnipresence in the sky," and Bentham's castigation of natural rights as "nonsense on stilts.")

A lot of "old nonsense" was done away with in Fichte, Hegel, Marx, Austin, Bentham, and Holmes. It was not until the aftermath of World War II, in confronting the Holocaust, that natural law stirred again in the conscience of the philosopher and the judge. If the Holocaust was evil, pure and simple, then there must be a good, pure and simple. If we shrink from thinking that the Final Solution could ever have been a valid human law because its purpose was so utterly perverse, there must be a purposive standard by which we can know which laws are indeed legitimate and which are not.

Rebirth of Natural Law

And so the revival began, kindling in different places: Jacques Maritain in France; Russell Kirk in the United States; and the Hart/Fuller debate. By the 1980s, natural law had once again become a philosophical discipline. Dozens of books and hundreds of articles poured out. Natural law philosophers spoke to one another and argued with one another. Approaches to natural law theory developed in competition with one another. Henry Veatch revived an Aristotelian approach to individual rights. John Finnis developed a phenomenological point of departure. Lloyd Weinrib attempted a radical Kantian revision of natural law theory. Natural law theorists engaged in debates and explorations with utilitarians, liberal theorists, natural rights thinkers, and communitarians to the benefit and maturation of each other.

It had been six centuries since we had seen this phenomenon.

What, in sum, are the hallmarks of this natural law school, newly revived, disparate as the approaches within it may be?

I have often heard people say, "I believe in natural law," as if it is some kind of creed. But natural law is not the object of belief. It is a conclusion of the reasoning mind. Faith grants us the truth beyond reason. There, the "I believe" rings out beyond the visible cosmos. Natural law, on the other hand, is bounded by the universe of reason. Whatever may be the truth beyond reason must come from a different source.

Others, on the other hand, think that natural law is a set of values that come to us intuitively. But natural law is not that either. The confusion between intuitionism and natural law often arises because natural lawyers like to speak about self-evident truths, just as the Declaration of Independence did. But "self-evident" does not mean "instantly apprehensible" without thinking. Self-evident truths are not objectivized feelings. They are rational axioms.

Rather, a self-evident truth is one in which a value (knowledge, for example) is seen, upon reflection, as self-evidently good—a good that is not instrumental, not merely a means to some other thing, but something that is good in itself. When reflected upon, knowledge proves its own worth by its very nature. It is a good; it is worthy to be pursued.

If, for example, I impart to you during a conversation something that you did not know before or did not understand in quite the same way, something will "click" in your mind. Your mind will almost automatically embrace or, in a biblical sense, cleave to the new knowledge simply as knowledge. Knowing is, in the experience of the mind, self-evidently good. And that, in its way, is also a natural law moment.

Natural law, then, is not a faith. It is not intuition. Natural law is an entire philosophy, and philosophy is hard work. It takes a deep, disciplined, and thorough philosophy to arrive at the principles of the natural law.

The school of natural law holds that we can reasonably reflect on the nature of the human person, on his relationship with others, on the manner in which he develops, on the purpose of his actions, on his place in scheme of reality, and on the nature of reality itself. We can derive from that certain fundamental moral principles that apply to men and women in their actions and interactions. They are "natural" (from the nature of things) "laws" (rules of behavior). These first principles of right behavior apply most particularly to the human person as a social being, to ourselves as a political community. The obligations of natural law apply to how men and women make human laws and to what those laws are. Both the internal structure of the law and its purpose are concerns of the natural law. In its most famous claim, natural law speaks to the rightness and wrongness of human laws.

Natural law distinguishes between power and authority. Ultimately, natural law finds the freedom of the human individual as rooted in the good, and political authority as contingent upon that human freedom. Natural law not only judges what human laws ought not to be passed, but it also illuminates the benign face of the law; it looks to those laws that ought to be enacted to assist human persons in the flourishing of their free individual personalities. Natural law is not only imperative, it is aspirational.

Finally, natural law speaks to the person as a whole, not divided between mind and body, or engaging in action without purpose. It seeks to locate the good of every person not in the comfort of the senses, but in the flourishing of all one's faculties. And it asserts that an individual can only truly flourish when individuality is realized through moral action.

Practical Application

Modern natural law has reached a point of maturity where the application of its principles to the particular problems of political society is ripe.

Are we then in the midst of another cultural natural law moment? Perhaps some of the applications of natural law to our present social malaise may advance the prospect, but we are hardly there yet. Let's be realistic. Natural law respects reality.

The dominant movement in current intellectual life is deconstructionism, an ancient skepticism dressed up in modern linguistic form. Like Sophism, deconstructionism holds that there is no overriding truth outside of the individual's own subjective preferences. Reality is only the extension of one's will-directed construction of one's own universe. Or, as the Supreme Court opines, "At the heart of liberty is the right to define one's own concept of existence, of meaning, of the universe, and of the mystery of human life."[1] Deconstructionism promises only the realm of privacy for the untrammeled exercise of one's will. At bottom, it connects no person with any other. I believe further that it connects no person with himself, and that it leaves one on the edge of the abyss of nihilism.

In contrast, natural lawyers claim that morality is not so much to be defined as to be discovered; reality is not created but apprehended.

When a philosophy (even one like natural law) is in the ascendancy, intellectual fatigue and impatience with the imperfections of any human system slowly bring on criticism and perhaps even rejection. But when order threatens to break down altogether, then the mind reaches back to the stability of principle. Humanity cannot abide error for too long, for error produces a disintegration, a disorder of the soul, and a disorder of society. We can live a complex life; we can live a life of contradictions; but we cannot live an absurd life. That is our nature. And that is why a modern natural law moment is needed.

Whenever the choice of subjective relativism and objective truth have come into contest, whenever the choice is one or the other, man will ultimately opt for the truth, no matter how discomfiting it may be. Just look at whom we choose for heroes.

> Is it Antigone or Creon?
> Socrates or Alcibiades?
> Is it Ruth who embraces the One God despite the humiliation it brings, or her sister-in-law Orpah, who remains comfortable with the pagans?
> Is it Lincoln or Douglas?
> Solzhenitzen or Breznev?
> Jesus or Pilate?

How we will know when natural law's cultural moment has returned, when the search for moral and practical truths is not disdained but pursued with passion? Perhaps the wisdom of Jack Benny may be a guide. Many decades ago Jack Benny had a radio show in which he pretended to be forever thirty nine years old; he also pretended to be the world's stingiest tightwad. In one radio skit, Jack is walking alone at night in an unsavory neighborhood when he is confronted by an armed robber. "Your money or your life!" the robber rasps. There is a long radio pause. "I said, 'Your money or your life!'" the robber repeats. Another pause. Finally Benny exclaims: "I'm thinking! I'm thinking!"

We find Jack Benny's answer funny because of the absurdity of comparing a wallet of dollars to the inestimable value of his life. Unless we know life to be a higher value, the situation isn't funny. Nobody listening to Jack

Benny's mock concern for his money nodded gravely and said, "Well, of course, that's his choice."

It is also humorous because we know that Jack Benny is really kidding. After all, if such a person were seriously measuring his money against his life (and we've heard of some instances where that has happened), we would say that he was foolish, or crazy, or impulsive, or stupid. But if he were serious about it, it would not be funny.

Today we hear not "Your money or your life," but "My money or your life," "My convenience or your life," "My career or your life," "My comfort or your life," and it is distinctly unfunny.

When then will we know that a new natural law moment is with us?

Perhaps we shall know that natural law's cultural moment has returned when we can laugh again, when on hearing someone say, "My money or your life," we know that, like Jack Benny, it's only a joke.

NOTE

1. Planned Parenthood of Southeastern Pennsylvania v. Casey, 112 S.Ct. 2791, 2807 (1992).

PART TWO

Natural Law and the Individual

Privacy

David Novak

The Issue of Privacy for Contemporary Natural Law Theory

Even among themselves, contemporary natural law theorists are divided over the issue of privacy. The issue of privacy has both positive and negative connotations for those of us engaged in natural law theory at this point in history. These connotations have to be sorted out in order for any natural law theorist to be able to develop a coherent approach to the whole issue.

Totalitarianism

On the one hand, the issue of privacy is one that affects many natural law theorists positively. Many of us recognize that the greatest historical stimulus to reflection on natural law here and now has probably been the experience of political totalitarianism in this soon-to-be-concluded century. Surely, a significant part of that experience has been the total disregard for human privacy evidenced by totalitarian regimes, whether Fascist or Communist. Areas that have traditionally been regarded as outside the public control of the state, such as the intimacies of religious life, family life, and friendship, have been regularly and systematically invaded and almost destroyed by recent totalitarian regimes.

The hallmark of all of these regimes has been their total denial of truth as that which transcends all human invention and to which, therefore, all human invention is answerable. In such regimes, everything is answerable to the immanent power of the state and its authorities. They establish what is true, neither discovering nor receiving truth from what is beyond themselves. Accordingly, any sphere like religion, family, or friendship, when it claims to derive its legitimacy (i.e., its truth) from sources essentially outside the control of the state, cannot be tolerated in principle by a totalitarian regime. They must be radically redefined and then socially reconstructed by the state.

The denial of truth and of the personal freedom we associate with privacy seem to be necessarily related in any conceivable political context.

Without the intention of truth, freedom becomes anarchy that is destructive of any rational order and thus rightly to be feared. Indeed, it is this very fear entailed by limitless freedom that totalitarian regimes exploit in their drive for total power, which, as Plato and Hobbes recognized, can only come from those frightened enough to give freedom away.[1] And without freedom, truth has no way of appearing in the world.[2]

The intuitive horror that the experience of totalitarianism elicits on the part of most morally earnest people has been a powerful stimulus for some of the more gifted of them to affirm cogently that which has been so brutally and irrationally denied—*viz.*, the transcendence of truth and the limit on total social control of human persons that we have come to designate as privacy. It is no accident that victims of Fascist and Communist totalitarian tyranny in our own time such as Jacques Maritain, Emmanuel Levinas, Jacques Ellul, and Pope John Paul II have become prominent natural law theorists (understanding the term more broadly than is usually done) in and for our time.

The "revolutionary" character of their respective thought has done much to belie the old dismissal of natural law theorists as simply apologists for the *ancien régime* in one way or another. Indeed, to the chagrin of some more traditionally "pure" natural law theorists, all of these thinkers (and others less prominent) have not been afraid to link the classic idea of natural law with the distinctly modern idea of natural rights, even though much more theoretical work is required in order for this marriage to be one of more than just rhetorical convenience.[3]

I mention that specifically because the *right to privacy* is by now certainly taken to be a "natural right," no matter how much that is still debated by American constitutional scholars. It has by now gone beyond a matter of modern political conceptual debate and become a matter of modern political vocabulary. In other words, political theorists (among whom natural law theorists are undoubtedly to be counted) can continue to debate the normative meaning of privacy. Still, they can hardly deny its normative necessity in the modern world without ultimately becoming advocates of some form of distinctly modern totalitarianism, however much they might think that they are restoring some premodern society more pristine than anything available at present.

Liberalism

On the other hand, the issue of privacy also affects many natural law theorists negatively. Certain prominent forms of liberalism, having roots that stretch all the way back to the beginnings of modernity, have elevated privacy from the level of *a* right *within* a larger societal context to that of the foundation of *all* rights and duties. One can best see this by looking at the radically individualistic claims made for privacy by many liberal theorists. Comparing the newer view of privacy with more classical views of it, we see that the essential difference between them depends on the introduction of the idea of autonomy or practical self-sufficiency into political discourse.

Classical views of privacy are not founded on the basic self-sufficiency of the individual. For the classical natural law theorist, the realms of the private and the public are not totally separate. Every individual is a person necessarily imbedded in a range of multiple relations. Therefore, no one is really independent in anything but a relative sense; no one is truly autonomous. Autonomy can only be the property of God, who is capable of "*creatio ex nihilo.*" It is a property no creature should attempt to achieve, let alone assume it already possesses.[4] To view any individual as being independent of relationality per se is a total abstraction, like viewing a point outside of a line, a line outside of a figure, a figure outside of a body.

What privacy means here is that no human person is simply a part of one relationship to the exclusion of all others. Each range of relations makes certain claims upon the person. Thus the realm of the private, which for the ancients was largely the domestic realm (*oikos*), limits the full domain of the realm of the public, which for the ancients was the realm of the city (*polis*), just as the city limits the full domain of the family.[5]

Autonomy and its Limits

Privacy is itself a relative term. Thus I have a right to privacy *from* the state in certain aspects of my family life (such as the choice to marry, the choice of whom to marry, the choice to have children, the choice to limit the number of children, etc.). It would be an unwarranted extension of the authority of the state as a public institution to invade an area of human existence that it must largely leave alone if that area is to remain intact. The state's right to invade this area of human relationship is only justified when it can be shown that political rights, which are beyond the realm of familial authority, are being violated. This would be the case, for example, when children—born or unborn—are being abused.

The same would be the case in terms of friendship. The state has no right to determine who my friends are to be without simultaneously destroying the realm of friendship altogether. The state's right to invade this area is only justified when it can be shown that political rights, which are beyond the realm of friendship, are being violated, such as when friends are conspiring against the safety or integrity of the society itself.

And the same would be the case in terms of religion. The state has no right to determine how I am to worship or not worship God. This would simultaneously destroy the free assent of faith (which always implies the free rejection of any faith or of some one faith) that faith itself, as distinct from conventional religious behavior, requires for its very integrity. The state's right to invade this area is only justified when it can be shown that political rights, which are beyond the realm of any religious community, are being violated—e.g., when people are being held prisoner in religious communities or being subjected to other forms of abuse in them. In all of these cases, we see an affirmation of freedom of choice, indeed freedom of choice with impunity, but we do not see the type of foundational autonomy that many liberals have seen as the ground of both freedom and responsibility.

Even though the term "autonomy" is usually taken in its Kantian sense (i.e., all moral law is self-legislation), the foundational autonomy of which I am now speaking is far more radical than what Kant advocated. Kant still correlated moral right and moral duty, and he did so based on his view of human nature and its essential sociality. In contrast, foundational autonomy, advocated by many contemporary liberals, asserts that in the most fundamental practical sense, I am alone. As such, I am free to do whatever I please, which means that my nature is essentially amoral and coequal with my power. My nature is essentially asocial. Thus my privacy is myself; everyone else is truly a stranger.[6]

Public Responsiblity

My public involvement is a necessary evil. Its value is purely instrumental. Public responsibility is that limit on my activity that I am willing to negotiate together with others in society in return for a mutual nonaggression pact among ourselves called the social contract. It is, in effect, delayed gratification. I take less now in order to be able to keep it longer. The state is what we establish in concert to make sure that no one can cheat on this contract with impunity.[7]

Since such private, selfish persons cannot expect any trust from one another, and thus cannot constitute a community among themselves, they must create the state *de novo* as a totally external institution, which stands over and above all of them to enforce necessary political order. The state as this alien entity (heteronomy) stands over against its citizens in their privacy (autonomy) just like a police officer stands over and against potential criminals in order to frighten them into obedience of the law. And because institutions and their bureaucrats have a way of quickly developing institutional interests of their own, the citizens whom they regulate subsequently develop as much distrust of this external, alien institution as they have for each other as potentially aggressive strangers (*heteroi*).

How much this political bargain costs me in terms of my private power, which is now constituted as my "natural right," runs the gamut from the maximalism of Hobbes to the minimalism of Nozick, with everybody else coming in somewhere in-between. In this overall view, then, all my relations are not what I am already imbedded in but, rather, what I can possibly create by and for myself. Nothing transcends me. Thus anyone advocating this overall view would be hard-pressed to argue how he or she could not be an atheist, just as, conversely, any natural law theorist would be equally hard-pressed to argue how he or she could be an atheist. For it is hard to conceive of such radical immanentism with a god (Judeo–Christian or even Platonic), as it is hard to conceive of its transcendent alternative (i.e., natural law) without a god.

The human insufficiency of this type of political philosophy has been emphasized by many, even many who are not natural law theorists and who would most likely deny any such appellation even by association. Indeed, the attack on this notion of radical individualism has of late been coming from those loosely called "communitarians." From what I have read, it seems that the communitarian critique is more phenomenological than theoretical. It well points out what a thin view of human existence liberal individualism actually presents. But we need more than phenomenology to persuade us just how we can properly balance the public and private spheres by principles encompassing them both, and thereby place them both in a rational relation. Natural law theory can, however, pick up on the insights of the communitarian critique of liberal individualism as an opening to the presentation of what its advocates have always regarded as being perpetual truth.

Privacy and Suicide

Many constitutional scholars have questioned the whole notion that there is a "right to privacy" in the United States Constitution. Yet it is well-known that this notion lies at the very heart of the Supreme Court decision in *Roe v. Wade*[8] in 1973 that permitted elective abortion in our society.

Roe v. Wade

That *Roe v. Wade* is a landmark decision is a matter of general agreement precisely because it assumes a certain philosophical stance that is bound to attract some and to repel others. One would be hard-pressed to find any other such landmark decision that has not had the same political effect.

Roe v. Wade has become so quickly institutionalized because it reflects a philosophy held by many in our society, whether having the political label "liberal" or "conservative" (the latter is usually libertarian when a natural law commitment is absent). In this view the greatest right, the one that is foundational, is the right to privacy, and the power of the state must regard itself as a means thereto. As Justice Brandeis summed it up most famously, it is the right "to be let alone."[9] That is why *Roe v. Wade* has been seen by subsequent courts as having the status of *stare decisis—viz.*, it already stands as precedent. About this, many natural law theorists would say with the ancient rabbis, "Sin begets sin."[10]

Nevertheless, despite its notoriety, *Roe v. Wade* does not present the most difficult challenge to the natural law theorist. It does not signify a total break between classical natural law and modern natural rights conceptuality. That is because, in the case of abortion (except in cases of a threat to maternal life), one can still argue that there is a separate, innocent victim of an act of aggression.

Until very recently, those in favor of elective abortion in our society confined their arguments to the question of the personhood of the fetus. By arguing that the fetus's lack of separate bodily space from that of its mother makes it part of her own body and thus not a person in its own right, they attempted to argue that abortion is a crime without a separate victim. Hence, by the criteria of foundational privacy, it is no crime at all.

By implication, however, if it could be shown that the fetus is a separate life from that of its mother (e.g., it has its own genetic code from the time of conception), then even by natural rights criteria, there would be a crime with a real victim. Thus it would be prohibited by the social contract with its minimal requirement of protection of innocent persons.

Liberty over Life

What has emerged of late, something that natural law adherents opposed to elective abortion have long suspected, is that the real reason behind the enthusiasm on the part of many liberals for elective abortion is precisely the fact that it is "elective." In other words, personal liberty, located in the right to privacy, is now presented as being more important than even the protection of innocent life. Thus, some advocates of abortion on demand are now admitting that the fetus might very well be more than a part of the body of its mother. However, because it is dependent on its mother for its life, she has the right to end that life if it interferes with the exercise of her own personal liberty.

Of course, here the supposed line drawn between abortion and infanticide disappears. That has created some degree of pause in the debate, for if dependence on another disqualifies one from the protection of society, as in the case of the infant's dependence on its mother's body and the infant's dependence on the attention of its caregiver (usually, but not always, its mother), then where do we locate just who is not dependent on others?

Is independence as liberty only the property of those who have the power to defend themselves? If that is the case, then even for such liberals the social contract has been irrevocably broken. No one would be safe any more. Any distinction between right and might would be destroyed. That is why carrying the argument this far requires more than just the precedent of *Roe v. Wade*, which was more circumspect in its conclusions, even if its hidden premise suggests more.

Suicide

On the other hand, though the extension of the precedent of *Roe v. Wade* to the permissibility of infanticide and beyond requires the introduction of some intermediate premises, the precedent of *Roe v. Wade* is logically sufficient to justify what is now called "physician-assisted suicide." This has been done in the recent decision of the United States Court of Appeals for the Ninth Circuit that declared the Washington state law prohibiting physician-assisted suicide to be unconstitutional on the grounds that it violated the guarantee of personal liberty in the Fourteenth Amendment to the Constitution.[11] It is exactly the same constitutional ground that *Roe v. Wade* invoked when it declared state laws prohibiting abortion to be unconstitutional. In Judge Reinhardt's decision, *Roe v. Wade* was the most important precedent. Yet in a case where the killer and the killed are one and the same person (the physician only being an authorized agent of the killer), the connection to a general protection of personal liberty is easier to make than in a case where, conceivably anyway, the one being killed is an actual victim of the aggression of a second party.

Indeed, many opponents of *Roe v. Wade* have pointed out that the very purpose of the Fourteenth Amendment was to prevent newly freed black slaves (slavery being outlawed by the preceding Thirteenth Amendment) from being made into chattel again by being denied the rights of all other citizens. Is not the powerless condition of the fetus similar to the powerless status of slaves? As such, *Roe v. Wade* actually contradicts the underlying principle of the Fourteenth Amendment, so it is argued by its opponents on constitutional grounds.

By looking at these two decisions, we can see that the Appeals Court decision is more convincing than *Roe v. Wade*, based on the same underlying premise in both cases. The distance between the premise and the conclusion in the Court of Appeals decision regarding physician-assisted suicide is shorter, hence logically tighter, than the distance between the premise and the conclusion in *Roe v. Wade*. That is because, in the case of abortion, there is a possible separation between criminal and victim, something that a punishable crime presupposes, but this is not the case with suicide.

Even the Talmud, basing itself as it does on biblical doctrines regarding divine creation and ownership of the universe, does not make suicide a punishable crime, although it is prohibited.[12] To do so would be to punish a victim as much as a criminal. But because suicide itself is prohibited, those assisting in a suicide, not being its victim, are to be punished on the grounds that "there is no agency for sin."[13] That would not be the case, of course, if one assumes that suicide is an exercise of a right to privacy and thus not a sin, punishable or not. In other words, any prohibition of physician-assisted suicide presupposes a prohibition of suicide, even if the violation of that prohibition is not punished in the absence of a second party being involved in it.

A Natural Law View of Privacy

The mention of *Roe v. Wade* and both its explicit and implicit connections to the permission of physician-assisted suicide is not part of any constitutional argument on my part. Even most lawyers are not constitutional experts, and I am not even a lawyer. My interest in this connection is philosophical—*viz.*, what an assumption of the foundational right to privacy entails. In other words, I am interested in uncovering just what the deeper presuppositions of both these legal decisions are and what they imply for natural law theory.

Reason and Religion

A frequent assumption about natural law is that it is essentially an idea formulated by Greek philosophers, initially by Plato, Aristotle, and the

Stoics. The contributions of the Jewish and Christian theologians who were also interested in the idea are regarded as subsequent endorsements and applications of a discovery of Greek philosophy. This is often done to counter opponents of natural law, who frequently charge that natural law is nothing but an elaborate apologetic for an essentially religious morality, a morality coming out of the particular revelation received and transmitted by a religious community. Attributing natural law theory to Greek philosophers seems to be part of an argument that wants to carefully separate reason from revelation and to designate natural law as "secular."

Of course, on historical grounds this location of the origin of the idea of natural law is quite shaky, inasmuch as gods are mentioned by Plato, Aristotle, and the Stoics, and that mention is not without normative significance. Although the revelation by gods is less precise a consideration in Greek philosophy than it is in biblical theology, one cannot rule it out. Plato, Aristotle, and the Stoics did use the traditional word from Greek religion, *theos*, when speaking of "God" or the "gods," and I do not think their use of this key word was at all disingenuous.

In the broadest sense, these gods made themselves known to their adherents by self-revelation. Therefore, it would seem that all classical natural law theory has some connection to revelation and cannot, therefore, be seen as totally separate from religion. When Hugo Grotius, considered by many to be the founder of modern natural law theory, said that we can have natural law "even if we say there is no God" (*etiamsi daremus non esse deum*), he was making a clear break with the classical tradition of natural law.[14]

What distinguishes natural law from the moral theology of Judaism or Christianity is that it is not based on the specific precepts of any scripture or tradition. Rather, it is the result of more general reflection on the nature of interhuman relations, which is human sociality. Its norms are derived from that reflection, which even revealed teaching must respect because it is the order of the world into which revelation comes as fulfillment, not destruction.

Revelation presupposes creation and its order (nature) as its necessary (but not sufficient) condition. Indeed, for theologians as otherwise diverse as Maimonides, Aquinas, and Calvin, natural law is the most immediately intelligible part of the larger divine law.[15] It is no accident, then, that virtually all contemporary natural law theorists are adherents of some religion of revelation such as Judaism or Christianity. (A possible exception would be those who are Kantians, assuming of course that one believes that natural law and natural rights can be synthesized as done by Kant and his followers. Thus Kantians could be seen as part of the natural law tradition.) That is so even if many of them are not formally theologians, so long as those who are theologians can cogently distinguish between theology and religiously influenced philosophy.

With this in mind, we now need to look at the question of suicide as being one that involves the interrelationship of three parties: (1) the individual human person, (2) the human community, and (3) God.

Injustice to the Community

A place to begin this part of our inquiry is to look at Aristotle's brief discussion of suicide in the *Nicomachean Ethics.*

> Now when a person kills himself in a fit of anger, he acts voluntarily in violation of right reason (*para orthon logon*); and that the law (*nomos*) does not permit. Consequently, he acts unjustly. But toward whom? Surely toward the state, not toward himself. For he suffers voluntarily, but no one voluntarily accepts unjust treatment. That is also the reason why the state (*polis*) exacts a penalty, and some dishonor is imposed upon a man who has taken his own life, on the grounds that he has acted unjustly toward the state . . . the just (*to dikaion*) and the unjust (*to adikon*) always imply more than one person (*pleiosin*).[16]

This passage only deals with the relationship between the individual human person and the state, which is the institution of fullest human community (*koinōnia*).[17] However, if we look at a strikingly similar passage from Aristotle's teacher Plato in the *Laws*, we see the relationship of the individual human and God as well as his or her relationship to his or her community. The striking similarity of the two passages enables me to interpret them in concert.

> Now he that slays the person who is, as men say, nearest and dearest of all, what penalty should he suffer? I mean the man that slays himself, violently (*bia*) robbing what Fate (*moiran*) has *alloted*, when this is not legally ordered (*taxases dikē*) by the State . . . . In this case, the rest of the matters concerning the rules about rites of purification and of burial come within the cognizance of the god, and regarding these the next of kin must seek information from the interpreters and the laws dealing with these matters, and act in accordance with their instructions; but for those thus killed the tombs shall be, first, in an isolated position . . . and with neither headstone nor stone to indicate the tombs.[18]

The notion that suicide, as the most extreme exercise of the right to privacy, is an injustice toward the state, as Aristotle put it, cannot help but suggest that the injustice here is one of depriving the state of one of its members. Accordingly, it seems to be the crime of robbery. But that, of course, presupposes that individual persons are the property of the state—i.e., they are public chattel of which the state is wrongly deprived by the private act of suicide. It is desertion of duty that the state alone determines in its own interest.

Yet is this not the very presupposition of totalitarian regimes, that human persons are their property, which those who embody the power of the regime can use or discard at will? Is this not the very historical stimulus that has made us so concerned with the right to privacy as the assurance of human dignity here and now? Surely, this fear is legitimate and deserving of the most serious answer.

Social Needs

Nevertheless, the fear is only justified if we assume that the injustice against the state is strictly that of robbery. For if that is the case, the state can just as easily mandate the suicide of those it considers useless or dangerous as it can mandate the life of those it considers useful or benign. However, if one regards the human person to be social *by nature*, then the function of the state is not to possess its citizens but to serve their social needs for each other. By identifying just what those needs are, natural law can be the criterion for judging which human regimes deserve the moral loyalty of their members and which do not.

The state is not an institution created by selfish individuals to stand over and against them because they do not trust anybody, even themselves. Humans are placed in society by forces greater than themselves, as Plato pointed out. They do not create society any more than society creates them. The function of the state as the most general institutionalization of human society is to order properly our mutual fulfillment of the needs of self and others. As the Bible puts it, each of us is "bone of my bone and flesh of my flesh," and each of us is a "helpmate" (*ezer*) for each other.[19]

Friendship and Loneliness

If these social needs of humans are coequal with their existence itself, then that existence itself is essentially to be with and for others. As a Talmudic sage put it, when he returned unrecognized to his old community after a long solitary absence, "either friendship (*haveruta*) or death."[20] In fact, that is the meaning of death. It is not "nonbeing," which is something no one has experienced or can even imagine. Instead, death is our own ultimate loneliness, our being abandoned to our ultimate privacy. It is the final being "let alone." Because we have all experienced loneliness, we can all imagine what ultimate abandonment means. That is why we fear death and do everything to postpone its inevitability. But can we do that without the concern and the help of the others *with* whom and not just *among* whom we live?

Our loneliness is so painful, so terrifying, that when we feel abandoned before death has actually arrived, we are tempted to take control and preempt its sting. Since loneliness *in extremis* is the very premonition of death, that control is our desire to cheat it of its robbery of our own power. In suicide, we become death and thus attempt to transcend being its victim. We want to die as we have lived, i.e., autonomously. Since we have believed in life that our dignity is to be autonomous, we now believe that we must die with that same dignity as we have lived. Death is no longer the ultimate horizon that teaches us that our essence is not to be in control but to make our peace with an order greater than ourselves.

Of course, now such a suicidal course of action is only advocated for those who are "terminal." But if death is our inevitable lot in the world into which we have been cast, then who is terminal and who is not can only be a matter of inherently imprecise degree, not one of essential kind. If death is the ultimate loss of control, and if that is the ultimate human indignity inconsistent with life as autonomous self-possession, then there is no reason to ban or even disapprove of suicide for any mortal, rational, human being. In fact, following this lethal logic, we should encourage, maybe even mandate (law being the last step in the process of social approval and disapproval) a time when the person bearing life is to dispose of it—*viz*., when it threatens to race beyond his or her control. Following this logic, is this not what is both good for ourselves and good for others, those others upon whom we become more and more a burden?

Isolation

This is where we are finally led when we assume that our privacy is foundational, that it is our most fundamental right. This insight was best explicated by one of the great founders of modern sociology, Emile Durkheim. In his classic study, *Suicide*, Durkheim wondered why suicide rates have risen so sharply in modern industrial societies. His answer was to propose his theory of *anomie*, which is the sense of being personally unconnected to others in a web of what we might call, following the contemporary anthropologist Clifford Geertz, a web of "thick" relationships.[21] It is the sense of loneliness that comes upon a person when he or she is increasingly seen by others and by oneself as a basically dispensable producer and consumer. In such a cold, uncaring environment, more and more desperate people sense that their own lives are simply more than they can bear alone. One might say, following Durkheim and paraphrasing T. S. Eliot, they cannot bear too much reality of being let or left alone.[22]

One need not follow Durkheim in his totally sociological view of human existence, a view that led him to conclude that even the human relationship with God is not really with transcendence but, rather, with the personification of the immanent power of society itself.[23] That could well be a perfect rationalization of the mixture of religion and politics that we find in totalitarian mythologies of nature or history. But we can, nevertheless, well appreciate his insistence that our own view of ourselves, our private vision as it were, is derived from our social relationships (he just did not see how far they extend).

When we are in our own private space, we are basically abstracted from the web of real social relations in which we are always situated from the cradle to the grave. To be let alone means our temporary gathering up of ourselves in free preparation for returning to the various types of relationships that ever claim us. Privacy, at best, is transitional.

Relationships that Destroy

It seems that there are two overall ranges of relationship that are destructive of authentic, social human personhood and thus encourage personal dissolution.

First, there is the totalitarian scheme that claims our total subservience and disposability for it alone. If any of us is better dead than alive for the state, it becomes our duty to eliminate ourselves even before the state has to bother itself with doing it. Thus it was no accident that the suicide rate of German Jews after 1933 dramatically increased—and that was years before the actual "Final Solution" of the death camps was implemented—when the society of which most of them had long believed themselves to be true members sent them the clear message that their presence was to be eliminated at any cost.

And second, there are the radically liberal regimes that send the message to their citizens that they are basically on their own, especially in situations when tempted with self-destruction. The message is "don't bother us." For here is where persons are the least self-sufficient, the most in need of help from others. In fact, is not our primary social need to be helped to control our own murderous tendencies? In the Bible, the first city is founded by Cain, the first murderer, who when left alone after killing his brother cries out, "My sin (*avoni*) is too great to bear."[24] The city is to protect him from both destroying again and being destroyed himself.

Social Support and Community

Along these lines, we can learn much from the example of the Hutterites, a Protestant pietistic community living in the upper midwest. It seems that the Hutterites—who constantly intermarry among themselves, thus narrowing their gene pool—have a high instance of manic-depressive illness, which many scientists think is genetically transmitted.

Manic-depressives have a high suicide rate, especially when they are in the depressive stage of their illness. Yet the Hutterites have an extremely low suicide rate. Why? That is so because when they notice the onset of the symptoms of depression they never leave the victims alone, and by so doing they get them though it. That is human community at its highest moral level. It is what natural law intends, even though the Hutterites would probably not consider themselves part of the natural law tradition for theological reasons.

When society regards itself as being charged by higher authority to care for each and every human life in its charge, is it not the prime responsibility of society to intervene—i.e., break into our privacy—when there is a strong probability that death might occur? For if society is charged to defend all lives against destruction, there is no longer any essential difference between suicide and homicide. Aggression is to be contained, irrespective of who the perpetrator is or who the victim is. Along these lines, is it an accident that history's most famous murderer, Adolf Hitler, died by his own violent hand, by the same means by which he delegated others to kill his victims? The fact that the criminal and the victim are identical is irrelevant, inasmuch as the law is to protect all persons and not discriminate in favor of any one of them over the other.

Any society that is basically indifferent to this charge quickly loses the loyalty of its more morally sensitive members. A society that does not care can hardly expect any loyalty from its members, inasmuch as it refuses to save them from their own private hell. And this society itself thus runs the risk of its own death by the indifference of more and more of its members. In the end, the very public edifice that private, autonomous individuals have erected to protect themselves from each other abandons all of them by refusing to protect each of them from himself or herself. In the end, who needs it at all?

NOTES

1. See Plato, *Republic*, 339C; Hobbes, *Leviathan*, ch. 13–17; Novak, D., *Jewish Social Ethics*. New York: Oxford University Press, 1992, 38–39, n. 1.

2. See Heidegger, Martin, "On the Essence of Truth," trans. J. Sallis, in *Martin Heidegger: Basic Writings*, ed. D. F. Krell. London: Routledge and Paul, 1977), 126 ff.

3. For the notion that this link is plausible, see, esp., Berlin, Isaiah, "Two Concepts of Liberty," *Four Essays on Liberty*. Oxford and New York: 1969, 129, n. 2. For the opposite view, see, esp., Strauss, Leo, *Natural Right and History*. Chicago: University of Chicago Press, 1953, 175 ff.

4. See Novak, D. , *Jewish–Christian Dialogue: A Jewish Justification*. New York: Oxford University Press, 1989, 148 ff.

5. See Aristotle, *Politics*, 1259a37ff.

6. See Nozick, Robert, *Anarchy, State, and Utopia*. New York: Basic Books, 1974, 32 ff.

7. See Plato, *Republic*, 358Eff.

8. 410 U.S. 113 (1973).

9. The origin of this famous slogan is in Warren, Samuel D., and Louis D. Brandeis, "The Right to Privacy," *Harvard Law Review* 4 (1890), 193.

10. *Mishnah*: Avot 4.2.

11. *Compassion in Dying v. Washington*, 79 F. 3d 790 (9th Cir. 1996).

12. *Babylonian Talmud*: Baba Kama 91b.

13. See *ibid.*: Kiddushin 42b.

14. See Grotius, *De Belli ac Pacis*, 1.10. For a more conservative view of Grotius, though, see Chroust, Anton-Hermann, "Hugo Grotius and the Scholastic Natural Law Tradition," *The New Scholasticism* 17 (1943), 26 ff.

15. See Maimonides, *Guide of the Perplexed*, 2.40; Aquinas, *Summa Theologiae*, 2/1, q. 94, a. 4 ad 1; Calvin, *Institutes of the Christian Religion*, 2.7.10 and 4.20.16.

16. *Nicomachean Ethics*, 1138a10–22, trans. M. Ostwald. Indianapolis: Bobbs-Merrill, 1962, 143 ff.

17. See Aristotle, *Politics*, 1253a30ff.

18. *Laws*, 873C-D, trans. R. G. Bury. Cambridge, Mass.: Harvard University Press, 1926, 2:264–267; Novak, D., *Suicide and Morality*. New York: Scholars Studies Press, 1975, 7 ff.

19. Genesis 2:23, 18. For the notion that marriage is the first human community in both the chronological and qualitative sense, see Soloveitchik, Joseph B., *The Lonely Man of Faith*. New York: Doubleday, 1992, 40 ff.

20. *Babylonian Talmud*: Taanit 23a.

21. See Durkheim, Emile, *Suicide*, trans. J. A. Spaulding and G. Simpson. Glencoe, Ill.: The Free Press, 1951, 241 ff.

22. See Eliot, "Burnt Norton," *Four Quartets*. New York: Harcourt Brace, 1943, 4.

23. See Durkheim, *Elementary Forms of the Religious Life*, trans. J. W. Swain, trans. New York: Free Press, 1947, 236 ff.

24. Genesis 4:13; see *ibid.* v. 17.

Nature, Morality, and Homosexuality

ROBERT P. GEORGE

In *Virtually Normal: An Argument About Homosexuality*,[1] Andrew Sullivan, the young, "gay," British, Roman Catholic former editor of *The New Republic*, has argued eloquently and intelligently for dramatic revisions of natural law thinking and public policy regarding sexual morality and marriage. It is incumbent upon natural law theorists and, indeed, anyone who is inclined to support traditional ideas about sex and marriage, to take Sullivan's challenge to the natural law tradition very seriously. My aim in this essay is to engage his arguments about nature, morality, and homosexuality.

Homosexual acts have long been condemned as immoral by the natural law tradition of moral philosophy, as well as by Jewish and Christian teaching. Sullivan argues that these condemnations are rooted in a failure to recognize that, for somewhere between 2 percent and 5 percent of the population, homosexuality is, in a sense decisive for the moral evaluation of homosexual conduct and relationships, "natural." But (as Sullivan asks) what is a "homosexual"? And what, precisely, is the sense in which homosexuality is "natural"?

Being Homosexual

Sullivan approaches the first question autobiographically. At about age ten he began to feel what he describes as a "yearning" which "was only to grow stronger as the years went by." Although initially "not sexual," it was, nevertheless, "a desire to unite with another: not to possess but to join in some way; not to lose myself but to be given dimension." This is, of course, a perfectly normal experience. In Sullivan's case, however, there was something not entirely normal about the way this yearning developed: namely, as a desire to be united not only emotionally but also physically with a person of his own sex.

Sullivan recognizes that his experience may differ in various respects from that of other homosexuals. In particular, he observes that the experience of female homosexuals tends to differ from that of males in that "it is more often a choice for women than for men; it involves a communal longing as much as an individual one; and it is far more rooted in moral and political choice than in ineradicable emotional or sexual orientation." Nevertheless, he says, even many lesbians report experiences not entirely unlike his own. He concludes that homosexuality, whatever the form of its expression, "is bound up in that mysterious and unstable area where sexual desire and emotional longing meet; it reaches into the core of what makes a human being who he or she is."

Thus, Sullivan puts into place a crucial premise of his argument for the value and moral validity of homosexual conduct: namely, that for people like him the fulfillment of a longing for emotional and physical union with someone of the same sex is critical to the success of their lives. For a homosexual, such fulfillment is, Sullivan goes so far as to suggest, the very thing "which would most give him meaning." It is in this sense that homosexuality is "natural" for homosexuals.

So, Sullivan reasons, homosexual genital acts, far from being "unnatural," are, or at least can be, naturally fulfilling for people whose fundamental yearning is to unite with someone of the same sex. Such acts, Sullivan supposes, can be truly unitive, and thus valuable, in the same way that heterosexual intercourse can be unitive and valuable.

Many people believe that sexual intercourse has value only in the context of marriage, or at least that marital intercourse has special meaning and value. Sullivan himself holds this view.[2] When combined, however, with his proposition that some people are homosexual "by their nature" and with the proposition which he thinks follows from it (namely, that for such people homosexual genital acts can be unitive and fulfilling), it leads to the social and political conclusion that society should accept and provide for marriages between same-sex couples. And this conclusion is one that Sullivan presses with particular vigor.

If homosexuality is "natural" in a morally normative sense, then homosexuals are, as Sullivan says, "virtually normal": "virtually" in the sense that homosexual orientation is comparatively rare—certainly no more than one person in twenty, and perhaps as few as one person in fifty, is homosexual (so, in a merely statistical sense, heterosexuality is the "norm"); "normal" because being homosexual is no more *ab*normal than, say, being black, or Jewish, or having red hair.

If, as Sullivan argues, homosexual relationships and conduct are naturally fulfilling and as such morally good, then it follows not only that "marriage should be made available to everyone, in a politics of strict neutrality," but also that military positions should be made available to homosexuals and heterosexuals on a nondiscriminatory basis, as should positions as teachers, coaches, and counselors in public schools. In Sullivan's view, law and government may no more legitimately draw distinctions between homosexuals and heterosexuals than they may distinguish between blacks and whites, Jews and gentiles, or redheads and brunettes. Thus, Sullivan calls for more than the mere *toleration* of homosexuality in and by the institutions of public life. As his demand for "gay marriage" makes clear, he believes that these institutions are morally obliged to treat homosexual relationships as equal in worth and dignity to socially approved heterosexual relationships.

The Limits of Legislation: Alternative Political Views

At the same time, Sullivan opposes extending civil rights laws to forbid discrimination based on sexual orientation into the private realms of housing and employment. He argues that liberals, who would bring the coercive force of law to bear to overcome intolerance of homosexuality in the larger society, have strayed from liberalism's own principles. "Liberalism," he declares, "is designed to deal with means, not ends; its concern is with liberty, not a better society." Contemporary liberals, in their zeal to free homosexuals (and members of other minority groups) from the consequences of prejudice, have, Sullivan suggests, "created a war within [liberalism] itself." They have breached the traditional liberal commitment to public neutrality between competing visions of what makes for, and detracts from, a valuable and morally worthy way of life. In practice, then, liberalism has become a threat to the very idea of private liberty it celebrates in theory.

Sullivan's argument proceeds by engaging ideas and arguments about the morality and politics of homosexuality advanced not only by "liberals" and "conservatives," but also by more extreme parties on each side—viz., "prohibitionists" and "liberationists." While acknowledging that his categories are "ideal types" whose tenets few people subscribe to in pure form, he subjects each to detailed criticism. His own view, unsurprisingly, fits into none. Sullivan is, in the end, not so much a "neoconservative," as he is sometimes said to be, as a sort of conservative liberal, saying "yes" to "gay marriage" and to open homosexuals in the military and schools, and "no" to state-sponsored affirmative action and the legal prohibition of private discrimination based on sexual orientation.

Liberal Views

Liberalism, whether in the form Sullivan criticizes or in his own conservative version of it, contrasts sharply with "gay liberationism," which scoffs at bourgeois values and seeks to subvert mainstream institutions (such as marriage and the family), as opposed to integrating homosexuals fully into them. Sullivan's "liberationists" eschew the argument that homosexuality, and homosexual conduct, are natural. They refuse to grant to "conservatives" the proposition that human nature has determinate content or any sort of moral normativity. They celebrate the plasticity of human nature and practice a "queer politics" which goes in for "outings," "speech codes," "censorship," and "intimidation." As Sullivan depicts it, liberationism tends to philosophical nihilism and political authoritarianism. Gay liberationists are the sort of people who give homosexuality a bad name.

Conservative Views

"Prohibitionists" and "conservatives" are Sullivan's classifications for people who judge that homosexual conduct is morally bad and believe that social policy ought to reflect that judgment. Conservatives differ from prohibitionists mainly in their tolerant attitude toward acts of "private" immorality. They strongly oppose the villification of homosexuals and typically favor the repeal of laws against sodomy. Moreover, conservatives tend not to be especially uncomfortable in dealing with homosexual friends and acquaintances who do not flaunt their homosexuality. The only real demand they make is that active homosexuals respect the sensibilities of others and be discreet about their sexual relationships to a degree that married people need not be.

At the same time, conservatives oppose "gay marriage" and other forms of official recognition and approbation of homosexual conduct and relationships. Although they tend to avoid the moralistic rhetoric of prohibitionists, conservatives share the moral belief that a life of active homosexuality should not be put forward as any sort of model of virtue.

Sullivan attacks the conservative view on two fronts. First, he challenges, as we have seen, the premise that homosexual acts and relationships integrated around those acts are morally bad or, indeed, morally inferior in any way to upright heterosexual conduct. (This challenge, obviously, cuts equally against the prohibitionists, who favor a more aggressive policy of discouraging homosexual activity. I shall therefore defer discussion of it until I turn to Sullivan's engagement with prohibitionism.) Second, he challenges the conservative belief that homosexuality can, much less should, be kept private. He claims that "the old public–private distinction upon which the conservative politics is based" has been eviscerated by the rise of the "gay rights" movement. With large numbers of homosexuals "out of the closet," the cultural basis of conservative politics is collapsing; "its bluff is being slowly but decisively called."

What is the conservative to do? One possibility is to join Sullivan and other nonliberationist proponents of "gay rights" (such as Bruce Bawer, Gabriel Rotello, and Stephen Macedo) in encouraging "conservative trends among homosexuals and a co-optation of responsible gay citizenship." To do this, however, the conservative must, in effect, lay aside moral qualms about homosexual conduct and accept something like Sullivan's ideal of the "virtuous homosexual" who reserves sex for stable, loving, monogamous relationships and embraces other "family values."

Above all, according to Sullivan, the conservative who takes this route should support the campaign for same-sex marriage as the best way to channel homosexual desire in the proper direction and encourage "a responsible homosexual existence." His only other option, Sullivan believes, is to join the prohibitionists and, especially, "the religious fundamentalists who do not share conservatism's traditional support of moderate and limited government."

Religion

Contrary to what this last comment, shorn of its context, may suggest to the reader, Sullivan's chapter on prohibitionists is mainly concerned with Catholic appeals to rational moral principles of natural law, rather than evangelical arguments from revealed truth. Sullivan treats these appeals with respect, noting that the tradition of thought about natural law (of which the Catholic Church is today the principal institutional exponent) "has a rich literature, an extensive history, a complex philosophical core, and a view of humanity that tells a coherent and at times beautiful story of the meaning of our natural selves." To his credit, Sullivan denies that prohibitionism's principled moral opposition to homosexual conduct can be dismissed as a "phobia" or written off as "bigotry." At the same time, he argues that neither philosophical nor theological arguments against homosexual acts can survive criticism.

Scripture

Sullivan concedes that both the Jewish and Christian scriptures appear to condemn homosexual genital activity. As he points out, however, in our own time, pro-"gay" critics have "reinterpreted" the relevant scriptural passages in efforts to show either that what is being condemned is something other than sexual misconduct or that the condemnation pertains only to ritual impurity and not to morality as such. Sullivan relies on the work of some of these critics, though he is forthright in acknowledging his own lack of professional competence to judge their claims. I, too, am no expert in biblical interpretation. Still, I would point out that some of the work on which he relies, particularly certain arguments advanced by the late John Boswell, has come in for scathing criticism from distinguished scholars (including some who share Boswell's and Sullivan's moral and political views about homosexuality) for "politically correcting" the Bible and Jewish and Christian history.[3]

Where Sullivan is prepared to concede that a biblical text condemns homosexual conduct on moral grounds, as in the case of St. Paul's Letter to the Romans, he argues that what is being condemned is not anything related to *homosexuality*—as we now know and understand it—but, rather, "the perversion of heterosexuality." According to this argument, St. Paul, being ignorant of the fact that some people are "by their nature homosexual" (this presumably having been a discovery of modern psychologists), perceives perversion in all homosexual acts, whereas, in truth, there is perversion only in the homosexual acts of persons who are by their nature heterosexual.[4]

The Meaning of Human Nature

This argument is dubious. Its premise, that Paul and the people of his time simply "assume that every individual's nature is heterosexual," trades on an equivocation on the meaning of the term "nature" and its cognates. It is implausible to suppose that Paul, as a Pharasaical Jew and a Christian, understood people's natures to be constituted, in any sense relevant to moral judgment, by their *desires* (even those deep and more or less stable emotional desires Sullivan calls "yearnings"), sexual or otherwise. (This is not to deny that Paul considered it "natural" for people to experience bad as well as good desires, including sexual desires.)

The view that human nature *is* ultimately constituted by emotional desires, while not unknown in the ancient world, is prominent today largely because of the profound influence of Thomas Hobbes[5] and, especially, David Hume[6] on the intellectual life of our culture. It was, however, rejected by the greatest pre-Christian philosophers, and I see no evidence of it in Paul's letters or in the writings of other Jews and Christians in the premodern world. So it is anachronistic for contemporary critics, such as Sullivan, to suppose that writers like Paul understood human nature to be constituted more or less as they believe it is—namely, by deep and fairly stable emotional desires—and then to claim that the early writers simply failed to understand that some people are "by their nature" homosexual.

In fact, Sullivan's whole argument against "the prohibitionists," and, by implication, much of his argument against "the conservatives," assumes that they understand people's "natures" to be constituted in the essentially Humean way that Sullivan and other liberals believe human nature(s) to be constituted. In fact, however, the "conservatives" as well as the "prohibitionists" reject the Humean understanding of how human nature is constituted as a *mis*understanding. Thus they need not and—in my own case and in the cases of "prohibitionists" and "conservatives" cited by Sullivan with whose work I am familiar—do not deny, as Sullivan thinks we must deny, that genuine homosexual orientation exists.[7]

But if one's nature is not constituted by one's basic emotional desires, what is it constituted by? What is it that is fundamental about each of us as human persons and rightly motivating of us?

Let us get at these questions by considering Sullivan's analysis of natural law argumentation, particularly as it has been advanced in recent statements of the Catholic Church on homosexuality and homosexual genital acts. He thinks that he has caught the *magisterium* of the Church in a contradiction. Unlike St. Paul (as Sullivan, Boswell, and others read him), contemporary churchmen recognize that homosexually oriented persons exist; such persons are not merely heterosexuals who, for whatever reasons, choose to engage in homosexual acts. But, Sullivan suggests, if the Pope and Cardinal Ratzinger acknowledge that some people's "natures" are homosexual, how can they continue to insist that homosexual acts violate natural law?

The answer is that the Church has a view about human good and the constitution of human nature which is much more like St. Paul's (as I read him)—and Aquinas's and, for that matter, Plato's—than it is like Sullivan's or Hobbes's or Hume's. The Church teaches that a person's nature, in the sense relevant to moral judgment, is constituted by human goods which give him *reasons* to act and to refrain from acting, and not by *desires* which may, rightly or wrongly, also provide motivation.[8] These "natural goods" are "basic" inasmuch as they are ends or purposes which have their intelligibility not merely as means to other ends, but as intrinsic aspects of human well-being and fulfillment. Far from being reducible to desires, basic human goods give people *reasons to desire things*—reasons which hold whether they happen to desire them or not, and even in the face of powerful emotional motives which run contrary to what reason identifies as humanly good and morally right.[9]

This understanding of human nature and the human good has been applied to questions of homosexual conduct by John Finnis, among others, whose views Sullivan classifies as "conservative." For Finnis, as for the broader natural law tradition, the immorality of homosexual genital acts follows by implication from the intrinsic immorality of all forms of non-marital sex.[10]

Marriage and Non-Marital Sex Acts

Marriage, according to Finnis, is one of the basic human goods. As such, it provides a noninstrumental reason for spouses to unite bodily in acts of genital intercourse. This bodily union is the biological matrix of the multi-level (bodily, emotional, dispositional, and even spiritual) relationship which is their marriage. Marital acts, while (necessarily) reproductive in type, are not merely instrumental, as St. Augustine seems to have supposed, to the good of having children (or avoiding sin).[11] Nor are they mere means of sharing pleasure or even promoting feelings of closeness, as many contemporary liberals think.[12] Rather, such acts realize the intrinsic good of marriage itself as a two-in-one-flesh communion of persons.

> The union of the reproductive organs of husband and wife really unites them biologically (and their biological reality is part of, not merely an instrument of, their *personal* reality); reproduction is one function and so, in respect of that function, the spouses are indeed one reality, and their sexual union therefore can *actualize* and allow them to experience their *real common good—their marriage*. . . .[13]

If this view, or something like it, is sound, then it is plain that oral or anal sexual intercourse, whether engaged in by partners of the same sex or opposite sexes, and, indeed, even if engaged in by marriage partners, cannot be marital. (This moral insight, if such it is, accounts for provisions of both civil and canon law according to which marriages cannot be consummated by such acts.)[14] Only acts of the reproductive type (whether or not, as Finnis explains, they are intended to be, or even can be, reproductive in effect) can actualize (and, in law, consummate) marriage. Other sexual acts cannot be maritally unitive because they do not unite the partners biologically, making them truly two-in-one-flesh.[15]

Moreover, masturbatory and sodomitical acts, by their nature, instrumentalize the bodies of those choosing to engage in them in a way that cannot but damage their integrity as persons. Inasmuch as nonmarital sexual acts cannot realize any intrinsic common good, such acts cannot but be willed for instrumental reasons. And in such willing, "the partners treat their bodies as instruments to be used in service of their consciously experiencing selves; their choice to engage in such conduct thus dis-integrates each of them precisely as acting persons."[16]

Moral Evaluation

Of course, this will not be considered morally problematic by people who hold an essentially dualistic conception of human beings as nonbodily persons who inhabit nonpersonal bodies which they "use" as "equipment."[17] (And dualists of a conservative bent will be quick to point out that they support not just any instrumentalized sex, but only that directed toward such valuable ends as emotional closeness and intimacy.) But those who reject the idea that the nature of human beings is constituted by their basic emotional desires tend to be the very people who reject person/body dualism. Start the list with John Finnis and Cardinal Ratzinger.

Sullivan devotes two or three pages to criticizing Finnis, whose bravery, honesty, and intelligence in arguing about homosexuality he praises. His focus, however, is on what Finnis says about the social and political implications of homosexuality and its legal treatment, rather than his more fundamental argument that homosexual conduct is intrinsically nonmarital and immoral. I have sketched that argument (all too briefly) here, not to defend it from its liberal critics—which I and others have done elsewhere[18]—but simply to show how it rejects—from start to finish—the conception of human nature as constituted by emotional desires which Sullivan wrongly assumes is shared by natural law theorists who claim that homosexual acts are morally bad.

Catholic Teachings

Once we see that "prohibitionists," such as Cardinal Ratzinger, and "conservatives," such as John Finnis, in fact reject the Humean conception of how human nature is constituted, Sullivan's charge that the Church's recognition of the reality of homosexual orientation is inconsistent with its continued condemnation of homosexual acts loses its force. Indeed, it becomes clear that the Church's view of homosexual desire (and the homosexual condition) as "disordered" (in that it *inclines* people to sin) is perfectly consistent with its ringing affirmation of the intrinsic worth and dignity of *all* persons, not excluding those who happen to be homosexual. In this light, Cardinal Ratzinger's 1986 statement deploring "violence and malice in speech or action" against homosexual persons is hardly the "stunning passage of concession" Sullivan describes it as being. Rather, it is a simple reminder of the all-embracing scope of Christ's command: "Love thy neighbor."

Sexual Abstinence

In the end, I think, Sullivan rejects the teaching of his Church (and mine) that homosexual acts are intrinsically immoral, because he has come to believe that the sublimation of sexual desire to which the Church calls those whose homosexual inclinations make marriage a psychological impossibility alienates people from themselves and "leads to some devastating loneliness." For Sullivan, it is celibacy that is "unnatural," at least for people from whom it is demanded because of a sexual orientation they did not choose, rather than, say, a religious vocation they did choose.

Of course, different people will consider (and even experience) the onerousness of sexual abstinence differently, depending upon their grasp of the reasons for exercising sexual self-restraint. And people's judgments as to whether such reasons obtain will likely vary, depending on their understanding, however informal and implicit, of the human good, of what is truly fulfilling of human persons.

It is entirely understandable that someone whose self-understanding is formed in accordance with the characteristically modern conception of human nature and the human good would be dubious about the proposition that there are morally compelling reasons for people who are not married, who cannot marry, or who, perhaps, merely prefer not to marry, to abstain from sexual relations. For Sullivan and others who share this self-understanding, sexual abstinence seems not only pointless but emotionally debilitating and even, in some sense, dehumanizing.[19]

They should at least consider, however, that the modern conception does not hold a monopoly on the allegiance of thoughtful men and women. The alternative conception of human nature and its fulfillment articulated in the natural law tradition (and embedded in one form or another in historic Jewish and Christian faith) enables people who critically appropriate it to understand themselves and their sexuality very differently. Of course, the adoption of this (or any other) view, even if sound, cannot by itself effect a change of sexual orientation or simply eradicate homosexual or other morally problematic sexual desires. However, it can and does render intelligible and meaningful the struggle to live chastely, irrespective of the strength of such desires and regardless of whether one is "gay" or "straight," married or single.

NOTES

1. New York: Alfred A. Knopf, 1995. All page references in the text are to this work.

2. See Sullivan's letter to the editor in *Commentary*, March 1997, responding to Norman Podhoretz's article, "How the Gay Rights Movement Won."

3. Daniel Mendelsohn demolishes many of the claims made by John Boswell in the latter's *Same-Sex Unions in Premodern Europe* (New York: Villard Books, 1994) in "The Man Behind the Curtain," *Arion*, III: 3 (1996), pp. 241–73. See also Shaw, Brent, "A Groom of One's Own," *The New Republic*, July 18/25, 1994, pp. 33–41; and Young, Robin Darling, "Gay Marriage: Reimagining Church History," *First Things*, No. 47, November 1994.

4. On St. Paul's teaching regarding the "unnaturalness" of homosexual acts, see Satinover, Jeffrey, *Homosexuality and the Politics of Truth*. Grand Rapids: Baker Books, 1996, pp. 151–52.

5. "The Thoughts are to the Desires as Scouts and Spies to range abroad, and find the way to the things desired." Hobbes, Thomas, *Leviathan*, pt. 1, ch. 8 (1651).

6. "Reason is, and ought only to be, the slave of the passions, and can never pretend to any office, other than to serve and obey them." Hume, David, *A Treatise of Human Nature*, bk. 2, pt. 3, sec. III (1740).

7. At the same time, because the phrase "homosexual orientation" is used in ways that render its connotation uncertain, I think it generally preferable to speak of homosexual attraction, inclination, desires, tendencies or dispositions. On the "radically equivocal" character of the phrase as it is deployed in contemporary political debate, see Finnis, John, Law, Morality, and "Sexual Orientation," *Notre Dame Law Review*, Vol 69 (1994), sec I. pp. 1049–1051.

8. Thus, Aquinas says that "the good of the human being is in accord with reason, and human evil is being outside the order of reasonableness." *Summa Theologiae*, I–II, q. 71, a. 2c, on which see Finnis, John, *Natural Law and Natural Rights*. Oxford: Clarendon Press, 1980, p. 36.

9. On basic human goods as reasons for action, see George, Robert P., "Recent Criticism of Natural Law Theory," *University of Chicago Law Review*, Vol. 55 (1988), pp. 1371–429. For my critique of the "naturalism" of Michael Perry—a prominent Catholic thinker who, I maintain, reduces human goods to matters of psychological satisfaction—see George, Robert P., "Human Flourishing as a Criterion of Morality: A Critique of Perry's Naturalism," *Tulane Law Review*, Vol. 63 (1989), pp. 1455–74.

10. See Finnis, "Law, Morality, and 'Sexual Orientation,'" sec. III, pp. 1053–55.

11. See St. Augustine, *De bono coniugali* (9.9). For a critique of the Augustinian view, see George, Robert P., and Gerard V. Bradley, "Marriage and the Liberal Imagination," *Georgetown Law Journal*, Vol. 84 (1995), pp. 301–20.

12. See, for example, Macedo, Stephen, "Homosexuality and the Conservative Mind," *Georgetown Law Journal*, Vol. 84, pp. 261–300. For a critique of the liberal view, see George and Bradley, "Marriage and the Liberal Imagination."

13. Finnis, "Law, Morality, and 'Sexual Orientation,'" p. 1066.

14. See George and Bradley, "Marriage and the Liberal Imagination," pp. 307–09, and the authorities cited therein.

15. For a further explanation and defense of this claim, see George and Bradley, "Marriage and the Liberal Imagination," id. Please note that a sexual act's being reproductive in type is a necessary, though not a sufficient, condition of its being marital. Adulterous acts, for example, can be reproductive in type and even in effect, but (obviously and by definition) are non-marital.

16. Finnis, "Law, Morality, and 'Sexual Orientation,'" pp. 1066–67. See also George and Bradley, "Marriage and the Liberal Imagination," pp. 313–18. The argument is further developed in Lee, Patrick, and Robert P. George, "What Sex Can Be: Self-alienation, Illusion, or One-Flesh Union," *American Journal of Jurisprudence*, Vol. 42 (1997).

17. On the reliance of liberal sex ethics on person–body dualism, see George and Bradley, "Marriage and the Liberal Imagination," n. 32, p. 311. For arguments that dualism of this sort is philosophically untenable, see the works cited therein.

18. See George and Bradley, "Marriage and the Liberal Imagination;" Lee and George, "What Marriage Can Be," Finnis, John, "The Good of Marriage and the Morality of Sexual Relations," *American Journal Jurisprudence*, Vol 42 (1997).

19. By the same token, many people who share this understanding find not just abstinence but also sexual *fidelity* to be pointless or even debilitating. It is a standing challenge (coming from both "liberationists" and "conservatives") to Sullivan and others who maintain that advocacy of same-sex "marriage" can be consistent with belief in the requirement of marital fidelity to identify a rational principle (or set of principles) consistent with this uderstanding which condemns "open" marriages and promiscuity in general as immoral. Of course, it is clear that some supporters of same-sex "marriage" do not, in fact, oppose promiscuity. After interviewing Sullivan, the editor of *The Harvard Gay and Lesbian Review* stated his own opinion on these matters:

> The attempt to sanitize same-sex marriage for tactical reasons has resulted in a kind of studied silence on the subject of sex. . . . We end up soft-pedaling sex in favor of "commitment." And while the discussion of sex within marriage has been avoided, the discussion of non-marital and extra-marital sex has also largely been missing. . . . And yet, in talking about an institution that most Americans define as fidelity to a single partner for a lifetime, how can we avoid discussing sexual promiscuity and serial monogamy and the myriad ways that long-term gay couples have defined their relationships. I for one know relatively few gay male couples whose relationship is not "open" to some extent. Gabriel Rotello and Andrew Sullivan . . . have regarded same-sex marriage as a possible antidote to gay male promiscuity and wildness—which it may well be, though I think it's just as likely that gay marriages would liven up the institution [of marriage] as submit to its traditional rules (which suits me fine).

Harvard Gay and Lesbian Review: A Quarterly Journal of Arts, Letters & Sciences, Vol. 4 (1997), p. 4.

Bioethics and Human Life

WILLIAM E. MAY

Human freedom and natural law go together like love and marriage. Just as the love of man and woman requires marriage if this love is to be conjugal (i.e., the love of husband and wife, persons who have made one another irreplaceable and nonsubstitutable),[1] so human freedom of choice needs natural law if persons are to choose well and thus make themselves to be *good* persons.

Marriage is the institution that protects conjugal love and allows it to develop. Similarly, natural law protects and perfects freedom because it frees persons from making blind or arbitrary choices and enables them to choose in accordance with the *truth*. At bottom, natural law can best be understood as consisting in ordered sets of true propositions of a practical nature meant to help us choose well. Natural law directs us to the goods perfective of human persons and enables us to distinguish alternatives of choice compatible with respect for these goods and the persons in whom they are meant to flourish from alternatives that are not so compatible.

Among the goods of human persons to which we are directed by truths of natural law is the good of human bodily life, obviously a good of crucial importance in issues of bioethics. Human bodily life is a good *of* human persons and not merely, as unfortunately many contemporaries regard it, a good *for* human persons. Obviously, the way we understand the good of human bodily life is critically important in the assessment of bioethical issues.

In this essay, I shall explore the nature of human choice, the first practical principles and first moral principles of natural law, and their application to the good of human bodily life.

Human Freedom of Choice, Human Acts, and Self-Determination

Human acts have *existential* significance because they are concerned with human existence. They are concerned with human existence because in and through them human persons determine their lives, their very selves, and their existence as moral beings.[2]

Human acts are not mere physical events in the material world that come and go, like the falling of rain or turning of leaves. Although human acts usually entail behavioral performances in the physical world that come and go—e.g., shooting guns, having sex, entering data on a computer, pulling the plugs on life-preserving machinery—these acts are far more than performances of this kind, for at their core is a free, self-determining *choice* whereby a human person gives to himself or herself his or her identity as a moral being. Human acts, in other words, not only *get things done* in the material world; they also *get things said*—i.e., they reveal something about the one who freely chooses to do them.[3] Moreover, human acts as freely chosen abide within the one who chooses to do them as a disposition to further choices of the same kind, until a contradictory kind of free choice is made.[4]

To illustrate: I make myself *to be* an adulterer by freely choosing to commit adultery, and I remain an adulterer, disposed to engage in adulterous acts, until, by another free and self-determining choice, I repent of my freely chosen adultery. Even then I remain an adulterer, for I have, unfortunately, given myself that identity. However, now I am a *repentant* adulterer, one who has, through free choice, given to himself a new kind of identity, the identity of one who repudiates the freely chosen adultery, repents of it, and resolves, through free choice, to amend his life and *to be* a faithful, loving spouse.

In short, we make ourselves *to be* the kind of persons we are in and through the acts we freely choose to do. Thus we can say that our actions are like "words" that we speak and through which we give to ourselves our moral character or our integral existential identity, one shaped by our own free choices.[5]

We are free to choose what we are to do and, by so choosing, to make ourselves to be the kind of persons we are. But we are not free to make what we choose to do to be good or bad, right or wrong. We can choose badly; we can freely choose to do what we know we ought not to do. If we are honest with ourselves, we must admit that at times we freely choose to do what we know we ought not to do. That this is so makes it clear that our choices—although they are *self*-determining and settle the question "what kind of a person am I?"—do not and cannot determine the moral rectitude of our freely chosen deeds or settle the question, "Is this choice morally good or morally bad?"

We choose well when we choose to do the good; we choose badly when we choose to do the bad. But how can we determine, prior to choice, which alternatives are morally good and which are morally bad? That determination can only be made on the basis of practical truths—i.e., truths about what is to be done. But this is precisely what natural law is, for natural law can best be understood as consisting in ordered sets of true propositions about what is to be done.

Natural Law: Truths About What Is to Be Chosen and Done

Starting Points for Deliberating about What to Do

I begin with the first truths of practical reason which function as starting points or *practical principles* for deliberating about what is to be chosen and done. The fundamental practical principle or truth is that *good is to be done and pursued, and its opposite, evil, is to be avoided.*[6] No one who understands the meaning of "good" can fail to give assent to the truth of this practical principle, because human choice and human action—whether morally good or morally bad—is rational, not irrational, and rational action has a point, a purpose, and ultimately some point or purpose that the one choosing it deems good or beneficial.

The principle that good is to be done and pursued and its opposite is to be avoided, moreover, is not vacuous. It is specified by principles or practical truths identifying basic forms of human flourishing which are the goods to be pursued, realized, and protected through human choice and action.[7] Here I make no effort to provide an exhaustive list of such goods, but among such goods—and these are recognized by everyone of every age and culture as *goods*—are life itself and health, knowledge of the truth and appreciation of beauty, friendship and harmony with other human persons.[8] Principles of practical reasoning of this kind—the principles that comprise the first set of truths of natural law—are used by everyone who considers what to do, however unsound or bad his or her conclusions might be.

Everyone—whether morally good or morally bad—wants to justify personal choices and actions to oneself and others, and seeks to do so by appealing to the goods identified in principles of this kind. For example, a research scientist seeking to discover new truths in the field of biology and medicine may engage in unethical experiments on human subjects—using them as guinea pigs, for instance—and may seek to justify (better, to rationalize) this action by appealing to the good of knowledge and the future benefits that new knowledge will bring to the human community. Similarly, the mobster who rubs out Ma Fia before she can rub him out seeks to "justify" or "rationalize" his behavior by appealing to the good of life—*his life*, which he seeks to protect by killing a person whose continued existence threatens or imperils this good in him.

As this brief explanation shows, the first practical principles of natural law or practical reasoning include the principle that good is to be done and pursued and the principles identifying the forms of human flourishing that are the goods to be pursued. This first set of natural law principles are truths of a practical nature that human persons, as intelligent beings, take into account in thinking about what they are to do if they are to do anything intelligently and rationally. But these first principles of practical reasoning are not, in themselves, normative principles or truth. They do not, of themselves, enable us to distinguish between alternatives of choice that are *morally good* and alternatives of choice that are not. For that, we must move from first practical principles to first moral or normative principles of natural law.

First Moral Principles: Truths for Discriminating Between Morally Good and Morally Bad Choices

Jews and Christians have articulated the first principle of morality in religious language. They have expressed it in the twofold command that we are to love God and to love our neighbor as ourselves.[9] We love our neighbor by willing that the goods of human existence flourish in that person: we will that our neighbor live, be healthy, come to have knowledge of the truth, appreciate beauty, and live in fellowship and harmony with others.[10] And we do not love if we will that our neighbor be dead or diseased or maimed or deprived of an education, or of any of the real goods that contribute to his full flourishing as a human person.

One way of articulating this fundamental requirement of morality in nonreligious language is the following: *in voluntarily acting for human goods and avoiding what is opposed to them, one ought to choose and otherwise will those and only those possibilities whose willing is compatible with a will toward integral human fulfillment.*[11] In other words, the basic moral requirement of natural law is that human persons, in making free choices, recognize and respect what is really good, both in themselves and in others. Their hearts ought to be open to what is truly good and perfective of human persons, namely, to the goods identified by the first practical principles of natural law or practical reasoning.

This first moral principle of natural law in effect simply expresses the *integral directiveness* of all the first principles of practical reasoning—i.e., the principle directing us to pursue and do what is good and avoid what is opposed to it and the principles identifying the basic forms of human flourishing as the goods that are to be pursued and done through human choice and action.

The matter can be put this way. Morally good alternatives of choice are consistent or compatible with *all* the principles of practical reasoning, with *all* the goods to which we are directed by them, although they promise participation only in *some* of the goods toward which these principles direct choice and action. For instance, the proposal to prepare this essay is consistent with or compatible with all the principles of practical reasoning, although it promises participation in only some goods of human existence—e.g., knowledge of the truth, fellowship and harmony with the participants in this colloquium—but not all goods of human existence. Thus the choice to prepare this essay is a morally good choice. Morally bad alternatives of choice, on the other hand, while consistent with and compatible with some good or goods of human existence and with the principle or principles directing action in their behalf, are not consistent with or compatible with other goods of human existence and with the practical principles directing choice and action on their behalf. Thus an experiment on human subjects using them as guinea pigs may be consistent with or compatible with the good of knowledge of the truth, but it is not consistent with or compatible with the good of interpersonal harmony—of fellowship, friendship, and justice with others. It is thus a morally bad alternative of choice and action.[12]

Just as the first principle of practical reasoning or first truth of natural law—*good is to be done and pursued and its opposite avoided*—is specified by identifying the basic forms of human flourishing or goods of human existence, so too the first moral principle of natural law can be further specified by principles identifying ways of choosing that are *not compatible* with a will toward integral human fulfillment or with a love and respect for all the goods of human existence. These natural law principles or specifications of the first principle of morality exclude alternatives of choice that ignore, slight, neglect, arbitarily limit, damage, destroy, or impede basic goods of human persons. One principle of this kind is the Golden Rule, or the principle of fairness. Another is that we ought not to adopt by choice the proposal to damage, destroy, or impede what is really good either in ourselves or in others, either out of hostility to that good or because the continued flourishing of that good impedes our participation in some other good that we arbitrarily prefer.[13]

Specific Moral Norms

In the light of the first moral principle of natural law and its specifications, it is now possible to articulate more specific moral norms. These norms identify specific objects of human choice as being compatible with or incompatible with the fundamental normative or moral principles of natural law. Examples of such specific norms are those requiring us to keep our promises and to forbear killing innocent persons or punishing persons for crimes that they have not committed.

Many specific moral norms, while true, are not absolute or exceptionless. They are nonabsolute because they are open to further specification in the light of the same moral principles (the truths taken up in the previous section) in whose light they are derived. Promise-keeping is an example. We are obliged to keep our promises in light of the good of interpersonal harmony, the first principle of morality, and its further specification by the Golden Rule or the principle of fairness.

Promises and the cooperation they foster, however, often concern goods other than interpersonal harmony. When keeping a promise would harm those goods, and if these goods could be protected by breaking the promise *without being unfair* or *violating the Golden Rule*, then the obligation to keep the promise ceases. Thus, for instance, if I promise to meet a friend for breakfast on a particular morning and on leaving my house find a person seriously injured on my sidewalk, I would not be obliged to keep my promise. My friend would understand why, for my friend would not regard it unfair for me to break the promise in order to protect the good of life and health in this seriously injured neighbor. My friend, in the same situation, would want the same care from me too, because this is required by the principle of fairness or the Golden Rule. In other words, the truths generating the norm that promises are to be kept likewise generate exceptions to this norm.

But some specific moral norms—for example, the norm requiring us to forbear intentionally killing innocent human persons—are absolute, without exceptions. Norms of this kind are absolute because nothing which could further specify the kind of human action which the norm concerns would prevent it from violating the first principle of morality itself and its specification that we are not to adopt by choice proposals to damage, destroy, or impede what is really good. One could not freely adopt such a proposal by choice without willing that evil be.[14]

Is Human Bodily Life an Instrumental or Intrinsic Good?

Among the goods of human persons to which we are directed by the first principles of natural law is the good of human life. Among the specific moral norms of natural law is the norm requiring us to forbear adopting by choice proposals to destroy the life of innocent human persons.

These are "practical truths"—i.e., truths concerned not with *what is*, but with *what is to be chosen and done*. But mistakes in particular practical judgments—which terminate the process of moral deliberation which begins with the principles of practical reasoning or natural law and its requirements—at times arise because of faulty speculative or factual judgments. Among such judgments are those concerning the status of human bodily life. Is human bodily life merely a good *for* persons and instrumental to them or is it a good *of* persons, intrinsic to them and constitutive of their being? This question is intimately related to the question, are all or only some members of the human species persons?

It is not possible here to give adequate attention to these important questions, and my handling of them must be somewhat summary.

Those who hold that bodily life is merely an instrumental good, something good *for* the person and not a good *of* the person, regard it as a necessary condition for personal life but not, of itself, an integral component of personal life. Those who hold this view basically consider the human person to be an entity aware of itself as a self, capable of relating to other selves or conscious subjects, and capable too of having interests and rights. Bodily life, they hold, is a precondition for personal life and, as a precondition for it, of instrumental value. But if a living individual member of the human species is as yet incapable of being consciously aware of itself and of relating to other conscious subjects, then this entity cannot seriously be regarded as a person. It follows, therefore, that intentionally depriving this entity of its bodily life cannot be regarded as the intentional killing of a human person.[15]

Similarly, some members of the human species have, unfortunately, irretrievably lost their capacity for conscious awareness and for relating meaningfully to other conscious subjects. One can then say that their personality has been extinguished and that the life they live lacks all personal qualities and is merely vegetative in character. Since the lives of these individuals are no longer of any benefit to them, insofar as they do not enable them to participate in truly *personal* goods, one can conclude that there is no need to keep them alive. Hence all means of preserving life are optional and inappropriate inasmuch as the life preserved is of no inherent value and indeed can be regarded as a burden. No wrong is done if this useless and burdensome life is terminated, either by acts of omission or by acts of commission. To the contrary, it may very well be a wrong to preserve bodily lives of this kind, lives of no value even to those whose lives they are.[16]

This way of conceiving bodily human life is widespread in our culture today and is obviously quite central in arguments advanced in support of euthanasia, assisted suicide, abortion, and other matters.

Its principal problem, however, is that it is dead wrong and presupposes a dualistic understanding of human beings. The claim that human bodily life is only instrumentally good, a good *for* persons and not *of* persons, implies that the human person or some parts of the human person are one thing (the conscious subject aware of itself) and that a person's living body is quite another thing. Since this implied position splits the person in two, it is rightly called dualism. But dualism is false.[17]

Intrinsic human goods are not possessions of persons but rather the fulfillment of their being. In an instrumental view of the goodness of bodily life, bodily life is not part of the intrinsic good of the human person. But bodily life is, in fact, intrinsic to the human person and not merely a possession of the person. Were it merely a possession of the person, then a person, on breaking his or her arm, could hardly say that he or she had hurt himself or herself; rather, one would have to say that one had damaged one's property. Again, were the body and bodily life things distinct from the human person, then an attack on one's body would not be an attack on one's person but rather on one's property. Such a position becomes absurd.[18]

Life is not merely one process among others, a process which can be distinguished from breathing, feeling, choosing, talking, and so on. Rather, the life of a person is indistinguishable from the person's very reality and permeates all his or her parts and activities.

The human person is more than the human body, but the body of the human person is integral to the being of the human person, and when that body dies, the *person* dies. Should we mourn the loss of a mere material body? Do we not, on the death of a loved one, grieve over the loss of a person? We may hold that, in addition to the mortal remains of the person which we may bury or cremate, there are immortal remains, but those immortal remains (the spiritual soul) are not the whole human person, for the human person is a body person, not a spirit person, and his or her body is integral to his or her *being* as a person.[19] Thus an attack on the body and bodily life of a human person is an attack on the person.

The dualism underlying the view that human bodily life is merely an instrumental good, a good *for* the person but not *of* the person is indefensible. The good of life to which we are directed by first principles of natural law includes human bodily life, and the personal life protected by the moral norms generated by natural law principles includes bodily human life. That truth is the bedrock principle in all bioethical issues.

NOTES

1. In *The Ethics of Sex* (New York: Harper & Row, 1963), p. 108, Helmut Thielicke correctly states: "not uniqueness establishes the marriage, but marriage establishes the uniqueness." By this he means that the irreplaceability and nonsubstitutability—the utter uniqueness of husband and wife—is established by the act of consent, of free choice, that brings marriage into being and makes the man and the wife no longer separate individuals with their own lives to live but husband and wife, *spouses*, with a common marital life to live. As Vatican Council II put the matter, marriage, "the intimate partnership of married life and love . . . is rooted in the conjugal covenant of irrevocable personal consent" (*Pastoral Constitution on the Church in the Modern World ((Gaudium et Spes))*, n. 48). On this point, see my *Marriage: The Rock on Which the Family Is Built* (San Francisco: Ignatius, 1995), ch. 1.

2. This truth is developed masterfully by Germain Grisez in many places. See, for instance, *The Way of the Lord Jesus*, Vol. 1, *Christian Moral Principles* (Chicago: Franciscan Herald Press, 1983), pp. 41–61. Grisez, along with Joseph M. Boyle and Olaf Tollefsen, offers a dialectical defense of free choice vs. determinism in *Free Choice: A Self-Referential Argument* (Notre Dame, IN: University of Notre Dame Press, 1976); see in particular pp. 122–77.

3. See the very fascinating treatment of this in Herbert McCabe, O.P., *What Is Ethics All About?* (Washington/Cleveland: Corpus Books, 1969), especially pp. 90–94. This work was published in England under the title *Language, Law, and Ethics* (London: Sheed & Ward, Inc., 1969).

4. See Grisez, *Christian Moral Principles,* pp. 50–55; also see my *An Introduction to Moral Theology* (rev. ed.: Huntington, IN: Our Sunday Visitor, 1994), pp. 26–30.

5. On character, see Grisez, *Christian Moral Principles,* pp. 58–59. In his encyclical, *Veritatis Splendor,* Pope John Paul II beautifully develops the self-determining character of human acts as freely chosen. See in particular nn. 65–67 and 71. He explicitly affirms that human acts "do not produce a change merely in the state of affairs outside of man, but, to the extent that they are deliberate choices, they give moral definition to the very person who performs them, determining his most profound spiritual traits" (n. 71). He then cites a marvelous passage from St. Gregory of Nyssa's *De Vita Moysis*, II, 2–3 (PG 44.327–28), in which Gregory says: "All things subject to change and to becoming never remain constant, but continually pass from one state to another, for better or for worse. . . . Now, human life is always subject to change; it needs to be born ever anew. . . . But here birth does not come about by a foreign intervention, as is the case with bodily images . . . ; it is the result of a free choice. Thus we are in a certain way our own parents, creating ourselves as we will, by our decisions."

6. On this see St. Thomas Aquinas, *Summa Theologiae*, 1–2, q. 94, a. 2. In this important question Aquinas begins by making an important analogy between the precepts of natural law, which pertain to reason as ordered to action (*ratio practica*), and the first principles of demonstration, which pertain to reason as ordered to speculative inquiry or knowledge for the sake of knowledge (*ratio

speculativa). He says that just as *being* is the first thing that we grasp intellectually with regard to knowledge of reality (i.e., with respect to what is), so *good* is the first thing that we grasp intellectually with regard to action (i.e., with regard to what is to be through human choice and action). He then says: "Therefore, the first principle in practical reason is that which is founded on the meaning (*ratio*) of the good, which meaning is, *the good is that which all things desire*. Therefore, this is the first precept of [natural] law, namely, that *good is to be done and pursued, and evil is to be avoided*. And upon this [precept or 'proposition' of practical reason] are based all other precepts of natural law, namely, that all those things belong to natural law that practical reason naturally grasps as goods to be done [and pursued]." [emphasis supplied]

7. In *Summa Theologiae*, 1–2, 94, 2, Thomas Aquinas, after articulating the first precept of natural law as good is to be done and pursued, and evil is to be avoided, goes on to say that practical "reason naturally apprehends as goods, and consequently to be pursued in action, all those things to which man has a natural inclination, and things contrary to them [reason naturally apprehends] as evils to be avoided."

It is important here to note that Thomas does *not* say that our "natural inclinations" constitute natural law. Rather, he says that the real goods of human existence to which human beings are naturally oriented are grasped "naturally"—i.e., nondiscursively—by practical reasoning as the "good" that is to be done and pursued. In other words, Aquinas holds that the basic precept of natural law—good is to be done and pursued and its opposite, evil, is to be avoided—is specified by identifying real goods of human persons. According to him, our "natural inclinations" dynamically orient us toward specific aspects of human flourishing or well-being, and practical reason "naturally" apprehends these aspects as "good" and therefore to be pursued in action. In this text Aquinas goes on to distinguish three levels of natural inclinations and basic human goods. On the first level there is in us a natural inclination to the good in accordance with the nature we have in common with all substances. The good to which we are naturally inclined at this level is that of being itself, and since, as Thomas elsewhere (ibid., 1, 18, 2) notes, the being of living things is life itself, the relevant human good here is that of life itself. At another level there is in us a natural inclination "to more special goods according to the nature we share in common with other animals." The relevant good here is the union of male and female and the handing on and educating of new human life. Finally, Aquinas says, there is in us an inclination "to the good according to the nature of reason, which is a nature proper to man: thus man has a natural inclination to know the truth about God, and to live in society. . . ."

The list of basic goods identified by Thomas in *Summa Theologiae* 1–2, 94, 2 is not intended by him to be taxative or exhaustive; it is rather an illustrative list, as indicated by the fact that he uses such expressions as "and the like" and "of this kind" in speaking about the goods he names.

Finally, it is essential to keep in mind that Aquinas was no dualist or "tri-ist"—i.e., he did not think that a human being is composed of two or three distinct natures. Rather, the one human nature has different levels; it is a complex nature, embracing substantive, animate, and rational components.

8. Germain Grisez and his colleagues, John Finnis and Joseph Boyle, have

for many years attempted to account fully for all the fundamental or basic goods perfective of human persons, the goods which, when grasped by practical reason, serve as "starting points" or "principles" for intelligent human action, for deliberating about what is to be pursued through human choice and action. Grisez identifies eight such goods: (1) life itself, including health and the handing on of life; (2) knowledge of truth and appreciation of beauty; (3) satisfaction in playful activities and skillful performances; (4) self-integration or harmony among various aspects of the self; (5) practical reasonableness and authenticity (harmony among moral reflection, free choices, and their execution); (6) justice and friendship or harmony among human persons; (7) religion or harmony between humankind and God or the "more-than-human-source of meaning and value"; and (8) marriage. For an account of the first seven of these goods see Grisez, *Christian Moral Principles*, pp. 115–39, and the essay coauthored by Grisez, Boyle, and Finnis, "Practical Principles, Moral Truth, and Ultimate Ends," *American Journal of Jurisprudence* 32 (1987), pp. 107–08. In 1993 Grisez published Vol. 2 of *The Way of the Lord Jesus, Living a Christian Life* (Quincy, IL: Franciscan Press). In it he argues persuasively that marriage is a distinctive basic human good, irreducible to any others. In his earlier work he had regarded marriage as a complex of the good of interpersonal harmony or friendship and the good of human life. However, he now holds—and for very good reasons—that it is a distinct human good. Finnis and Boyle concur with him. I too hold that these eight forms of human flourishing are goods perfective of human persons, irreducible to other goods.

It is important to recognize that the principles of practical reason (of natural law) directing us toward these goods are *not* moral principles—i.e., principles enabling us to distinguish between morally good and morally bad alternatives of choice. These principles render human choices and actions rational or intelligent. Even immoral choices are rational and intelligent, and evildoers appeal to principles of this kind to rationalize their behavior.

9. Thus in Deuteronomy 6:4 we read: "Hear, O Israel: the Lord our God is one Lord; and you shall love the Lord your God with all your heart, and with all your soul, and with all your might. . . . " And in Leviticus 19:17 we read, "You shall love your neighbor as yourself." Consequently, when Jesus was asked which is the greatest commandment, he replied: "You shall love the lord your God with all your heart, and with all your soul, and with all your mind. This is the great and first commandment. And a second is like it, You shall love your neighbor as yourself. On these two commandments depend all the law and the prophets" (Matt 22:37–40; cf. Mk 12:28–34; Lk 10:25–28; Rom 13:9; Gal 5:14).

In the light of this religious tradition, it is therefore easy to understand why St. Thomas explicitly identified the twofold command to love God and neighbor as oneself as the "first and common precept of natural law" to which the specific norms of the Decalogue are to be referred as conclusions are referred to their principles (see *Summa Theologiae,* 1–2, 100, 3, ad 1).

Aquinas did not explicitly distinguish between the precepts or first principles of natural law identifying basic forms of human flourishing as the goods to be pursued and its first moral principle or the principle of love of God and neighbor and specifications of this principle such as the Golden Rule. However, a patient reading of relevant texts in *Summa Theologiae* 1–2, 94 and 100, especially 100, 1, 3, and 11, will show that he clearly identified the love command as the first moral principle of natural law and that he included such moral norms as the Golden Rule among the first and common precepts of natural law. For an exegesis of relevant Thomistic texts on this matter, see my *An Introduction to Moral Theology,* pp. 49–53 and texts cited there.

10. It is, in my opinion, instructive to note that John Paul II, in *Veritatis Splendor*, explicitly related the precepts of the Decalogue concerned with our neighbor to the love commandment, making it clear that we can love our neighbor only by respecting the *goods* perfective of our neighbor. Thus he wrote: "The different commandments of the Decalogue are really only so many reflections of the one commandment about the good of the person, at the level of the many different goods which characterize his identity as a spiritual and bodily being in relationship with God, with his neighbor, and with the material world. . . . The commandments of which Jesus reminds the young man are meant to safeguard the *good* of the person, the image of God, by protecting his *goods*. . . . " (n. 13; cf. nn. 50–52, 67, 99). On this see my essay, "*Veritatis Splendor* and Natural Law: From First Principles to Moral Absolutes," *Rivista Teologica di Lugano,* 1.2 (1996) 193–215.

11. This is the way Grisez formulates the first principle of morality or the first moral principle of natural law in *Christian Moral Principles,* p. 184.

12. On this see Grisez, *Christian Moral Principles,* pp. 184–89; Grisez, Finnis, Boyle, "Practical Principles, Moral Truth, and Ultimate Ends," pp. 127–29.

13. Although Thomas Aquinas, in his articulation of natural law, did not explicitly identify moral principles further specifying the first principle of morality, which he articulated in terms of the twofold command to love (cf. *Summa Theologiae,* 1–2, 100, 3, ad 1), he did include, among the "first and common principles" of natural law, such principles as "do unto others as you would have them do unto you; do not do unto others as you would not have them do unto you"—or the Golden Rule (cf. ibid., 1–2, 94, 4, ad 1) and "evil is to be done to no one" (cf. ibid., 1–2, 95, 2). Principles of this kind would seem to further specify the twofold command to love and to serve as premises in light of which the truth of the precepts of the Decalogue can be shown (on this, cf. ibid., 1–2, 100, 1, 3 and 11, and my *An Introduction to Moral Theology,* pp. 49–53).

The problem here is how one proceeds from the first principle of morality to specific moral norms. Aquinas did not give much consideration to this matter, holding that one "immediately," "with but little consideration" could come to grasp the truth of specific moral norms such as those found in the Decalogue, in the light of the "first and common precepts of natural law"—i.e., in light of the precepts directing us to act in behalf of human goods, to love God and neighbor, to do evil to no one, to act fairly. Grisez has sought, in his development of natural law thought, to develop this issue quite explicitly and clearly by articulating "modes of responsibility"—i.e., moral principles more specific than the first principle of morality, but more general than specific moral norms. In his earlier writings (e.g., *Contraception and Natural Law* [Milwaukee: Bruce, 1964]) Grisez expressed these requirements of natural law in both affirmative and negative ways. In his most recent writings, in which he continues to develop natural law thought, Grisez articulates these "modes of responsibility" negatively. He does so because formulating them in this way shows that it is impossible for them to come into conflict, because one can simultaneously forbear choosing and acting in an infinite number of ways. The function of these moral principles, which help specify the first principle of morality, is to exclude ways of choosing incompatible with a will toward integral human fulfillment. Hence they are articulated negatively rather than affirmatively. On this see Grisez, *Christian Moral Principles*, 189–92, 205–26.

14. On the movement from the first moral principle and its specifications or modes of responsibility to specific moral norms and on the reasons why some specific moral norms are not absolute whereas others are, see Grisez, *Christian Moral Principles,* pp. 251–68; see also my *An Introduction to Moral* Theology, pp. 79–81.

15. This understanding of human bodily life and of human personhood is clearly set forth by Joseph Fletcher, Peter Singer, Michael Tooley, and many other moral philosophers and theologians today. Thus, in his *Morals and Medicine* (Boston: Beacon Press, 1960, p. 211) Fletcher writes: "Physical nature—the body and its members, our organs and their functions—all of these *things* are a part of 'what is over against us', and if we live by the rules and conditions set in physiology or any other *it* we are not men, we are not *thou*. . . . Physical nature is what is over against us, out there. It represents the world of *its*" [emphasis in original]. The same understanding of bodily life is set forth by Peter Singer in many writings. See, for instance, his *Rethinking Life and Death: The Collapse of Our Traditional Ethics* (New York: St. Martin's Press, 1994), especially pp. 190–92, where he articulates the requirements of the "first new commandment," to wit, that we must "recognise that the worth of human life varies" and that "life without consciousness is of no worth at all." Basically the same view is integral to the ideas set forth by Michael Tooley in his *Abortion and Infanticide* (New York/Oxford: Oxford University Press, 1983). Obviously, this way of understanding human bodily life regards it merely as an instrumental good, a good *for* the person, not of the person. Consequently, this understanding of the value of bodily life goes hand in glove with the view that not all living human beings or members of the human species are persons. Rather, only those members of the species actually capable of conscious life and of having interests are persons.

16. One theologian who holds this view, Richard McCormick, S.J., thus claims that human bodily life is a "good to be preserved precisely as the condition of other values,"—i.e., consciously experienced values. Consequently, in his opinion, the criterion to determine whether medical treatment is obligatory or not must be based on the quality of the individual's life, on the burdensomeness of the individual's life, not the burdensomeness of the treatment employed. Thus McCormick can say: "It is the kind of, the quality of the life thus saved (painful, poverty-stricken and deprived, away from home and friends, oppressive) that establishes the means as extraordinary. *That* type of life would be an excessive hardship for the individual" [emphasis in original]. *How Brave a New World? Dilemmas in Bioethics* (Garden City, NY: Doubleday, 1978), p. 347.

This dualistic understanding of the human person and instrumental character of bodily life is also brought out clearly by Daniel Maguire, one of the leading champions of mercy killing and assisted suicide in the United States today. In a passage quite reminiscent of the blatant dualism espoused by Fletcher (cf. previous endnote), Maguire had this to say: "Birth control was . . . for a very long time, impeded by the physicalistic ethic that left moral man at the mercy of his biology.

He had no choice but to conform to the rhythms of his physical nature and to accept its determinations obediently. Only gradually did technological man discover that he was morally free to intervene creatively and to achieve birth by choice. The question now arising is whether, in certain circumstances, we may intervene creatively to achieve death by choice or whether moral man must in all cases await the good pleasure of biochemical and organic factors and allow these to determine the time and manner of his demise. . . . Could there not be circumstances when it would be acutely reasonable . . . to terminate life through either positive action or calculated benign neglect rather than await in awe the dispostions of organic tissue?" Maguire answers this rhetorical question in the affirmative, and no wonder, given his understanding of human bodily life. The passage is found in his essay, "The Freedom to Die," in *New Theology No. 10: The Ethical and Theological Issues Raised by Recent Developments in the Life Sciences*, ed. Martin E. Marty and Dean G. Peerman (New York: Macmillan, 1973), pp. 188–89.

17. A good recent critique of dualism can be found in David Braine, *The Human Person: Animal and Spirit* (Notre Dame, IN: University of Notre Dame Press, 1992). For a brief but incisive critique, see Grisez, *Christian Moral Principles,* pp. 137–39.

18. Some might claim that the phrase, "I hurt myself," used to describe what occurs when one breaks one's arm, is merely metaphorical. They would counter by saying that a person, for instance, who loses a finger in an accident does not say, "I have lost a part of myself," but rather, "I have lost my finger." Moreover, we do not consider a person who has suffered the loss of a finger or arm or leg to be less of a person.

In responding to such counterclaims, it should be pointed out that the person transcends the sum of his parts—and this is why we do not regard a person who has lost a finger or arm or leg as less of a person for having suffered this loss. But nonetheless, the person who has suffered the loss of a finger or arm or leg has suffered harm to himself, to his bodily integrity. Surely, attacks on the body of a person are regarded as attacks on the person and are treated more severely than attacks on the person's property. The human persons I love are not merely conscious subjects inhabiting bodies, but are flesh-and-blood beings. I come into *personal* contact with them by *touching* them, and some touches are "offensive" because they violate the person's integrity and personal inviolability.

19. Consequently, Thomas Aquinas, commenting on St. Paul's first letter to the Corinthians, declared: "homo naturaliter desiderat salutem sui ipsius, anima autem cum sit pars corporis hominis, non est totus homo, et anima mea non est ego; unde licet anima consequatur salutem in alia vita, non tamen ego vel quilibet homo" (*Super Primam Epistolam ad Corinthios lectura*, XV, lec. ii, no. 925).

Education: Nature, Nurture, and Gnosis

John E. Coons

Every natural law theory recognizes two distinct but related forms of goodness that can be realized by human choice. The first consists of behaviors; conduct is good if it satisfies principles and rules deriving from what it is to be human. The second—the personal perfection—is the moral identity one can acquire as one chooses among possible behaviors. Historically, most but not all versions of natural law have taught that the human actor must correctly grasp the good of the first sort in order to achieve that of the second. No one advances in moral self-perfection while mistaking bad acts for good. This view has the practical appeal that it identifies certain people as bad. It might also be true.

On a closely related point, natural lawyers are unanimous: Rational actors are fallible. In making choices humans can mistake either the facts or the rules that govern conduct, and they can do so without culpable self-delusion. The most diligent search for the objective good can turn up wrong answers. It might, for example, be truly wrong to withhold certain information from the police, but the most earnest pilgrim could conclude otherwise and act accordingly. The majority of natural moralists would think the pilgrim morally diminished by this good-faith error.

For all its venerability, this view of the good person is intellectually shaky. Natural law does, of course, entail the premise that behavior itself is good or bad apart from how we judge it. But that premise does not necessarily imply that bad actions make bad people. Such a conclusion would be consistent with the premise but not required. An utterly different view, but one still consistent with the premise, would be that persons become morally good by diligently seeking the correct behavior, that honest mistakes in no way diminish personal goodness. The seeker perfects himself even while making a hash of the practical order that he tries to serve. Such a disjunction between the good of acts and of actors is plausible. Nor does it risk the common good; the belief that moral self-perfection depends upon one's serious pursuit of natural justice is an appropriate incentive for citizens.

I need names to distinguish these competing models of personal goodness. The view that requires correct knowledge of right answers I shall call "natural gnosticism"; the one that is satisfied by a diligent quest for those answers will be identified by various forms of the noun "obtension" (the O.E.D. allows us to enlist this old word).[1] These two images of the good person are quite distinct; translated into policy, it would not be surprising if they should imply different regimes for education.

Natural Gnosticism

Each view (the gnostic and the obtensional) claims to be the correct understanding of natural moral perfection, and it will be helpful to identify the place each holds among the various nature-based theories of the good person. A four-set breakdown of natural law theories serves this purpose. (It is a confection of Patrick Brennan's and mine.)[2] Two types are clearly gnostic, each fusing the good of the act with the good of the actor; in order to fare well morally, one must discover and do correct deeds. The third type of natural law is less perspicuous, but probably agrees. The fourth rejects the gnostic fusion, allowing self-perfection by obtension.

Aristotle and Aquinas represent the first of these natural traditions, which I shall call common sense. For Aristotle, the actualizing of the natural finality of the human person is an achievement of the intellect. Indeed, it is the inferior mind of the "natural slave" that limits his moral horizon, denying to the slave the free person's fuller access to eudaemonia.[3] A millennium and a half later Aquinas added a refinement; innocent ignorance concerning a fact can cancel the moral self-injury of an objective error. But its effect is merely to excuse. The actor's futile effort to find and do the real good is never perfecting.[4] If Oedipus strove for the best, his honest mistakes nonetheless left him a moral washout. This view finds contemporary expression in the language of "moral luck" that is preferred by philosophers such as Thomas Nagel and Bernard Williams.[5]

The common sense tradition was and still is widely criticized as lacking a ground of obligation. The scrutiny of natures may help to identify the act that would be proper, but "who sez" that we should observe it?[6] Responding to this criticism, Suarez and others identified God as the source of obligation and thereby solidified what Brennan and I call the classic position.[7] A discernible divine command gives natural law its obliging force, making it our task to realize the right relations (or matches) among created natures. These matches are disclosed by our reflection upon sense data and upon various self-evident propositions. Suarez et al. concede, however, that only some of the correct behavior is self-evident. Under certain circumstances actors can be invincibly ignorant of the right way. This is a pity, for again comes the gnostic turn; "such ignorance cannot exist without guilt." Indeed, "the existence of a precept obliges a man to know it." The classic position offers the misinformed no hope of moral fulfillment.

The third school of nature is a work of our times; its version of self-perfection is "integral human fulfillment" (or, here, simply "integration"). The edifice of John Finnis, Germain Grisez, and others, it has deserved and received considerable academic attention.[8] As a moral system, it is founded upon a set of seven or eight basic human goods (knowledge, friendship, play, religion, etc.). Integration is less plainly gnostic than the first two sets. Or, more accurately, integration at first seems to recognize that all persons have knowledge sufficient for full self-perfection.

True, our realization of the basic goods through the search for correct behaviors is a contingent intellectual achievement; fallibility is still in play even as, with intelligent creativity and freedom, we act to achieve practical reasonableness. But fallibility is consistent with the view that we achieve self-perfection by obtension. Indeed, at one stage, the integrationists make the prospects of the invincibly ignorant seem identical with those of the moral cognoscenti. Speaking of reason's proper attitude toward the basic goods, Finnis declares "the first principle of morality":

> Insofar as it is in your power, allow nothing but the basic reasons for action to shape your practical thinking.[9]

This might suggest that reasonableness is necessary to personal morality but *only insofar as it is in your power*. Integration flirts with the obtensional conclusion that diligence is the efficient instrument of moral self-perfection.

This intimation, however, fades in the succeeding description of integral human fulfillment as the achievement of natural personal goodness. Integration requires that the human actor avoid the neglect of any one good; "participating in all human goods *well*" is necessary to full moral development of the self.[10] There is a certain harmony of the basic goods that must be achieved, and a person's intention to get it right is merely necessary and not sufficient. Unless I misread Finnis and Grisez, the interior commitment of the actor is not sufficient where he fails to achieve this state of objective concordance. My fear increases as they emphasize the role of religion in clarifying the terms of integral human fulfillment.[11] Correct perceptions of the integrated good enhance personal moral perfection; and, alas, these are insights that some will have in abundance and others will lack through no fault of their own.

Later I shall speak of the consequences of believing in one theory of personal goodness or the other. It will then be clear why I hope that my impression of the integration school as gnostic is simply a misunderstanding. Meanwhile, let me emphasize that the belief in moral self-perfection by honest effort in no way impugns the value of nature as a guide to reason in the necessary and unending search for correct behavior. Indeed, where obtension proceeds without divine revelation, its typical methods of inquiry are those of natural law; fulfillment of the natural good of correct actions is exactly what one must "put forward as a reason" to one's own free and responsible will.[12]

Moving Natural Law Inside

What Brennan and I had sought in the first three versions of natural law emerges without ambiguity in the work of Bernard Lonergan.[13] To put it simply, Lonergan looks for moral perfection of the person inside the self. This is not, of course, a fall into solipsism. Like every other natural lawyer, Lonergan holds fast to the reality of the good that is to be realized by conduct; that reality is the very object of moral quest. The actor remains responsible *to* the external good. The question is: responsible *for what*?

Not for correct answers, says Lonergan, who begins the vindication of honest error with a grudging concession of the fallibility of the moral self. This weakness of ours does not, of course, excuse or even diminish the cognitive burden of the moral pilgrim. Quite the opposite. To recognize that our minds typically fall short of full apprehension is only to intensify the duty to search. Because moral choice remains a step into the obscure, our hard-won cognitive advances serve mostly to confirm the darkness that by nature we are commissioned to oppose.

What is, however, clear to every person, and only this, is that we have been born free creatures who are made to say yes or no to the obligation to seek the real good. Putting it back into Aristotle's terms, it is precisely in saying yes to the imperative to search that we actualize our potential for moral self-perfection. Our finality lies in becoming one who is committed to the task. There is no higher natural perfection. The honest seeker reaches sufficient moral reality in the perceived content of his own committed subjectivity. He grasps whatever his mind can bring in from the cold to be judged. He may be wrong about the content of the moral truth of the extended world. His judgment, nevertheless, achieves full integrity by ardently affirming that elusive truth as its object. His moral grasp exceeds his cognitive reach. Lonergan calls this achievement "authenticity."[14]

I should emphasize that this effort of mine to squeeze the prodigy that is Lonergan into a nutshell is untrue to his own distinctively exhaustive method and is justified here only by necessity. Lonergan is his own best advertisement for the generative toil that is required of the successful (or unsuccessful) seeker of objective moral truth. I am content here to quote these few lines from *Insight*:

> Will is good . . . in the measure that antecedently and without persuasion it matches the pure desire both in its detachment from the sensitive subject and in its incessant dedication to complete intelligibility. A will less good than that is less than genuine; it is ready for the obnubilation that takes flight from self-knowledge; it is inclined to the rationalization that makes out wrong to be right. . . . In brief, as man's intelligence has to be developed, so also must his will. But progress in willingness is effected by persuasion, persuasion rests upon intelligent grasp and reasonable judgment, and so the failure of the intellect to develop entails the failure of the will.[15]

It is risky for a humdrum lawyer to declare that this move to the inside is important to the future of natural law moral theory, but so I see it. Natural law has been prodigal in its concentration on externals, often on the most contestable particularities of behavior. Like waves lapping the rocky shore, its progress in identifying clearly correct rules is barely discernible. At the same time, its gnostic assessment of self-perfection has caused natural law unconsciously to preach a moral hierarchy of persons, hierarchy that is foreign to the sensibilities of many of its own faithful. Perhaps the flourishing of these several great traditions might be restored by a turn to the one perspicuous law that is both given and fulfilled inside us. I accept the need for and the truth of rules of behavior. By all means, keep telling us *what* is good; but meanwhile reconsider *who* is good. On that question there is territory yet to be mapped by the moral psychologists of natural law.

Lessons for Education

The Rescue of Dignity and Equality

My assignment is to reconsider the implications of natural law for the political economy of schools. Specifically, then, what do our competing natural theories of moral self-perfection have to say about the curriculum and the organization of schools? Presumably, the individual natural law educator will teach children only that version of moral self-perfection in which he believes and will debunk the one in which he disbelieves. Thus, there will be agreement in one respect and conflict in another about curriculum. The broad consensus that holds among natural lawyers regarding the content of the external good (correct behaviors) will be represented in all schools. On the other hand, regarding what it is that suffices for moral self-perfection, there will be the sharpest division in their respective messages.

Consider the stakes in this schism. The division implicates core elements of the Western understanding of how humans stand in basic relation to one another. A teacher's choice between the obtensional and gnostic forms of moral self-perfection determines the coherence of several premises that are generally taken for granted in the classroom; these premises include human dignity, equality, and community. That choice will also affect the political design of a school system.

Dignity I begin with the implications for the concepts of human dignity and equality. Most natural law pedagogues tend to be universalist and inclusive in spirit; they would prefer that children learn a story of mankind in which natural moral perfection is an equal-opportunity enterprise. In pursuing this purpose, they very frequently resort to the concept of dignity which they regard as both intensely positive and common to all human persons. Unfortunately, one primary victim of moral gnosis is human dignity.

Linked historically to the *Imago Dei* of *Genesis*, dignity is something lodged in the specific human faculties of reason and free will. Among the creatures it is the human person alone who through reason can seek the terms of obligation to others and thereby realize himself. Dignity resides in this capacity for moral self-perfection through quest and choice. The problem with this idea is that, again, the grasp of correct answers to moral questions is plainly contingent upon circumstance. One person's apprehension of the relevant facts and rules (and the opportunity to reflect upon them) differs greatly from another's. Reason is ours, but differentially so; and if reaching correct answers is the necessary entree to personal moral perfection, dignity becomes relativized. It obtains only as a hierarchy of individual capacities. We all have dignity, but you have more. Dignity is transmogrified into the medium of indignity.

This tendency of gnostic naturalism to relativize the human capacity for personal goodness is curiously confirmed in the current revivals of Aristotelian ethics. Happiness, we learn, consists in thriving intellectually, socially, and economically. Our natural finality can be had only by objective moral success. Humans are not perfected by struggle but by getting it right, an outcome which depends in great measure upon brains and luck. We witness a surprising convergence of John Finnis and Martha Nussbaum.

When it is understood thus as a hierarchy, dignity also cancels any theory of a descriptive human equality, for equality requires a capacity for personal goodness that is uniform in degree. Mere *possession* of a capacity to advance morally by grasping discrete aspects of the objective good will not serve. The problem is not that we are fallible, but that we are fallible in degrees that vary by luck and native acumen. In order for our capacity for moral self-perfection to be uniform in degree, it would have to be purged of its gnostic elements and reconceptualized as the ability to be diligent in the search for the real good. That is a talent that might be evenly shared.

Bell Curve Traditional natural lawyers recently confirmed their unconscious bent for moral aristocracy by participating in the spectacular overreaction to Herrnstein and Murray's *Bell Curve*.[16] Whether accurate or not in its empirical claims about the distribution of cognitive power, that book was plainly received by many as a message about human worth; these critics understood it as an implicit assertion of a natural hierarchy of moral capacity. The gnostic temptation was at work. How easy it is for the sophisticated to imagine that sophistication itself is the moral category! When this gnostic bent inhabits a mind already committed to a putative belief in human equality, the effect is painful intellectual tension. It is not easy to serve both hierarchy and equality.

I concede that the contribution of gnostic natural law to the relativizing of dignity and to the subversion of equality has been trivial compared to that wrought by "enlightenment" theories. The most hierarchical of all moral conceptions is the notion that we invent our own morality; in such a world, it is the clever whose moral horizon is the most expansive. Sophistication multiplies the selves that any of us can choose to be.

Nevertheless, gnostic natural law has unwittingly abetted this ideological tendency; celebrating the moral potency of the intellectual, it has paradoxically endorsed Nietzsche's catalogue of those qualified to be Ubermensch.[17] With him the gnostic affirms the moral apotheosis of the smart. True, the natural law hero does not invent a strictly personal morality; nevertheless, this hero has the right mental stuff for finding the authentic mother lode and thereby achieving greatness. A gnostic president once identified such a person for the graduates of Yale as "the best and the brightest."

If this be the truth of our world, then we are bound to teach it to our children, with its clear implication that the gifted child holds the key to a moral transcendence that is unavailable to the dull. The effect of this gnostic teaching upon the pupils' perception of one another is quite predictable. School (indeed, life) becomes a moral Calvinism in which the elect are a subcategory of the smart.[18]

Re-Picturing Community

The educator who would introduce natural law into the curriculum is, thus, forewarned. Delivered in its traditional intellectual modes, natural law provides its students a hierarchical moral perception of one another and of adults. Its gnostic criteria of moral fulfillment create an undertow of condescension for the stupid and the barbarian. Only by teaching obtension can natural law find a home in a democratic school. As we continue to identify the benign implications of obtension, it is hard to be indifferent to the choice between natural law theories.

A few more examples of these implications can be sketched here, giving primary attention to the idea of human community, as it would be portrayed for the child. Regarding the definition of community, I am going to make an assumption that is largely intuitive (and, of course, problematic). I am confident that this assumption can be defended as a truth of both human psychology and linguistic usage, but here I shall simply assert it as follows: In order for the reality that is named community to hold, the most marginally rational person—the most wretched and disadvantaged member—must be perceived to have a capacity for moral and/or spiritual self-fulfillment (and, conversely, degradation) that is as plenary as that of the most gifted and fortunate. In other words, the belief in human equality and the rejection of moral gnosticism are definitional to community.[19] The original Hasidics may have taught something of the sort as a reaction to the elitism of the learned.[20] Where humans are perceived to stand in a hierarchical order of moral perfectibility, the Brahmin and the outcast may achieve coexistence or even society; but community will elude them.

I shall not try to answer once for all the additional question of whether community, when properly defined, requires belief in the equality of *outsiders*.[21] The members of certain human clusters do in fact see nonmembers as deficient in moral potential. My present disposition is to include such self-defining moral elites within the definition but to demote them to a distinctly inferior status in the taxonomy of communities. It will be convenient simply to call them "elites," so long as that term is understood to be pejorative. Members of self-regarding moral elites are by definition incapable of belonging to any community that includes perceived inferiors; of course, in specific practical matters elites can cooperate with such communities.

By contrast, individuals who do accept the descriptive equality of all rational humans are capable of membership in an indefinite number of particular communities. And any community in which this belief is shared by all members is entitled to the label "genuine." This does not imply that genuine communities all share the same ultimate purposes, lifestyles, or rules of right behavior. Quite to the contrary, believers in universal human equality can cluster on the basis of disparate ideologies, religions, ethnicities, professions, or like differences that can set communities in practical conflict with one another. Put another way, although they are genuine, such communities can be *exclusive* in important social or ideological dimensions. Nevertheless, as we shall see, conflict between and among these groups has a meaning for their members that is crucially different from the meaning that is attached to such conflicts by members of gnostic elites.

Equality of Believers It is my impression that the world of Roman Catholicism is one locus of the belief in universal equality.[22] If I am correct about this, Catholics constitute a large and useful example of the impact of the obtensional versus the gnostic interpretation of human nature upon group attitudes toward outsiders. Let us assume (this is not so audacious) that the population of believing Catholics also satisfies whatever other criteria a reasonable person might think necessary to constitute a genuine community. In that event, their belief in a natural human moral equality locates Catholics (qua Catholic) in two genuine communities—one exclusive, one universal.

They are, first of all, a community to and among themselves; their church claims authoritative access to correct answers, and assent to that ecclesiastical authority is a criterion of membership. Exclusivity is no trivial matter for them. Their orthodoxy triggers meaningful obligation. In their own view they are bound (and nonbelievers are not) to give the teaching authority of their community a presumption of correctness. When engaged in the quest for correct moral answers, assent to this presumption operates as the practical threshold of the good conscience that is necessary and sufficient to moral self-perfection; the obtending believer cannot reject an ordinance of the church merely because he or she has vague reservations.

By the same token, even the most anguished and honest apostasy on a serious moral issue sets the individual outside this exclusive community. The dissenter emigrates from the cluster that upholds the authority of the church. Because that authority is vaguely defined, there will be practical disputes about who is in and who is out. But the principle is clear enough: The doctrinal emigré asserts that the ecclesiastical authority is wrong; in this person's eyes the exclusive community that accepts it is deluded about its reliability. The act of emigration is thus the invitation to a new and somehow more discerning community. It initiates a plurality of exclusive communities (even though each may aspire to the old name).

Finally, the exclusive community that consists of continuing believers also asserts a special commission and duty of their church to teach *all* mankind whatever can be known of moral truth. But do believers then suppose that outsiders have a reciprocal duty to give priority to these specific moral messages because of their source? I take it that, in the Catholic view, the answer is no. Every human is already obliged by nature to seek the objective moral good wherever he or she can find it. The unbeliever or emigré thus has the duty—the natural duty—to consider Catholicism's moral answers on their merits, along with whatever other wisdom is available; but for the unbeliever they can carry no special presumption of truth. Rome is seen as but one of the world's many representatives of the Tao. The element of community in such a relationship seems very thin.

Nevertheless, precisely in recognizing human equality, the Church has embraced a principle that makes its own moral answers about behavior irrelevant to the *goodness of the person*. Its commitment to moral self-perfection by obtension entails the richly communal message to the outsider that one who honestly concludes that the Church is wrong (on whatever issue) is bound in conscience to *reject* it. Moreover, it is exactly by doing so in response to conscience that one achieves the fulfillment willed for all by the Church. Even in the midst of the most intense conflict, real human connection among enemies remains possible. To the eyes of the insider, the conscientious outsider remains a full partner in that ultimate natural community consisting of all moral pilgrims. And this vision of unity holds even as the outsider honestly refuses the authoritative message of the exclusive community.

Genuine Community Nothing turns upon my using Catholics as the example. This relation between their exclusive but genuine community and its ideological competitors is merely one very large and vivid instance of the subsurface harmony that is everywhere generated and sustained by the assent to universal human equality. In their deepest meaning, the inevitable quarrels among genuine but exclusive communities thus reduce to disputes within the human family. These convulsions, however destructive in the economic and social order, never risk the moral integrity of either the individual or the community that is mankind.

Genuine community thus implies deep respect for the members of groups, however much their beliefs conflict with either accepted public values or one's own. This is specifically a respect for *persons* and not for their ideas or practices when these are perceived as false or evil, though, of course, this very respect for the person is a primary guarantee that the ideas themselves will receive fair consideration. In the midst of their inevitable conflicts, all exclusive but genuine communities understand the social order (domestic and international) to consist of persons of equal moral perfectibility and of inscrutable goodness who interact through social and political processes to determine exactly which accommodations will best sustain the common good. There will always be political losers, but in such a moral culture the losers will less often be selected by raw majoritarian power. Being respected themselves, they will be the more willing to respect and to sustain the unending responsiblity for practical judgment.

As it emerges from gnosticism, natural law prepares itself to teach genuine human community. It could have no more urgent mission to the children of the world.

Tolerance Reconsidered

The belief in moral self-perfection by obtension also presents the opportunity to reconceive the pedagogy of human tolerance within those schools that accept nature as authoritative. I do not pretend to see this matter whole and will suggest only the starting point. Again, it entails the severability of the two realms of the good: the world of behavior and that of the moral self as it chooses behavior.

I continue to assume the reality of good and evil in human conduct; the discussion here prescinds from all relativist versions of tolerance (e.g., moral neutrality). Whatever else tolerance implies, it means the sufferance of the real evil of bad behavior for the sake of some good of a higher order than the one threatened by whatever is to be tolerated.[23] When it willingly suffers pornography, the individual or the society does so for some high-minded reason—e.g., that free expression is crucial to the quest for truth. We suffer the bad for the sake of the good. On this our two versions of self-perfection agree.

Note that tolerance so conceived is a behavioral good with an external and objective status. It is a state of affairs that occurs whenever one person or a set of collaborators achieves the correct ordering of two objective goods that are in mutual conflict. For example, by regulating the sport of boxing the state might achieve the level of violence that, given the circumstances, is truly optimal.

Tolerance, however, also occurs as a moral state of the *person.* A moral actor can be tolerant. Whether or not an individual actually achieves this condition in a specific case can depend upon whether one's theory of personal goodness is gnostic or obtensional. Given the gnostic premise, only the person who discovers and wills the correct priority among conflicting goods could deserve the label "tolerant." By contrast, obtensional natural law would identify the tolerant person as that man or woman who searches diligently for the correct behavioral ordering. By effort alone the obtending person is already as morally enhanced as he could be by discovery of the right answer. As an aspect of the person, then, tolerance is a subspecies of obtension; it is generated by the free commitment to seek the external good in those specific cases where it will consist in the correct ordering of two goods that are in conflict in the behavioral order.

Moralities of Persons and Nations If it were simply one aspect of obtension, there would be nothing special to say about tolerance. It is in this respect no different from, say, justice, which also has its external and internal forms of perfection. What might make obtensional tolerance relevant to the pedagogy of natural law is its capacity to improve and clarify the rough analogy that educators often invoke between the moralities of persons and nations. That analogy is rough precisely because political collectivities necessarily act by consensus and must consider many other factors beside the law of nature. Nonetheless, educators commonly evaluate nations by the same human criteria that they apply to individual actions. It is as if the teachers were natural lawyers and the nations were persons. Whole societies get judged for their tolerance. Sweden tends to turn up at one end, China at the other.

Accepting this propensity of educators to personify societies as moral actors, the shift to an obtensional viewpoint offers a fresh perspective upon which nations could qualify as tolerant. From the gnostic point of view, the answer emerges as a straightforward calculus of government policies toward sex, drugs, cults, abortion, or what have you. If the policies of the society tend to be unusually proscriptive, the nation is intolerant. By contrast, viewed in obtensional terms, the tolerance quotient would allow for disjunction between the correctness of the nation's objective policy and the goodness of the (personified) society. The tolerant society would be the one that does its best to get a correct priority among conflicting goods—given the way it is able collectively to discern them. Singapore thus could be as tolerant as the United States.

Indeed, it could be more so. For tolerance, again, is the sufferance of a perceived evil. And here the evil is a collective perception: a consensus in the society sees certain behavior as bad and yet to some degree allows it. If, instead, it were simply a case of collective indifference, there would be nothing to tolerate. Take this hypothetical: Singaporeans become convinced that homosexual behavior is evil. For the sake of some other good, they nonetheless allow it. That would be a case of tolerance. On that same issue Americans might have no collective conviction; in allowing such behavior, the Unites States would not be tolerant but merely indifferent.

If an objectively repressive society can be tolerant, has the word lost its meaning? One does have to be careful not to transmute the Nazis into tolerant folk on the ground that they took seriously the correct ordering of values. Perhaps it is enough to say that, far from trying to order objective goods correctly, their specialty was to deny their existence. Taking Nietzsche seriously, Nazis needed no moral judgment beyond their determination of the Fuhrer's will. Still, I wish I saw a brighter line between the repressive but tolerant society on the one hand and the totalitarian society on the other.

And there are other problems here. For the present I only want to stress the heuristic payoff that comes from judging both individuals and societies not only by what they allow and proscribe but by the quality of the effort that leads them to judgment. Strictly speaking, collectivities cannot obtend at all. But natural lawyers, who so often judge a society's deeds, might well make the additional effort to judge the integrity of its search. By judging nations in their own terms as well as by objective universals, they could advance the insight of their own students, stirring an appreciation for the moral challenges faced by political actors.

Organizing Schools for a Nation of Natural Lawyers

I turn at last from these cosmic ideological concerns to the practical question that better explains my being invited to contribute to this symposium.[24] How would natural lawyers go about organizing and financing formal systems of schooling? As to this, a good deal depends upon the sort of society natural law might be assigned to educate. Two social extremes will serve to illustrate my view of the matter.

The first is a purely hypothetical society, one in which most adults believe in the moral authority of nature. They are—as it were—St. Paul's Gentiles, as yet uncorrupted by Hobbes and Richard Rorty. They are Poles, Eskimos, Ethiopians, and Celts; they are socialists, flat taxers, free traders, and monarchists; they are of every religion and none; they even disagree about how to teach what every one of them agrees should be taught. And, like every community of natural lawyers, they divide into gnostic perfectionists on the one hand and obtensional perfectionists on the other. In spite of all this diversity, what they agree on is (1) the reality of a behavioral good as preached by Aristotle, Aquinas, Leo Strauss, or Henry Veatch, and (2) the capacity of at least some persons, using reason, to identify parts of that good.

Call it a natural moral culture. How will this nation organize its schools, and will the gnostics and their obtensional opponents find something in this practical activity that they can agree on? In truth, regarding the regulation and structure of education, disagreement between them should be hard to find. At least on the central question of *moral content*, all natural systems (in whichever camp) seem to support principles—and even rules—of behavior that are roughly similar. In new and disputed cases, they conduct the search for the right answers in ways that, at least to my amateur eyes, seem compatible. This hypothetical society would prescribe schools that teach this moral content and this method of moral inquiry. In practical terms, there would be little in such a regime to dissatisfy even the gnostics.

In all other respects, the school system would be varied and dynamic. Having witnessed the consequences of state monopoly, no serious contemporary educator could still aspire to Plato's *Republic* on the ground that it is natural. In regard to the form and content of schooling, outside the moral dimension subsidiarity would be cherished, and the family would decide. Subsidized by society—and aided by professional advice—parents of every sort would exercise the kind of responsibility that nourishes the family relation and the civic virtues. In such a regime, competition among pedagogical methods would enhance the mastery of the behavioral good. At the same time, it would nourish social unity amidst ideological diversity; encouraged by the trust of the community, parents typically would appropriate this expression of confidence and return it to the social level, affirming the bond among peoples of very different political, ethnic, and religious outlooks. On all these points there would be no division between gnostic and obtensional natural law.[25] Of course, if such a society ever existed, it is long extinct.

Nurturing the Child's Personal Perfection in a Morally Pluralistic Society

The practical distinctions between gnostic and obtensional versions of education become more obvious once morality goes plural. To the natural gnostic, the present American moral scene is a great frustration. Every child in the public school incurs a direct and substantial injury, exactly to the extent that he or she believes the school's message of indifferentism (or worse). In the gnostic view of things, the child cannot achieve a personal perfection that rises above the behavioral content of his or her moral beliefs. One is not actually doomed by moral misinformation (if smart or lucky, the child may see through it), but heaven help the credulous child in the hands of the present school system.

Of course, there are islands of authentic natural teaching in both the public and private sectors. But one encounters them by chance, or, if parents have the capacity to pay, they seek them in the market. The state could subsidize the choices of the poor; but even a general system of scholarships would not remedy the problem. For, in this society, the families themselves are in disagreement about the objective good. Given a subsidized freedom to educate, many parents would still corrupt their own children with false teaching. To the gnostic, this scene is one of hopeless moral derangement both of personal goodness and of the common good.

By contrast, the obtensional interpretation of pluralism is less tragic; indeed, a family-based system of education could be understood (for this society) as a reasonable approximation of the natural ideal. At first this difference between the competing theories is not so clear. Insofar as behavioral evil gets taught in a pluralist system, the obtensional and gnostic camps agree that education is injuring the common good; all of us regret the damage to justice and the social order from teachers who portray real evil in positive terms.

What is distinct about obtension is that it denies that any teaching—bad or good—can affect the capacity of the *child* to reach moral self-perfection. It sees that *unjust societies and false ideas do not make bad persons*. The capacity of individuals to say yes or no to the quest for the real good is unaffected by exterior circumstances, including miseducation. Even if one fails to find the objectively correct way, this in itself is no threat to personal moral achievement, so long as one fulfills the obligation to look for it. The world may be the worse for my works, but I can be morally fulfilled by having tried my best.

This invulnerability of the moral person allows a more hopeful interpretation of the fate of children who are victimized by the schools. So far as I am concerned, it also presents a thoroughly realistic interpretation of the responsible self. The only tragedy for any human person is deliberately to reject the authority of the real good to demand full commitment of our personal resources.

If the moral prospects of children are invulnerable to wrong ideas about behavior, should we stop worrying about the ethical content of their education? Of course not, for obviously the *common* good is also at stake. We would all like to live among fellow citizens (whatever their personal goodness) whose education helps them to tell the difference between good and bad deeds. In a pluralist society, natural lawyers must keep looking for the system that will maximize the citizens' grasp of the common good. I shall at the end return to the criteria of such a system.

The Child's Viewpoint But stay a moment with the child. An important clarification remains to be made about the relation between the school system and the personal moral perfection of the student. Take the child's view of this issue. His ultimate moral invulnerability may console the rest of us, but it does not make the child indifferent to the form and content of the school's message. To the contrary, the child's natural capacity (and duty) to seek the good provides a strong ethical claim to a legally protected right of a very specific sort. That claim is a clear implication of the obtensional premise, as I shall now try to show.

Every rational child is aware both that good and evil are real and that his own grasp of correct behavior is inchoate and marginal. The child is also aware of the basic obligation to inform his conscience and to follow it. This two-sentence description of what in fact is a dense moral ontology serves my present purpose. The point is that the child is consciously responsible to obtend, and—as a beginner—has a specific responsibility in the search for right acts to desire the best adult source of moral advice.

It is a natural responsibility to try to become an efficient detector of the objective good; every child *ought* to want his or her moral education to commence in a relation of subordination that will aid the search for what one is by nature bound to seek. This involves no paradox. The child may remain morally invulnerable to anything except his own free abandonment of the quest for the good. However, for the time being this means only that the child's own authenticity as a seeker depends upon a willing pupilage to the most reliable moral authority that is available.

Moral Dependency Even a morally pluralistic society could understand this obligation of the child to seek the most efficient moral dependency. At least among ordinary people in America, the strong convention survives that all of us are obliged to search for answers that are correct, whether we like them or not. True philosophical skeptics are rare. Given this starting point, unless some countervailing reason appears, society owes every child a subordination to whichever adult sovereignty is most likely to encourage and assist the search for the content of the behavioral good that the child is obliged to will as the ideal.[26]

The obvious difficulty here is the moral pluralism of the potential sovereigns. Who among this menagerie of American adults is qualified as the leader to whom the child has a natural right? The state itself obviously is disqualified. Precisely to the extent that society lacks consensus regarding the good life, there can be no governmental candidate for the role of tutor. This, of course, is a primary reason that state schools fail; their moral curriculum can be little more than the private confection of professionals and lobbyists. Often, its highest objective is to avoid offense to any organized group.

But are not the parents even worse candidates for the role of moral sovereign? Here, again, the gnostic is torn by the prospect of twenty conflicting versions of sexual, economic, social, political, medical, religious, and intellectual good—all being thrust upon helpless infants in whatever school is chosen by their parent. Woe to the child and woe to the society the child will one day create!

Parental Authority Obtension, by contrast, would separate these two questions about the child and the society. It concedes that parental authority over choice of school would result in the teaching of a smorgasbord of specific behavioral goods; some of these will conflict with every version of natural law, posing real risks to the social order and even to the individual child's material welfare. In such cases, woe, indeed, to society. None of this, however, poses the slightest risk to the child's capacity for moral perfection. Indeed, the child is not only invulnerable; in one crucial respect he is positively benefitted by the sovereignty of the parents, however misguided their leadership. For it is this relationship alone that guarantees to the obtending child a message that is responsive to his own moral impulse. Parents may differ about the content of the good; what they agree on is that there is in fact a good to be sought.

This is a trait that is specific to the role of parenthood. It may disappear temporarily, say, at the office, where economic actors can be driven to believe pro tem in a Hobbesian world. It may disappear in the academy; professors—however correct their behavior—sometimes get promoted for talking like moral skeptics. In the home, by contrast, the reality of the good is indestructible. The most nihilistic parent is quite incapable of telling her child that there is no correct (or incorrect) way. Parenthood is the pulpit of objective morality, if only as the instrument of parental survival.

Again, the actual content of parental notions about morality is protean, and many a child receives bad ideas. What he never hears is that the good is his to invent. And so the child is always invited to obtend—to seek the real good, just as his nature requires. A system of education could do worse for the child. Ours presently does. In a pluralist state, only monopoly schools with a captive clientele could survive preaching the bogus good of moral neutrality.

Obtension, Parental Choice, and the Common Good

In this final part I continue to assume a pluralistic moral order (such as the United States) and an obtensional as opposed to a gnostic view of natural self-perfection. Turning from the personal moral fulfillment of the child, I now consider aspects of the objective common good (including the child's material welfare). How should we think about and plan for formal systems of schooling that, amidst diversity, can still teach the commutative and distributive justice of natural law?

In proposing an answer, I verge upon the very task I have often found so troublesome in natural moral inquiry. I admire the method and the metaphysics but find them inconclusive. Though often confident about the correctness of specific actions, all too seldom can I spot their illative connection with the human nature that I claim as my premise. My own practical judgments often seem less an inference from nature than from revelation; and when the latter seems sufficient, on grounds of efficiency I tend to abandon the natural side of the inquiry. I say this not to discourage anyone's pursuit of nature straight to the end; perhaps, for most people, obtension (the quest for the right conduct) can be managed in no other way. Henry Veatch is quite right: "If morals and ethics are not based on nature or reality, then what else are or can they be based on?"

I only want to warn that I am not very good at this sort of thing, nor am I always certain that I am talking the talk of natural law. A consolation here is that we need not get to the level of personal behaviors. Leave it to authentic natural moralists in schools of their own design to find and teach the specific objective good. My task is only to suggest a general system that is congenial to such schools and could exist within a pluralistic society; it is an inquiry into the practical politics of natural law.

The Ideal System The ideal system is suggested by substantive premises about nature, including the three already identified: descriptive human equality, equal human dignity, and genuine community. Each implies the other; together they tell us something about the natural organization of schools in a morally pluralistic society.

Specifically, the core responsibility of a nature-based ethic is to teach not only correct behavior but, first of all, the complex truth of human unity. Elite gnostic communities must be shown the possibility that the rest of us enjoy the same capacity as they for moral self-perfection. Individuals and groups who are ideological competitors of one another must grasp the intellectual structure of a descriptive human equality and appreciate its plausibility. Most of the churches will teach this sort of thing as revelation, but it is natural law that will make equality and its implications available to secular reason. In this project the state is not a reliable ally, and moral relativists are the enemy.

It will be a proper work of the naturalists to evangelize the warring groups by producing graduates who are able to distinguish the moral persons of their enemies from the evil of their policies. Success will depend upon the existence and example of a socially supported system of educational providers that, in its own constitution, affirms the message of human moral equality. Natural law thus has the vocation to persuade the larger society on practical grounds to adopt such an organic structure as public policy. The practical political objectives that sell the program of peace, stability, liberty, etc., will be wholly natural but will also appeal to persons of the most diverse philosophies, even including moral relativists.

The political chance for establishment of such a system is suggested by the contemporary and very visible popular concern for the teaching of objective morality; "virtue" is again a public good. Though the protagonists in this debate differ about the content of good, their common affirmation of its existence provides a major pillar of human equality. The society must now express this deep agreement about human nature in an institutional way, and no technical or financial difficulty bars that end. The school system may be plural regarding behavioral details while yet providing a unifying conception of the moral perfectibility of all persons. That is, the school system can be allowed to express the natural disjunction that obtains between the subjective and objective moral orders. Only such an economy of education could deserve the support of parents from incompatible moral communities.

The technical features of the system can be quite varied, so long as parents of all income levels are assured practical access to the types of schools they prefer. This qualification is extremely important. The historic system of state schools in this country, contrary to its own mythology, has divided children by income class. Thus, any system of family choice that is not plainly tilted toward the poor will be business as usual. It will effectively contradict the hoped-for allegiance to human equality. Unnecessary limitations upon the choices of nonrich families will be interpreted as new instruments of gnostic hierarchy. Such a "reform" will simply reproduce the instabilities and group hostilities of the existing order. The natural lawyer's strategy, then, will include specific techniques that level the playing field for all income classes. Here I shall simply assume the adoption of such protections.[27]

Social Stability Earlier I noted that, in a theoretical society that is committed by consensus to a natural law ethic, such a system would probably contribute to social stability. We must now ask whether that would be true in the very real context of moral pluralism, and here we encounter dissent. The critic is located principally in the school establishment, but deserves recognition. Though the particular issue is at a great remove from our starting point in nature, the spirit of natural law inquiry requires at least a skeleton response. I offer it as my conclusion.

In a pluralist society, does parental sovereignty bring us together or tear us apart? First of all, there is at least some insight available from those sometime friends of natural law, the empiricists. What they think they have learned from systematic study of private (i.e., family-chosen) schools that serve lower-class children is that educational choice correlates with tolerance and democratic behavior as well as with academic success.

Controlling for class differences, separate studies headed respectively by Greeley[28], Coleman[29], and Bryk[30] have over thirty years consistently found that low-budget religious schools graduate students who, along with the three Rs, have been taught to play by the rules in social and political affairs, to be tolerant and law-abiding, and to participate in civic life. The opponents of family choice have offered no data to rebut these claims. Hence, at worst, the reports of the experts are consistent with the conclusions I shall now report as my own; these are propositions drawn from professional and practical experience in the public and private sectors of education here and abroad since 1961.

Family Choice When the family is empowered by the larger society to choose the school and thus to monitor its own moral messages, its social connections are stabilized and enhanced in two ways—one internal, the other external. Internally the child and parent, who have already spent five years together, see their special relationship extended painlessly into the formal world of large institutions. The settled function of the parental advocate and protector is maintained. At the same time, the strangers who operate the school never are forced into the role of sovereign. Instead, they remain free to act as the professional agents they were trained to be. As a consequence, they are able to relate to the parents as coordinating equals.

The child thus retains confidence in his only unconditional sponsor, and the message of the school remains consistent with that of the home. The parents avoid the indignity of being required by their poverty to yield the child up to an alien system of values. Authority and responsibility remain linked, and the parent gains the strongest incentive to learn about education and to monitor its course. The family members continue to function qua family in relation to one another. Education is transformed into a profamily institution.

Meanwhile, viewed externally, this deliverance of the family from the moral randomness of public monopoly allows the parent and child to maintain an open and positive attitude to the school and to the other families who have chosen freely to be there. Perhaps, under special historical conditions, conscription to the moral melting pot actually nourished social peace. If so, it has long since ceased to do so. The captive aspects of the existing state system have become the guarantee not of mutual respect, but of conflict among the distinctive groups and between all those groups on the one hand and, on the other, those who presently impose upon them the moral curriculum (neutral or otherwise). Conscription tends to close the eyes of both child and parent to the real good that it is the child's natural duty to seek in others. No doubt moral insight sometimes transcends incarceration, but its natural home is not the ideological barracks. For this purpose the ideal is a free system in which children and families can follow their consciences to the school that teaches the moral truth as they perceive it.

It is true that family choice does not fully liberate the child. His liberty remains important, whatever one's version of natural moral perfection. I shall not revisit the details of our duty to honor the child's free nature, but only repeat the punch line: the child's best hope of practical moral freedom lies in a formal subordination to those who know and care for him and who will themselves be losers in the end if he does not achieve moral maturity. Paradoxically, children have their best hope of authentic liberty within the parental sovereignty.

I concede that, under a system of parental choice, at the margin of society there would be cadres, who would continue to teach hatred and who would then be aided by tax dollars. Even if the new system strains to exclude such groups, the First, Fifth, and Fourteenth Amendments will very properly give them a strong de facto protection. One must assess the social risk posed by these surviving islands of rage and weigh it against the equivalent risk that is presently represented in the monopoly schools of the state.

Family choice would not eradicate the freedom to hate; but it would eliminate a primary reason to do so. The existing system *is* that reason; it is a hate-generating device. Realistic parental fears of ideological submersion are a rich source of xenophobia. Families most willingly support the freedom of their ideological enemies when their own freedom is guaranteed in the same social bargain. As responsible moral beings, parents have by nature the best reason to wage social peace through choice, even as they conscientiously (and properly) wage cultural war through words. Even as they accomplish their own moral self-perfection, they would simultaneously honor the common good as their universal ideal. What could be more natural?

NOTES

1. To obtend is "to put forward as a reason." By a scant extension, I apply the word to the actor's subjective presentation to oneself of a justifying external purpose. The "ob" and the "ten" crudely suggest the outside/inside aspects of this moral quest that perfects even the actor who mistakes the behavioral good of the particular circumstances. According to the *O.E.D.*, the noun form appears in Samuel Johnson's dictionary of 1755. Some such term is needed to distinguish this version of moral self-perfection from that of the gnostics; other candidates are welcome.

2. Coons, J., and P. Brennan, "Nature and Human Equality," 40 *Am J. of Jurisprudence* 287 (1995); *By Nature Equal: The Anatomy of a Western Insight* (Forthcoming, Princeton University Press, 1998).

3. Aristotle, *The Politics*, I.2, 1252a31–34; I.5, 1254b20–23; I.13, 1260a12; III.9, 1280a33–34.

4. *Summa Theologiae*, Ia, q.19, a.2, ad 3. Question 19 is generally relevant to the question. And see Porter, Jean, "The Subversion of Virtue," *Annual of the Society of Christian Ethics* 23 (1992), pp. 25–26.

5. See their respective essays in Statman, Daniel, ed., *Moral Luck*. New York: SUNY Press, 1992. Each bears the same title as the collection, that is, "Moral Luck." Nagel is at p. 57; Williams at p. 35.

6. See, e.g., Arendt, Hannah, *On Revolution*. Harmondsworth: Penguin, 1977, p. 190.

7. *See* our "Nature and Human Equality," *supra*, note 2, pp. 306–12, where the sources of the Suarezian quotes are specified.

8. Ibid. pp. 312–19.

9. Finnis, John, "Natural Law and Legal Reasoning," 38 *Cleveland State Law Review* 1 (1990), p. 3.

10. Finnis, John, *Fundamentals of Ethics.* Washington, D.C., Georgetown, 1987, p. 72.

11. See Hittinger, R., *A Critique of the New Natural Law Theory.* Notre Dame, 1987, pp. 93–154.

12. See *O.E.D.*, *supra*, note 1.

13. Our views of Lonergan appear along with the documentation in "Nature and Human Equality," note 2, *supra*, at pp. 319–32. See also Coons, J., and P. Brennan, "The Idea of a Descriptive Equality: Lonergan Explains Jefferson," 12 *Lonergan Workshop* 45 (Boston College, 1996).

14. Lonergan, Bernard, *Understanding and Being: The Halifax Lectures on Insight* (2d. ed., The Collected Works of Bernard Lonergan, Vol. 5) (1988), p. 172.

15. Lonergan, Bernard, *Insight: A Study of Human Understanding* (4th ed.). San Francisco: Harper and Row, 1958 pp. 691–92.

16. Herrnstein, Richard, and Charles Murray, *The Bell Curve: Intelligence and Class Structure in American Life.* New York: The Free Press, 1994.

17. "Be robbers and conquerors, as long as you cannot be rulers and owners, you lovers of knowledge! Soon the age will be past when you could be satisfied to live like shy deer hidden in the woods. At long last the pursuit of knowledge will reach out for its due: it will want to *rule* and *own*, and you with it." "*The Gay Science*," in W. Kaufmann, ed., *The Portable Nietzsche.* New York: Viking Penguin, 1984, pp. 97–98 (emphasis in original).

18. Among the other ideological victims of natural gnosticism is the idea of servant leadership. No doubt we barbarians need direction from the intellectuals, but not for any superior capacity of theirs to be good persons. It is, rather, for their ability to illuminate for us the empirical choices that face the society and to help us evaluate them in reasoned dialogue about the common good, a conversation in which all rational persons are obliged by their nature to participate. It is Everyman's responsibility to deploy the insights of the gifted as he participates in social life, seeking (with Lonergan) to become authentic by dedication to the task. The smart people are merely working for and with the rest of us as we search together for the natural moral good of the extended world.

Still another victim is the idea of human greatness. Centuries of enlightenment have taught us to identify the great person in the manner of Carlyle's hero. He (or the very occasional she) is the one whose (good?) deeds of statecraft or intellect have altered the visible course of history. I am prepared to join the gnostics in the celebration of good deeds, but I think it a dreadful corruption to teach school children that there is some special connection between large enterprises and large souls. What they ought to learn is that we have insufficient evidence for any natural hagiography of good persons. Moral prodigies may lurk in the least visible quarters. To admire persons simply for their deeds would be a non sequitur.

19. Milton posed the problem for Adam: "Among unequals what . . . harmony or true delight . . . which must be mutual. . . ." Milton, J., *Paradise Lost*, Book VIII, 425–26. New York: Viking Press, 1949

20. See Telushkin, Joseph, *Jewish Literacy.* New York: William Morrow Co., 1991, pp. 214–18; Stephen Wylen, *Settings of Silver: An Introduction to Judaism.* Mahwah, N.J.: Paulist Press, 1991, pp. 250–57 and (bibliography) 378.

21. The reader may wish to consult "The Responsive Communitarian Platform," 2 *The Responsive Community* 4 (Winter 1991–92).

22. The present pope, in his critiques of errant theologians, has repeatedly emphasized that good intentions do not transmute bad acts into good. However, nothing in *Veritatis Splendor* or the new *Catechism* requires Catholics to suppose that mistakes about content prevent the diligent but mistaken actor from advancing personal moral perfection by sincere choices. The pope's restraint on this point reaffirms the theme of Vatican II that the invincibly ignorant conscience is to be followed "without thereby losing its dignity." *Gaudium et spes*, section 16. This does not *prove* a Catholic commitment to descriptive equality, but it is hard to find explicit rejections of the concept.

23. I am wholly content in this respect with the views of Budziszewski, J., *True Tolerance*. New Brunswick: Transaction Publishers, 1992.

24. The most accessible version of my views on schools may be Coons, J., "School Choice as Simple Justice," 22 *First Things* 15 (1992).

25. However, my earlier observations about the potentially demoralizing effects of gnostic teaching upon community would apply here. The promotion of moral hierarchy in some schools and equality in others deserves assessment; it is neglected here for reason of space and because of its limited relevance to a real world containing no society of the sort described.

26. An obtensional argument for the child's right is elaborated in Coons, J., "The Religious Rights of Children," in J. Witte, ed., *Religious Human Rights in Global Perspective, Vol. II: Religious Perspectives*. The Hague: Martinus Nyhoff, 1996, 157.

27. For a full-dress technical description, see Coons, J., and S. Sugarman, *Scholarships for Children*. Berkeley: Institute of Government Studies, 1992.

28. Greeley, A., and P. Rossi, *The Education of Catholic Americans*. Aldine: Chicago (1966); Greeley, A., W. McCready and K. McCourt, *Catholic Schools in a Declining Church*. Kansas City: Sheed & Ward, (1976).

29. Coleman, J., and T. Hoffer, *Public and Private High Schools*. Basic Books: New York (1987).

30. Bryk, A., V. Lee, and P. Holland, *Catholic Schools and The Common Good*. Cambridge: Mass: Harvard University Press (1993).

Family, Nurture, and Liberty

DAVID F. FORTE

When I was six or seven, growing up in Somerville, Massachusetts, my father took me on the bus and the MTA into Boston to walk the Freedom Trail. It was his practice to try to do something alone with each of his three sons on succeeding Saturdays. As we progressed along the Trail, smelling the dust and exhaust fumes of old Boston, my father walked me back into the eighteenth century. We strolled over the Common and looked into Old South Church (the Tea Party started here, he pointed out), down to the Old State House (the Massacre happened in front of it), Fanueil Hall (stopping for lunch nearby at Durgin Park), and up to North Church (the lanterns signaling Paul Revere looked out to the Back Bay, which was water then, he explained). At each stop, he would have me picture the people, the conflicts, the emotions, that accompanied the Revolution. It was a time of wonder for me. The names of Otis, Hancock, Revere, the Adams cousins, and even Crispus Attucks were impressed into my mind.

This, you should know, was shortly before the Southeast Expressway had cut through Haymarket Square, destroying parts of the Italian and Chinese neighborhoods of Boston, and long before the gentrification of Quincy Market. To find the eighteenth century, my father and I had to wend through the vegetable carts and butchers' stalls, avoiding the roaring delivery trucks in far greater profusion than can be seen there today. History then had to be found and imagined. It had yet to be cleaned up and placed beside the boutique and atrium restaurant.

Since that time, history has always been an exercise in imagination to me, as I attempt to transfer myself into the person and time I am reading about. Even in his eighties, my father and I exchanged history books and articles. When he visited Ohio, we took automobile treks to find the Old Northwest Territory, Connecticut's Western Reserve, and the industrial revolution. We were the best of friends in our shared quest to know, and we enjoyed each other's company immensely.

Now I suggest that if you who read this had a reasonably happy childhood, there was some moment (or moments) of similar awakening for you. As it was for me, I should think that that event would be but one small instant in a rich texture of experiences, events, and discoveries that you, your parents, your siblings and relatives, and your childhood friends created and shared. In that texture, I, like you, found and pursued my particular identity, which was exactly what my parents hoped would happen.

Since that time, neither I nor you have stopped in formation of our selves. And I, like you, continue to seek to make that self "better:" in the skill of our respective crafts, in our physical well-being, and—perhaps most importantly—in our moral actions. Or, if we don't, we know that we ought to (I really must begin exercising soon). We have setbacks, but the quest continues. We all, I suggest, spend our lives constantly seeking to become better persons.

Now, if that last sentence strikes you as reasonable, then I welcome you to the world of natural law. For what we have jointly found reasonable in that sentence is the following: (1) that we are "beings," existing over time and in place; (2) that we are aware of our "beingness," that is to say, we are each a "self;" (3) that at the root of our being is an individual personality that is unique and can never be replicated; (4) that we all strive to make our selves better, physically, materially, intellectually, and morally; (5) that succeeding in making ourselves better is an exercise in judgment, based on our capacities and on the manner in which we interrelate with our environment and other persons; (6) that we could not have formed our personalities as we have without some vital caring assistance of other persons; and (7) that we know all this by reflecting upon our (and others') lives—that is to say, upon our shared human experience.[1] Each of those propositions is a staple of a natural law philosophy; each comes from a manner of reasoning that is more reflective than analytical, though no less logical.

Nurture

What my father did for me that Saturday, and what my parents and other relatives did for me every day of my childhood, was to nurture me. They gave direction, encouragement, example, and material sustenance so that I could "do all I was capable of doing," as the stock phrase goes. Whatever potentiality for excellence they divined in me, they sought to nurture; that is, they tried to provide me with the basis for my own individual achievement.

It was not mere altruism that my parents gave to me, but the broader virtue of nurture. Altruism, defined as giving to another without thought of gain for oneself,[2] is a drier concept than nurture. I can conceive of altruism at arm's length, a distant form of assistance—modern welfare structures, for example.[3] Nurture requires a complex and subtle relationship and, usually, some degree of intimacy. Nor is it ordinary friendship. Or if it is friendship, it is at least a special form of friendship. Aristotle described friendship as seeking the good of the other;[4] but the kind of good that nurture seeks is the self-realization of the other. Nurture, therefore, requires more than kindness and certainly more than pity. It depends upon empathy, and is a special form of action taken at the moral behest of empathy.[5]

True, like altruism, nurture seeks to benefit another and, like friendship, it seeks the good of the other. The good it seeks, however, is an excellence of accomplishment in any of the arts of life, whether knowledge, productivity, aesthetics, or moral acuity.[6] Nurture looks to the particular endowments of the individual and seeks to provide the basis for that individual's instantiation of his own identity. It fosters growth, "perfects, advances, furthers" the good that is in the other person, to "unfold more completely" his latent capacities.[7] It respects the individuality of the other person. Think, for example, of how parents enjoy describing the unique personalities of each of their children.[8]

Individual Responsiblity

Nurture is not, however, doting kindness. It does not serve another's wants or desires, but rather it looks to another's needs.[9] By "needs" I mean that ensemble of requirements—material, emotional, and moral—that supports a particular individual's achievement of any range of life's goods.[10] Nurture can, therefore, include a real component of discipline, for ultimately, it is the habit of self-discipline that permits us to accomplish anything of personal note. Put another way, nurture assists another person in his particular participation in and among life's objective goods.[11]

Under the theory of natural law, there are certain values that are objectively good for the human person: life, knowledge, virtue, craft, aesthetics, community, and so on. (There is some variation in the litany, depending upon the theorist.) Nonetheless, the manner of accomplishing or participating in these goods is fully individual. Further, since the manner of participation is a matter of personal judgment, it is also a matter of personal responsibility. One can know how well one is doing in the effort for a greater involvement in the goods of life; that is to say, one can know (if one reflects on it) whether one is indeed becoming a better person. Accordingly, one could also fairly judge whether another person was "wasting his talents" or "becoming a credit to himself."

Parents tend to blame themselves for the moral and material failings of their children. Indeed, nurture, like all moral actions, needs judgment, craft, and practical reasonableness to be successful. It requires enormous subtlety, a sense of timing and proportion, and a notion of how to measure success in increments. A nurturing parent is daily called upon not only to perceive and exploit opportunities for the child, but to control and mitigate any damage that can occur from all sides, even from the parent's own missteps.

All of us can recall attempts at nurture that have failed because of lack of knowledge or poor execution. Nonetheless, nurture, strictly speaking, cannot be said to have failed simply because the recipient turned out to be a ne'er-do-well. That nurture is directed to the self-realization of the other person means that the other person has a responsibility for his relative range of successes and failures. In nurture, one gives for the good of the other. If the other fails to "make good" on the gift (absent a misfortune or harm not of one's making), it is that person's failure, not the parents'.

Empathy

Nurture, like many other forms of assistance to others, depends upon empathy, a concept noted by moral philosophers such as Aristotle, St. Thomas Aquinas, David Hume, and Adam Smith.[12] But it is more than just associating oneself with another's particular needs. ("If I were hungry and on the street, I would want a hot meal.") Rather, nurture's empathy is one that not just identifies oneself with the other, but respects the other's particularity. It sees the other as a *self* like my self, unique and having its own special gifts. Thus, although I have little talent in graphic arts, if I see my four-year-old son delighting for hours in drawing and molding, I shall seek an opportunity for that talent to develop according to its own potentialities.

Finally, the giving of nurture, though directed at the individual good of the other, is necessary for the moral self-realization of the giver as well. It is an act of moral excellence that requires empathy, judgment, restraint, and respect for the other person. As we would have been hampered in developing each of our respective identities had we not received nurture from someone else, so too, without opportunities to dispense nurture, we would be unable to achieve our own moral individuality. Thus, in one sense, the egoism/altruism dichotomy[13] associated with altruism is false; under natural law's conception of human excellence, one cannot instantiate one's own unique personality without (at the same time) engaging in helping others to do the same. It is not a quid pro quo. The two are bound up indissolubly in the same activity.[14]

Nurture, then, is a universal necessity and, if the principles of natural law hold true, a universal moral command. It is applied, like all moral commands, in particular circumstances. Although the term is most commonly used regarding parental obligations toward children,[15] the need for differing kinds of nurturing and the obligation to be a nurturer continue throughout our lives. It is not, as Kohlberg suggested, a transient stage on the way to adult Kantian moral independence.[16] Nor is it a moral attribute, as argued by Gilligan, primarily limited to the female gender.[17] That we may see it most concretely actualized in mothers does not mean that nurturing does not go on in other forms and other relationships.[18] A good teacher nurtures. A good lawyer is a nurturer. Even a child, in dazzling moments of insight, nurtures his mother or father.

Social Policy

If nurture is a universal moral norm derived from natural law, then what does that augur for the law, the polity, and social policy?[19] Can we find a system that not only protects persons from the evil and careless acts of others, but encourages and supports nurturing relationships upon which moral excellence and human happiness depend? Such a system would run counter to the egoism that seems to dominate much of the political spectrum today.

When rights become simple powers and not requirements for the practice of moral excellence; when educational policy becomes pressure-group controlled and is not directed toward the nurturing of the child or the parent/child relationship; when the poor are treated as objects and not as subjects with potentialities of individual self-realization; and when individuals are taught to perceive of themselves primarily as members of victim groups and not as unique individuals with capacities for accomplishment, a governmental attitude encouraging nurture would be an appropriate (if perhaps unwelcome) antidote. Such a governmental policy should also respect an environment where nurturing relationships already flower and be wise enough to leave it alone.

Nurture and Natural Law

First some preliminaries. What do I mean by "natural law?" In this essay, I shall, in general, limit my discussion to the perspectives offered by philosophers in the Aristotelian school, which is about as mainline a natural law theory as one can find. Let us begin our brief excursus with some working definitions that accord in general with the views of many of the traditional natural law theorists.

Nature, we can say, is the way things are and why they are what they are (e.g., what is a manatee, and why is it different from other water mammals?). Laws in the broadest sense are rules, either describing (or predicting) how things act in fact (e.g., the phases of the moon) or (for purposeful agents) how they ought to act (i.e., moral rules). Laws enacted by the state are an amalgam of authoritative rules, a portion of which declare how persons are to act. In short, laws seek to regulate human behavior toward some end. Ultimately, natural law asks what is the end of human nature and how laws can assist humans to fulfill that end.

Moral and Legal Norms

The tradition of natural law is based on the argument that moral and legal rules can be derived from a reflection on human nature.[20] Conceptions of the relationship of nature to humanity and to law differ among many philosophers in the tradition.[21] Most, however, start with an idea of human nature,[22] and from that conception seek to find the norms by which human law should be formulated.[23] That approach is the hallmark of the Aristotelian school.

The norms are normally derived by a reasoned reflection on human life and existence in its individual and social aspects. Once derived, those primary normative principles are available to guide both the lawmaker and the individual, either imperatively or aspirationally, into proper modes of action. Thus, the natural law tradition rejects arriving at moral and legal norms from the more narrow utilitarian concept of human nature as driven by a pleasure/pain calculus. Likewise, the tradition (usually) rejects the Kantian route of arriving at imperatives rationally and independently of a conception of nature.[24] Whether state of nature/law of nature theorists like John Locke are part of or opposed to the natural law tradition remains contested.[25]

Although proponents of natural law sometimes disagree as to its source, content, and justification, natural law seems to fulfill the continuing need of the Western legalist to have some touchstone by which to judge the goodness or badness, or even perhaps the validity or invalidity, of positive law.[26] Accordingly, if nurture is a moral excellence, we can judge whether the legal system is assisting or hindering that good. We can assay whether certain social programs are, in the true sense of the word, justified.

Whether or not positive laws are justified is one of the primary utilities of natural law theory.[27] If a positive law formally and substantively meets the standard of justification, the natural lawyer normally concludes that the law so promulgated carries with it an obligation of the subject to obey.[28] Thus, the notion of "the rule of law" morally binding all to obey justified positive enactments (as opposed to the arbitrary power of a person or group compelling obedience solely by coercion) is commonly a necessary attribute of most natural law theories.[29] As Aristotle put it, "[H]e who asks Law to rule is asking God and Intelligence and no others to rule; while he who asks for the rule of a human being is bringing in a wild beast."[30]

Whether a positive law is justified or not is, of course, question begging. Consequently, natural law philosophers are almost invariably drawn to the issue of justice; to elucidate justice, they usually require an implicit or explicit theory of rights. And a theory of rights returns one to a reflection on the nature of the human person.

Nature of Natural Law

The circularity of the reflective process (although not necessarily one of circular logic), beginning and ending with the concern of what it is to be truly human, often takes the natural law theorist into fields of enquiry beyond philosophical logic. These theorists have used history, theology, science, and art to illuminate the central enquiry.[31] Yet despite the wide-ranging openness of the natural lawyer to different perspectives on what constitutes the essence of the human enterprise, many modern observers who have had contact with the idea of natural law have the impression that it is a narrow and static set of rules, something like a philosophical Decalogue. In casual conversation among academics, the question is often heard, "Do you believe in natural law?" as if it is a creed and not a reasoned theory.[32]

Some think of natural law as a self-contained set of immutable principles, anthropomorphically operating as Holmes' "brooding omnipresence in the sky,"[33] a stern demigod high in the legal mythos handing down laws to humans or judging which human laws shall stand.[34] That inaccurate image of natural law may in fact derive from our notion of law imbued in us by positivist legal philosophers of the last two centuries. If law is a command backed by a sanction, then natural law must be (if it existed) a Calvinist higher order meticulously regulating how people can construct their affairs.[35] People often impute to others what they see in themselves.

In fact, most natural law philosophers not only have a broader attitude as to what constitutes "law" than do the positivists; they also emphasize the contextual manner in which the principles of natural law operate.[36] If human nature is a constant, the human personality is radically individualistic. If the social realm is an essential element of every person's "humanness," the variety of interpersonal experiences is nonetheless infinite.[37]

There is a further particular harm that comes from a static image of natural law, besides its inaccuracy. It sees law as essentially restrictive and not enabling. In contrast, for many natural law theorists, the notion of natural law does not restrict the function of law, but enlivens it: "[T]he law first educates men and then empowers them to decide," wrote Aristotle.[38] In other words, the law (properly formulated) nurtures.

Nurture and Rights

For natural lawyers, the ethic of caring has traditionally been termed "subsidiarity," meaning assistance.[39] "Nurture," I think, is the better descriptive. Nurture not only comprehends the obligation to assist, but also connotes the supportive, interpersonal, and individualistic kind of relationship that the natural law tradition affirms.[40]

What then are the human needs that need nurturing? And who, in the indeterminable variety of possible relations and circumstances over time, has an obligation to meet these needs? When can the state compel me to be my brother's keeper? It seems clear we cannot assist everyone equally. As St. Thomas Aquinas puts it, "No man is sufficient to bestow a work of mercy on all those who need it."[41] Not only would such a task be impossible, it would be destructive of one's own individuality. Nor, on the other hand, can we become totally isolated, even by choice, from assisting anyone else's beneficial objectives or from accepting the dependency we have on others for the constitution of our own lives and identities.[42] Where to begin? Where to draw principled limits?

First, we should assume, as did the ancients, that for nurture to have any place in a social order, the first rule must be: at the least, do no harm.[43] One cannot harm and nurture at the same time.[44] But harm presupposes that another enjoys fundamental immunities. Thus a theory of rights must provide a source of necessary immunities (including the loss of certain immunities when one threatens another with harm). As we discover what we may, or perhaps must, do *for* other people, we must set limits on the means we utilize, on what we can do *to* them. Assistance can only be based, therefore, on aiding the good of the other. Assistance that purports to use harm as a "necessary means" to someone else's good would not only be an invasion of right, it would be illogical and contradictory to its purpose. In a word, it would be immoral.

Furthermore, a theory of needs-based obligations without a theory of immunities could be used to justify a regime of positive rights, seemingly with no protection against a state that smothers individual rights in the name of benefiting citizens and leaves virtually no room for the constitutive activities of the individual human personality.[45] A bare theory of negative rights, on the other hand, provides little protection for the fragile network of supportive relationships upon which each of us depends.

The rub is this: if we have too weak a theory of rights, the individuality of the person could be swallowed up in an enforced obligation to assist others and society. If we have too strong a theory of rights, we divide and separate humans from one another, break essential connections between them, and, indeed, make weaker, not stronger, the individual human identity. A governmental policy that increases separation in the name of individual rights breaks the nurturing connections upon which human individuality ultimately depends. The dilemma for the natural law theorist is in reconciling a theory of needs with a theory of rights. A natural law theory must therefore combine the notion of individual right with individual good for there to be a coherent ethic of assistance.

Nurture and the Good

Just how does the Aristotelian school of natural law arrive at its notion of an objective human good, which would include the value of nurture? Putting aside the preliminary arguments (mostly epistemological) that lead ultimately to its major operating premises, the Aristotelian natural law school holds that things in nature are in motion (i.e., transition, change, development). It holds that every thing moves (either by its own internal mechanisms or by external force) from potentiality to actuality; that the nature of every thing distinguishes what its particular potentialities are;[46] that there is a point (or state) of flourishing that every thing could enjoy if its potentialities were fully actualized (its end, or *telos,* which is its "good"); and that one can define what the appropriate state of flourishing would be for any class of things (healthy red oak trees, for example). Furthermore, every individual thing within a class has its own, never to be repeated or duplicated, aspect of flourishing (no two mature, fully grown red oaks are the same).[47] What then is the nature of being human? What is a person's end? What "good" does one strive for?

Now, because the Aristotelian image of things in motion toward an end does not comport with the conceptualizations of modern science,[48] some of the more recent advocates of the Aristotelian school simply short-circuit that process and move directly toward discussing human nature.[49] But they come to the same general conclusions as Aristotle did. Retaining, therefore, the position that things in the world are knowable through human observation and that their coherence is apprehensible to human reason, the modern natural law advocates maintain, like Aristotle, that the nature of the human being is to seek happiness and well-being through the practice of virtue. The practice of virtue is the state of flourishing, the end, the good, the perfection of human potentialities that human nature aims at, even though the achievement of the end is by voluntary action and not by any predetermined "natural" mechanism.[50] Hence (putting aside the practical relevance of good and bad fortune), an individual is the responsible agent of the achievement of one's own natural end (i.e., the practice of virtue) and can be appropriately blamed or praised, depending on how well one acts in achieving it.[51]

That there is a more phenomenological methodology to the observation of human nature today is not contradictory to the reasoned reflection on human experience that Aristotle himself espoused.[52] In any event, the modern advocates of natural law arrive at the same outcome that Aristotle did: the end (the state of human flourishing) of all humans is happiness; happiness consists of the practice of virtue (actually, happiness attends the practice of virtue); virtue is a habit of moral action toward oneself and others (classically, the search for truth and the practice of justice, courage, and benevolence).[53]

To achieve the state of well-being wherein virtue may effectively be practiced, a number of elements are necessary. There must be a state whose structure both allows and assists the practice of virtue. The coercive and educational force of law must be used (indeed, can only be used) to enforce justice (protect one in the enjoyment of one's rights); to help provide an infrastructure (economic, educational, military, and the prevention of natural harms) in which the individual's physical well-being and exercise of virtue can flourish; and directly to induce and assist the individual in the practice of virtue.[54] In other words, the objective of law is to seek the common good—that is to say, the good (a state of human flourishing) that is common to all persons (in their respective individualities).[55]

Nurture and Human Flourishing

What then are the elements of human flourishing, and how does nurture relate to them? To begin, let us see how contemporary natural law theorists distinguish human needs from human goods.[56] Henry Veatch lists as human needs:

> food, clothing, shelter; association and companionship with others; knowledge and understanding; and opportunities for rest and relaxation, and for aesthetic enjoyment, for the practice of religion, and, indeed, for the so-called finer things in life.[57]

Elsewhere Veatch articulates a more extensive rendering of needs, but in the end he emphasizes that "the mere possession" of these things "is not the whole story." The question is how wisely and intelligently these things are used in the ultimate moral obligation of living well and virtuously.[58]

Human Goods

How does one live well and virtuously? It is by participation in the self-evident goods of human existence. John Finnis offers the following list: knowledge, life, play, aesthetics, friendship, practical reasonableness (constructing a life's plan), and spirituality.[59] Needs, therefore, are instrumental. I need sustenance in order to live, books in order to learn. Goods, on the other hand, are goods in themselves, valuable because the state of human flourishing only occurs according to one's participation in those goods. In that sense, listening to Mozart's Jupiter Symphony is noninstrumental; it is an aesthetic experience in and of itself.

Goods, of course, can at times be instrumental. I can listen to the Jupiter Symphony as I study for my music appreciation exam. But some things are both needs and goods at the same time. Life itself is a good that is also a necessary instrumentality for the enjoyment of all other goods.

Nurture is similar. Nurture is a need of all persons to develop their individual potentialities. We are all perpetually dependent to a greater or lesser degree on other persons in the achievement of life's goods. Life requires sustenance, knowledge requires teaching, aesthetics requires example, friendship requires friends, play requires playmates, spirituality requires a relationship with some transcendent other, productivity requires reliable partners. In this sense, a person cannot be a person without the nurturing assistance given by another. Nurture is as much a requirement as is safety.

The Need to Nurture

At the same time, the giving of nurture is a moral good necessary for one's happiness. It is easily granted by natural lawyers that one's flourishing cannot occur without other persons to interact with. But there is more to interacting with other persons than there is in interacting with paints and a canvas, or with a profit and loss sheet, or with a Spring field in need of plowing. When I interact with another person, I interact with another self. I experience the other, intersubjectively, as, *in essence*, equal to myself.[60] And thus, the "good" of the other person is as important to me as is my good. Indeed, my own flourishing cannot succeed without my participation in the flourishing of others. In sum, I cannot pursue my own individual flourishing without offering nurture to others. In the very act of nurturing another, I experience my self more concretely. If a governmental policy works to deny me nurturing opportunities, it denies me an essential part of my human flourishing.

In sum, the obligation to nurture derives from a notion that the human person requires, as an essential element of one's individual human identity, the receiving and giving of assistance, and the alternate engagement in and disengagement from interpersonal relationships. The ancient and medieval proponents of natural law were fully at home with the idea in their notion of obligations and more specifically in their definition of friendship. Aristotle concluded that a friend is one who seeks the good of the other, and that no person could achieve happiness (our natural end) without virtuous friends.[61] In his long, fatherly, and preachy letter to his son, away at school in Greece, Cicero admonishes that

> everything that the earth produces is for man's use; and as men, too, are born for the sake of other men, that they may be able mutually to help one another; in this direction we ought to follow nature as our guide, to contribute to the general good by an interchange of acts of kindness, by giving and receiving, and thus by our skill, our industry, and our talents to cement human society more closely together, man to man.[62]

Or as the even more pessimistic Pufendorf put it,

> [A]ll the advantages that attend human life today derive from men's mutual assistance. There is nothing in this world, save the great and good God Himself, from which greater advantage can come to man than from man himself.[63]

It is in inducing and assisting the individual in the practice of virtue that requirements of nurture arise. In Finnis' words, the degree of human flourishing depends upon "the quality of interaction among persons."[64] Nurture is perhaps the highest quality of interaction among persons, for its objective is to provide supportive assistance that enables the other person independently to flourish, to achieve excellence in his particular practice of the virtues.

Nurture and the Law

From these observations it follows that a society that increases the opportunities for nurture also increases the chances for human happiness. How can the laws assist? Seeing that the perfection of persons lay in their practice of moral virtue, many of the ancients looked to the state for the necessary means. Eventually, Cicero hoped, men "would do of their own accord what they are compelled to do by law," but the nature of human appetites was such that a well-run state was of absolute necessity.[65] Aristotle expected that education, directed by the family or the polity, would train the person in moral virtue. But for those who did not respond to such encouragement, who looked only to their selfish impulses, he taught that the coercive power of the state had to restrain them.[66] Some modern Aristotelians, on the other hand, are almost Lockean in their defense of individual rights against the state[67] and insist that the needs of human persons, no matter how great, do not give rise to positive rights with claims on others to assist.[68]

The modern Aristotelians have a point. Granted that co-operation and nurture should be encouraged in a society, the fact is that the practice of nurture is so individual, so dependent upon the nuances of a relationship at any one time, that it would seem foolish if not arrogant of the state to try to define and enforce when assistance should be given. After a winter storm one December, for example, my two sons and I built a stegasaurus dinosaur out of snow in the backyard. We all three engaged in the human good of play. To do so, we had prior "needs" of certain things. We needed snow (an element of good fortune), and life, and health. We also needed a backyard, and leisure, and knowledge of what a stegasaurus looked like (which meant we needed education, the result of other persons' participation in research and knowledge, and books, and a system of free communication). To be available to me, all of this had to come from the fruits of work and an efficient economic system. Building the stegasaurus was fun, and it also provided my sons with training in co-operation, the development of motor skills, the manipulation of a material element, an experience in aesthetics (it was a pretty good stegasaurus), and some good exercise. How could any state have "constructed" such a range of circumstances so that those opportunities would have been available for me at that time? How could I justify using the coercive mechanism of the law to take sufficient property from other persons to satisfy my needs of time and a backyard to make snow sculptures?

Rather, it seems evident from historical observation that a legal system that guarantees a wide range of personal activity (economic and otherwise) in life's goods provides the most fertile basis for the kind of society that is conducive to the practice of moral virtue. But certainly, that cannot state the end of it. Even if we have a (relatively) free economic society where the myriad forms of nurture can best thrive, we also have a milieu where greed, selfishness, isolation, and self-destructiveness can also thrive. That, too, comes from the evidence of human experience. Is the state without any writ to go beyond mere prevention of harm and actually encourage (or even sometimes compel) other-regarding behavior of individuals? If a parent can have a range of discipline over a child while still morally respecting the dignity and individuality of the child, cannot society (through appropriately constructed means of consent) discipline its adult members while still respecting the dignity and individuality of each person?[69]

Law and Virtue

The answer of natural law is, within fairly severe limits, affirmative. The state can assist in the formation of a virtuous society.[70] There are two justifications for the limited intervention of the state to improve the moral activities of the individual: need and coordination. In each case, the purpose of state action is to assist the recipient of aid in the achievement of his (morally justified) life's plan and to educate the giver, by discipline or example, in appropriate moral conduct. Whether the enforced giver accepts and internalizes the lesson is that person's responsibility.

All this is based on the fundamental reality that nurture is relational, radically individualistic, and has the best chance to flourish in a society in which the material, temporal, and other opportunities for mutual support are available. By and large, therefore, because of the infinite range of circumstances and relationships necessary for nurture to thrive among humans, a limited state and a wide range of personal liberties is necessary. That is a logical conclusion supported by empirical observation of how individuals thrive in free political and economic societies. But it does not follow that the state therefore has no right to educate me in the proper exercise of my freedom (i.e., using it toward the exercise of virtue toward others), for the law necessarily sets an authoritative standard. Nor does the notion of a limited state necessarily prohibit it from inducing me to achieve a higher level of participation in life's goods (e.g., subsidizing museums rather than rock concerts).

Assistance

I require liberty to participate more fully in the objective goods of life, but there is no one pathway of human flourishing for me to the exclusion of all others. It is not true that only I know which options are best (I make mistakes). That comes too close to the utilitarian fallacy. Rather, if I flourish through the practice of moral virtue (my human "end") by pursuing a worldly craft well, for example, it does not matter fundamentally what I do, so long as I do it as excellently as I can. Freedom is essential in choosing and executing a life's plan in which the ensemble of life's goods works best for me, but I cannot do it alone. I am not omniscient or all-powerful. Neither authoritarianism nor radical individualistic autonomy can be justified by the notion that there is only one particular way for me.

I am a law teacher. I attempt to pursue my craft in a spirit of excellence. I attempt to practice moral virtues in the manner of teaching and researching. Suppose that I had innate talents for mathematics. Suppose, because of life's accidents, harms, or whatever, I never knew I had those talents. Suppose that had I pursued math, I would have been a far better astrophysicist than I am a teacher. Does that mean I am not flourishing? That my life is a failure? That I cannot practice virtue? Suppose I must give up teaching through illness, or because the law school closes, or because I must devote more time to the upbringing of my family. Does that preclude me from the practice of virtue? Rather, does it not mean that life would offer me opportunities for the practice of other virtues (courage or fortitude, for example), rather than intellectual wisdom? I may have a life's vocation, but its epiphany is in the daily living of it.

Liberty is a necessary requirement for the moral practice of practical reason in forming a life's plan based on craft and virtue. Only justifiable and proportionate reasons (war and a draft, for example) can limit that necessary freedom. If, for such justifiable reasons, my liberties are lessened, no wrong has been done to me (unless the war is unnecessary). If, for justifiable and proportionate reasons (public education, for example), some of my property is taken through taxation, no wrong is done to me (unless those in charge spend my compelled contribution unwisely or public education, as is often the case today, harms children's prospects).

In sum, a wide range of liberty is necessary to achieve human flourishing. Any intrusion into that liberty must be justified. And an intrusion is justified only if it is based upon the same objective good that my right to freedom of action is based upon. The objective good of human flourishing is the touchstone upon which liberty, limited government, and limited intrusions are all based. Further, that intrusion is subject to the natural law rules of prudence. If the state fails to increase the chances for liberty and moral flourishing by its intrusion, it commits a double wrong: against me and against those it has purportedly sought to assist.

The Justification for Limited State Assistance

I now turn to when such limited intrusions by government can be justified under natural law theory. The first justification is because of need. Can the need of another be such to justify depriving me of any of my individual rights, and if so, which rights and how much? And if I grant that some needs of others can justifiably intrude upon my rights, how can I do so without losing any justification for negative rights altogether? That is the great apprehension of many modern natural law writers. As defenders of the limited state, they reasonably fear that any justification for the imposition of claims against individuals based on need would logically destroy the basis of negative rights and immunities. Forcing a person to give lawfully obtained property or time to benefit another person invades immunities with seemingly no logical stopping point.[71]

Limiting Need-Based Rights

But there is a logical stopping point. St. Thomas Aquinas articulated how positive rights based on need can be both justified and limited. Asking whether it is lawful to steal through stress of need,[72] Aquinas answers in the affirmative. "[I]n a case of extreme need, . . . that which [a man] takes for the support of his life becomes his own property by reason of that need."[73] It is noteworthy that Aquinas does not say that the theft is excused. He says that there is no theft. There is, in fact, no taking of another's property because need has made it the taker's property "by reason of that need." How did the property holder lose the right to his own property?

To begin with, it should be emphasized again that in the Aristotelian tradition, rights are derivative of the good. They do not exist independently of the good. Aquinas is not saying that needs, in and of themselves, give rise to a right. Fundamental goods do. Based upon the logical requirement of universalization (shared by other traditions, such as the Kantian and natural rights schools), the recognition of a good or end to human existence necessarily obliges me to respect that good in others as well as in myself. Consequently, the good of life gives rise to a right to life, the good of knowledge to free communication, the good of seeking the spirit to freedom of religion, the good of practical reasonableness to a wide range of liberties, and the good of friendship to freedom of association. These are universal rights because the fundamental goods are universal.

Thus, under natural law it is the good, not the existence of other negative rights, that defines the limits to rights. I have no right to take another person's life for the benefit of a friend, because life is an objective good of the other person. I have no right to associate in order to commit a crime, because association is for the mutual benefit (in all moral things) of its members.

For Aquinas, property is a real right, but it is a human right, an instrumentality for the accomplishment of individual moral virtue.[74] One element of moral virtue is to assist others in need (to the extent one can without impinging on one's own morally legitimate uses). But since one cannot succor everyone in need, it is left to the individual to choose whom to aid in charity. Aquinas does not construct general positive rights out of need, because most needs are inchoate in relation to any individual. He is clear that in those circumstances, no specific duty can be said to attach.[75] The needs are too general and contingent. Thus, because of the moral good involved in certain specific relationships, assistance to members of one's family or to friends is normally morally preferable to that of strangers.

But where a person's life intersects with your own, even for a moment, and he is in dire need of food, for example, you have a moral obligation to save that person out of your "superabundance," that is to say, out of property you can spare to meet his need without proportionate danger to you (i.e., causing yourself to starve).[76] In that situation, because of the specificity of the two selves (you and the starving person at one place in time) and the utter dependence of the other person upon you, the duty you have to help is no longer inchoate, but specific. By force of circumstance, it vests. If you have a specific duty to provide sustenance at the time, that person has a specific right to it.[77]

It follows, therefore, that in cases of extreme need, where one's moral obligation would incontestably require one to assist another (there being no practical alternative except your aid), a specific duty has arisen and a claim-right derives from it. Indeed, in law, we fasten such duties to parents in the raising of their children, simply because that relationship is such that specific duties can be attached to it. There is no reason why the principle should not apply to other specific relationships (even if not contracted for) that arise in other arrangements of life. If the need is dire and manifest, and, because of the lack of alternatives, the duty to assist is specific, the moral duty gives rise to a right of assistance, and the state could justifiably enforce that assistance.

Coordination

The second justifiable mechanism by which the state could assist the practice of virtue is through the notion of coordination. Unlike state of nature theorists and proponents of other egoist-based political theories, natural lawyers have never had much trouble in justifying (to themselves at least) the legitimacy of the state. It exists because it is an efficient mechanism of coordinating material needs among persons; because it can protect persons from harm; because it can assist those in the performance of their moral duties, individually as well as collectively; because it fulfills the moral needs of persons for social/political interaction; and because, properly run, it can provide moral exemplars to the citizens.[78]

By a reasonably responsive manner of eliciting consent, the state may direct resources gathered from the citizens to projects that advance the common good, that is, things which assist individuals to achieve moral excellence in their particular life's plans. Thus, building an infrastructure of highways, of water distribution, of a sound currency, of education, or of care for the hungry or ill can legitimately be coordinated by the state. The state may encourage certain morally beneficial activities: tax-exempt status for philanthropic or religious organizations, for example. It may encourage productive associations or aesthetics (perhaps by spending more money, within reason, on a public building simply to make it more beautiful).

Those who administer the state are under the moral obligation to be true to their craft as well. Governmental programs should not be maintained because they benefit the self-seeking interests of administrators (or of groups of citizens). If the good can be more efficiently achieved by nonregulation, or by less regulation, the state (i.e., those in authority) would be morally bound to withdraw. More accurately, because the good of interrelationships is best obtained by the freedom to construct and pursue those relationships, the obligation is on the state to justify any intrusion designed to make those relationships more morally productive.

In light of recent social history of the United States, it is clear that state policies have positively worked against the moral flourishing of individuals. State actions from welfare to legal restructuring of the Constitution by the courts have weakened the family, the primary mechanism for successful nurturing. In past decades, natural law writers have looked to the state to intervene to prevent private violations of natural law norms between persons. Today, however, state intervention is often itself the mechanism of fracturing society and weakening the moral bonds between persons. The presumption should be, therefore, absent a justifiable purpose and a reasonable realistic prospect for success, that we should leave the moral flourishing of the individual under natural law to the care of oneself and to private associations like the family.

Conclusion

The state cannot take the place of nurturing acts between individuals. It can assist in the formation of those relationships. It can seek to prevent the vulnerabilities present in intimate relationships from resulting in harm (spousal abuse or abortion, for example), but it cannot construct its own alternative to how humans can beneficially interact. It can coordinate the generic basics of security, subsistence, and education; it can encourage patterns of nurturing (parental involvement in education, a wider range of information available in abortion decisions, and welfare policies that reward bonding and independence); it can seek to prevent harm (rescuing those in need); but it cannot regulate the variety of interpersonal decisions upon which effective nurturing depends. In sum, the state is morally obliged to respect the goods that come from a reasoned reflection on human nature. And those goods, including nurture, depend upon the individual's own commitment to excellence.

Epilogue

While I was first completing this essay, word arrived that a beloved uncle of my wife's had died. He had suffered for some time from amyotrophic lateral sclerosis (ALS). During the years, as the use of his body progressively diminished, he maintained a gentle and infectiously happy spirit that was his hallmark in more vigorous days. He privately brooded about many things, but never complained about his illness, continuing on with a quiet fortitude. He saw himself through his children's college graduations and the marriage of his daughter. During his last months, his family drew around him, chatting with him, washing and feeding him. He dictated letters to his wife and children. One Saturday, he died suddenly and peacefully in the middle of the day. He had, throughout, continued to nurture and be nurtured; even in the last stages of his illness, his humanity flourished.

The best thing society could do in those circumstances was, perhaps, to coordinate appropriate medical care, and otherwise to leave the intimacies between that man and his family alone and unrestrained. For in the end, the act of nurture is an act of love; and nurture, mutually given and received, is a celebration. A society whose laws encourage nurture calls out of us the best parts of our humanity.

NOTES

1. In this, I, of course, differ *toto caelo* from the deconstructionists and other antinomians who hold that reality is unknowable or that, at best, it is constructed through our own will-directed rationality. Instead, I adhere to the realist tradition in philosophy and begin without justification or any felt need for justification on the ground that human co-rationality and intersubjectivity give us access to reality, permit us to understand reality as it is and as it is experienced by humans, and to make arguments and reach conclusions about reality that we can convince one another of. In other words, the philosophers of the natural law tradition approach philosophy the way ordinary persons approach life: it's there, and despite its difficulties, it can be understood.

2. *See generally*, 1 E. STAUB, POSITIVE SOCIAL BEHAVIOR AND MORALITY: SOCIAL AND PERSONAL INFLUENCES (1978); C. DANIEL BATSON, THE ALTRUISM QUESTION: TOWARDS A SOCIAL PSYCHOLOGICAL ANSWER (hereinafter cited as C. BATSON, THE ALTRUISM QUESTION)(1991).

3. *See* MARVIN OLASKY, THE TRAGEDY OF AMERICAN COMPASSION 167–199 (1992).

4. ARISTOTLE, THE POLITICS 293 (T. Sinclair, trans. Penguin ed. 1962, 1979).

5. *See C. Daniel Batson, How Social An Animal? The Human Capacity for Caring*, AMERICAN PSYCHOLOGIST, March 1990, pp. 339–40.

6. The ultimate goal is that of self-realization, a continuous process of becoming. JOHN FINNIS, NATURAL LAW AND NATURAL RIGHTS (hereinafter cited as FINNIS, NATURAL LAW AND NATURAL RIGHTS) 96 (1980).

7. SARA RUDDICK, MATERNAL THINKING: TOWARD A POLITICS OF PEACE 82–83 (1989).

8. Nor can we say that nurture is only an instinctive response of the human animal to preserve his gene pool for future reproductive success. The wide practice of abortion (and indeed of contraception) militate against nurture being merely an instinctive response to increase the chances of survival. Rather, nurture has to be a moral command, bred of our sense of our human selves and identities. And like all moral commands, nurture may be well or ill practiced.

9. To the question whether something is good because one desires it, or whether one desires it because it is good, Aristotle decided upon the latter, but his notion of desire in this case was the organism's seeking to have its natural good

actualized, rather than in having its range of pleasures increased. HENRY B. VEATCH, ARISTOTLE: A CONTEMPORARY APPRECIATION 101 (1974).

10. Needs, in this sense, are objective. They are "goods" in need of satisfaction. To take a personal predilection, a person may want potato chips, but need broccoli. Or, a person may want to watch MTV, but need to study her math.

11. FINNIS, NATURAL LAW AND NATURAL RIGHTS, *supra* note 6, at 64, 84, 96, 100, 104.

12. *See* the useful summary in C. BATSON, THE ALTRUISM QUESTION, *supra* note 2, at 17–32.

13. *See id.*, at 1–58.

14. It follows, of course, that Nietzsche and Ayn Rand are totally wrong, and perversely so. Each found charity to be destructive of the ego's own accomplishments. *Id.* at 26–27, 214. In fact, not only does the philosophy of natural law dispute this, I believe that human experience shows it to be false. Just listen to parents discussing the activities of parenting with one another, or more directly, listen, if you could, to the private conversations at the end of the day of a mother and father discussing their interrelated roles in raising their children. In the very quest to nurture the children, each parent defines his and her own moral personality. (And, in the same process, the mother and father nurture one another.)

15. Often, however, in the nature vs. nurture debate, nurture loses its richer meaning and becomes merely a synonym for behavior that is influenced by a child's environment rather than by his genetic makeup. *See, e.g.*, George W. Barlow & James Silverberg SOCIOBIOLOGY, BEYOND NATURE/NURTURE? REPORTS, DEFINITIONS, AND DEBATE (1980).

16. For Kohlberg, nurturance seems to occur at stage three in moral development: "Good boy orientation. Orientation to approval and to pleasing and helping others. Conformity to stereotypical images of majority or natural role behavior, and judgment by intentions." 2 LAWRENCE KOHLBERG, THE SCIENCE OF MORAL DEVELOPMENT 44, 147 (1984).

17. Gilligan does not use the term nurture, but an "ethic of care." For example, she writes, "The ideal of care is thus an activity of relationship, of seeing and responding to need, taking care of the world by sustaining the web of connection so that no one is left alone." CAROL GILLIGAN, IN A DIFFERENT VOICE 62 (1982).

18. Even Aristotle noticed the particular excellence in the virtue of friendship that mothers had for their children because of their greater capacity for empathy ("one who share's his friend's joys and sorrows"). ARISTOTLE, ETHICS (Book IX) 293 (J. Thomson, trans., 1955, 1980). When I was a second year law student, my instructor, Judge Jack Weinstein, invited his evidence class to attend one of his trials at our convenience. The one I attended was a negligence suit by two teenage boys who had been blinded as children when they had set off some dynamite caps while playing by a railroad track. After the jury panel had been seated, the judge asked the plaintiffs to enter the courtroom. The two boys, carrying white canes, were guided in. At the moment we all saw them and their scarred eyes, gasps of dismay swept through the panel. One woman immediately stood up, her eyes moving between the judge and the plaintiffs, and said in a voice that was emotional but resolute, "Your honor, I am a mother. I don't know how any mother can be objective in this case. I know I couldn't." The judge excused her from the panel.

19. Because I am limiting the scope of my enquiry to nurture and the modern natural law ethics, I am placing to one side the enormous literature on "social justice." For the same reason, I must also hold in abeyance commentary or analysis on the debate in current feminist literature on the ethic of caring.

20. It was Plato, Aristotle, and the Stoics that made the notion of nature the grounding for morality, and eventually, law. EDGAR BODENHEIMER, JURISPRUDENCE 6–14 (rev. ed. 1974).

As long as that proposition that nature and law are interrelated has been maintained, it has, of course, been contested. The Sophists, for example, asserted that nature and law were opposed to one another. *Id.*, at 5–6. Kant, in contrast, held that nature could never be a source of moral rules, while the modern philosophies of utilitarianism and positivism remained skeptical of the natural law enterprise. *Id.*, at 61–62. *See, e.g., Jeremy Bentham, A Critical Examination of the Declaration of Rights, in* THE WESTERN IDEA OF LAW 502–506 (J.C. Smith & David N. Weisstub, eds. (1983); HANS KELSEN, WHAT IS JUSTICE? (1957). Nonetheless, the natural law tradition persists. Since 1980, in particular, there has been an effusion of significant natural law writing. *See, for example*, CHARLES COVELL, THE DEFENCE OF NATURAL LAW: LAW AND JUSTICE IN THE WRITINGS OF LON L. FULLER, MICHAEL OAKESHOTT, F.A. HAYEK, RONALD DWORKIN, AND JOHN FINNIS (1992); ROBERT GEORGE, NATURAL LAW THEORY: CONTEMPORARY ESSAYS (1991); DAVID GRANFIELD, THE INNER EXPERIENCE OF THE LAW: A JURISPRUDENCE OF SUBJECTIVITY (1988); JOHN FINNIS, NATURAL LAW AND NATURAL RIGHTS (1980); RUSSELL HITTINGER, A CRITIQUE OF THE NEW NATURAL LAW THEORY (1987); ALISDAIR MacINTYRE, AFTER VIRTUE, A STUDY IN MORAL THEORY (1981); DOUGLAS B. RASMUSSEN & DOUGLAS J. DEN UYL, LIBERTY AND NATURE: AN ARISTOTELIAN DEFENSE OF LIBERAL ORDER (1991); HENRY B. VEATCH, HUMAN RIGHTS, FACT OR FANCY? (1985); LLOYD L. WEINREB, NATURAL LAW AND JUSTICE (hereinafter cited as WEINREB, NATURAL LAW AND JUSTICE) (1987).

21. *See, for example*, HITTINGER, A CRITIQUE OF THE NEW NATURAL LAW THEORY (hereinafter cited as HITTINGER, CRITIQUE) (1987), and DAVID GRANFIELD, THE INNER EXPERIENCE OF THE LAW: A JURISPRUDENCE OF SUBJECTIVITY (1988). Some natural lawyers, such as Herbert Spencer, perceive humanity as an aspect of nature and urge that human laws reflect that fact. *See, e.g.* HERBERT SPENCER, THE PRINCIPLES OF ETHICS (1897, 1978). Others, like Lon Fuller, see natural law as part of a more focussed inquiry on what constitutes the nature of law itself. LON FULLER, THE MORALITY OF LAW 96–106 (1964).

22. Sometimes equated with human good, derived from reason. *See* FINNIS, NATURAL LAW AND NATURAL RIGHTS, *supra* note 6, at 35–36.

23. John Wild defines natural law as "a universal pattern of action, applicable to all men everywhere, required by human nature itself for its completion." JOHN WILD, Plato's MODERN ENEMIES AND THE THEORY OF NATURAL LAW 64 (1953). In a similar vein, Ronald Garet offers that natural law is "a theory that associates its claims about the ordering of basic social relations with claims about human nature. Natural law theories elaborate a vision of human nature and attempt to make that vision available to political philosophy." *Ronald R. Garet, Natural Law and Creation Stories*, in RELIGION, MORALITY, AND THE LAW (NOMOS XXX) 218 (J. Pennock & J. Chapman eds. 1988). I think it evident that even those who look at nature generically and those who concentrate on the internal nature of law are both centrifugally pulled into the human focus. I earlier suggested that Fuller's defense of his theory against the criticisms of H.L.A. Hart pushed Fuller into acknowledging the dependency of his view on a moral theory of human action. *See David F. Forte, Natural Law and Natural Laws* (hereinafter cited as *Forte, Natural Law and Natural Laws*), 26 UNIVERSITY BOOKMAN 75 (1986). Another author has suggested that Hart's minimal theory of natural law is far stronger than even Hart apparently believed. *See* DANIEL W. SKUBNIK, AT THE INTERSECTION OF LEGALITY AND MORALITY: HARTIAN LAW AS NATURAL LAW (1990). By human nature, I mean the commonality of humanness shared by all individual men and women at all stages of their biological existence.

24. *See* VEATCH, HUMAN RIGHTS, *supra* note 20, at 11–33. Note also Veatch's and Hittinger's criticism of John Finnis and Germaine Grisez on whether norms can indeed be deduced from human nature as it is, or whether a "Kantian turn" towards rationalism is a useful supplement. *Id.* at 93–104. *See* also, WEINREB, NATURAL LAW AND JUSTICE, *supra* note 20, at 108–15.

25. *See* VEATCH, HUMAN RIGHTS, *supra* note 20, at 4–10. One study finds nearly everybody in the natural law tradition. *See* FRANCIS H. ETEROVICH, APPROACHES TO NATURAL LAW FROM PLATO TO KANT (1972). The general argument of Weinreb is that the state of nature theorists eventually led Western thought away from a focus on the concept of nature to the state as the source of law. *See, generally*, WEINREB, NATURAL LAW AND JUSTICE, *supra* note 20. For an intermediate position, *see* A. JOHN SIMMONS, THE LOCKEAN THEORY OF RIGHTS (1992).

26. To Georgio del Vecchio, for example, "The conception of absolute justice is one of the fundamental needs of the human mind." GIORGIO DEL VECCHIO, THE FORMAL BASES OF THE LAW (hereinafter cited as DEL VECCHIO, FORMAL BASES OF THE LAW) 14–15 (J. Lisle trans. 1914, 1919), while d'Entrèves declared, "Natural law is the outcome of man's quest for an absolute standard of justice." A.P. d'Entréves, NATURAL LAW 93 (2d rev. ed. 1970, 1972).

27. Yves Simon makes the connection succinctly: "nothing would be right by enactment if some things were not right by nature." YVES R. SIMON, THE TRADITION OF NATURAL LAW 118 (1965, 1992).

28. *See, e.g.*, FINNIS, NATURAL LAW AND NATURAL RIGHTS, *supra* note 6, at 314–20. For an enlightening critique of the natural law position *see*, KENT GREENAWALT, CONFLICTS OF LAW AND MORALITY 159–94 (1987).

29. *See id.*, at 270–76.

30. ARISTOTLE, THE POLITICS, *supra* note 4, at 143. And Giorgio del Vecchio writes: "It is not without deep-seated reason that in all ages and countries the idea of natural law, that is, one founded on the very reality of things and not on the simple 'placet' of the legislature, has been cultivated." DEL VECCHIO, FORMAL BASES OF THE LAW, *supra* note 26, at 15.

31. The works of Aristotle, Cicero, and Grotius are some classical examples. *See, e.g.* ARISTOTLE, THE POLITICS, *supra* note 4; ETHICS, *supra* note 18; CICERO, DE OFFICIIS (W. Miller trans., Loeb Lib. ed. 1913, 1975), CICERO, DE RE PUBLICA (C. Keyes, trans., Loeb Lib. ed. 1928, 1977); GROTIUS, THE RIGHTS OF WAR AND PEACE (De Jure Belli ac Pacis) (A.C. Campbell, trans. 1901, 1979).

32. According to Alf Ross, the Scandinavian positivist, "Natural law seeks the absolute, the eternal, that shall make of law something more than the handiwork of human beings and exempt the legislator from the pains and responsibility of decision." Elsewhere, he concludes, "Such an attitude to life is typically infantile." ALF ROSS, ON LAW AND JUSTICE 258, 228 (1958, 1974). Jeremy Bentham was more pithy, calling natural law "nonsense on stilts." *Jeremy Bentham, Anarchical Fallacies*, in 2 WORKS OF JEREMY BENTHAM 105 (J. Browning ed. 1962).

33. Holmes actually made the remark about the common law, not natural law, but the negative image is the same. *So. Pacific Co. v. Jensen*, 244 U.S. 205, 222 (Holmes, J., dissenting)("The common law is not a brooding omnipresence in the sky but the articulate voice of some sovereign or quasi sovereign that can be identified.")

34. "The natural-law doctrine undertakes to supply a definitive solution to the eternal problem of justice, to answer the question as to what is right an wrong in the mutual relations of men." HANS KELSEN, WHAT IS JUSTICE? 137 (1957).

35. Roscoe Pound describes natural law as an ideal law to which "the positive law, the body of norms, that is, authoritative models of patterns of decisions, should be made to conform." ROSCOE POUND, JUSTICE ACCORDING TO LAW 6 (1951, 1973). He tags this ideal law as "positive natural law." *Id.* Russell Hittinger appropriately rejoins, "[I]t is a mistake to envisage natural law as a ready-made body of law (a meta-positive law, as it were) to which the problems of human positive law can immediately be referred." *R. Hittinger, Introduction*, in YVES R. SIMON, THE TRADITION OF NATURAL LAW xxvii (1965, 1992).

36. "When [fundamental principles of justice] are modified under changed circumstances, moral duty also undergoes a change, and it does not always remain the same." CICERO, DE OFFICIIS, I.x.32, *supra* note 31, at 33.

37. *See* VEATCH, HUMAN RIGHTS, *supra* note 20, at 108–12.

38. ARISTOTLE, THE POLITICS, *supra* note 4, at 143. That more complete conception of natural law has its own problems. What it gains in catholicity and flexibility, it may lose in trenchancy. Respectful positivist critics of natural law sometimes find the flaw not in its rigidity but in its lack of rigor. *See, generally*, JOSEPH RAZ, PRACTICAL REASON AND NORMS (1990).

39. FINNIS, NATURAL LAW AND NATURAL RIGHTS, *supra* note 6, at 146.

40. As Finnis defines subsidiarity, "[T]he proper function of association is to help the participants in the association to help themselves or, more precisely, to constitute themselves. . . ." *Id.*

41. SAINT THOMAS AQUINAS, ON LAW, MORALITY, AND POLITICS 191 (W. Baumgarth & R. Regan, S.J., eds. (1988). Aquinas also stated, "Absolutely speaking it is impossible to do good to every single one: yet it is true of each individual that one may be bound to do good to him in some particular case. Hence, charity binds us, though not actually doing good to someone, to be prepared in mind to do good to any one if we have the time." 2 ST THOMAS AQUINAS, SUMMA THEOLOGICA (hereinafter cited as AQUINAS, SUMMA THEOLOGICA) (Pt. II-II, Q. 31, Art. 2, Reply Obj. 1) 1321 (Fathers of the English Dominican Province, trans. 1947).

See JUDITH SHKLAR, THE FACES OF INJUSTICE (1990) for an argument that one's obligation to others is more wide-ranging. For a discussion of others who hold that one's responsibility to others is universal, *see* FINNIS, NATURAL LAW AND NATURAL RIGHT, *supra* note 6, at 195.

42. FINNIS, NATURAL LAW AND NATURAL RIGHTS, *supra* note 6, at 141–50.

43. "The first office of justice is to keep one man from doing harm to another, unless provoked by wrong." CICERO, DE OFFICIIS, *supra* note 31, I.vii.20, *supra* note 31, at 23.

44. Simply because someone does not like something, or believes it is painful, does not mean there is harm. Properly proportioned discipline (of children and adults) is not a harm if done towards encouraging the development of moral habits. Aristotle is blunt: "[T]he man who lives in accordance with his feelings would not listen to an argument to dissuade him, or understand it if he did. And when a man is in that state, how is it possible to persuade him out of it? In general, feeling seems to yield not to argument but only to force." ARISTOTLE, ETHICS, (Book X), *supra* note 18, at 336.

45. *See* VEATCH, HUMAN RIGHTS, *supra* note 20, at 179–80. In the draft Ukrainian Constitution, for example, Article 24 guarantees equality, but permits special privileges if established by law. Article 40 permits freedom of expression unless it rouses religious hatred. Article 10 declares that "private property is inviolable," but Article 48 contains the reservation: "The exercise of the right of ownership must not contradict the interest of society as a whole or of individual citizens." Draft Constitution of the Ukraine, prepared by the working group of the Constitutional Commission of the Parliament of the Ukraine, January 1992.

46. Or in some cases, what they can be, depending on the nature of action taken upon it, as a block of stone can be a statue or a paper weight, according to the purpose and execution of the craftsman.

47. A cogent and far more sophisticated restatement of the Aristotelian argument can be found in VEATCH, HUMAN RIGHTS, *supra* note 20, at 58–67.

48. *See* C. BATSON, THE ALTRUISM QUESTION, *supra* note 2, at 67–73. Those Cartesian premises of modern science have their own problems in attempting to describe nature as it really is. *See* VEATCH, HUMAN RIGHTS, *supra* note 20, at 222–249; and *Forte, Natural Law and Natural Laws*, *supra* note 23, at 75–79.

49. Or, in the case of Finnis, fundamental human goods discoverable by practical reason. FINNIS, NATURAL LAW AND NATURAL RIGHTS, *supra* note 6, at 35–36.

50. VEATCH, HUMAN RIGHTS, *supra* note 20, at 82–83.

51. *Id.* Good fortune may assist, but ultimately every person is responsible for the excellence of his own life.

52. "For the starting point is the *fact*; and if this is sufficiently clear there will be no need to ascertain the reason why. Such a person can easily grasp first principles if he is not already in possession of them." ARISTOTLE, ETHICS, (Book I), *supra* note 18, at 67. John Finnis' method of apprehending the basic goods of life has a similar methodology. *See* FINNIS, NATURAL LAW AND NATURAL RIGHTS, *supra* note 6, at 64–69. *See, generally*, WILLIAM A. LUIJPEN, PHENOMENOLOGY OF NATURAL LAW (1967).

53. ARISTOTLE, ETHICS, (Book I), *supra* note 18, at 75–76; (Book 2), at 103–106 (relating an expanded list of virtues and vices to the moral mean). CICERO, DE OFFICIIS, I.v.15, *supra* note 31, at 17.

54. ARISTOTLE, ETHICS, (Book X), *supra* note 18, at 338.

55. "[T]he securing of a whole ensemble of material and other conditions that tend to favor the realization, by each individual in the community, or his or her personal development." FINNIS, NATURAL LAW AND NATURAL RIGHT, *supra* note 6, at 154. The common good, of course, includes justice, i.e., the protection of one's negative rights and liberties. DOUGLAS B. RASMUSSEN & DOUGLAS J. DEN UYL, LIBERTY AND NATURE: AN ARISTOTELIAN DEFENSE OF LIBERAL ORDER (hereinafter cited as RASMUSSEN & DEN UYL, LIBERTY AND NATURE) 143 (1991).

56. Many philosophers begin with the individual qua individual, eliminating the accidents of contemporary society and construct from there what one's rights and obligations necessarily must be, or what one would necessarily agree to be bound by. A natural law theorist, on the other hand, may survey life as actually lived and arrive at certain "needs" or "goods" as fundamental to being human. Compare JOHN RAWLS, A THEORY OF JUSTICE 11–22 (1971) and FINNIS, NATURAL LAW AND NATURAL RIGHT, *supra* note 6, at 81–85. Although that enquiry sometimes overlaps with a utilitarian assessment, the natural law theorist generally views human needs and goods as generic and objective, and not a numeric compilation of so many subjective preferences. *See*, for example, MacIntyre's criticism of utilitarianism. ALISDAIR MACINTYRE, AFTER VIRTUE, A STUDY IN MORAL THEORY 62–64 (2d ed. 1984).

57. VEATCH, HUMAN RIGHTS, *supra* note 20, at 117. Edgar Bodenheimer notes that common human traits include the need for food, the sex drive, the need for security and safety, for recognition and esteem, for love, and for knowledge. EDGAR BODENHEIMER, PHILOSOPHY OF RESPONSIBILITY 54–56 (1980).

58. VEATCH, HUMAN RIGHTS, *supra* note 20, at 79–80. Even when considering the problem of desperate needs, Veatch continues to be tugged by the principle of individual responsibility. *See id.*, at 182–83 (arguing that individuals are ultimately responsible for providing for their own needs).

59. FINNIS, NATURAL LAW AND NATURAL RIGHT, *supra* note 6, at 59–90 (1980). Similarly, Germaine Grisez's list of human goods are

> Human life, including health and safety, all the arts and skills that can be cultivated simply for the sake of their very exercise, beauty and other objects of aesthetic experience, theoretical truth in is several varieties; friendship, both as relationship in immediate liaison and organization in larger communities; the use of intelligence to direct action; the effective freedom to do what one chooses with the whole force of an integrated personality; and a proper relationship to the fundamental principles of reality—i.e. to God. Germaine Grisez, A New Formulation of Natural Law against Contraception, 30 THOMIST 343–44 (1966), quoted in VEATCH, HUMAN RIGHTS, *supra* note 20, at 96–97.

60. GIORGIO DEL VECCHIO, JUSTICE, AN HISTORICAL AND PHILOSOPHICAL ESSAY 77–78 (Lady Guthrie, trans. 1952, 1956).

61. ARISTOTLE, ETHICS, (Book IX), *supra* note 18, at 293, 303–307.

62. CICERO, DE OFFICIIS, I.vii.22, *supra* note 31, at 25.

63. SAMUEL PUFENDORF, ON THE DUTY OF MAN AND CITIZEN ACCORDING TO NATURAL LAW 34 (M. Silverthorne, trans. 1991).

64. FINNIS, NATURAL LAW AND NATURAL RIGHTS, *supra* note 6, at 22.

65. CICERO, DE RE PUBLICA, I.ii.2, *supra* note 31, at 17.

66. "In general, feeling seems to yield not to argument but only to force." ARISTOTLE, ETHICS, (Book X), *supra* note 18, at 336.

67. As Veatch puts it,

> no agency of society, of family, of friends, or of whatever can make or determine or program an individual to be a good man, or program him to live a life that a human being out to live. Instead, attaining one's natural end as a human person is nothing if not a "do-it-yourself" job. VEATCH, HUMAN RIGHTS, *supra* note 20, at 84.

For John Finnis, there are absolute rights, derived from the absolute obligations one owes another never "to choose directly against any basic value, whether in oneself or in one's fellow human beings." FINNIS, NATURAL LAW AND NATURAL RIGHT, *supra* note 6, at 224–25. In contrast, Veatch holds that rights derive not from our obligations to others, but from our obligations to ourselves. Quoting from another philosopher, Veatch asserts

> I ought to develop my own potential for flourishing. So, others ought not to prevent me from developing my potential. So, by the principle of universalizability everyone has such a right. Gilbert Harman, Human Flourishing, Ethics, and Liberty, 12 Philosophy and Public Affairs 307–312 (1983), quoted in VEATCH, HUMAN RIGHTS, *supra* note 20, at 165 n. 26.

Rasmussen & Den Uyl deduce a range of primary Lockean rights not from one's pursuit of the good, but from the inherent *potential* of every person to pursue the good. Thus one who is acting against his own perfection still has as much right to liberty as does the well-motivated person. RASMUSSEN & DEN UYL, LIBERTY AND NATURE, *supra* note 55, at 109.

68. "My answer must take the simple form of a simple denial that individuals have any positive rights. There are no such things." VEATCH, HUMAN RIGHTS, *supra* note 20, at 180.

69. Rasmussen & Den Uyl hold that such a proposition cannot instill virtue, for there is no free choice involved, and, in fact, instills the wrong lessons: that state action is the answer to all of life's problems. RASMUSSEN & DEN UYL, LIBERTY AND NATURE, *supra* note 55, at 212–213. They overlook the educative role of the state as exemplar and the human mechanism of virtue as the habit of acting rightly that Aristotle so trenchantly observed. ARISTOTLE, ETHICS, (Book II), *supra* note 18, at 91.

Further, the objection that forcing a person to assist another does not increase the subject's virtue is true but irrelevant. If one should question what logic there was in forcing other to act virtuously, since virtuous action requires voluntariness, the answer of the ancients, was, in effect, that substantively, without the coercion, the subject was not about to act virtuously anyway. There was another person in need who should have been provided for. So at least the substantive need is fulfilled, and the form of the virtuous act is maintained. Furthermore, because of law's educative function, the habit of acting helpfully to another may eventually be internalized so that subject will act voluntarily and morally after all. ARISTOTLE, ETHICS, (Book X), *supra* note 18, at 337–38.

70. For an extraordinarily thorough examination of the relation of the political order to virtue in history, *see* PAUL A. RAHE, REPUBLICS ANCIENT AND MODERN: CLASSICAL REPUBLICANISM AND THE AMERICAN REVOLUTION (1992).

71. For Veatch, Rasmussen & Den Uyl, the good of practical reasonableness or even the ultimate human good of constructing a life of individual participation in the range of human goods necessarily requires the enjoyment of an extremely wide range of liberty. Indeed, any interference with legitimate (i.e. non-harmful) choices by a free person would need to be justified. VEATCH, HUMAN RIGHTS, *supra* note 20, at 206; RASMUSSEN, LIBERTY AND NATURE, *supra* note 55, at 108–09.

72. 2 AQUINAS, SUMMA THEOLOGICA (Pt. II-II, Q.66, Art. 7), *supra* note 41, at 1480–81.

73. *Id.* (Reply Obj. 2), at 1481.

74. "Things which are of human right cannot derogate from natural right or Divine right." *Id.*, at 1480.

75. Aquinas is specific: "Yet he that is able to give food is not always bound to feed the needy." 2 AQUINAS, SUMMA THEOLOGICA (Pt. II-II, Q.71, Art. 1), *supra* note 41, at 1497.

76. Or causing another in your care to starve. One never can seek to do good through harm.

77. Aquinas concludes,

> Nevertheless, if the need be so manifest and urgent, that it is evident that the present need must be remedied by whatever means be at hand (for instance when a person is in some immediate danger, and there is no other possible remedy), then it is lawful for a man to succor his own need by means of another's property, by taking it either openly or secretly nor is this properly speaking theft or robbery. 2 AQUINAS, SUMMA THEOLOGICA (Pt. II-II, Q.66, Art. 7), *supra* note 41, at 1481.

78. The verbal summary is mine, but the concepts are evident in ARISTOTLE, THE POLITICS, CICERO, DE RE PUBLICA, and FINNIS, NATURAL LAW AND NATURAL RIGHT.

Part Three

Natural Law and the Government

The Axioms of Public Policy

HADLEY ARKES

Tom Stoppard has characters in one of his plays lamenting the untimely, tragic death of a young philosopher, removed from the scene by a murder, just before a conference at which he was scheduled to speak. One colleague, in a surge of sentiment, says, "Poor Duncan. . . . I like to think he'll be there in spirit." And the other adds—yes, "if only to make sure the materialistic argument is properly represented."

Amnesiacs and Philosphers

In this age of reconstruction, antifoundationalism, and fifty-seven varieties of relativism, it is no longer surprising to find undergraduates, or even their professors, floating in the same benign haze. "Do I contradict myself? Ah, then I contradict myself." Kant remarked long ago on those philosophers who sought to marshal reasons in the most cunning way for the sake of "proving by reason that there is no such thing as reason."[1]

In our own day, it is no longer even a novelty to find the skeptic who is prepared to doubt his own existence. "I have a right to believe that I don't exist." The reflex of the philosopher is to ask, Who is the bearer of that right? The one who does not exist? Have we reached now a new stage in ontology? Have we arrived at a point where people adorned with formal schooling no longer detect even a trace of contradiction in asserting the presence of rights without the presence of entities who bear those rights? I recall a late colleague of mine who professed at times not to know that he himself existed—though he was bitterly certain that the check from Blue Cross was late.

Daniel Robinson has remarked in this vein that the amnesiac suffers doubt as to *who* he is, but no trace of doubt *that he is*. In that respect, the amnesiac grasps, without much self-consciousness, the axiom that eluded even the redoubtable Descartes. Descartes' curious oversight here was pointed up, in his characteristic, penetrating, and witty way, by Thomas Reid. As Reid remarked, "A man that disbelieves his own existence, is surely as unfit to be reasoned with as a man that believes he is made of Glass":

> There may be disorders in the human frame that may produce such extravagancies, but they will never be cured by reasoning. Des Cartes, indeed, would make us believe that he got out of this delirium by this logical argument, '*Cogito ergo sum*,' but it is evident he was in his senses all the time, and never seriously doubted of his existence; for he takes it for granted in this argument, and proves nothing at all. I am thinking, says he—therefore I am. And is it not as good reasoning to say, I am sleeping—therefore, I am? or, I am doing nothing—therefore, I am? If a body moves, it must exist, no doubt; but, if it is at rest, it must exist likewise.[2]

Rights and Existence

But the condition of the skeptic becomes ever more curious when the radical skepticism is attended by the most emphatic claims about the existence and standing of his rights, which do not apparently invite even a hint of skepticism. For some reason, the impassioned undergraduate and the committed feminist think that their deepest political interests are at stake. Their liberties and their freedom to live without the burden of judgments cast by others seem to hinge on the prospect of resisting the claim, on the part of people in authority, to know any "true" propositions about "nature" or about the principles of right and wrong.

In the new orthodoxy of the Left on the campuses, there is of course no "human nature." What people have been pleased to describe as nature is really "socially constructed," varying from one place to another according to the vagaries of the "local culture." And yet the people who hold to this view have not betrayed the slightest hesitation in casting judgments on other cultures when it has come to denouncing the treatment of women in other places or condemning the regimes in South Africa or China. Apparently they have had no trouble in piercing through the screens of local cultures and identifying the beings who count as "women" in these places. And they seem to move quite as readily, without strain, in identifying the "wrongs" done to these women as women.

I have had the occasion more than once to call attention to this curious mix of positions and to extract this lesson: that for the Left on the campuses, there are "human rights" to be vindicated in all places, but strictly speaking there are no "humans." And since there are no moral truths, there are no "rights" that are truly rightful. "Rights," under this construction, must be nothing more than the conventions that are arranged from place to place, according to the temper of the local majority.

Just why anything in the agenda of feminism or the rights of women or anyone else should be advanced by a groundwork of this kind must remain one of mysteries of our own age. But the distraction of mind here reflects something that has run well beyond the cluster of undergraduates and their tutors, something that has seeped into our law and jurisprudence. For what is engaged here, I think, is not simply a kind of tin ear for inconsistency.

Founding Principles

What I think we are seeing represents a notable detachment from the generation of the American Founders in this respect: there seems to be a detachment of our jurisprudence from nothing less than the axioms of understanding—from that stratum of necessary truths that forms the very ground of our reasoning. "In disquisitions of every kind," said Hamilton, "there are certain primary truths, or first principles, upon which all subsequent reasonings must depend. These contain," he explained, "an internal evidence which, antecedent to all reflection or combination, commands the assent of the mind."[3]

In a line offered in passing, in one of his opinions (*McCulloch v. Maryland*),[4] John Marshall apologized to his readers for taking so much time in demonstrating propositions that should be recognized as axioms. Marshall understood, and he assumed his readers understood, that certain axioms had to be in place before it was possible to carry out a "demonstration." Marshall and the Founders also understood that a "self-evident" truth was not evident to every self who happened down the street. It was a truth that had to be grasped *per se nota*, as something necessary in itself—precisely in the way that Hamilton said it needed to be grasped. In that respect, Marshall and Hamilton were reflecting the teachings that ran back to Aquinas on the first principles of our understanding and the principles, then, of natural law.

The evidence is written plainly in the works of the Founders not only that they were attentive to the axioms of our understanding, but that they were capable of incorporating them, elegantly, in the judgments they wove. But I deliver no news when I simply note that, in our own day, the most mature and schooled judges have shown the most serene blindness to those foundations of moral judgment, or the axioms of the law. For a quarter century, that obtuseness has actually furnished the grounds of jurisprudence in whole new fields. To take one notorious example, Justice Harlan turned a fortune-cookie maxim into a new building block in our law when he declared, in *Cohen v. California* (in 1971) that "one man's vulgarity is another's lyric." Twenty years later, Judge Sarokin could declare in New Jersey that "one man's hay fever is another's ambrosia."

In the interval, the judges had deeply absorbed the teaching that came along with the bromide: namely, that speech on matters of moral significance is irreducibly subjective and emotive. As Justice Harlan said, there were no principled grounds for making distinctions between the speech that was obscene or assaulting, on the one hand, and the speech that was innocent and inoffensive, on the other. In short, we could not make discriminations any longer on the content of the speech.[5] Fed now by that lesson, grown-ups bedecked in robes on the Supreme Court profess that we cannot tell the difference, say, between a burning cross and a cross used for devotional purposes; or that we cannot distinguish between the destruction of a damaged flag and the desecration of a flag.

We have been afflicted of late by a malady that was virtually unknown at the time of the Founding, and that is a certain obliviousness about the very axioms of a regime of law, or the first principles of moral and legal judgment. My argument here is that there are serious confusions of policy, which have become more than minor irritants, but confusions that seriously skew the conditions of justice. These confusions can be traced directly to confusions that enter at the very root of the law, in the things that should serve, for jurists, as the axioms of their understanding.

I would suggest, as I push this matter a bit further, that certain controversies we encounter today over matters of public policy are confusions that are swollen out of scale precisely because people are confounding uncertainties over policies, or applications, with the fundamental axioms that make the law both intelligible and practicable. As a notable example, we seem to be afflicted today with arguments that would deflect us from any regimen of regulation over the arts, from movies to drama to painting and sculpture. For some reason, the regulation of this domain is thought to be far more perilous for a republic than the regulation, say, of factories or brokerage houses.

The superstition seems to be widely diffused in the land that the law lacks, in the domain of the arts, the standards of judgment that it can summon far more readily when the object of regulation happens to be the manufacturies of pharmaceuticals or automobiles. But as I shall try to argue, the law does not encounter, in this field, any problem more inscrutable than it encounters anywhere else. We are often encouraged to hold back the hand of the law out of a false diffidence about the standards of judgment. In this holding back, we make a grievous mistake at several levels, not the least of which is this: A certain perplexity is bound to arise, in any field, when we seek to move from the principles of right to the regulations of positive law that can apply to practical cases.

It must always be legitimate to raise questions about the aptness of regulations or their faithfulness to the principles that inspire and justify them. But when it comes to the arts and the dangers of censorship, we allow ourselves to be intimidated, beyond the merits, by cases. Our perplexity in devising regulations, in defining obscenity or pornography, is taken as an occasion for raising doubts about our capacity to define the wrong itself and to understand the very ground of the law. The inclination then has been to recede altogether from this critical domain in our culture, or the character of our public entertainments. We give, in other words, a false dominion to our perplexity, and we affect blindness to the most fundamental, necessary things we know about the grounds, or the structure, of the problem.

Axioms of the Political Structure: The Whole and the Part

I write then of "structure" and the principles that bear on the structures of political life. And I say "political" life rather than the structure of the American regime or a constitutional order because it seems to me that the Founders understood this matter on a level that ran beyond the American Constitution. This problem touched on understandings that were antecedent to the Constitution, precisely because they were axiomatic.

In *The Federalist* No. 80, for example, Alexander Hamilton took note of the obvious point that, in a union of many parts or components, it was only to be expected that some of the parts may show an inclination to policies that were "incompatible with the interests of Union, and others with the principles of good government." Hamilton was on his way to making the further point that "controversies between the nation and its members or citizens, can only be properly referred to the national tribunals." "Any other plan," he said, "would be contrary to reason, to precedent, and to decorum." By "decorum" he meant, in the classic sense, the appropriate or reasonable scale of things. And that point, he said, would "rest on this plain proposition, that the peace of the WHOLE ought not to be left at the disposal of a PART."[6]

Detached from the circumstances of any case, reduced to its pure, abstract qualities as a principle, the proposition, as Hamilton expressed it, strikes us instantly with its force as an axiom. And yet the circumstances of the case do indeed often get in the way. They may draw us to the questions of justice enmeshed in the injuries of the parties. They may divert us from the fact that, beyond the drama and the clash of parties, there are axiomatic propositions at stake, which can be ignored only at the cost of a deeper injustice and a graver injury.

Public Policy

And so, when the Roosevelt Administration was moved to extend diplomatic recognition to the Communist regime in Russia, the administration had to make itself and the American courts accomplices in carrying out Bolshevik schemes for the confiscation of property. The immediate question then was whether the property held by Russian nationals and corporations, and deposited in banks in New York, would be delivered over to Stalin's government. With the completion of the diplomatic "arrangements," institutions in New York would be encouraged to behave with suitable courtesies, as though they were operating in accordance with that oxymoron called "Soviet Law."

I once suggested to readers that the moral dimensions of the problem might come out more fully if we supposed for a moment that the case involved the recognition, in the late 1930s, of a Nazi government in Germany. Let us suppose that the regime in Germany had confiscated the property held by Jewish nationals and, in the process of extending recognition to the new government, the courts in New York were compelled to act as engines of enforcement, attached now to the Nazi laws. They would churn into action then, divesting American residents of their property if they happened to be Jewish refugees from Germany.[7]

One could understand why the courts in New York might stage a resistance, just as they staged a resistance in this case. As Justice, and later as Chief Justice, Harlan Fiske Stone would try to brake this willingness to move, with such dispatch and thoroughness, in overriding the public policy of New York State. On the matter of public policy, his colleagues needed no convincing. It was quite as clear, at least, to Justice George Sutherland that this kind of arrangement would readily run afoul of the Fifth Amendment, with its protections against the taking of private property without just compensation. The arbitrary seizure of property offended principles that were deeply embedded in the American Constitution. No one suffered the least doubt that this seizure of property would have engaged a severe challenge on the part of the judges if it had arisen in our domestic law. But the judges understood that they could not disturb this particular policy without undoing the settlement that was bound up with the recognition of the Soviet government.

Primacy of the Nation

Whether it truly conduced to the well-being of the United States to enter these diplomatic relations with the regime in Russia might have been an open question. But it could not possibly have been a question within the reach of judges and courts. These decisions on the granting or withholding of diplomatic recognition were bound up with the calculations of military policy and the securing of the nation. Clearly, in a republican government, decisions involving the peril and safety of the nation had to be lodged entirely in the hands of officers who bore a direct responsibility to the electorate, those people whose lives were at stake in these decisions.

George Sutherland would write for his colleagues in that case of *U.S. v. Belmont*[8] on the recognition of the Soviet regime. One can hardly imagine that Sutherland suffered even a moment of doubt about the wrongness of the Bolshevik decrees. He could have harbored no doubts then about the wrongness of those laws that the American government was pledging itself to honor and enforce. Nor would he have doubted the essential rightness of that public policy in the State of New York that posed the last, slender obstacle to the completion of this settlement. And yet Sutherland was obliged to say, with the unequivocal force of the axiom that must reign, that

> in respect of all international negotiations and compacts, and in respect of our foreign relations generally, state lines disappear. As to such purposes the State of New York does not exist.[9]

As far, then, as foreign policy is concerned, we might say that "there is no New York." That is precisely because, as Hamilton explained, "the peace of the WHOLE ought not to be left at the disposal of a part." When Hamilton sought to explain in this way the understandings that had to be built into the Constitution, he was not really explaining principles that were peculiar to the American Constitution. He was explaining, rather, principles that were bound up with the very logic of a constitutional government, or a government restrained by law, even if they were never made explicit in the Constitution.

Necessary and Proper Authority

Hamilton could hardly contain his incredulity mingled with outrage when certain anti-Federalist writers railed at the Necessary and Proper Clause, and found, in that clause, a license for new powers of unbounded reach. But as Hamilton managed to show, in a model of teaching,

> The intended government would be precisely the same if [the Supremacy Clause and the Necessary and Proper Clause] were entirely obliterated . . . . They are only declaratory of a truth which would have resulted by necessary and unavoidable implication from the very act of constituting a federal government, and vesting it with certain specified powers.[10]

Hamilton moved along this chain of reasoning: A political association is marked by the presence of law. It is the distinct nature of law that it forms "a rule which those to whom it is prescribed are bound to observe." It is the nature of law, then, that it implies *supremacy*. It must displace personal choice; it may properly override the policies of subordinate associations:

> If individuals enter into a state of society, the law of that society must be the supreme regulator of their conduct. If a number of political societies enter into a larger political society, the laws which the latter may enact, pursuant to the powers intrusted to it by its constitution, must necessarily be supreme over those societies, and the individuals of whom they are composed. It would otherwise be a mere treaty, dependent on the good faith of the parties, and not a government, which is only another word for POLITICAL POWER AND SUPREMACY.[11]

All of this would be in place even if there had been, in the Constitution, no Supremacy Clause or Necessary and Proper Clause. In fact, all of this could be said without knowing anything about the character of the American Constitution or of the government in America. These were propositions that had to be true of anything bearing the character of a government marked by the presence of law, and a government that absorbed in itself the moral premises of a regime "restrained by law": that government would understand, from the beginning, that there were rightful and wrongful ends; that a government rightly constituted would not claim the authority to exert its powers for all manner of ends. The government would claim a right to seek only decent and lawful ends, and therefore it would begin with a sense that certain ends, and certain powers, are beyond its lawful reach. It would seek to do, as Hamilton said, only the things that were "necessary" to its ends and "proper" to do.

When Hamilton wrote in *The Federalist* No. 80, he was contemplating the collision of powers in a union that contained a central government along with thirteen states. But when he observed that "the peace of the WHOLE ought not to be left at the disposal of a PART," his observations were not tied to the American scheme of federalism. What he says, in *The Federalist* No. 80, could have been said quite as aptly by Aristotle, in explaining the principles that were immanent in his own schema of constitutions or regimes.

As we may recall, Aristotle divided his types of regimes, on one axis, according to the concentration or dispersion of power: whether rule was exercised by the one, the few, or the many. But then the second and more decisive axis divided the regimes between the legitimate and the illegitimate, the decent and the corrupt. The corruption or perversion of power was taken, as its root, as a transmutation in the nature of the thing. And what was that transmutation? The polis was public in its nature and its ends, and it was corrupted when rulers made use of their power to favor their *personal* ends or their *private* interests. Rather than directing themselves to a common good, a "public" good, or a good of the whole, the corrupt rulers directed themselves mainly to the good of a "part." On that critical matter hinged the distinctions between kingship and tyranny, aristocracy and oligarchy, commonwealth and democracy (the decent or the corrupted form of rule by the many).

But my point is that the original understanding of the polis began with an understanding of the difference between the public and the private, between a good that was common or universal and a good that was merely personal or private. This awareness then of a tension between the part and the whole is simply endemic in the notion of a government bounded by the moral law.

These considerations may be rudimentary or axiomatic, but as we have had ample occasion now to see, they are not always obvious. Their violation can become the source of vast perils: the peace of the whole nation would be disrupted by a war with the Indian tribes, and the nation could not permit itself to be drawn into war because a state would not restrain its own inhabitants from warring on the Indians. Whether the national government was right or wrong to recognize the government under Stalin, the peace and security of the whole nation were engaged in the diplomacy of that move. It could not be disrupted by officials in New York, who were beyond the reach of voters in all the other states.

The Contingent and the Permanent: A Rule "Uniform and Invariable"

I strain then to point out that these instructions offered by Hamilton and others among the Founders do not offer merely rules of prudence or skill, even though they seem to form a manual of statecraft. They are propositions that fold in moral premises, or nothing less than the "axioms of understanding," along with their counsels of prudence. Justice Joseph Story remarked, in his later years, that he had "heard Samuel Dexter, John Marshall, and Chancellor Livingston say that Hamilton's reach of thought was so far beyond theirs that by his side they were schoolboys—rush tapers before the sun at noon day."[12] The difference would show itself at times in deft turns of reasoning, struck off quickly without strain, but marking unmistakably a mind whose reach ran just a bit beyond their own.

Many people will recall that Marshall's argument in *McCulloch v. Maryland* tracks rather closely along the lines of the statement that Hamilton had prepared for Washington on the constitutionality of the national bank. Marshall's argument followed Hamilton's almost exactly, except for one notable thing. Here, as in other instances, a turn in the argument revealed that the reader was dealing, in Hamilton, with a mind in a rather different register.

The Rule of Necessity

Hamilton's statement on the bank had been prepared for the purpose of countering an argument assembled by Jefferson in opposition to the bank. The main lines of argument over the national bank and the "necessary and proper clause" are by now familiar. Hamilton would distinguish the different levels in the meaning of "necessity": the term could certainly mean indispensably necessary, in the sense of being utterly essential. But in ordinary language, the term could also mean "no more than needful, requisite, incidental, useful, or conducive to."

Jefferson insisted that, when it came to the federal government, the rules of construction should be quite restrictive. In this setting of a strictly limited government, "necessary" would mean something like absolutely necessary. A measure would come within the "necessary and proper" clause only if it were so necessary that its absence would render the grant of power nugatory.[13] But more than that, as Hamilton pointed out, Jefferson's understanding of "necessity" would depend on a reading of circumstances, including things that might be casual or temporary. Jefferson suggested that it could not strictly be necessary to have a national bank when there were already in existence state banks performing the same functions. But in casting his argument in that way, Jefferson had incorporated, as Hamilton said, "an idea which alone refutes the construction."

Jefferson had fallen into the most serious confusion about the levels of the argument. If taxis are readily available, there may be no need for me to buy a car. If they are not available, I may find it necessary, in the circumstances, to buy a car. But all of that is quite separate from the question of whether I possess a certain freedom, or right, to purchase a car. I may have that right, but with cabs readily available, it is not necessary for me to exercise it. Still, the fact that I have no need, under the circumstances, to exercise this right can hardly be taken as a waiver of my right.

In the same way, the existence of state banks might make it unnecessary for the national government to create a national bank. But as Hamilton remarked, those banks in the states are "institutions which happen to exist today, and for ought that concerns the government of the United States, may disappear tomorrow." Whether there is a right, in the national government, to create a bank could not rest on anything as conditional or contingent as whether the states happen to create or dissolve their banks. As Hamilton put it, "The *expediency* of exercising a particular power, at a particular time, must indeed depend on *circumstances*; but the constitutional right of exercising it must be uniform and invariable—the same today as tomorrow."[14]

To see the matter from the other side, it is possible to imagine a constitution for a central government meant to be tightly circumscribed. We might imagine that the constitution tries to encompass an operating rule of this kind: "No function should be performed by the central government as soon as the function is supplied, in any place, by one of the states." But it should be clear that *this rule itself could not be contingent upon anything done within the states.* Within its own terms, it would have to be, as Hamilton said, "uniform and invariable."

If the question, then, is whether the government has a claim to exercise the means to its own ends, that part of the problem cannot be contingent. Jefferson would have had to concede that point in principle when he entered upon any discussion of the "necessity" of the means in any case. In that event, Jefferson had been laboring against himself. His strenuous argument had to presuppose precisely the premise that he fancied he was resisting. And that is why, as Hamilton remarked, his argument revealed a "*radical* source of error in the reasoning."[15]

I take it that no one would really doubt the caliber of Jefferson's mind, and so we may take the case as an example to us all. Even the most urbane and gifted among us may find themselves falling at times into mistakes that touch the axioms of our understanding. In matters of law and public policy, those mistakes at the root may also touch matters of moral consequence. In that same vein, I would like to draw a few separate examples on some of the matters that have vexed us recently. I would put before us the possibility that we find our judges and commentators falling into confusions, in the style of Jefferson, over matters that really should be axiomatic. Or, as in the style of Jefferson, they may be confusing principles with things that are merely contingent.

On Hominoids, Delayed, Early and Incorrigible: The Principle of Identity

I was a bit surprised, a few years ago, to receive an invitation to address the Catholic bishops in their workshop on the matter of "delayed hominization." It appeared that many people in the Church were getting quite concerned over these new arguments, which were taken up even by some Jesuits armed with degrees in biochemistry.

Delayed Hominization

The purport of these arguments was to cast up a caution against regarding the human embryo as human from its first moments as a zygote, or even in the chimera stage. The contention was that the zygote is still wanting in the attributes that are necessary to its completion as a human being. Those attributes needed to be supplied by molecules from the mother, conveyed to the zygote only after it is implanted in the uterine wall.[16] Up to this point, we find a progressive division of cells, with changes so marked that it becomes hard to say that the first cell is really the "same being" as that complex cluster of cells. The notable break comes when that colony of cells is suddenly transformed into that one, ontologically distinct human being. But according to this argument, the zygote is not the same being, or the same person—and it is nearly laughable to suggest that it claims the same moral or ontological standings as the being who fills out its features after it is implanted on the wall of the uterus.

The purpose behind this minor flexing of genius I take to be quite evident. The biochemists and philosophers who would urge upon us a "larger" view seem to be concerned to detach people from the temptation to protect the being in the womb from its earliest moments. And when the argument is pressed by certain Jesuits, the design seems to be to encourage the Church to temper its opposition to abortion, which seems to be so unseasonably adamant.

I remarked to the bishops that this was a case of merging new biology with old fallacies.[17] The proponents of "delayed hominization" were utterly persuaded that those early clusters of cells could not be the same as that unique being who emerged at the end of the process. I suggested that we attach a name to that new being: we might call her Wendy Himmelstein. Some of these commentators are convinced that those ungainly cells are not Wendy Himmelstein. And yet the people who wish to forego the advent of Wendy Himmelstein seem to know precisely which cluster of cells they must strike at if they would prevent the emergence of Wendy Himmelstein. There would seem to be, then, a relation of identity between those cells and Wendy Himmelstein.

Identity

The argument, of course, becomes more refined, but as refined as it becomes, it can never get around the fact that we have here the ancient problem of identity. Socrates sitting is the same as Socrates standing. The Brown who was caught embezzling tells us that he has undergone a conversion; he is, now, no longer the same as the one who had embezzled. If we punish him, we would be punishing the wrong man. His conversion may be welcome and, for all we know, some new, improved soul is inhabiting the body we identify with Brown. But we are in fact souls embodied. We are obliged to treat Brown, in all of the phases of his life, as the same man moving through different phases, some of them with a moral refurbishing. But the thing that connects, in all of these phases, is Brown himself, his continuing existence, as the repository of his lengthening record of experience.

For many of us, the anchor of our own knowledge may come with the child's recognition that I am, today, the same person as I was yesterday; that the experience of the day before belongs to me. We deal here with one of the axioms of our understanding and, indeed, of our being. The biochemists and philosophers who are straining their genius on the scheme of "delayed hominization" are elaborating arguments that cannot reach any matter of moral consequence, for they run up against axioms which cannot be evaded or dislodged.

Federal Authority

In a column sometime ago in *Crisis* magazine, I recalled a conversation with a friend and former adviser to George Bush. He was apparently growing weary of the strain created in the Republican Party over the issue of abortion, and he turned to me at one moment to ask, earnestly, "Why can't we just keep this out of national politics?"

It was a long explanation as to why the matter simply could not be returned to the states at this moment, but I remarked to him that we might possibly strike a deal to remove this issue from the federal government if he and his friends truly meant the entire federal government, the courts as well as the Congress. Could he get his friends to sign on to a series of measures invoking the powers of Congress under Art. III, Sec. 2, and altering the jurisdiction of the federal courts on the issue of abortion? Or when they talk about removing this issue from national politics, do they really mean "remove from the politics of abortion the institutions that show an interest in restricting the 'right' to an abortion?"

Are the courts, after all, not part of the federal government? In a curious way, a certain screening seems to take place on this issue. What is conveniently blocked out is a set of axioms that may begin with Chief Justice Marshall's dictum in *Cohens v. Virginia*: "[T]he judicial power of every well constituted government must be co-extensive with the legislative, and must be capable of deciding every judicial question which grows out of the constitution and laws."[18]

Corollary: any question or subject that may come, properly, within the authority of the courts, must come properly within the jurisdiction of the legislature. And, by extension, any subject of legislation must come within the reach of the executive, who bears the responsibility to enforce the laws.

As anyone with a remote interest in constitutional law knows, a nice question has arisen about the grounds on which Congress could legislate on the matter of abortion if that subject were returned, fully, to the arena of legislation. Conservatives were content to avoid the question for a long while by assuming simply that the issue would be returned to the states.

Recently, Professor Lawrence Tribe flexed his usual genius in order to produce the implausible argument that the Commerce Clause would provide a ground on which Congress could fill out the protections for the right to choose an abortion. Some of us have sought to show that the same, implausible device of the Commerce Clause would work even more powerfully to protect the children in the womb.[19] Under this head we have even been willing to invoke that hoary old case of *Wickard v. Filburn*[20] and say: even though this is but one abortion, it becomes part of a pattern that encompasses, each year, about 1.3 million abortions.

If the federal government could restrain Roscoe Filburn from growing wheat, even for his own consumption, on his own farm, the government could just as plausibly restrict those "private" acts of abortion that make up a massive national volume of abortions. After all, to remove that many infants from the American market is to depress, gravely, the market for bassinets, diapers, and baby food, to say nothing of the demand for colleges and weddings in later years. Liberals were hardly very mirthful when conservatives were willing to use the same, formulaic arguments under the Commerce Clause as the supposed ground for the recent bill on partial-birth abortions.

Jurisdiction

But none of these gestures is in vain. The young, conservative lawyers on the Judiciary Committee in the House of Representatives would not have plucked that rationale out of the air if there had been a clearer consensus among the lawyers about the constitutional ground for the legislation. And yet here again we may be, as Henry James says, the victims of perplexities from which a single spark of direct perception might have spared us.

The subject of abortion has been ruled dramatically, preeminently, by the federal courts for nearly three decades. With the premises of John Marshall, we might ask how the subject of abortion could come properly within the reach of only one branch of the federal government. If the federal courts bear, persistently, an authority to address the question of abortion in all of its dimensions, that same authority could hardly stand in any more diminished version in the hands of the Congress or the President.

I understand, of course, that there may not always be this equivalence in jurisdiction among the branches. I have already recalled George Sutherland's understanding that the courts could not reach certain questions of constitutional rights if they arose in the course of recognizing foreign governments or deploying the military forces. Even if constitutional rights were embroiled in these cases, this was not a domain in which judges, in the United States, should dare to meddle. They would have to give way to other officers bearing a comparable responsibility, no less than that of judges, to preserve the Constitution.

I suppose it should follow that, in certain cases, the understanding may run in the other direction: There may be matters within the reach of the court that may not come within the reach of the legislature or the executive. I register my openness to that argument, but I await it. And until it arrives, we would stand on far sounder ground if we stood with the axioms suggested by Marshall: We would be far more warranted in assuming that, if the Supreme Court finds a ground in the Constitution for vindicating the constitutional rights of a litigant, the Congress may find the ground for its own jurisdiction in precisely the same part of the Constitution.

We may wait, then, for metaphysicians of the law to tell us whether the right to an abortion is anchored in the Fourteenth Amendment, the Ninth Amendment, the Commerce Clause, or the clause on Letters of

Marque and Reprisal. But while we are waiting, we may content ourselves with this dictum: Whatever now furnishes the ground on which the federal courts may reach the matter of abortion in all its phases, that same ground must be quite as serviceable in supplying the authority to Congress to legislate.

Thinking Again the Unthinkable: The Elementary Case for Censorship

The issue of abortion holds the central place in what has been called, loosely, the "culture wars" in this country. The recognition seems finally to have taken hold that it really is not "the economy, stupid." The major fault lines between the parties turn on moral questions that are routinely subordinated to "the economy," in large part because the capacity to speak in public on moral questions seems largely to have vanished from the political class.

In a public life so arranged, the media have been willing to anoint as "moral mavens" people who merely use the M-word, even if they are offering mainly chatter about these questions. And so Senator Bob Dole can be credited with audacious stands when he merely rails at Hollywood over something called "values." But neither from his lips nor from his texts does there spring a proposal for legal restraints or censorship, even in the mildest version.

In the Hall of Improbable Characters, the exhibit containing such figures as the Zany Insurance Salesman and the Diffident Stock Broker, we now have the Culture Warrior. He is, evidently, a creature given to high sentiments, emphatically sounded. At the same time, he seems quite careful never to take any of his "moral" arguments seriously enough to engage the law. But as even John Stuart Mill understood, "we call any conduct wrong, or employ, instead, some other term of dislike or disparagement, according as we think that the person ought, or ought not, to be punished for it."[21]

The traditional connection between morality and law may be conveyed in this way: If we came to the recognition, say, that it was wrong for parents to torture their infants, we are not apt to conclude that, therefore, "we ought to offer the parents tax incentives in order to induce them to stop." If we genuinely bore the conviction that the torture of infants was wrong, that conviction would express itself more aptly in an imperative or a command. We would forbid the torturing of infants, for everyone, for anyone. Which is to say that we would forbid it with the force of law.[22] The so-called warriors, or moral leaders in the new culture wars, seem to find their arts of warfare in striking moral postures, without the logic or conviction of moral judgments.

Anyone who has been schooled in the primers of prudence knows that the law need not be heavy-handed in order to teach its lessons. As Aquinas remarked in this vein, the purpose of the law is to lead us to virtue, not suddenly, but gradually. Even the mildest form of censorship may nevertheless plant the principle that the arts and popular entertainment may be subject to serious moral restraint. And the use of the law offers a discipline that may restrain even the voluble outpourings of the culture warriors. It is one thing to jawbone about Hollywood, with complaints freely emitted; it is quite another to make clear to the public the standards of judgment we regard as serious enough that we would defend them in a court of law.

What holds us back, of course, is not merely a want of audacity, for many people have been willing to court hostility as the price of speaking out. A much more serious inhibition arises from a certain diffidence that we can settle now, in our public debates, a consensus on any standard to define obscenity or depravity in the arts. But this is precisely where I would suggest that we are held back now by a certain confusion over principles and contingencies. It is worth drawing us back to some of the propositions that should stand at the root of the problem.

In the first place, every device, every empirical thing, and every activity can be part of a means–end chain directed to a wrongful end. A pen can be used to defraud or to pardon an innocent man. The knowledge of driving a car can be directed to the end of saving lives in an ambulance or driving for the Mafia. Is it conceivable then that the arts—painting, plays, movies—form the only activity under the sun that stands utterly, purely, without moral consequence?

For my own part, I do not think I have ever known an artist who regarded the arts as morally impotent. One way or another, the artists think they are engaged in a project of affecting the sensibility of their audiences and the culture that envelops us. That is to say, they do not betray the slightest doubt that the arts have moral consequence. But if the arts can ennoble, it must follow that they have the capacity to debase. If they can recruit our sentiments to love what is admirable, they can employ many of the same arts for the purpose of making us suggestible to the things that are shady, corrupt, evil.

Those general propositions do not, of course, translate themselves quite yet into regulations. But the problem here is hardly different in nature from the problem we would encounter as we tried to explain, in a regulation, the things that might count as malpractice at the hands of dentists and accountants. There would seem to be no particular strain at this moment in settling restraints on what may be shown directly about violence. There are no pictures, on the screens, of faces shot partly off or of intestines splattered. In fact, it is remarkable as to how broad the restraints have been. As recently as the 1940s or 1950s there seemed to be comparably little strain in recognizing certain boundaries for the films on matters of sexuality. It seemed to be understood, for example, that if one pictured teenagers involved in a sexual relation, it was a portentous situation, freighted with significance. It was not something to be depicted as routine, expected, legitimate, or as a matter of little consequence.

Shades of Meaning

These things seemed not to need saying because there was, at the time, a firmer understanding of just why it was problematic to encourage those kinds of intimacies among youngsters, who were quite remote from any state of mind that attended the commitments of marriage. A movie that represented these kinds of involvements as natural and legitimate would not have required, for its decoding, the subtle arts of a professor of literature. The implicit message in the film could have been spotted readily by truck drivers and their wives.

As it happens, we are so constituted that even people without college degrees can be quite sensitive to these moral shadings. Truck drivers may be no less acute than professors in recognizing when they are being insulted or treated in a demeaning way. People at all levels of education understand the shades of meaning built into our ordinary language, especially as they touch upon the things that are being commended or condemned, applauded or derided. And that is why trials over insults and defamation have fallen well within the arts of juries drawn from ordinary people.

But to remind ourselves of that point is to recall precisely why the project of censorship need not be beyond the wit of a board composed of ordinary folk. It would not require a jury composed of professors of art in order to decode the meaning of a crucifix anchored in a vat of urine. A jury composed of truck drivers as well as professors could make for an interesting mix, and their disagreements may make it hard to produce decisions except in the clearest cases.

Boards and juries make mistakes, and so they may work under rules that suggest, "When in doubt, presume on the side of freedom." But even if they convict rarely, they may teach, on those rare occasions, some clear lessons to the community. As they flex their moral judgment, they remind us that the arts are no more immune to moral judgment than the arts of bartenders and chiropractors. And if they do not presume to reach everything, they may encourage us to reflect seriously on these matters for ourselves, even in those places involving the arts where the law does not reach.

Moral Judgment

My point again is that we run the risk here of confusing principles with the perplexities involved in defining what is obscene in any case. And as we do that, we talk ourselves into the false notion that the arts are delivered to some transcendent place, beyond the restraints of the law and the reach of moral judgment.

Of course, for the votaries of postmodernism, radical feminism, or the orthodoxies that now reign on the American campuses, this problem dissolves as a problem. For people of this persuasion the arts are of course removed to a realm beyond moral judgment, but largely because there are no moral truths to pronounce in this domain or in any other. The problem persists only for those people who have not been snared by the secular religion of cultural relativism or one of its common varieties.

The problem remains intelligible then as a problem mainly for people who are persuaded, one way or another, that there are indeed moral truths in the world that reflect something more than local conventions. Some of these people may be shaky in the grounds of their conviction, but they have at least the sense that the Ten Commandments were not meant to be merely municipal regulations for the immediate vicinity of Mt. Sinai. Some of them go so far as to speak of "exceptionless moral norms"; others take on a more Kantian vocabulary in talking about categorical wrongs, anchored in the laws of reason. Others may recoil from the Kantian language, and make some purring sounds about Aristotle, Leo Strauss, and the need for prudence. But they are convinced that they are, most emphatically, not utilitarians or relativists. One way or another, they are attached to the notion of natural law or natural rights, and yet they find themselves falling into a dispute, often quite intense, over the deep layers of significance that are supposed to separate these two notions.

He Who Cannot Be Further Divided: The "Individual" and Rights

To the outsider looking on, it would appear to be a quarrel within the same family. Or, as Henry James would put it, these two sides would seem to represent chapters in the same book. For in either case, their position hinges on principles of right and wrong that have a cognitive standing of their own. They would be, as the saying goes, not subjective and merely personal, but objective, impersonal, and in that respect, universal. These principles of judgment cannot be dependent, for their validity, on the votes of majorities; their goodness, or rightness, cannot be reduced to the things that give us pleasure. These attributes, which they share, strike many of us as the ingredients that are truly decisive; they are far more critical than the things that divide these people from the relativists gliding by all around them.

Yet we know that the people who attach themselves to natural law in one school or another can be very much aware of differences running deep. There may be an inclination to think that these principles of moral judgment are grounded in "nature," but people may split into wings over the question of whether we make our way to "nature" by generalizing, in an inductive manner, from the pattern of our species written in the human record. Others insist that we cannot draw necessary truths or first principles on the basis of induction, for on the basis of induction we can produce only statements of probability.[23]

Kant warned about the temptation to deduce principles of moral judgment from "the particular natural characteristics of humanity" or "the particular constitution of human nature."[24] And more recently, John Finnis has denied that principles of natural law would have to be inferred from propositions about human nature. "They are not inferred from facts," he has insisted. "They are not inferred from metaphysical propositions about human nature, or about the nature of good and evil, or about the 'functions of a human being.'"[25]

Even among writers sensitive to these distinctions, there has been a further division over the supposed difference between natural law and natural right. My friend, the redoubtable Ernest Fortin, stated the point quite sharply years ago in a review of Finnis. Fortin recorded the judgment, held by a number of Catholic writers, that natural rights and natural law are quite compatible; that indeed, "the modern rights doctrine is simply a perfected version of the old natural law doctrine."[26]

But Fortin persists in seeing the most striking differences that separate them. In his construction of natural law, human beings are seen as social and political creatures who find their natural place in a political community. In fact, that larger whole is quite necessary to their standing and integrity as persons. "They form a larger whole," he writes, "to which they owe their primary allegiance and outside of which for the most part they are nothing." They may be identifiable as individuals, but they are "nonetheless intrinsically ordered to a determined end or ends that cannot be actualized without the collaboration of others."[27]

Individual Persons

In contrast, natural rights find their anchor in individual persons, beings who stand quite complete on their own as entities and the bearers of rights. In fact, those rights precede the polity or civil society. And for the end of securing those rights, these individuals

> 'enter' into a society that is entirely of their own making. All rules governing their relations with one another and all principles of justice are ultimately rooted in rights and derive their efficacy from them.[28]

In his usual savvy way, Fortin has caught the sense of things, or the nuances that may be readily overlooked. But there is also a danger of getting swept up in the metaphors, and becoming, as Mrs. Malaprop once put it, "as headstrong as an allegory on the Nile."

I am reminded of another remark of Daniel Robinson's, about commentators getting caught up in an expression that has seized the imagination of scholars: that painters, during the Renaissance, discovered perspective. Are we to suppose, he asked, that people up to that time were walking into walls and falling off hills? The fact of the matter is that the awareness of space and time, and therefore of perspective and dimension, is simply part of the constitution of our natures. The understanding is anchored within us, and anchored in the same way, as an axiom of our practical reason, is the understanding of individuals as the bearers of rights.

The shift from "natural law" to "natural rights" would seem to mark, on the surface, a shift from an accent on obligations to an accent on rights or on the claims of individuals. In that sense, the notion of natural rights may absorb all of the maladies that have been ascribed in our own day to so-called "rights talk": a relentless stream of claims for the privileges and freedoms of individuals, against the wider claims of the community, or against the principles that justify a restraint on freedom. And yet, it is hard to see how the shift in emphasis can mark any alteration in the underlying logic, after all, of moral terms.

In his lectures on jurisprudence, James Wilson noted that passage in which Blackstone had observed that "the law, which restrains a man from doing mischief to his fellow citizens, though it diminishes the natural, increases the civil liberty of mankind. . . ."[29] To that observation Wilson responded with a simple question: "Is it part of natural liberty," he asked, "to do mischief to anyone?"[30] Wilson was simply drawing here on the axiom, expressed by Lincoln and Aquinas, that there cannot be a "right to do a wrong." Even in the state of nature, as Wilson understood, one did not have the right to murder or steal or "do mischief." Even in some nether world outside of civil society, there could not be a coherent claim of a right to do a wrong. But if we understand the logic of a wrong, we understand, by implication, a corresponding right. If people did not have the right to do a wrong, we might as aptly say that even people in the state of nature had a *right not to be wronged.*

Rights and Obligations

Indeed, among the Founders it was quite common to do the translation running either way. Hamilton learned his natural law from Vattel in his writings on the law of nations, and in Vattel, it was clear, rights were simply derived from duties or obligations:

> [T]he natural law gives us the right to all those things without which we cannot satisfy our obligations; otherwise it would oblige us to do what is impossible, or rather it would contradict itself, by prescribing a duty and at the same time refusing us the sole means of fulfilling it. However, it is clear that these means must not be unjust in themselves, or such as the natural law absolutely prohibits.[31]

Of course, Vattel's own discussion of rights was cast mainly in terms of the rights of princes. But there was a strong accent also on the obligations of princes, their duties under the laws, and the limits of their powers. "A prince," said Vattel, "is, therefore, strictly bound not only to respect them, but also to uphold them."[32] One can be bound only by a law of reason, or a moral principle, which commands one's respect. If the prince is strictly obliged then not to punish anyone without a law or a hearing, we might as aptly say that people are regarded, operationally, as possessing a *right* not to be punished without a law or a hearing. No doubt, the matter may sound differently when described as a right or as the function of a duty; but it is hard to see how the underlying logic can be anything other than the same.

Nor is there anything in the logic of rights that confines it to single persons, as opposed to those aggregates of persons who make up associations, private and public. There may be rights then of communities, bodies politic, or even the rights of a Squash Club to confine its facilities to its dues-paying members. But as James Wilson reminded us in his elegant opinion in *Chisholm v. Georgia*, a state may be bound by the law, because the individual, the free man, may bind himself to the laws, and what is a state, after all, but an "aggregate of free men?" And "the sovereign," as Wilson said, "when traced to his source, must be found in the man."[33]

As we survey those things in the landscape that may bear the attribution of rights, we would indeed notice rights of corporations and associations. But the inquiry would naturally drive us to the bearers of rights that are finally indivisible, irreducible, incapable of further individuation. In a word, the individual. Under certain circumstances, with systems of assignment and allocation, it might be said that Jones has a right to receive a kidney, under fair terms, if these goods are being distributed. But it would be hard to say that the kidney has a right to refuse or accept its transfer. With the individual person, we would seem to reach the irreducible bearer of rights.

Yet, we also know—in fact, we must know—that in relation to the community at large, there is an immanent possibility of a tension between the interests of Jones, or the rights of Jones, and the rights of the community. The understanding seems to be settled now, even among the tribe of ethicists and utilitarians, that it would not be warranted to punish an innocent person simply to appease the hunger of the public for vengeance. Even among primates rather skeptical these days of moral truths, the utility of punishing someone—anyone—seems to be overridden by the insistence that we not feed the appetite of the public by punishing an innocent person.

In our own day, we have come to argue in a more rigorous way about racial discrimination, in a manner that runs well beyond the willingness of people thirty or forty years ago to settle these matters on the basis of generalizations and probabilities that seem, in ordinary life, quite good enough. On the basis of the aggregate data, we know that, for the present moment, the crime rate figures rise in any area to the extent that there is an increase in the population of young black males. And yet we understand that nothing in these aggregate data would furnish a ground of justification for barring from the neighborhood the black family seeking to move in next door. Even communitarians suffer no strain in recognizing that the individuals who compose this family deserve to be treated on their own terms, for what they themselves have done; that they do not deserve to absorb disabilities, *as individuals*, on the basis of what is known in the aggregate about the racial group of which they happen to be members.

George Gilder once collected some rather powerful aggregate data that described the condition of that hapless creature known as the single male: bachelors were twenty-two times more likely than married men to be committed to hospitals for mental disease (and ten times more likely to suffer chronic diseases of all kinds); single men had nearly double the mortality rate of married men and three times the mortality rate of single women; divorced men were three times more likely than divorced women to commit suicide or die by murder, and they were six times more likely to die of heart disease.[34] The data are plain and convincing: these creatures cannot be left to themselves. And yet no one seems to suppose that anything in these data provides the grounds for overriding personal freedom and assigning these men to brides.

I take it as plain as anything can be in this world that no one would think of prescribing such a thing—and I take it as equally clear that no one would attribute our aversion in this matter to the notion that, somehow, as "moderns," we have been shaped in our sensibilities by Hobbes. It requires just a moment's reflection to remember that there is no tension here, between the just treatment of the individual and the aggregate good of the community, that was not already contained in that encounter, long before Hobbes, when Abraham negotiated with God over Sodom and Gomorrah:

> That be far from Thee to do after this manner, to slay the righteous with the wicked, that so the righteous should be as the wicked; that be far from Thee; shall not the Judge of all the earth do justly? [Genesis, 18]

They may not be, at all times, the best of company, but the late news is that individuals are here to stay. We must suspect that they and their rights were a part of the moral landscape even before historians discovered "individualism." Their claims, their rights and wrongs, may be cast in the language of duties or rights, and they may be enlarged or diminished, but at their core the logic of these rights has remained the same. It will not be altered by the shifts that take us back and forth between natural law and natural rights. On the other hand, this estimate I strike off for you now may be discounted by the recognition that "I am not the man I used to be." But my friends here would draw their deeper comfort in recognizing, as they would instantly, that in the nature of things that cannot be true, and it never will be.

NOTES

1. Kant, Immanuel, *Critique of Practical Reason* [1788]. trans. Lewis White Beck. Indianapolis: Bobbs-Merrill, 1956, p. 12; p. 12 also of the standard edition of the Royal Prussian Academy.

2. Reid, Thomas, "Inquiry into the Human Mind," collected in *The Works of Thomas Reid*. Edinburgh: MacLachlan, Stewart, 1896, p. 100.

3. *The Federalist* No. 31. New York: Random House, n.d., p. 188.

4. 17 U.S. (4 Wheat.) 316 (1819).

5. Harlan's opinion in the Cohen case, and the fuller teachings surrounding it, are treated at length—and I do mean at length—in my book *The Philosopher in the City* (Princeton: Princeton University Press, 1981), pp. 63–74, set within a larger discussion on civility and the restriction of speech, pp. 23–91.

6. The *Federalist* No. 80, supra, note 3, pp. 516–17.

7. I set up this argument in my book, *The Return of George Sutherland*. Princeton: Princeton University Press, 1994, pp. 212–25, especially pp. 224–25.

8. 301 U.S. 324.

9. Ibid., at 331.

10. Hamilton, *The Federalist* No. 31, pp. 198–99.

11. Ibid., p. 201.

12. Quoted by MacDonald, Forrest, *Alexander Hamilton: A Biography*. New York: Norton 1979, p. 314.

13. See Hamilton's opinion on the constitutionality of the Bank, in Kurland, Philip B., and Ralph Lerner, *The Founders' Constitution*. Chicago: University of Chicago Press, 1987, Vol. 3, pp. 247–50, at p. 249.

14. Ibid.; italics in the original.

15. Ibid.; italics in the original.

16. Professors Carlos Bedate and Robert Cefalo have stood among the doctors of biology and obstetrics who have offered this argument:

> The information used for the development of a human embryo involves more than the zygote's chromosomal genetic information, namely, the genetic material from maternal mitochondria, and the maternal or paternal genetic messages in the form of messenger RNA or proteins. In terms of molecular biology, it is incorrect to say that the zygote possesses all the informing molecules for embryo development; rather, at most, the zygote possesses the molecules that have the potential to acquire informing capacity. That potential informing capacity is given in time through interaction with other molecules. . . . [W]hen the molecules interact, the result is . . . a completely new and different molecule. . . .

See Bedate, Carlos A., and Robert C. Cefalo, "The Zygote: To Be or Not Be a Person," *Journal of Medicine and Philosophy* 14, (date) pp. 641–45, at 642–43.

17. My fuller argument was contained in the piece, subsequently published, "On 'Delayed Hominization': Some Thoughts on the Blending of New Science and Ancient Fallacies," in Smith, Russell E., (ed.), *The Interaction of Catholic Bioethics and Secular Society*. Braintree: Pope John Center, 1992, pp. 143–62.

18. 19 U.S. (6 Wheat.) 264, at 384 (1821).

19. See my piece, "Have Argument, Will Travel," *Crisis* (June 1993) pp. 14–15; and my chapter, "The New Jural Minds: Rights Without Grounds, with Truths, and without Things That are Truly Rightful," in Sarat, Austin, and Thomas

R. Kearns (eds.), *Legal Rights: Historical and Philosophical Perspectives.* Ann Arbor: University of Michigan Press, 1996, pp. 177–203.

20. 317 U.S. 111 (1942).

21. Mill, J. S., *Utilitarianism.* Indianapolis: Bobbs-Merrill, 1957 [1861], p. 61.

22. This connection between the logic of morals and the logic of law, treated here with such compression, is considered more fully in my book *First Things.* Princeton: Princeton University Press. 1986, ch. II.

23. This is a matter I review in some detail in my book *First Things*, Ch. IV and V.

24. Kant, Immanuel, *Fundamental Principles of the Metaphysics of Morals* [1785], trans. Thomas K. Abbott. Indianapolis: Bobbs-Merrill, 1949, pp. 42 and 58.

25. Finnis, John, *Natural Law and Natural Rights.* Oxford: Clarendon Press, 1980, p. 33.

26. Fortin, Ernest, "The New Rights Theory and Natural Law," *The Review of Politics*, 44 (1982), pp. 590–612, at 591.

27. Ibid., p. 594.

28. Ibid., p. 595.

29. Blackstone, William, *Commentaries on the Laws of England.* Chicago: University of Chicago Press, 1979; originally published in 1765, vol. 1, bk. I. ch. 121–22.

30. Wilson, James, "Of the Natural Rights of Individuals," in *The Works of James Wilson.* Cambridge: Harvard University Press, 1967, vol. II, pp. 585–610, at 587.

31. de Vattel, Emmerich, *The Law of Nations, or The Principles of Natural Law.* (Washington: Carnegie Institution, 1916 [originally published, 1758]), p. 14.

32. Ibid., p. 22.

33. See Wilson in *Chisholm v. Georgia*, 2 Dallas 419 (1793), at 456 and 458.

34. I cite these figures in my book *The Philosopher in the City.* Princeton: Princeton University Press, 1981, p. 254. And the main citation there is to Gilder, "In Defense of Monogamy," *Commentary* (November 1974), pp. 31–36, at 32.

Legislation

TERRY HALL

Much of the recent resurgence in the theory of natural law focuses on discussions on jurisprudence and constitutional interpretation.[1] Questions concerning the essential characteristics of a legal system, the notion of the rule of law, the criteria for adjudicating appellate claims, as well as of original intent, strict constructionism, and judicial activism typically frame natural law inquiries. In this paper I wish to explore the relevance of the concept of natural law at the front end, so to speak, of the legal process. I propose to treat the question of how, and to what extent, principles of natural law might legitimately apply to the activity of legislating, of actually making law in the sense of *originating* prescriptions and proscriptions by which a political community arranges its affairs.[2] I propose, further, to place my discussion in the context of Aquinas' treatment of law in the so-called "Treatise on Law," contained in questions 90–108 in the *prima secundae* of the *Summa Theologiae*. I do this because Aquinas gives an uncommonly provocative and insightful set of terms and distinctions by which to guide reflection on the topic. While his discussion of the issues is not as ample as we might wish—he does not pause to cross every "t" and dot every "i"—it does comprise a more extended discussion of the essential principles involved than do most engagements with our theme.

Before discussing more specific issues, we would do well to remind ourselves of the general framework within which Aquinas places his discussion of natural law. Two general considerations are especially pertinent here: first, what I shall refer to as the essential system requirements of law, or what all law must exhibit in order to compel recognition as law; and second, the several kinds and levels of law and their relationship to each other in a hierarchical order. Both considerations are crucial to an understanding of what Aquinas understands by the concept of natural law.

System Requirements of Natural Law

We begin with the familiar definition of law that occurs in the four articles of Question 90 of the *Summa Theologiae,* Ia–Iae, and summarized in

Question 4—*viz.*, that law is "nothing else than a certain ordinance of reason for the common good, made by him who has care of the community, and promulgated." This is an extraordinarily compressed definition. To grasp its significance we must try to spell out what it intends to delineate, namely, what we may characterize as system requirements for legal prescriptions that compose not just a miscellany but a bona fide *rule of law*—what Aquinas refers to as *lex*.[3]

Law as a Work of Reason

Law is a rule of human action in the sense that it measures human conduct according to a reasonable standard, which standard discloses what secures, maintains, and furthers the common good. That law is ordained by reason implies (1) that it is not arbitrary or capricious; (2) that it is more universal than particular; and (3) that it is public, or accessible to any human agent possessing reason or intelligence. This last feature is of capital importance, for it amounts to saying that, in the context of human communities, law, for Aquinas, is not coeval with revelation. It is, of course, congruent with revelation and with Scripture. Properly constituted, it does not contradict revelation.[4]

Yet the making of law for human society turns out to be very much more than just canvasing Scripture. This opens up the possibility that natural law legislation can be undertaken with a minimum of theological commitments. Further, there is space for natural law prescriptions and proscriptions to recommend themselves to those who do not share the religious and theological views of those who have made them. Aquinas notes St. Paul's assertion, in Romans 2:14, that "the Gentiles, who have not the law, do by nature those things that are of the law" (*S.T.* Ia–IIae, Quest. 90, Art. 1). This is because law can be understood to be a work of natural intelligence or reason, a faculty in which every human being shares, regardless of one's particular religious commitments or lack thereof. Since reason is at work in the making of law, reasons can be given which are publicly accessible. Natural law legislators are not ineluctably theocrats.[5]

There is another important sense in which the making of law conforms to reason—or, more precisely, in which genuine law must bear the mark of rationality. Aquinas says that, in determining the content of particular laws, the lawmaker is involved in making what is analogous to an artisan (*artifex*) making a house (*S.T.* Ia–IIae, Quest. 95, Art. 2). The immediate point St. Thomas is establishing here is that a builder is engaged in constructing not "house in general" but a particular house. Every house will necessarily exhibit a finite range of features, will exemplify a certain kind of shape, and will be composed of certain sorts of materials and not others. But just what specific shape an actual house will take and what materials will be used in its composition must be determined on the occasion of its construction. This, Aquinas says, is an activity of practical and not speculative reason. It is fabrication, reason in making.

There is, however, an additional point to be noticed here, though Aquinas does not pause to make it explicit. In speaking of an *artifex*, an artisan, Aquinas is using a term that connotes skill in making. The house, and analogously the law to which Aquinas directs our attention, must therefore be thought of as well-constructed, a good product of the builder's craft. Good laws—laws properly speaking, I think St. Thomas would say—no less than good dwellings are the outcome of practical reason's capacity to order the materials of their composition in an ordered way. In the case of a house, the order imposed on the materials is for the sake of the purpose that guides the building, namely, that of providing shelter against the elements. Likewise, legislation as a rational activity involves attention to certain requirements of competent, durable construction.

Some sense of what is involved comes readily to mind. In well-constructed legislation, the actions and agents being addressed will be clearly defined, such that the scope of the law is as unambiguous as possible. Further, just as a well-constructed house must be accommodated to its surroundings—it is not rational to build a house on a steep slope susceptible to rock slides—so also the legislator as artisan must take care that the particular law being crafted fits in well with the system of law already in place. If it is inconsistent with established laws, people will be placed in a quandary as to which law is supposed to guide their conduct; further, the inconsistent elements of law will tend to subvert each other.[6]

The more poorly made a law is, the more deficient it will be as an instrument serving to promote the common good. This is a deeper sense in which law is, or should be, the work of reason: sustained attention to detail is crucial. To close out the building analogy, we might say that ill-constructed law provides inadequate "shelter" for citizens in their day-to-day civil transactions with others.

Law as Promoting the Common Good

As we have seen, genuine law is concerned with the common good. It aims at furthering the common good and sometimes at removing impediments to the common good. Laws that are prejudicial to the community as a whole or that aim directly at advantaging a particular group of persons while disadvantaging another group of persons fail to be oriented to the common good. For instance, a law requiring the conscription for military service only of poor men or African-Americans would fail the common good test. Even if the law were inadvertently to advantage and disadvantage persons in this way, it would be *prima facie* injurious to the common good. A lawmaker who legislates for the sake of a merely partisan good thus fails in the discharge of his public office.[7]

Law as Durable and Public

Further, the reasonableness of law must be disclosed in a durable way: it must be promulgated. The great exemplar of law in the classical world, Roman law, was characterized by the phrase *ratio scripta*: written reason.[8] As promulgated, or written down and conveyed to a public setting, law measures actions beyond the initial occasion of its formulation and beyond the confines of the venue in which it is first announced.

Law as Eventuating from Authoritative Office

Law properly so-called is also made by appropriate parties, the agents of the law, who by their special office possess the prerogatives of making law. As an ordinance of reason, and therefore in principle capable of being promulgated by anyone, its *authoritative* character is secured only by eventuating from an established and acknowledged office—*viz.*, by one who is specifically and formally charged with the care of the common good. On this point Aquinas observes that a private person is hampered in the attempt to lead another to the achievement of personal good, to virtue, inasmuch as the former can only advise the latter, having no effective coercive power to inflict penalties for recalcitrance to or inadequate compliance with admonishments to virtue.

Even a father, who does possess a degree of coercive power—by his superior strength, among other assets—even a father should be understood not as an author of laws in the strict, most precise sense, but of "certain commands and ordinances" (*S. T.* Ia–IIae, Quest. 90, Art. 3, ad 3). Typically, such commands are given on a specific, particular occasion and are exhausted on the occasion of their pronouncement. And even if a father should formulate a more general rule of action—that is to say, a *standing* rule meant to apply to many and future occasions, and which consequently exhibits the generality of law *per se*—still, these would in Aquinas' estimation not be law in the precise sense. They would not be directed to the common good in its widest application.

Kinds of Law

The second main preliminary set of remarks on the character of law Aquinas sets before us is that there are several kinds of law which are related to each other in a hierarchical way. Thus Aquinas avers that natural law faces two ways, as it were: toward the eternal law by which God rules the cosmos, on the one hand, and in which it participates; and toward human, positive law on the other hand, to which it is properly related as principle to further determination.

Eternal Law and Natural Law

By its participation in eternal law, natural law is fixed, unchanging, everywhere and always the same. Yet natural law is not simply coincident with eternal law, inasmuch as natural reason does not have within its purview the whole, the community of the cosmos. Natural reason is ineluctably enmeshed in temporality, in the shifting circumstances of day-to-day engagements—of what is to be done on *this* occasion and in *these* circumstances—even though the rule and measure it affords is a stable and permanent focus.

The natural law comes before us in these texts of Aquinas as a sign and illumination given to us, through the agency of rational intelligibility, for the discernment (*discernere*) of "what is good and what is evil" (*quid sit bonum et quid malum*; *S. T.* Ia–IIae, Quest. 91, Art. 2). This discernment is to be understood not so much as a kind of passive reception of its object analogous to physical sight, nor as an intuition, but rather as an achievement. We must bring about discernment through attentive reflection on a particular situation, in the light of the fundamental principles and precepts of the natural law which are available, so to speak, in advance of these situations. In other words, natural law awaits determination to specific practical situations in which human beings are called upon to act and to do.

The eventual outcome of this engagement of discernment is human or positive law. This discernment is to proceed (somehow) against the background of the eternal law, which means that positive law properly made is linked to the former. Human law cannot be, for Aquinas, understood as freestanding, but must be seen as nested within a broader conception of law that is as wide as the cosmos itself.

From Natural Law to Human Law

Taken by itself, natural law is insufficient for guiding humans in their diurnal intercourse with one another. One must descend, as it were, to a lower level still if the rule of law grounded in a natural standard is to be made effective. Now Aquinas considers the suggestion that natural law, precisely because it participates in the eternal law that governs the whole, *is* sufficient for the ordering of all human affairs (*S. T.* Ia–IIae, Quest. 91, Art. 3).

This suggestion implies that there is no need for human, positive law—no need, in effect, for what we have been calling discernment. A crucial issue is at stake here. If the natural law is by itself a sufficient guide for ordering human community, then there is no *work* for human legislators to do beyond the essentially simple registration of its authoritative prescriptions. Lawmaking would really be only the discovery of what nature in fact teaches, and this discovery would be a relatively easy, direct recognition. Lawmaking as arduous, deliberative, involving the weighing of alternative courses of action and policies, of attempting to foresee and protect against unintended consequences: all of this would not come into play. In other words, on this view human law is superfluous.

Human Law as a Determination of Natural Law: The Sphere of Legislative Reasoning

Aquinas, however, rejects the suggestion that a further engagement of lawmaking, beyond the recognition of the principles of the natural law, is unnecessary on the grounds that reason functions in its practical engagement analogously to the way it proceeds in its speculative activity; in both cases it works its way from principles to conclusions—that is, from the general to the particular. This assertion is immediately qualified, however, in an important way. In both intellectual engagements, there is required an effort of reason (*per industriam rationis inventa*), a rationally guided reflection; we are not in possession of the knowledge of the particular by nature. In the practical domain, the intellectual activity of making law involves what Aquinas calls a determination: human legislators are required to determine the application of general norms to specific situations. The crucial point is that human legislation under the guidance of natural law is not an activity of logical deduction.

This is why one must be careful when reading the statement that reason, in both its speculative and its practical activity, proceeds from principles to conclusions. Taken by itself, the statement inclines us to understand the operation of practical reason as too narrowly logical—that is, as an exercise in deductive reasoning. In the exercise of deduction, a conclusion is drawn as *necessarily* following from its premises. In a valid deductive argument, the conclusion is implicit in the premises and has only to be drawn out explicitly. In a sound deductive argument, owing to the truth of the premises, the conclusion is necessarily true. This, of course, is the essence of a syllogism.

Necessity, however, is not present in the application of the principles of natural law to particular situations. Here we are in the realm of the singular and contingent (see *S. T.* Ia–IIae, Quest. 91, Art. 4). "Wherefore," Aquinas continues, "human laws cannot have that inerrancy that belongs to the demonstrated conclusions of sciences" (*S. T.* Ia–IIae, Quest. 91, Art. 3, ad 3). This recognition in its turn implies that we should not expect the same certainty and definiteness to obtain in every genus. Human legislation is not a demonstrable science. In this spirit, Heinrich Rommen warns against thinking that a *jus naturale more geometrico* is possible.[9]

Content of the Natural Law: First Precepts

With respect to the actual content of the natural law, Aquinas gives as its controlling principle the precept that "good is to be done and pursued and evil avoided" (*S. T.* Ia–IIae, Quest. 94, Art. 2). Human action is structured so as to take place under the aspect of the good (*sub rationi boni*) or of what is desired as good; this is what it means to be a human agent possessing intelligence. We act, will, and choose for the sake of an end that, correctly or incorrectly, we believe will satisfy a natural desire, which satisfaction will perfect us in our nature as *human* agents (ibid.).[10]

From this *primum præceptum*, or first precept, several others follow according to the order of our natural inclinations. These amplify and flesh out the primary precept of the natural law. They direct us to (1) take care (exercise "foresight," be provident) in order to preserve human life; (2) take care to continue the species through sexual intercourse and the education of offspring; and (3) exercise our rational nature by seeking to know the truth about God and by living in civil peace with others of our kind (ibid.). Regarding the third amplificatory precept, Aquinas goes on to say that the fulfillment of our nature requires that we should "shun ignorance [and] avoid offending those among whom one has to live, and other such things regarding the [third-mentioned] inclination" (ibid). He does not stop here to spell out these latter things, but contents himself with noting that whereas there are many such natural law precepts (*multa præcepta legis natura*), all share in one common root (*radix*; ibid., ad 2).

Natural Law Legislation—The Application of Discernment

Let us now move from these general considerations of the content of the natural law to a more precise discussion of the activity of discernment. We have seen that Aquinas emphasizes that in applying the most general principles of the natural law to particular legislative situations we are engaged in an exercise of practical and not speculative reason. And we have seen that this involves not deducing a conclusion from premises but discerning the application of a rule of action; it is a determination, not a deduction. Here we recall the example of the artisan building a house.

Now, whereas some further amplification of the general principles of the natural law are brought to light by deduction, most, it seems, will certainly not be. As an instance of the former—that is, of deductive legal reasoning—Aquinas says that the precept that one ought not to kill another person "may be derived as a conclusion from the principle that 'one should do harm to no man'" (*S. T.* Ia–IIae, Quest. 95, Art. 2). But the legislator who comes to the task of setting down penalties for transgressing this law cannot deduce these from any more general natural law precept or principle: "[T]he law of nature has it that the evildoer should be punished, but that he be punished in this or that way is not directly by natural law but is a certain determination of it" (ibid.). The penalty must be determined, not deduced, analogously to the manner in which the builder determines that a house should have oak walls instead of stone, be one story in height instead of two, and be dome-shaped instead of square.

Aquinas fixes this point more securely when he notes that Aristotle says that some things that are legal (or conversely illegal) in a system of law were originally a matter of indifference, the example being that of determining the amount of ransom to be paid for a captive. Once set down in law, however, the prescription is no longer to be treated as a matter of indifference, but as a normative enactment. That this law, and the law stipulating the punishment for murder, could have been otherwise—are contingent and not necessary—does not suffice to lessen the obligation to obey.[11]

Instructive in this regard is Aristotle's conviction that murder itself is simply wrong, or wrong in all circumstances.[12] Initially, in the actual and dense particularities of the legislative process, the lawmaker has considerable (though not unlimited) room to maneuver. He must decide what law to enact in circumstances in which prudential rather than strictly logical considerations are more in play.

Applying General Principles

The guidance given to the legislator by natural law is not as exact and extensive as we might wish. It means that the lawmaker will often—perhaps we should say generally and for the most part—be in a situation in which, even if seeking to legislate in accordance with the natural law, a choice exists among a number of specific prescriptions. The general principles of the natural law will not themselves determine what should be legislated in these situations. So there will be a measure of uncertainty as to what is the best, most just legislative enactment.

The guidance that Aquinas does pause to offer is itself most general in application. He says, for instance, that "[t]he general principles of the natural law cannot be applied to all men in the same way on account of the great variety of human affairs, and hence arises the diversity of positive determinate prescriptions/proscriptions. The general principles of the natural law will not themselves be laws among the various people" (*S. T.* Ia–IIae, Quest 95, Art. 2, ad 3).[13] Whereas the natural law teaches us that everywhere and always good is to be done and evil avoided, that people must avoid harming their fellows, and that life and property must be safeguarded, their concrete exemplification must take account of shifting and variable circumstances. Inasmuch as the sought-for common good is pursued within a nest of contingent particulars, the common good, Aquinas says, "comprises many things" (*bonum [commune] . . . constat ex multis*); consequently, law must be attentive to the variability of "persons, occupations, and times" if it is to enable the political community to endure through time (*S. T.* Ia–IIae, Quest. 96, Art. 1).

Restraint

Additionally, there is a certain measure of restraint of which legislators ought to be mindful. "The purpose of human law," St. Thomas avers, "is to lead men to virtue, not suddenly but gradually" (*S. T.*, Ia–IIae, Quest. 96, Art. 2). Legislators should therefore take care not to frame laws that might impose an undue temporal burden on imperfectly virtuous citizens by demanding too much of them within too short a frame of time.

Well-crafted law will, under certain circumstances, take what might, from the standpoint of principle alone, seem the long view. It might not be possible, judged from the standpoint of prudence, to extirpate slavery in one fell swoop—perhaps even to expunge abortion in every situation in which it appears attractive. Rather, such evils might have to be phased out gradually, by hedging them about with various restrictions and regulations, as well as outright prohibition in some circumstances. Tolerating an abortion right in law in circumstances (and, let's say, only in such circumstances) where the life of the mother is at risk might seem to some to be an unacceptable attenuation of the natural law. Yet in certain legislative contexts, this might be a compromise necessary to prohibit abortion in other circumstances. The compromise decision reached is not premised on the admission that the unborn in certain situations cannot claim protection under the natural law. Rather, the decision proceeds from a different conviction, namely the prudential judgment that this legislative enactment is the best that can be obtained under the circumstances of a democratic legislature and strongly divided public opinion.

Others might reach the contrary judgment, that no compromise with prochoice legislators is justifiable and that an absolute prohibition on abortion, in all situations, is the best policy. These persons might judge that prochoice legislators have less political clout and that the American people are more resilient than the cautious legislator judges to be the case. My point is that it is not the case that the first natural law legislator is less committed to natural law principles than the second, and that two prudential judgments guided by the same fidelity to principle sometimes are discrepant. Knowing when to compromise on a legislative agenda is part of the skill of the legislator–architect, which is no less a part of the virtue of a natural law legislator than any other kind.

Prudence

How is one to determine when these considerations ought to be in play in the deliberations of the natural law legislator? The only answer is that prudence must decide. Aquinas' practical advice to legislators is thus at once both sparse and profound, and can be summed up in the admonition: exercise prudence.

The picture of natural legislating that his account provokes is thus considerably more complicated than that presented by Plato in the *Republic*. There, in Book VI, Socrates asserts that rulers in the ideal polis will rule by, first, looking away from the daily affairs of the political community and toward the Good; then, equipped with this vision, they will, like painters taking their bearings from a paradigm or template, turn back to the daily affairs of *res publicae* and sketch in the details of the laws.

The Thomistic natural law perspective does not portray the legislative task so simply. Yves Simon makes the point we are pursuing in a more pointed way when he says that "between law and action there always is a space to be filled by decisions which cannot be written into law." He continues:

> If law is a premise rather than a conclusion, if, universally, law admits of no immediate contact with the world of action, the ideal of a social science which would, in each particular case, procure a rational solution and render governmental prudence unnecessary is thoroughly deceptive. Whatever the science of man and of society has to say remains at an indeterminate distance from the world of action, and this distance can be *traversed only by the obscure methods of prudence*. . . . [T]he requirements of prudence [are] to extend, in the obscurities of contingency, the work of reason down to immediate contact with the world of action.[14]

Reason

We may close out these considerations by noting that St. Thomas says that "it is right and true for all to act according to reason, and from this principle, it follows as a proper conclusion that goods entrusted to another should be restored to their owner." However, a case might well occur when restoring the deposit would be harmful to the community and therefore unreasonable; and, being unreasonable, the return would subvert the natural law ("to the natural law belong those things to which a man is inclined naturally, and among these, it is proper to man to be inclined to act according to reason"). The good in this case ought not to be returned. The controlling principle of the natural law in such cases "will be bound to fail the more according as we descend further into detail, e.g., if one were to say that goods held in trust should be restored with such and such a guarantee or in such and such a way, because the greater the number of conditions added, the greater the number of ways in which the principle may fail, so that it be not right to restore or not to restore" (*S. T.* Ia–IIae, Quest. 94, Art. 4).

Let us note in closing that when Aquinas says that the natural law principle governing such cases fails when one is engaged in the density of particular contingent occasions of human actions and relationships, he does not mean that the natural law fails in applicability, that it becomes on the occasion null and void. Rather, he means that the principle itself cannot tell one whether it is right or not right to return the deposit. The natural law principle does not yield a conclusion as the outcome of a logical exercise in justice. Once more, the relevant natural law principle is applied prudentially.

Aquinas sets before us the reasonable legislator, not the rationalistic legislator in the mode of Kant, who (at least in some moments) spoke of the availability of a moral compass that would point infallibly, as it were, to true moral North.[15] I take it that for St. Thomas there is no such moral compass available to legislators.

Applications

Enough, perhaps, has been said to orient us to the main thrust of Aquinas' account of natural law at its most fundamental level. We turn now in this final section to a consideration of some specific applications of the natural law teaching to concrete legislative situations. What manner and degree of illumination might natural law commitments actually provide a legislator—not a moral philosopher or a legal theorist concerned with articulating controlling principles and precepts, but one who is involved in the drafting of specific statutes in law, or, alternatively, is engaged with the question of whether to support or oppose with his vote a particular legislative proposal. Everything Aquinas has said is spoken not as a person occupying a legislative office, but as a theorist of law. How can one engaged in the practical activity of legislation take bearings from the natural law? Or to put the question in a slightly different way: How close does one stand to the natural law?

Remote Cases

At first glance, it might seem that what we have said about Aquinas' understanding of the natural law offers scant relevance to the enterprise which engages legislators in a large and complex society such as our own. With respect to some issues, the legislators seem to stand at a considerable distance. Should they support or oppose legislation to reduce the capital gains tax? Should they support or oppose abolishing price supports for dairy farmers? Should they support or oppose the creation of a federal Office of Justice Assistance and Research? Or, to adapt an example Aquinas employs, should one oppose or support a crime bill that increases the prison term for possession of crack cocaine tenfold over penalties for possession of other forms of the drug?[16] Without an excessive amount of ingenuity, one *can* refer each of these questions back to the overarching principles of the natural law. People need to eat in order to preserve their life, and they need to nurture their children, and so having a plentiful supply of milk serves this naturally sanctioned end. Civil peace in significant degree depends on the effectiveness of law enforcement agencies, which effectiveness is enhanced by an adequate data bank of empirical information.

Well, then, *must* price supports be kept in place? Even when the federal budget has swelled to the danger point, threatening (so some economists assert) the economic viability of future generations? *Must* another government bureaucracy be created, with additional strain, too, on the nation's ability to remain solvent? Lowering the capital gains tax might increase the ability of business enterprises to expand and hire new workers, affording economic self-sufficiency to larger numbers of people—but might also widen the gap between rich and poor and thus foster envy, resentment, and alienation among less affluent citizens, thereby weakening their perception that they too are encompassed within the common good. It might also shrink federal tax revenues to the point where resources for fulfilling national obligations—social security, for example—are lacking.

Even though it is possible to refer each of these cases back to more general principles—and thereby show the pertinence of natural law principles to particular legislative issues—the distance between the principle and the application is so considerable that the exercise offers little guidance for deciding what should be done. Two legislators, both committed to these overarching natural goods, may surely disagree on whether to support the proposed legislation in these cases without jeopardizing their fidelity to the natural law. Different outcomes for each of these policies can with plausibility be suggested.

The point is that in many—perhaps the majority—of the legislative decisions facing a lawmaker, natural law commitments might seem not to be of special help in reaching a decision on what legislation should permit or prohibit. Indeed, it seems evident that two people, both of whom admit the natural law *foundations* of all human law, might well disagree on whether a specific proposal should or should not be enacted into law. Their disagreement at this level of law does not entail their disagreement at the more fundamental and remote level of primary principle.

Proximate Cases: Abortion and the Life Issues

In other sorts of cases, the proposed law has not a remote but a more proximate connection to natural law principles. The so-called "life issues" —most notably abortion and physician-assisted suicide—are among the clearest instances. In the case of abortion, the argument is rather straightforward. Everything living has a natural inclination to preserve itself in being. (*S. T.* I–II, Quest. 4, Art. 2) Further, the education of offspring is likewise a precept of the natural law (ibid.). Knowledge, this precept seems to imply, is a good of our nature, and its acquisition requires assistance from others who possess it already. Life is a good in and of itself, as well as a condition for the acquisition of other goods of our nature. Abortion violates these precepts. No legislator can tolerate laws permitting abortion without violating the natural law and thus without forfeiting his commitment to it.

The preceding assertion was advanced without qualification, as the analyses of Aquinas' understanding of the precepts of the natural law seems to require. "Harm no one" is for him a fundamental moral teaching, no dispensation from which human law can legitimately allow. So it would seem that for the natural law legislator this is the end of the matter, with no further call upon his deliberative faculties: life is an inviolable natural good, which must trump every proposal to dispense with its protection, no matter what the circumstances.

In most abortion situations, I think this natural law argument is true. There are, however, situations where unusual and complicating factors are present: for instance, when the mother's life would have to be forfeit if she were required to carry the child to term; in the case of incest; and perhaps in the case of a pregnancy as the result of rape. Natural law commitments are just as clear and compelling in these cases, are they not? The right to life of the fetus trumps everything else, does it not?

Yet Aquinas also teaches that the framing of law should take into account the capacity of people to bear its prescriptions: "[L]aws imposed on men should also be in keeping with their condition, for, as Isidore says, law should be 'possible *both* according to nature *and* according to the custom of their country.'" Those laws are ill-framed which seek to lead citizens to virtue all at once, suddenly, and not progressively. Such laws can impact citizens the way new wine impacts old wineskins, causing the container to burst. Such laws can defeat their own purpose of leading people to virtue by causing too many to despise them and "from contempt [of them] break out into evils worse still" (*S. T.* I–II, Quest. 96, Art. 2, the *corpus* and the reply to objection 2).[17]

In the judgment of the legislator it might be the case that criminalizing abortion in all circumstances, including those in which the life of the mother would be at risk, falls into the category of "too great a burden." Note that Aquinas in the passage quoted says that human laws should be congruent both with the natural law and with customs that have long held sway. In fact, the American legal tradition has never outlawed abortion in all circumstances; the states have typically granted an exception from prosecution for women whose fetus poses a threat to their own life.[18]

To be sure, abortion in such instances would clearly constitute harm to the fetus. But prohibiting it would just as certainly constitute harm to the mother. That a natural law legislator might judge a prohibition in such cases to impose too heavy a burden seems to me to be in keeping with the principles Aquinas has set forth. This does not, of course, commit one to tolerating abortion in many other situations; and in fact, I think the same natural law legislator must be opposed in most, perhaps all, cases where the life of the mother is not at risk. Cases of rape and incest do not require an innocent person to die, though they do involve emotional trauma that it would be grossly insensitive to ignore. Without attempting to offer an analysis of such cases, let me just say that the factors of burdensomeness and custom could legitimately come into play in a natural law analysis.

In terms of the current situation in the United States, our legislator might well reach the judgment that prohibition with exceptions for life of the mother and/or incest and/or rape is the best one can hope for in terms of legislative achievement. A colleague with equally strong natural law commitments might disagree. My point is that mere appeal to natural law precepts seems insufficient to settle the issue as an issue in natural law legislation. And Aquinas seems to have anticipated such cases.

Proximate Case: Contracts

The law of contracts is another case where natural law analysis can play an illuminating role. Now, one might argue that the law of contracts, the rule that requires certain kinds of promises or pledges, is simply and most essentially an economic matter—that an economic system not sheltered under the legal recognition of the probative force of contractual agreements cannot function properly to distribute goods and services. But there is a more powerful justifying formulation than this.[19]

A contract is a species of promises, and the keeping of promises supports and nurtures trust in social transactions. Making a promise and then failing to fulfill it is tantamount to theft. A society that permits theft announces that its members will by their fellow citizens be routinely placed at risk in their persons and possessions. This encourages suspicion as the abiding way of regarding one another. Without trust the bonds that unite people in cooperative interactions must be absent. No society can endure under such conditions. That persons will be required to fulfill promises made in the furtherance of meeting the material necessities of life is thus a condition for human life to subsist.[20]

The exigencies of our condition, our nature, render us unable to sustain our life without the aid of others. Aquinas says that, notwithstanding the need for trust, some "are prone to vice and not easily amenable to words."[21] For some, that is, their word is not their bond. Such individuals must be restrained by the fear of punishment by law. One's word must be one's bond. As Hadley Arkes puts it, "the morality of contract . . . [stands] antecedent to the laws on contracts."[22]

We might note in passing that this principle which seems so plainly probative (so "natural") was on the verge of being eclipsed during the Depression by an act of Congress that would have compelled a bank holding a mortgage to relinquish control of land to a debtor still in lien to the bank. This amounted to a law allowing the taking of property without agreed compensation to be paid. In effect, it would have permitted the abrogation of contract.[23] Some members of Congress opposed the legislation precisely on grounds of subversion of trust. Without invoking the term, their reasoning constituted an appeal to natural law precepts.

Proximate Cases: Pornography

Regulation of pornography furnishes another instance in which natural law reasoning finds its controlling precepts lying close at hand. Briefly, the argument would run as follows. Programs broadcast over television channels or available without restriction on the Internet that comprise sexually explicit and coarse acts tends seriously to frustrate the healthy expression and use of the sexual side of human nature because it subverts the privacy on which the latter depends. Sexuality has fundamentally to do with intimacy, and therefore with the private domain of human transactions. As both Plato and Augustine understood, some things are not proper for the eyes of others to see.[24] The broadcast of portrayals of sexual intimacies says in effect just the opposite: that sex is not an engagement of intimacy but is voyeuristic. Voyeurism subverts intimacy, and thereby obstructs the passion on which the family is founded. A society which is inattentive to the conditions under which families flourish places itself at risk. The restriction and regulation of pornography therefore finds a reasonable warrant within natural law lawmaking.

Refuting the Charge of Vacuity

In all of these cases the most essential point is not just that a natural law perspective leads one to oppose certain legislative proposals and to support others, and in some cases to tolerate what one would rather not see tolerated, but that it connects the opposition, support, or toleration to a principled understanding of what is good for humans. It provides one with reasons and a certain course (a "direction") of reasoning. It enables one to oppose the practice on grounds other than mere taste and opinion. By doing so, it invites others to reason along.

These considerations suffice to rebut the old charge that natural law principles and precepts are vacuous, that the natural law is woefully indeterminate as regards legislation. The latter charge against natural law theorists has been made often enough. Kai Nielsen, for instance, states boldly and flatly that the first principle of natural law—good is to be done and evil avoided—is so vacuous that it "[cannot] possibly be the foundation of any morality or any legal system. It cannot tell us *what* is good or what we ought to do or *what* is bad and wrong." The principle, he argues, is a nonsubstantive premise and "substantive moral conclusions cannot be drawn from nonsubstantive premises."[25]

To this objection one might make at least two immediate replies, if only to set the terms of the debate on a more precise basis. First, and to repeat: applying the natural law is not an activity of drawing conclusions from premises in an exercise of deductive reasoning, but of making a more concrete determination of a general rule. Applying a rule to a case is not doing deductive logic. Second, the rule that we should seek and do the good must be understood in the context of the meaning Aquinas assigns to the pivotal term, "good." It means, of course, not just something we pursue as desirable, but that which perfects us, or completes us. It thus elevates us, raises us to a more ennobling level of life than we would achieve if we pursue the bad. This in turn implies that not every way of life or scheme of conduct can be countenanced.

The principle is not, *pace* Nielsen, "compatible with any and every moral code." Some putative "moral codes"—for instance, the German medical experiments during the 1930s and 1940s, with their guiding principle of *lebens unweltes lebens*, life unworthy of life—are not perfective in any sense of the term. On some questions to discern what is truly perfective, or most comprehensively perfective, may be difficult. To enact a statutory prohibition against the sale of cigarettes to adults may or may not promote the human good in a sufficiently comprehensive way. But the notion of the good as perfective rescues the charge that the controlling principles and precepts of natural law are empty, and therefore utterly useless as a guide. They are not empty, yet they are also not, so to speak, full. That is why there is need for human positive law in addition to the natural law.

It is worth attending to the fact that the full statement of the "good" principle is that good is to be done *and pursued.*[26] We constantly are in the situation of having to *seek* the good, to bring what is truly perfective for us as the beings we are to light. We do not know this, in all details, in advance, because we cannot hold before us all the actual contingencies in which deliberations must perforce occur.

A corollary to these two points against the charge of vacuousness is that whereas we should not overestimate the guidance natural law principles make available to us, neither should we underestimate it. Apart from the *substantive* content of natural law judgments, natural law *reasoning* should be appreciated as a valuable heuristic tool for those engaged in lawmaking. Natural law principles intimate a space within which the specific determinations of the legislative process can be carried out.

From the perspective of natural law reasoning, certain ways of disposing of legislative issues fall inside this space, while other ways of dealing with the issues, with tolerable clarity, fall outside. This last is so not because of the peculiar convictions or personal preferences of a particular legislative agent, but because some ways of disposing of an issue are incompatible with meeting the exigencies of human nature and thus are unreasonable. Thus natural law reasoning—for example, in dealing with the problem of abusive parents—will take care to locate the range of determinations that are consistent with the nature of the family. It will attempt to locate the space within which solutions are to be looked for and outside of which no appropriate solution can be found. So, for instance, one can argue that creating a legal right for children to sue their parents should be treated as outside the range of appropriate legislative responses, inasmuch as it would subvert the special intimacies of family life.

Conclusion

The principles of the natural law present an elevated plane to which we can look up, away from the particulars of the convoluted issues of the legislature, not in order to spy premises from which to make deductions or to gain access to the sort of clarity that obviates the need for prudential judgment and resolves all disagreements, but to remind ourselves of the proper reference point for engaging in legislative determinations. Use of the natural law perspective as a focal point of reference might serve to attenuate naked appeals to power, to parochial interest, to mere local aggrandizements. And where issues in law touch closely on natural law precepts, natural law reasoning can help make clear why the law must forbid or enjoin certain actions, notwithstanding differences of opinion on the matter.

Having a shared set of referents in natural law principles—so that natural law *reasoning* constitutes common terrain for pursuit of the good in the midst of ambiguity and disagreement—might not suffice to guarantee good laws, but it might provoke us to pursue them more fruitfully. Appeal to natural law principles and to the manner of prudent reasoning from them furnishes a shared mode of discourse about the law. It is not clear that anything else can supply us with this. Natural law principles and reasoning will not always be intimately involved in framing legislation, but if they are never turned to we will be the poorer. In that event, our citizens will be encouraged to understand lawmaking as merely an exercise in partisan interest. And that is a coarse and demeaning understanding of political life. Even when present most notably as a background notion, the natural law elevates the legislative process.

At certain crucial times in our political past it has been more than this, it has been in the foreground—the Lincoln–Douglas debates of 1858, in which Lincoln repeatedly argued that there is no right to do wrong, are a particularly revealing instance. If today's legislators reject the natural law principles and methods of reasoning, then it will be difficult for citizens to avoid understanding the laws under which they live as simply a reflection of partisan interests, unconnected with any sense of a principled insight into human affairs. We might be able to get along for a while as a cohesive political community, but the corrosive cynicism toward the law such an understanding seems inevitably to foster does not encourage optimism for the future of our attempt to live together in civic friendship, as more than merely strangers to one another.

NOTES

1. See, for instance, the collection of essays in George, Robert P., ed., *Natural Law Theory: Contemporary Essays*. Oxford: Clarendon Press, 1992, especially Part II: "Natural Law and Legal Theory." Earlier in this century, John Chipman Gray averred that law is not what legislators enact but what judges decide, so that until a court has pronounced on a matter there is, properly speaking, no law. It is a certain fact, Gray says, that "courts are constantly making *ex post facto* law." Gray, John Chipman, *The Nature and Sources of Law*. New York: Macmillian, 1909. Quoted in Letwin, Shirley Robin, "Modern Philosophies of Law," *The Great Ideas Today: 1972*. Chicago: Encyclopedia Britannica, 1972, pp. 121–22.

2. By "originating" law I mean what Aquinas terms the engagement of promulgating law, that is, producing publicly known rules that serve as the measure

of conduct deemed enforceable by the entire community for the furtherance of its common good. See *Summa Theologiae* I–II, Quest. 90, Art. 4. Citations from this text are from the translation of the Fathers of the English Dominican Province (New York: Benziger Brothers, 1947). Readers may also consult the recent reissue of the Benziger translation dealing with the questions on law under the title Saint Thomas Aquinas, *On Law, Morality, and Politics.* Indianapolis: Hackett, 1988, edited by William P. Baumgarth and Richard J. Regan, S.J. All subsequent references to the *Summa* will be provided in the body of this paper.

3. Aquinas's fourfold stipulation of the systemic requirements of law can be compared usefully with Lon Fuller's account of the "Eight Ways to Fail to Make Law" in *The Morality of Law*, revised edition. New Haven: Yale University Press, 1964. Fuller summarizes the eight requirements as follows: "The first and most obvious lies in the failure to achieve rules at all, so that every issue must be decided on an ad hoc basis. The other routes are: (2) a failure to publicize, or at least to make available to the affected party, the rule he is expected to observe; (3) the abuse of retroactive legislation, which not only cannot itself guide action, but undercuts the integrity of rules prospective in effect, since it puts them under the threat of retrospective change; (4) a failure to make rules understandable; (5) the enactment of contradictory rules or (6) rules that require conduct beyond the powers of the affected party; (7) introducing such frequent changes in the rules that the subject cannot orient his action by them; and, finally, (8) a failure of congruence between the rules as announced and their actual administration. . . . Certainly there can be no rational ground for asserting that a man can have a moral obligation to obey a legal rule that does not exist, or is kept secret from him, or that came into existence only after he has acted, or was unintelligible, or was contradicted by another rule of the same system, or commanded the impossible, or changed every minute." Ibid., p. 39.

4. For a discussion of this point, see D'Entreves, A. P., *Natural Law: An Introduction to Legal Philosophy*, revised edition. London: Hutchison University Library, 1970, pp. 39–40.

5. D'Entreves contends that the incorporation of Roman law into the medieval horizon of understanding and practice was possible only when the natural basis of law was fully accepted, which achievement was accomplished by Aquinas. "An immense task lay ahead of the medieval man. The present had to be secured, the past conquered. The lesson of Roman law was that the greatest of all legal systems had been based purely on reason and utility; the lesson of Aristotle, that the State is the highest achievement of man and the necessary instrument of human perfection. How could a Christian community be taught the elementary duties of good life and fellowship? If so great a body of wisdom had been discovered without supernatural help, if a basis was to be provided for human relations independently of the higher requirements of Christian perfection, surely there must be a system of natural ethics. Its cornerstone must be natural law." *Natural Law,* p. 42.

6. Former Congressman Jack Kemp often gave the following example of inconsistency in United States foreign policy laws regarding underdeveloped countries. Having been granted American aid to build roads to enable farmers to transport food to urban markets, some foreign governments proceeded to impose price controls on these same foodstuffs, in order to secure political support from urban

consumers. In many cases the price controls were set too low to provide farmers with sufficient incentive to produce crops at much more than a subsistent level. It seems clear that voting for continued foreign aid in these circumstances was in tension with the domestic price-control policy of the recipient countries. The two elements of public policy canceled each other out.

7. Thus Burke's defense of religious freedom in Catholic Ireland against Protestant persecution rested on the natural law requirement to take into account the common good of those affected by the proposed restrictions. In his "Tract on the Popery Laws," Burke argued that, "They have no right to make a law prejudicial to the whole community . . . because it would be made against the principle of a superior law, which it is not in the power of any community, or of the whole race of man, to alter." Quoted in Stanlis, Peter J., *Edmund Burke and the Natural Law*. Ann Arbor, MI: University of Michigan Press, 1958, p. 44.

8. See Brierly, J. L., *The Law of Nations*, 5th ed. Oxford: Clarendon Press, 1955, p. 19.

9. See Rommen, H. A., "In Defense of Natural Law" in *Law and Philosophy: A Symposium*, ed. Sidney Hook. New York: New York University Press, 1964, p. 117. Cf. d'Entreves's statement that "despite the stress which is laid upon the absolute and immutable character of the natural law, the notion of it seems to be curiously flexible and adaptable. Positive laws are not expected to be molded upon it as upon a rigid pattern. A considerable sphere of freedom is left to the human lawgiver in the interpretation of its general precepts." *Natural Law*, p. 46.

10. Cf. Aquinas's discussion of the good-directed structure of human action in *S.T.* I–II, Quest. 1, Arts. 5 and 6, in the *respondeo*.

11. The text from Aristotle is *Nichomachean Ethics* V, 7 1134b20.

12. *Nichomachean Ethics* II, 6 at 1107a11.

13. It is worth noting that Aquinas is replying to the objection that it cannot be the case that all human laws are derived from the natural law, for the (alleged) reason that while it is possible to give a reason for things derived from the natural law, it is not possible to give a reason for every legislative enactment of human law. If the objection were to hold, then there would be some statutes that both qualify properly as law and yet do not do so in virtue of their connection with the natural law. The focus of the objection seems to be a necessitating reason, and not just a justifying reason. It is a reason that is sufficiently strong to show that the enactment in question, and no other, is required by the principles of the natural law. I take it that it is just this sense of rationality that Aquinas is contending is not present and available to legislators in most of their activity.

14. Simon, Yves R., *The Tradition of Natural Law*, ed. Vukan Kuic. New York: Fordham University Press, 1965, pp. 83, 85 (emphasis added).

15. For Kant's use of the paradigm of the compass, see his *Grundlegung zur Metaphysik der Sitten* §1. Berlin: Felix Meiner Verlag, 1965, p. 22; English translation as *Foundations of the Metaphysics of Morals*, trans. Lewis White Beck. New York: Macmillan, 1959, p. 20.

16. "[T]he law of nature has it that the evildoer should be punished but that he be punished in this or that way is not directly by natural law, but is a certain determination of it." *S.T.* I–II, Quest. 95, Art. 2.

17. Aquinas gives prostitution as an example (drawing on Augustine). The

thrust of his argument is that the attempt to legislate the extirpation of prostitution might well bring about greater evils, given the weakness of human will. See *S.T.* II–II, Quest. 10, Art. 11.

18. See Louisell, David W., and John T. Noonan, Jr., "Constitutional Balance," in *The Morality of Abortion*, ed. John T. Noonan, Jr. Cambridge, MA: Harvard University Press, 1970, p. 230 and *passim*.

19. I rely here on the lucid analysis presented by Hadley Arkes, "That 'Nature Herself Has Placed in Our Ears a Power of Judging'," in *Natural Law Theory: Contemporary Essays*, ed. Robert P. George. Oxford: Clarendon Press, 1992, pp. 245–278.

20. Thus Aquinas observes that "we observe that man is helped by industry in his necessities, for instance, in food and clothing. Certain beginnings of these he has from nature, *viz.*, his reason and his hands, but he has not the full compliment, as other animals have to whom nature has given sufficiency of clothing and food." *S. T.* I–II, Quest. 95, Art, 1.

21. Ibid.

22. Arkes, "That 'Nature Herself Has Placed in Our Ears a Power of Judging,'" in *Natural Law Theory* p. 268.

23. For a discussion, see Ibid., pp. 260–262.

24. See, e.g., Socrates's portrayal, in *Republic* IV 439e–440a, of Leontius, the man who both wished to gaze upon human corpses and who realized the natural baseness of such a desire; also Augustine's discussion of *concupiscientia oculorum*, the lust of the eyes, in *Confessions* X, 35.

25. Kai Nielsen, "The Myth of Natural Law," in *Law and Philosophy*, pp. 124–25. See also J. R. Lucas, *Justice*, Oxford: Clarendon Press, 1980, p. 32, for a similar view: "Natural rights, like natural law generally, suffer from vagueness. They do not tell us where we stand, but only express a claim about where we ought to stand . . . there is a great problem of specification." A measure of the changed attitude toward the resources of the natural law perspective, outside of Catholic intellectual circles, that has occurred over the three decades since Nielsen published his astringent criticism can be found, among other places, in Lloyd L. Weinreb's *Natural Law and Justice* (Cambridge, MA: Harvard University Press, 1987). Though certainly not a Thomist, Prof. Weinreb's patience and respect in treating Aquinas's natural law theory is in striking contrast with Nielsen's thinly-veiled contempt for, and his preemptory dismissal of, the same. To hear Nielsen tell it, Aquinas's views possess scarcely a minimum of intellectual integrity.

26. I owe this last observation to a point made by Michael Platt in conversation.

Judicial Review

CHRISTOPHER WOLFE

Liberal political theory seems consistently unable to provide a coherent account of political life. Even in its best known form, the "antiperfectionist" liberalism of John Rawls, it cannot vindicate its claim to public "neutrality" about ultimate human goods.[1] Insofar as antiperfectionists have at least partly abandoned their claim to such neutrality, the formalistic notions of good that they have embraced fail to provide adequate theoretical foundations for their project.[2]

Perhaps it is not surprising, then, that natural law theory has emerged once more from the ashes to which it has been regularly reduced over the centuries. In its previous reincarnation, arising especially from the experience of totalitarianism and World War II, it took a neoscholastic form, especially in the writings of Jacques Maritain and Yves Simon.[3] In its contemporary reappearance, natural law theory is most associated with the (nonscholastic) writings of John Finnis and Germain Grisez and their collaborators,[4] although neoscholastic natural law remains on the scene as well.[5]

Natural law theory remains, for the most part, at the margin of American intellectual and public life, but on one occasion in recent American history it became a subject of some notoriety. In the hearings on the nomination of Justice Clarence Thomas for the Supreme Court, one of Thomas' earlier speeches embracing natural law and its relevance to constitutional questions became the center of considerable controversy. While the debate eventually fizzled out, partly because Thomas seemed to back off from his earlier comments and partly because it got lost in the succeeding brouhaha, it did occasion some discussion of the significance of natural law for American law. Around the same time a more interesting, if less publicly visible, debate occurred in the pages of *First Things*, with Harry Jaffa, Robert Bork, and Russell Hittinger squaring off on the issue of the relevance of natural law to judicial review.[6]

More recently, another *First Things* symposium, on "The End of Democracy?: The Judicial Usurpation of Politics," has occasioned considerable public debate.[7] The five authors (Robert Bork, Russell Hittinger, Hadley Arkes, Charles Colson, and Robert George) raised serious questions about the legitimacy of the American regime[8] on the basis of two overlapping considerations: first, the usurpation of legislative power by the judges (especially the Supreme Court), and second, the use of that power contrary to fundamental principles of natural law (e.g., with respect to abortion, euthanasia, and homosexual conduct). The symposium, which elicited some deep hostility even among some neoconservatives normally sympathetic to both *First Things* and these authors, was a reminder of the permanent possibility of tension or outright conflict between the prevailing principles of the American regime and transcendent standards of political morality.

In light of this recent debate, I shall examine various aspects of the topic of natural law and judicial review. I shall start with a brief discussion of the place of judicial review in natural law theory and shall argue that, like most other institutional arrangements, judicial review is not a necessary requirement for a good form of government, but that it may serve a useful function under some contingent circumstances. Then I shall turn to a more extended discussion of natural law in theories about judicial review, arriving at the conclusion that, in the American form of government, natural law may be relevant to some extent in the process of ascertaining the meaning of the Constitution, but that it ought not to be an independent basis for judicial review.

Judicial Review in Natural Law Theory

Does natural law theory either require or encourage the establishment of judicial review as an institutional feature of government? The first part of that question can be answered very briefly because natural law theory tends to be open to a wide variety of political institutions. It is difficult to think of *any* political institution that is "required" by natural law theory. Natural law focuses on ends and principles, for the most part, and institutions are typically means.

So, for example, in writings of the greatest representative of the natural law tradition, Thomas Aquinas, there is relatively little discussion of political institutions. It might be pointed out that this is because of the theological character of Thomas' work. That observation is true, but to some extent it begs the question: it fails to note the significance of the fact that, in Thomas' view, theology does not dictate specific political institutions. Moreover, not all of Thomas' work was theological. His commentaries on the works of Aristotle, for example, are an important part of his legacy, but Thomas' commentary on Aristotle's *Politics*, unlike those on metaphysics, ethics, and the soul, for example, was never finished. Other discussions of politics in Aquinas—*De Regimine Principorum* for example—seem to be very conventional or conservative, taking prevailing institutions as givens, rather than engaging in wide-ranging speculation about other possible institutions.

If we turn to Aristotle, on the other hand, there *is* extensive discussion of a variety of political institutions, suggesting something about how Aquinas would have dealt with issues of political institutions.[9] Even here, however, we discover that Aristotle's attitudes toward political institutions differ considerably from those which prevail today. Aristotle's political theory is divided into considerations of the best regime simply, the best practicable regime generally, the best practicable regime for a given set of circumstances, and how to make the best of a given regime. The institutions of the simply best regime are not spelled out in any detail, at least partly because the best regime is not so much a practicable model to be achieved as a guide by which to judge existing regimes.[10] The institutions of various practicable and existing regimes are discussed, but always with a recognition of their *contingent* character. Institutions have to be adapted to particular conditions, and the best institutions are those that fit their conditions best.

If classic natural law theory takes this attitude toward political institutions in general, then judicial review would seem to warrant the same treatment. Judicial review—the power of judges, in the course of their duty to interpret the law in cases, to refuse to give effect to (that is, to declare void) laws or other acts that are inconsistent with the nation's constitution or fundamental law—must be evaluated in the context of a particular form of government that is appropriate for the given circumstances of a given people at a given time. Sometimes it will be appropriate, sometimes it will not be so—depending on prudential judgments that are the province more of the statesman than the political theorist. The theorist can, however, make some observations as to the general conditions under which it will be advisable for a constitution to include the power of judicial review.

For example, natural law theorists have a healthy awareness of the darker side of human nature. Whether this awareness derives from theological notions of sin or from simple empirical observation of the human race, the deep and widespread disorder in and among human beings is evident. Moreover, the disorder is distributed throughout mankind, in the sense that no easily identifiable group of people—male or female, educated or uneducated, supervisor or worker, rich or poor, European or African or Asian or American, priest or philosopher or politician or judge—seem exempt from it. In light of this elemental fact, a theorist will be receptive to the notion of a mixed or balanced government, one in which all those who exercise political power are subject to some checks and balances (though the nature and extent of the appropriate checks are very debatable). Judicial review, insofar as it constitutes a check on power that is always subject to abuse, is potentially attractive to the natural law thinker, if it can itself be preserved from being abused.

When might judicial review be considered a valuable political institution? It might be attractive under conditions such as these: (1) there is a written constitution, which in general provides for a proper breadth of government power to perform its responsibilities and for prudent limitations on government, both structural (e.g., federalism) and explicit (e.g., constitutional prohibitions such as the Bill of Rights); (2) judges are constrained in their power of review by widely known and accepted principles of law; and (3) there is reason to believe that judges, insofar as they depart from the views of other government actors on constitutional issues, in cases where they are not otherwise constrained, are likely to make more prudent decisions than alternative decision makers.

Note, however, the extreme contingency of such conditions. A constitution that provides proper breadth of power in one generation might provide too little or too much in the next; limits on government that are prudent at one time might be either too extensive or insufficient at another. There are considerable variations in the degree of constraint that principles of law might impose on judicial power in any given set of circumstances. The mechanisms for enforcing constraints on judges may vary in their efficacy over time; the relative likelihood of prudent decisions by judges or by others (e.g., legislators, executives, administrative agencies, state and local officials, etc.) are likely also to vary dramatically in ways that are unpredictable. Generalizations about these issues are often likely to fail.[11]

In the actual historical circumstances of the United States, there is disagreement even after the fact among scholars about whether judicial review has, on the whole, been beneficial to our society. While the conventional view is that judicial review has been beneficial—a view manifested in the absence of any significant movement to eliminate the power—there have been well-known scholarly assessments that have questioned this view.[12]

The result of this discussion is to suggest that natural law theory has no definite stance on the question of judicial review. While it is a potentially valuable institution, its usefulness is highly dependent on contingent circumstances. Whether a given constitution should include the power of judicial review will be a question for the prudent legislator of a society's political institutions to decide.

Natural Law in Judicial Review Theory

Another way to approach the question of natural law and judicial review is to take the existence of judicial review as a given in our polity and ask whether natural law is relevant to the exercise of judicial review. More specifically, one might ask whether judges, in exercising the power of judicial review, should be able to invoke the natural law as a ground for invalidating legislative acts or other acts of government.

In this section, I hope to accomplish four things. First, I shall briefly describe the major occasions in American history when arguments about judges and natural law became prominent. Second, I shall look at two ways in which natural law can be seen in contemporary constitutional and legal analysis, drawing on Russell Hittinger's description of contemporary constitutional theory and Michael Moore's description of a natural law theory of interpretation. Third, I shall analyze a major contemporary debate among conservatives regarding the use of natural law by judges, in order to sort out various positions and what some of their strengths and weaknesses are. Fourth, I shall give what I believe is the correct use of natural law for purposes of interpretation of the Constitution, applying that understanding to the difficult case of abortion.

Judges and Natural Law in American History

There is, of course, an extensive history of this question in the United States. Let us look briefly at four elements of that history: "natural justice" judicial review, the rise and decline of economic substantive due process, the Frankfurter–Black incorporation/due process debate, and the Clarence Thomas nomination debate.

Natural Justice Judicial Review

The conventional starting point for discussion of natural law in American constitutional adjudication is a 1798 Supreme Court case, *Calder v. Bull*,[13] in which Justice Samuel Chase argued that:

> I cannot subscribe to the omnipotence of a state Legislature, or that it is absolute and without control; although its authority should not be expressly restrained by the constitution, or fundamental law of a state. . . . There are certain vital principles in our free Republican governments, which will determine and overrule an apparent and flagrant abuse of legislative power. . . . The

> genius, the nature, and the spirit of our state governments, amount to a prohibition of such acts of legislation; and the general principles of law and reason forbid them.[14]

It seems clear that Chase thought that these "general principles of law and reason" could be invoked by judges, independent of the text of the Constitution, to invalidate a law.[15] Justice James Iredell denied this, maintaining that

> if . . . the legislature of the union, or the legislature of any member of the union, shall pass a law, within the general scope of their constitutional power, the court cannot pronounce it void, merely because it is, in their judgment, contrary to the principles of natural justice. The ideas of natural justice are regulated by no fixed standard; the ablest and the purest men have differed upon the subject.[16]

Iredell here was not rejecting principles of natural justice—which, like virtually everyone in the founding, he believed in wholeheartedly—but only the notion that they might be invoked to ground an act of judicial review. One can easily believe in principles of natural justice without thinking that they provide the kind of *specific* guidance necessary to justify an act of judicial review.[17]

Calder v. Bull was only one example of what I have elsewhere called "natural justice judicial review."[18] During the first several decades of American history, there were a number of cases (about seven or so) in which the Supreme Court invoked "principles of natural justice" in one form or another. This has led Thomas Grey to argue that natural justice judicial review "was at least as well founded in the general thought and practice of the [founding] as judicial review of the now uncontroversial interpretative sort."[19]

I believe that Grey is wrong on that point. Natural justice judicial review was not only rare,[20] but perhaps more importantly, as James Bradley Thayer noted, natural justice judicial review "in no case within my knowledge has . . . been enforced where it was the single and necessary ground of the decision."[21] In each case, it was either *dicta* or tied to some reference to the letter of the Constitution as well. Matthew Franck's recent book, *Against the Imperial Judiciary*, while going too far in denying the existence of natural justice judicial review, presents extensive evidence to show the limited scope of judicial power in the early years of American history.

Moreover, the greatest constitutional justice of this time, Chief Justice John Marshall, while he employed natural justice judicial review in one case

(*Fletcher v. Peck*),[22] notably refrained from invoking it in subsequent cases (such as *Dartmouth College v. Woodward*).[23] While one can only speculate on the reason for this change, I think that it is likely that Marshall was ambivalent about natural justice judicial review for precisely the reasons Iredell gave. And while there was one invocation of natural justice judicial review later in the nineteenth century—in *Loan Association v. Topeka*,[24] discussed in *Davidson v. New Orleans*[25]—the idea basically died out, I think, for similar reasons.

Nonetheless, even the temporary and limited use of natural justice judicial review is an enlightening reminder that the founding generation were not Benthamite positivists. The Constitution was universally held to embody certain principles of natural justice, which were an essential foundation for its authority. While the "will of the people" was necessary for the Constitution's legitimacy, it was not sufficient. If natural law was not an independent ground for judicial review, it was the foundation for the Constitution, itself the ground for judicial review.

I should conclude by pointing out that the term "natural law," as used in the founding era by men like Chase and Iredell, primarily applied to Lockean natural rights thinking. The basic idea was that the fundamental law of nature is rooted in the universal desire for self-preservation, and this first law of nature is the basis for a right to self-preservation. But self-preservation cannot effectually be ensured if one is subject to the arbitrary will of another, and it is also endangered by the scarcity of nature. Self-preservation was therefore expanded into the venerable trilogy of "life, liberty, and property." These rights are too insecure in the state of nature, and therefore men enter into the social contract, erecting government with the limited purpose of securing those fundamental rights. This notion of "natural law," then, is more an Enlightenment form of it, though some people may have read it as being somewhat harmonious with more traditional forms, such as the Thomistic version that influenced Richard Hooker (often cited by Locke) and, to a limited extent, Blackstone.

The Rise and Decline of Substantive Due Process If natural justice judicial review died out, it can be argued that its disappearance was really more a transfiguration than a death, for the kinds of principles that were prominent in natural justice judicial review—especially the protection of property—were simply channeled into a new form of judicial review. The "new" form of judicial review was nominally tied to a constitutional provision, but like natural justice judicial review it had the open-endedness of a judicial review that was not immediately dependent on the document.

Edward Corwin argued that, from one perspective, Iredell decisively won out over Chase, since natural justice judicial review was abandoned; but, in another sense, Chase was the winner, since his principles of natural justice became the core of economic substantive due process.[26]

The due process clause was originally intended, I think, as a guarantee of the standing legal procedure.[27] Attempts to read it as a broad substantive guarantee founder on (1) the difficulty of explaining the use of the word "process" for a substantive guarantee and (2) the implausibility of such a broad guarantee being assigned the place the due process clause occupies in the overall structure of the Bill of Rights.

Nonetheless, from the very beginning of the nineteenth century there were efforts (primarily in state courts) to give due process clauses (or "law of the land" clauses that were widely regarded as its equivalent) a broader reading. This was accomplished, as a matter of interpretation, by focusing on the last word, *viz.*, due process of *law*. For example, in *Dartmouth College v. Woodward*,[28] Daniel Webster argued that: "By the law of the land is most clearly intended the general law; a law which hears before it condemns; which proceeds upon inquiry, and renders judgment only after trial." This sounds somewhat procedural, but Webster found it relevant to New Hampshire's unilateral altering of a college charter, which was hardly a procedural issue in the normal sense of the term.

The use to which the courts put the developing notion of substantive due process was similar to the use of natural justice judicial review: the protection of property rights. Corwin traces its development in state courts, culminating in the case of *Wynehamer v. N.Y.*, in which the high court of New York struck down a law that forbade the sale of liquor. There were certain legislative actions that could not be done "even by the forms which belong to due process of law."[29] This formulation appeared again the following year in the first formal use of substantive due process in a Supreme Court opinion. In the *Dred Scott Case*, the Supreme Court argued that the Missouri Compromise deprived citizens of their property (in slaves) and thus "could hardly be dignified with the name of due process of law."[30]

After the Civil War—and despite the unfortunate parentage of *Dred Scott*—substantive due process slowly developed in a series of cases, until by the end of the century the Court was explicitly striking down economic regulation on the basis of the due process clause, in cases such as *Allgeyer v. La.* and *Lochner v. N.Y.*[31] The era of economic substantive due process lasted from about 1890 to 1937.[32]

What is interesting for purposes of the present topic is that the justices who adopted this understanding of the due process clause did so with some reliance on natural law reasoning. Moreover, they considered that they were doing nothing innovative, but simply following the example of earlier American jurists. One of the best examples is a speech by Justice David Brewer to the New York State Bar Association in 1893.

> It may be said that this is practically substituting government by judges for government by the people. . . . But this involves a total misunderstanding of the relations of judges to government. There is nothing in this power of the judiciary detracting in the least from the idea of government of and by the people. The courts hold neither purse nor sword; they cannot corrupt nor arbitrarily control. They make no laws, they establish no policy, they never enter into the domain of popular action. They do not govern. Their functions in relation to the State are limited to seeing that popular action does not trespass upon right and justice as it exists in written constitutions *and natural law*. So it is that the utmost power of the courts and judges works no interference with true liberty, no trespass on the fullest and highest development of government of and by the people; it only means security to personal rights—the inalienable rights, life, liberty, and the pursuit of happiness [emphasis added].[33]

Note how easily Brewer slides "natural law" into conjunction with "written constitutions" and sees judges as protectors of both, apparently without any sense of the dramatic expansion of judicial power that is thereby entailed.

It is an unfortunate fact of American life that the standard-bearer of the forces opposed to this assertion of judicial power was Oliver Wendell Holmes, Jr.—the preeminent legal positivist and legal realist who exercised such an extraordinary influence over the minds of many noted legal thinkers of the first half of the twentieth century.[34] The misfortune lies in the fact that Holmes' intellectual proclivities gave a distinctly modernist—and unnecessary—ground for opposing economic due process. Opponents of *Lochner* and similar decisions might easily have said that the due process clause was a guarantee of legal procedure rather than substance and that, while the Founders had valued property rights, they did not intend the due process clause to be a general warrant for judges to strike down economic regulation that they considered unreasonable.

Holmes' more "evolutionary" thought led him to a different critique. Without rejecting the principle of substantive due process, he (wrongly)[35] conceded to his opponents that they accurately represented the mind of the Founders on issues of property rights, but then argued that it was necessary *not* to be too closely tied to that mind, that it was necessary to adapt the Constitution to the new exigencies of a new age.[36] Holmes himself generally employed this approach to justify deference to *legislative* adaptations of the Constitution. His intellectual descendants on the Supreme Court after 1937 (especially on the Warren Court) ultimately used the same rationale to justify judicial activism, in the form of "updating" and expanding various constitutional guarantees of freedom and equality (perhaps on the basis of a new and altogether different notion of natural law).[37]

The Court's experiment with economic due process was, as I have argued, a form of natural justice judicial review and a form of judicial legislation. By elevating the meaning of the due process clauses to an extraordinarily high level of generality (equivalent to "no government may *arbitrarily* deprive people of life, liberty, or property"), it was possible to tie judicial review nominally to a constitutional provision, while having a virtual blank check (or wild card—choose your own metaphor) for the judges to enforce their own vision of natural law principles.

"Natural law," in this context, then, was a somewhat expanded Lockean version, with an (over)emphasis on the right to economic liberty and to property. While the right of government to regulate property rights in the public interest was acknowledged (and, indeed, even during the era of laissez-faire jurisprudence from the end of the nineteenth century until 1937, the large majority of challenged government economic regulations survived Court scrutiny,)[38] "freedom of contract" came to hold a special position in American law. It is fair to say, I think, that the association of "natural law" with this form of laissez-faire thought helped contribute to its bad odor among twentieth-century intellectuals.

The Incorporation Debate The natural law–positivism dispute raised its head on the new, post-1937 Supreme Court in the context of a running debate on procedural due process between Justices Hugo Black and Felix Frankfurter. This was part of the debate over incorporation of the Bill of Rights guarantees into the Fourteenth Amendment, thus making them applicable to the states.

The background to the debate is well-known. The laissez-faire Court which had embraced substantive due process emphasized its application to economic matters, but did not confine it to that area. As early as 1884, in *Hurtado v. California*, a case regarding procedural due process, the Court had argued that the due process clause "must be held to guaranty not particular forms of procedure, but the very substance of individual rights to life, liberty, and property."[39] In the early twentieth century, the Court maintained, in *Twining v. N.J.* (1908), that due process included whatever was "a fundamental principle of liberty and justice which inheres in the very idea of free government and is the inalienable right of a citizen of such a government."[40] In 1930, the Court struck down a state conviction for failing to meet the demands of Fourteenth Amendment procedural due process, in *Powell v. Alabama.* The right to the assistance of counsel was said to be (at least in the circumstances of this case) "fundamental"[41] and therefore guaranteed by the due process clause.

Up to this point, any overlap between Fourteenth Amendment due process and the Bill of Rights was purely incidental. Then *Palko v. Connecticut* (1937) took the important step of describing the determination of what was fundamental (or "implicit in the concept of ordered liberty")[42] as a process of "earlier articles of the federal bill of rights [being] brought within the Fourteenth Amendment by a process of absorption"[43]—otherwise known as "selective incorporation." This set the stage for the Black–Frankfurter debate, most notably in *Adamson v. California*[44] *and Rochin v. California.*[45]

In *Adamson,* Black put forward the view that the framers of Section I of the Fourteenth Amendment had intended to apply the entire Bill of Rights to the states. The portion of his argument of particular interest for this paper is the part in which he lambastes "natural law":

> This decision reasserts a constitutional theory . . . that this Court is endowed by the Constitution with boundless power under "natural law" periodically to expand and contract constitutional standards to conform to the Court's conception of what at a particular time constitutes "civilized decency" and "fundamental liberty and justice."[46]

Black went on to contend

> that the "natural law" formula which the Court uses to reach its decision in this case should be abandoned as an incongruous excrescence on our Constitution. I believe that formula to be itself a violation of our Constitution, in that it subtly conveys to courts, at the expense of legislatures, ultimate power over public policies in fields where no specific provision of the Constitution limits legislative powers.[47]

He expressly connected this "natural law" thinking with the earlier economic due process cases, which were anathema to him:

> It must be conceded, of course, that the natural-law–due-process formula, which the Court today reaffirms, has been interpreted to limit substantially this Court's power to prevent state violations of the individual civil liberties

> guaranteed by the Bill of Rights. But this formula also has been used in the past, and can be used in the future, to license this Court, in considering regulatory legislation, to roam at large in the broad expanses of policy and morals and to trespass, all too freely, on the legislative domain of the States as well as the Federal Government. . . .[48]

Black finishes with a contrast between the two approaches:

> To pass upon the constitutionality of statutes by looking to the particular standards enumerated in the Bill of Rights and other parts of the Constitution is one thing; to invalidate statutes because of application of "natural law" deemed to be above and undefined by the Constitution is another. In the one instance, courts proceeding within clearly marked constitutional boundaries seek to execute policies written into the Constitution; in the other, they roam at will in the limitless area of their own beliefs as to reasonableness and actually select policies, a responsibility which the Constitution entrusts to the legislative representatives of the people.[49]

Justice Frankfurter's concurrence took up Black's challenge. A New Dealer himself, like Black, Frankfurter was nonetheless skeptical of Black's efforts to narrow judicial discretion so dramatically. Frankfurter does not reject the natural law tag, seeming to accept it when he argues:

> In the history of thought "natural law" has a much longer and much better founded meaning and justification than such subjective selection of the first eight Amendments or incorporation into the Fourteenth. If all that is meant is that due process contains within itself certain minimal standards which are "of the very essence of a scheme of ordered liberty," . . . putting upon this Court the duty of applying these standards from time to time, then we have merely arrived at the insight which our predecessors long ago expressed.[50]

The Court must exercise judgment to determine whether proceedings "offend those canons of decency and fairness which express the notions of justice of English-speaking peoples."[51] Frankfurter maintains that judges should not rely on "idiosyncrasies of a merely personal judgment" but "must move within the limits of accepted notions of justice."[52]

There is a profound irony in the attribution of natural law reasoning to one of the most devoted followers of Oliver Wendell Holmes, Jr., who despised natural law thinking.[53] Interestingly, the one time that Frankfurter uses the term in his opinion, he puts the phrase in quotes—as if to distance himself from it somewhat. Moreover, the reference to "the notions of justice of English-speaking peoples" seems to establish a more conventional standard, unlike the more universal standards typical of natural law.

And yet there is some sense in which one might legitimately consider Frankfurter's (and the Court's) approach a natural law argument. Whence does one derive the content of "notions of justice of English-speaking peoples" and other cognate notions? In the absence of any guidance from the constitutional text, is it not general notions of justice and decency that provide the substantive content of this form of procedural due process? That is, from one perspective, is not the Frankfurter approach a sort of "*substantive* procedural due process," in the sense that it is a rather generalized guarantee of "just" legal procedure, with the "interpreter" being responsible for fleshing out the content?

The Clarence Thomas Nomination Debate The most recent occasion for a significant public discussion of natural law and the Supreme Court was the 1991 nomination of Clarence Thomas. I say "occasion" advisedly, since I do not believe that the actual resulting discussion was particularly elevated.

Natural law became an issue because Thomas had given a number of speeches and written a number of articles in which he appeared to argue that natural law was decidedly relevant to American constitutional law. In particular, he cited Justice Harlan's dissent in *Plessy v.* Ferguson[54] as a good example of a judge rightly adverting to the higher law background to the Constitution (especially in the Declaration)—though Harlan did not explicitly cite natural law.

At the hearings on his nomination, however, Thomas appeared to back off his earlier ringing endorsement of the relevance of natural law to constitutional interpretation. Not only did he deny that judges could strike down laws on the basis of natural law principles not embodied in the Constitution—a view clearly consistent with his earlier arguments—but he said that natural law was of merely theoretical interest, without any practical impact on actual constitutional adjudication.

Thomas was willing, later, in an exchange with committee chairman Joseph Biden, to respond affirmatively to Biden's statement: "I don't see how any reasonable person can conclude that natural law does not impact upon adjudication of a case, if you are a judge, if you acknowledge that you have to go back and look at what the Founders meant by natural law, and then at least in part have that play a part in . . . adjudication. . . ."[55] But even this was hedged substantially, on the grounds that "the provisions they [the framers] chose were broad provisions, that adjudicating through our history and tradition, using our history and tradition evolve."[56]

This unfortunate backing off of the issue—which I strongly suspect was due primarily to the advice of his Bush Administration and Congressional "handlers" at the nomination hearings—short-circuited the opportunity for a substantial public debate on the issue. It was a missed opportunity to educate the American people. Such a debate could have helped to make the relevance and importance of natural law clear, while clarifying its limits as well. In the event, it turned out to be a nondebate.

Finding Natural Law in Contemporary American Law

As the Thomas nomination discussion suggested, the earlier ways of invoking natural law that I have described are generally in disrepute today. There is, however, another, quite different perspective, from which it is actually possible to characterize the main thrust of modern Court jurisprudence as a form of natural law, as Russell Hittinger does. According to Hittinger,

> Natural law is an order that: (1) reason does not make, in the sense that it is not an artifact of our own practical agenda; (2) is presupposed by legal and moral deliberation, and is brought to light by theory and reflection; and (3) is in some way normative for conduct and for our legal artifacts.[57]

As Hittinger points out, his is a very broad notion that "can come to include any moral theory about law that is not positivist."[58] In the contemporary era of American constitutional law, the central moral principle is autonomy.

The first post-1937 use of pure substantive due process was *Griswold v. Connecticut* (1965), which struck down a Connecticut prohibition of the distribution or use of contraceptives.[59] As Hittinger rightly notes, the true nature of the privacy right became clear only with *Eisenstadt v. Baird*, which gave it a thoroughly individualistic turn.[60] Eventually, in its most dramatic use of the right to privacy, the Court struck down all abortion laws in *Roe v. Wade*.[61] While the Court declined to extend the privacy right to include homosexual sodomy in *Bowers v. Hardwick* (on narrowly conventional grounds),[62] the Court's current understanding of the right is still quite broad, as a famous passage in *Planned Parenthood v. Casey*, reaffirming the central holding of *Roe*, shows:

> These matters, involving the most intimate and personal choices a person may make in a lifetime, choices central to personal dignity and autonomy, are central to the liberty protected by the Fourteenth Amendment. At the heart of

> liberty is the right to define one's own concept of existence, of meaning, of the universe, and of the mystery of human life. Beliefs about these matters could not define the attributes of personhood were they formed under compulsion of the State.[63]

One way to formulate this idea of natural law is to say (as Hittinger characterizes David A.J. Richards' autonomy-based theory) that "the only ontological standard to which we ought to attune our judgments is the generic notion of autonomous selfhood."[64]

Of course, one must qualify very general statements about "contemporary constitutional law." As noted, the Court has refused to work out fully the logic of "autonomous selfhood," as *Bowers* shows. And, whatever the importance of the *Griswold–Casey* line of cases, it is not the whole of contemporary constitutional law. The important allied area of church–state jurisprudence, for example, would have to be considered, and one would be hard-pressed to find any coherent theory to explain the Court's decisions in that area (much less any relationship between such a theory and the Constitution). To some extent, then, the modern Court's natural law is a rather *ad hoc* affair.

Hittinger's fundamental insight nonetheless remains sound and important to understand: if the Court has rejected older understandings of natural law as "the structure of moral understanding that must lie behind the text of the Constitution," some other theory will fill the vacuum and provide that structure.

Moore's Natural Law Theory of Interpretation One specific form of contemporary natural law theory harmonizes well with the broad outlines of contemporary law described by Hittinger, but differs in its unusual, explicit stress on moral realism.[65] This is Michael Moore's "natural law theory of interpretation." According to Moore, interpreters should (a) recognize that the general phrases of the Constitution (such as the Privileges and Immunities clause, the Due Process Clause, the Equal Protection Clause, and the Ninth Amendment) refer to "objective values," and (b) "develop theories about the nature of equality, liberty, liberties of speech and of worship, cruel punishment, and the like, in a never-completed quest to discover the true nature of such things."[66] "The framers," he says, "used such brief and general language because they thought they were referring to values whose rich natures would guide meaning."

Moore denies that "such moral realist interpretation . . . is so unconstrained that it amounts to an unwritten constitution."[67] First, "using the true nature of values in interpreting a text is not the same as using those values as the text." According to his theory, "the written document tells interpreters which values they are to seek via their best theories," which is "quite different from simply deciding for oneself what the relevant values are." This is "a constrained interpretive judgment."[68]

Second, he responds to the "epistemological skeptic,"[69] who, while conceding that there are moral rights and that the framers were trying to refer to them, argues that (a) it is harder to know the natures of such entities as rights (relative to natures of natural kinds, e.g., that of a tiger); (b) "because such rights are less knowable, there is also bound to be greater disagreement about those truths;" and therefore (c) "although there may be answers 'out there' about moral entities, they cannot significantly constrain judges. Moore essentially says that Madison and Hamilton were aware of this worry, and responded to it as we should: by trying to ensure that the courts are staffed by those few who had the skill and integrity to know such things, "who share the framers' belief in knowable right answers to moral questions and . . . have a good grasp of what those answers are."[70]

Moore is elaborating a natural law theory of interpretation, it should be emphasized; he is not advocating an appeal to natural law directly, apart from the Constitution. But Moore is typical of modern constitutional interpretation in attributing a very high level of generality to key constitutional phrases (e.g., due process, equal protection, and the Ninth Amendment), and in according great latitude to judges to flesh these generalities out according to their "best theories," so the difference between his use of natural law in "interpretation" is not substantially different from a direct appeal to natural law.

Moreover, his response to those he calls "epistemological skeptics" seems completely inadequate. If the only "constraint" on judges is that we should choose only those who *really know* "the right answers to moral questions," that establishes not so much constraints as parameters for conditions in which constraint is not necessary.

Moore's invocation of Madison and Hamilton is entirely misplaced. When *The Federalist* refers to the fact that only a "few men . . . in the society . . . will have sufficient skill in the laws to qualify them for the stations of judges," this was the context:

> There is yet a further and a weighty reason for the permanency of the judicial offices; which is deducible from the nature of the qualifications they require. It has been frequently remarked with great propriety, that a voluminous code of laws is one of the inconveniences necessarily connected with the advantages of free government.

> To avoid an arbitrary discretion in the courts, it is indispensable that they should be bound down by strict rules and precedents, which serve to define and point out their duty in every particular case that comes before them; and it will readily be conceived from the variety of controversies which grow out of the folly and wickedness of mankind, that the records of those precedents must unavoidably swell to a very considerable bulk, and must demand long and laborious study to acquire a competent knowledge of them. Hence it is that there can be but few men in the society, who will have sufficient skill in the laws to qualify them for the stations of judges.[71]

Note that the spirit of this passage is the need to confine judicial discretion, rather than to leave it to "interpreters to develop and apply their own best theory of the virtues."[72] The numbers are small because of the laborious work invested in mastering voluminous precedents, not because the truths of morality were known only to "an educated and morally fit few."[73] Moreover, this passage's reference to voluminous precedents suggests that Publius (Hamilton, in this case) has in mind ordinary common law judging, not the very special case of judicial review.

Much of Moore's analysis would arguably be relevant to the much broader question of constitutional interpretation *simpliciter*—unconfined to the context of judicial review. There *is* a need for a theory of interpretation that deals with relatively broad and vague constitutional provisions, such as the Privileges and Immunities Clause, and much of what Moore says might be admissible in a theory of interpretation for legislatures and executives, as they deal with such clauses.[74] But the context of judicial review, and therefore also the context of separation of powers, gives the question a different framework.

Here, what Moore calls "epistemological skepticism," and what I would rather call epistemological and republican humility, counsels that judges exercise judicial review only in clear cases, when acts are contrary to the "manifest" tenor of the Constitution, as Publius puts it.[75] In the last section, I hope to suggest grounds for such humility in the context of an older moral realist approach.

Conservatives, Positivism, and Natural Law

The Thomas nomination debate did stimulate an interesting, though less widely followed, exchange on natural law and judicial power, in the pages of the journal *First Things*.[76] In that debate, Judge Robert Bork, Hadley Arkes, Russell Hittinger, and William Bentley Ball laid out different, but sometimes overlapping, views on the place of natural law in adjudication. I shall use my analysis of the strengths and weaknesses of their positions to stake out my own position on the relevance of natural law to judicial review.

Bork argues that natural law may be useful in ascertaining the meaning of constitutional provisions, because interpretation requires us to look at the principles that underlie and animate those provisions. But he argues that natural law may not be used as a basis, independent of the Constitution itself, to strike down laws. He explicitly declines the honor of being considered a natural law exponent by virtue of his view that natural law is binding on the judge when it is incorporated into positive law. That view rests not on "the fitness of things" or "the logic of law," but on the statements of the Founders on the duties of courts and design of our government. He does, however, concede that perhaps the duty of the judge to fulfill his oath to operate according to law is itself part of natural law—i.e., the natural law requires the judge to confine himself to positive law.

Arkes is critical of positivists who argue that there are no standards of moral judgment apart from what is posited by the law, and he suggests that Chief Justice William Rehnquist and Bork have sometimes made statements that seem skeptical. For example, Bork has argued that "Truth . . . is what the majority thinks it is at any given moment precisely because the majority is permitted to govern and redefine its values constantly."[77] Arkes defends (against Bork's criticism) his earlier argument that Harlan's dissent in *Plessy v. Ferguson* was correct because, even apart from the Reconstruction amendments, judges "tutored in natural rights and committed to a 'government of consent'" could condemn segregation on the basis of the republican Guarantee Clause of the original Constitution.

Hittinger points out that conservative natural law proponents generally agree that modern Court invocations of natural law have been disastrous. He wants natural law considered "in the course of discerning 'what the framers and ratifiers meant,'" and would distinguish between natural law legal thinkers who want to import natural law into the Constitution and those who merely want to recognize it as part of the document's original intent—a distinction that he says Judge Bork sometimes does not make.

William Bentley Ball adopts the broadest view of judicial power in this debate, arguing that the American Constitution does not disturb the natural law and common law principle that judges have equity power, based on the Due Process Clause, to go beyond the letter of the law to protect substantive rights such as free exercise of religion. That modern judges have often appealed to a lower or unnatural law rather than a higher law should not lead us to abandon judicial power, leaving us at the mercy of legislatures.

Each side scores some points in this debate, but, just as importantly, there is more agreement than might appear at first sight, especially between Bork and Hittinger. Bork is absolutely right to distinguish between a denial of natural law-based judicial review and cultural relativism. In no way is there any logically necessary connection between these two phenomena. One can be a cultural relativist and be strongly opposed to judicial activism, as Professor Lino Graglia is, and one can be opposed to both cultural relativism and natural law-based judicial review,[78] as Bork and Hittinger (and I) are.

Rejection of judicial review based on natural law and not the Constitution, however, does not entail rejection of the use of natural law as embodied in the Constitution, and insofar as understanding of natural law is necessary to understanding the Constitution, as all the participants in this debate agree. For example, the exchange makes it clear that Arkes and Bork substantially agree on a certain use of the natural law, of what Bork calls the "method of reasoning from the implications of written constitutional principles to subsidiary principles."[79] For his part, Arkes acknowledges Bork's endorsement of looking at the "structure of moral understanding that must lie behind the text of the Constitution."

On the other hand, Bork undercuts his embrace of the more restrained use of natural law in his response when he argues at one point that knowledge of natural law in relation to original intent is mostly "academic." The main reliance, he says, is on the inquiry as to "what the words of the Constitution meant to reasonable men at the time of the ratification" and on "a great many secondary materials." But Hittinger's point is precisely that, given the widespread influence of a certain understanding of natural law at the time of the founding, "what the words of the Constitution meant to reasonable men" at that time will be understood more clearly if one keeps that understanding in mind; likewise, the "secondary materials" also reflect that understanding. Bork may be right when he implies that there will not be many cases in which "a particular version of natural law [can] demonstrate that the text's words mean something other than we might think today,"[80] but that is no warrant for reducing the correspondence of natural law and original intent to an "academic" question.

The agreement on the more restrained use of natural law should not obscure the differences on a broader use of it. Here I think that Bork and Hittinger are in general agreement in rejecting Ball's very broad interpretation of the Due Process Clause and also Arkes' more expansive reading of the Equal Protection Clause in his discussion of *Plessy* and *Brown*.

Having said all this—which generally endorses Bork's views—I must say that it is painful to hear Judge Bork say that he has never written a better line than "Truth . . . is what the majority thinks it is at any given moment precisely because the majority is permitted to govern and redefine its values constantly." I think it is clear that what Bork means is this: judges must take the positive law (Constitution and statute) as a "given" in their work—and therefore as the "truth"—even if such law happens to be morally wrong in an objective sense. But the line he wrote is an awful one, because what we typically mean—and what we should mean—by "truth" is not some conventional account of reality, but what reality truly is. So we ought to save the word "truth" for accounts of things that correspond with reality objectively, and not use it as Judge Bork used it in his earlier article (even if what he meant by it was right).

In a later article, Hittinger takes Bork to task for two other statements. The first appears in his 1971 *Indiana Law Journal* article: "If judges should claim . . . to possess a volume of the annotated natural law, we would, quite justifiably, suspect that the source of the revelation was really no more exalted than the judge's viscera." The second is in *The Tempting of America*: "in today's situation . . . there is no objectively 'correct' hierarchy to which the judge can appeal. But unless there is, unless we can rank forms of gratification, the judge must let the majority have its way."[81] Hittinger takes these to be statements supporting moral relativism or emotivism. I doubt that this is what Bork meant, but Hittinger cannot be said to read Bork's language unfairly.

Moreover, Bork fails to recognize Arkes' point when he "decline[s] the honor" of being considered a natural law judge by Arkes, on the grounds that Bork is articulating a natural law principle when he says "that natural law is binding on a judge only when incorporated in positive law."[82] I think that there is a serious problem of circularity in many originalists' appeals to original intent to show that original intent is the correct position for a judge to adopt. Bork says that his view does not rest on the fitness of things or the logic of the law, "but rather upon the statements at the founding of what the duties of courts are and upon the design of our government."[83] But Arkes can rightly respond: why should those statements and that design be determinative? And it is circular to respond: because of those statements and that design.

Ultimately, at some point, originalists must make a case that the design of the Constitution (including its limitations on judicial invocation of natural law) is good. That's why a pure positivist response on the question of judicial power is necessarily inadequate, though not legally inadequate. It would be sufficient for a judge to say that he took an oath to uphold the

Constitution, and the Constitution does not give him the power to invoke natural law independent of the Constitution. But, as Arkes says, at some point, if asked to explain why one should obey that oath, the judge must give a reason that goes beyond the positive law. Bork himself does: "I suppose it could be said that this duty of fulfilling an obligation is itself natural law. If so, it is a piece of natural law that requires the judge to confine himself to the positive law in all else."[84] Just right!—keeping in mind that Bork's confinement of the judge to the positive law is compatible with, indeed requires, *interpreting* the positive law with a discernment of "the structure of moral understanding that must lie behind the text of the Constitution."[85]

My overall evaluation of the debate, then, is this: Bork and Hittinger basically have it right. They agree that (1) natural law reasoning is relevant to interpretation of the positive law, insofar as it elucidates the "structure of moral understanding that must lie behind the text of the Constitution," but that (2) judicial invocation of natural law apart from its being embedded in the document (logically entailed by it) is improper for judges.

Bork wants to keep emphasizing the second proposition, and he is afraid that the judicial invocation of the natural law in the process of interpreting positive law (proposition one) will get out of hand and become the invocation of natural law independent of the Constitution that is rejected in proposition two. For his part, Hittinger wants to emphasize the first proposition, and he is afraid the second will be pushed to the point of excluding even the legitimate appeal to natural law reasoning validated in the first.

Bork's fears are not entirely unwarranted, since Ball and Arkes represent precisely the tendency that Bork fears: starting from an invocation of natural law to understand the Constitution, it is possible to move to a position of using it to supplement or transform the Constitution. Moreover, Hittinger, in an earlier article, had also used language in raising doubts about Bork's position that might have been interpreted to justify a broad judicial invocation of natural law. Bork's approach, he said, "would be to admit defeat on what is perhaps the most salient and valuable aspect of American constitutional law—the vindication of individual rights according to natural principles of justice."[86]

Likewise, Hittinger's fears are not entirely unwarranted, since Bork himself keeps saying things that feed his fears—e.g., "Truth is what the majority thinks it is at any given moment precisely because the majority is permitted to govern and redefine its values constantly," and his reaffirmation of that statement, "I never wrote a better line."

On a deeper level—one that goes beyond the issue of judicial review itself—Hittinger and Arkes are both aware that Bork's reliance on original intent to validate original intent is circular and, however much it might be a sufficient *legal* answer for a judge to give, it is inadequate as a defense of the whole enterprise of which the judge is a part. Bork might (rightly) respond that it is not the job or the obligation of the judge to provide the theoretical foundations for the Constitution (and the judge's job of interpreting it faithfully). But it is a task that someone must perform if the Constitution is to survive and, unfortunately, few people are doing it. Most contemporary constitutional scholars are doing the opposite, in fact: providing new theories for *not* abiding by the Constitution. That is why Judge Bork really is outside the mainstream of legal scholarship these days, to his credit. In such circumstances, the Constitution can use all the help it can get, and intelligent judges have the means to contribute to that necessary defense. In doing so, they will necessarily be invoking some conception of natural law. If this is not, strictly speaking, part of their judicial duties, it is an important task nonetheless.

Natural Law in Constitutional Interpretation

I have argued—and on this general point, I think Bork, Hittinger, and Arkes are in agreement as well—that natural law is relevant to constitutional interpretation, insofar as it helps to ascertain the fundamental principles underlying and animating the Constitution. How is this so?

It should be acknowledged that the influence of more classical forms of natural law thinking on the American Constitution was limited.[87] It did, nonetheless, have a significant role. While the structure of moral understanding that lies behind the American Constitution is largely, in my view, derived from Lockean political philosophy, it does include important elements from more classical forms of natural law. This is so partly because the understanding of Lockean philosophy itself was heavily mediated by the natural theology that Locke himself embraced in his texts and by the widespread and politically and socially influential Christianity that was the dominant religion at the time of the American founding.

Essential elements of the moral framework that the Founders by and large took for granted as the starting point of their political reflection were derived from classical sources. For example, these sources undergirded the idea of the family as the basic cell of society and supported the complex mixture of laws and social mores (at the state and local, rather than the federal, level) which regulated marriage and sexual conduct.

The relevance of these classical elements of American political and social life to constitutional law lies especially in the rational limits to liberty—the conditions for liberty, as opposed to license—that they provided. Autonomous selfhood was not the slogan of anyone in the founding.

On the other hand, conservative advocates of the classical ideal of natural law often tend to embrace judicial restraint in today's debates. So how is it possible for them to evade Michael Moore's charge of "epistemological skepticism," which he levies against originalist advocates of judicial restraint?[88] The answer to that question contains an important insight into classical conceptions of natural law, which we can begin to explore by examining Justice Iredell's comment that "the ablest and purest men have differed upon the subject."

Many interpreters have taken Iredell's comment to be a statement rooted in skepticism. They read it as saying: since our opinions about the human good (the content of principles of natural justice or natural law) are at such great variance, how can any of us reasonably claim to *know* the good with any certitude? If, as I contend, Iredell believed in principles of natural justice as strongly as other Founders did, why would he employ an argument of this sort?

The answer is to be found in the fact that natural law principles are self-evident and certain, but, for the most part, at a fairly high level of generality. They must be applied to concrete situations. And classic representatives of the natural law position made it clear that the more concrete the moral decision, the more it involved many contingent elements, and the less universal its prescriptions would be. Thomas Aquinas, for example, argues that

> The practical reason . . . is busied with contingent matters, about which human actions are concerned; and consequently, although there is necessity in the general principles, the more we descend to matters of detail, the more frequently we encounter defects . . . . [I]n matters of action, truth or practical rectitude is not the same for all, as to matters of detail, but only as to the general principles; and where there is the same rectitude in matters of detail, it is not equally known to all.[89]

For Iredell, with the version of natural law that he adhered to—a largely Lockean form of natural rights—that meant that there was, undoubtedly, a right to property, but that the particular legal enforcement of that right to property, especially regarding such specific questions as whether a state legislature that also exercised a kind of ultimate judicial power (as the

House of Lords did in England) could reopen a probate case, was much less certain. Given this kind of entirely reasonable doubt about contingent matters, denying judicial discretion to enforce principles of natural justice independent of positive law was perfectly reasonable and unrelated to any form of moral relativism. For similar reasons, those of us who strongly believe in natural law can reasonably deny judicial power to invoke the natural law independently of the positive law as a basis for judicial decisions.

There are, of course, other reasons for opposing natural law judicial review. For example, a reasonable estimate of the likelihood of judges having more accurate conceptions of the requirements of natural law is, in fact, "not very likely." For another, there is the importance of the rule of law, including judges themselves being subject to law, even a law that is in some respects deficient vis-a-vis the natural law. I want to conclude by looking more closely at a complex example of this last sort.

Judges, Natural Law, and Abortion

Even if natural law were taken as a norm for judges in a more limited sense—as relevant to the structure of moral understanding that must be taken to underlie the Constitution—how far can this legitimate use of natural law be pressed? A particularly interesting case of this kind concerns the question of abortion and the Fourteenth Amendment's Equal Protection Clause. I consider this to be a hard question (harder than I thought it was, when I first began thinking about it years ago).

The due process privacy right to an abortion created by the Supreme Court in *Roe v. Wade* has no constitutional foundation. It is an invention upon an invention upon an invention: a right to an abortion built on a right to privacy built on substantive due process, all of it without constitutional warrant. Nonetheless, it is not self-evident that the Constitution says nothing relevant to the abortion issue.

The Fourteenth Amendment to the Constitution says that, "No state shall . . . deny to any person within its jurisdiction the equal protection of the laws." A textualist reading of the Constitution would, I believe, focus especially on the use of the word "protection." That is, the phrase is not simply equivalent to "state laws shall treat people equally." Many laws (not all of them) *protect* people—protect their lives and property in particular. Sometimes those representatives of the state who are charged with the duty of enforcing those laws for the protection of people fail to discharge this duty. In such cases, those people whose security of person and property are jeopardized have been denied the equal protection of the laws.

This reading of the Equal Protection Clause fits well certain aspects of the historical situation confronting the framers of the Fourteenth Amendment. Law enforcement officials in the South hardly made the protection of the newly freed slaves—often subject to depredations by their former slave-masters and their followers—a high priority.

In the absence of such protection, it was essential that some mechanism exist for protecting these rights. The fifth section of the Fourteenth Amendment provided Congress with the legislative power to rectify this injustice arising from a failure to give equal protection of the laws to the newly freed slaves by providing some other, more effectual, means of protection (i.e., federal enforcement of such protection). (Note that, according to this reading of the amendment, the *Civil Rights Cases* of 1883 misunderstood congressional power from at least one perspective.[90] While the amendment was, in one sense, directed at state action and not merely private action, that state action included *inaction*, the failure to provide "the equal protection of the laws," and Congress had the power by appropriate legislation to deal with the failure, by means which included suppressing the illegal private action the state had failed to suppress—e.g., depredations of the Ku Klux Klan.)

The language of the Fourteenth Amendment, while conceived in light of the racial situation of the Southern states, was not confined to that situation—indeed, section one contains no reference to race whatsoever. The amendment established a principle that applied to denial of equal protection not only on racial grounds, but also on other grounds.

The question I want to raise, then, is whether abortion might not be precisely the *kind* of case that the Equal Protection Clause was intended to deal with. When states do not *prohibit* abortion, do they not thereby choose selectively to deny the equal *protection* of the laws to a class of persons?

The key question to answer would obviously be "do abortions kill 'persons?'" The key question would not, by the way, be "did the framers and ratifiers of the Fourteenth Amendment specifically have unborn children in mind when they passed and ratified the equal protection clause?" Chief Justice John Marshall dealt with this question long ago, when he argued in *Dartmouth College v. Woodward* that

> It is more than possible that the preservation of rights of this description was not particularly in view of the framers of the Constitution, when the clause under consideration was introduced into that instrument. . . . But although a

> particular and rare case may not, in itself, be of sufficient magnitude to induce a rule, yet it must be governed by that rule, when established. . . .The case, being within the words of the rule, must be within its operation likewise. . . .[91]

The Constitution establishes principles, and those principles apply to all cases which fall within their purview, even cases the framers did not specifically have in mind. (This was a corollary of the fact that the Constitution "was framed for ages to come, and is designed to approach immortality as nearly as human institutions can approach it."[92])

Does abortion fall within "the words of the rule?" It would seem to, if the law permits abortion, and if abortion kills a person. That is, it does if what is aborted is a "person." Is it a person?

It is very hard to resist the temptation to respond, simply, that what is aborted is a person. If one were to take Michael Moore's general approach, one would simply ask, "Is the fetus in fact—*really*—a person?" And the answer to that question is clearly "yes." A person is a kind of being that has the intrinsic capacity for reason and free will. Fetuses are incipient human beings, who have that capacity. Therefore, fetuses are persons. And laws which permit abortion are a denial of the equal protection of the laws to those persons.

In the final analysis, I do think that this line of reasoning is a "temptation"—for a judge. The judge's duty in interpreting the law is to do so in light of the ordinary meaning of the words, as they were understood by those to whom they were addressed. Did the ordinary person to whom the Fourteenth Amendment was addressed understand the word "person" in such a way that its general principle would require the inclusion of fetuses?

Note that this is somewhat different from asking, "Did that ordinary person actually think that fetuses were persons?" It is not inconceivable, for example, that medical knowledge at the time of the Fourteenth Amendment's passage and ratification was still limited enough that the actual facts about the fetus were still not fully known, and therefore factual judgments as to whether it was a person might actually diverge from the principle the Fourteenth Amendment established. (For the record, though, at least those people who knew the facts best at that time—the medical profession—did seem generally to believe that the fetus was genuinely a human life, which ought not to be destroyed.[93])

The question, no matter how it is phrased, is somewhat difficult to answer because the authors and ratifiers of the Fourteenth Amendment could use the word "person" without giving it any exact definition—a rough, commonsense notion of the term was sufficient for their purposes.

That is, they did not have to define their *principle* very exactly, in that respect.

In the absence of a more precise definition of the principle behind "personhood," and given the fact that many people did and do in fact doubt (however wrongly, in fact) whether a human person exists from the time of human conception, I argue that the Constitution lacks the kind of clarity that would be necessary for a judge to strike down a law permitting abortion. I point out, however, that Congress, in its power to interpret and enforce the Fourteenth Amendment, is not bound within the limits that the principles of republicanism and separation of powers place on judicial review. Congress, then, would have the right to say that a fetus is "really" a person and to act to give it the equal protection that it is so often denied. Ultimately, Congress should do precisely that, for reasons that parallel closely Lincoln's admonition that the national government ought to maintain the principles of the Declaration—the principles of natural justice, of the natural law—and keep the country on the path to the elimination of slavery. The main difference is that, unlike Lincoln confronting the slavery issue, today we have a Fourteenth Amendment that can reasonably be invoked by Congress to prohibit abortion.

Conclusion

My own understanding, then, regarding judicial invocations of natural law as a basis for judicial decisions—one that would typically be regarded as a textualist original intent position, but which could perhaps be most accurately described as a "real meaning theory" of judicial review[94]—is that there is no legitimate ground for the invocation of natural law independent of the Constitution as a ground for judicial review. However, there is a legitimate role for natural law in the proper exercise of judicial review in the United States, if it is confined to serving as an aid to interpretation of the Constitution, insofar as the Constitution itself embodies a certain understanding of natural law. Even in the context of its use as an aid to interpretation, moreover, judicial review should still be exercised with legislative deference. The arena in which natural law might—and should—play a more extensive role is the broader area of interpretation of general constitutional guarantees by the legislature and executive, and action to pursue justice within the confines of the Constitution, in their legitimate lawmaking capacities.

Of course, there is an even broader arena where considerations of natural law inevitably play a central role—an arena highlighted by the *First*

Things symposium on "The End of Democracy?: The Judicial Usurpation of Politics." Ultimately, there must be some standard by which the justice and legitimacy not only of particular policies, but of the overall regime itself may be evaluated. This question requires a complex prudential judgment regarding the theoretical and actual distribution of power in a government, the appropriate role of popular consent, and the character of the nation's major public policies and social practices—all in the light of both universal principles of political morality, what is possible given the particular circumstances of a given people, and likely alternatives to the existing regime. In effect, everyone must make this kind of judgment, if only by default (simply accepting the legitimacy of the current regime). There is no escape from such judgments, and that is why overt discussions of natural law may wax and wane, but natural law itself will remain a permanent fixture of political life.

NOTES

1. See, for example, the analysis of a variety of contemporary liberal theorists in George, Robert, *Making Men Moral.* Oxford: Clarendon Press, 1993.

2. Ronald Dworkin provides an example of this turn in liberal theory, in his Tanner Lectures. See Wolfe, C., "The Egalitarian Liberalism of Ronald Dworkin," in *Liberalism at the Crossroads*, eds. Wolfe, C., and Hittinger, R. Rowman and Littlefield, 1994, and "Liberalism and Paternalism: A Critique of Ronald Dworkin," 56 *Review of Politics* 615 (Fall 1994).

3. See, for example, Maritain, Jacques, *Scholasticism and Politics.* New York: Macmillan, 1940; and *Man and the State.* Chicago: University of Chicago Press, 1951; and Simon, *The Philosophy of Democratic Government.* Chicago: University of Chicago Press, 1951.

4. See Finnis, John, *Natural Law and Natural Right.* Oxford: Clarendon, 1980; and Grisez, Germain, *The Way of the Lord Jesus.* Franciscan Herald Press: Vol. 1, 1983, Vol. 2, 1993. See also George, Robert, *Making Men Moral.*

5. See, for example, Hittinger, Russell, *A Critique of the New Natural Law Theory.* Notre Dame: University of Notre Dame, 1987; and McInerney, Ralph, *Aquinas on Human Action.* Washington, D.C.: Catholic University of America Press, 1992.

6. *First Things* (March 1992), pp. 16–20; (May 1992), pp. 45–54.

7. *First Things* (November 1996), pp. 18–42.

8. The word "regime," in this context, means the comprehensive, fundamental "constitution" (small "c") of a given people or nation. The word, given currency by students of Leo Strauss, following his perceptive study of classical political philosophy, emphasizes the integration of a nation's "form of government" and its "way of life," elements that modern political philosophy tends to separate.

9. It is true that Aristotle is not a natural *law* thinker. As Leo Strauss

argues, Aristotle falls in the category of natural right thought, and while these two categories overlap considerably, they are not identical. I do think, however, that the more one descends into discussions of political detail, the more Aquinas and Aristotle were likely to be in substantial agreement, taking into consideration the differences of the worlds in which they lived.

10. Another factor in the institutional underspecification of the simply best regime is that institutions, like law, are made on the basis of generalizations which do not always hold. That is one of the weaknesses of law, from the standpoint of perfect justice, though the generality of the law is a strength from the standpoint of approximating justice for the most part, in the best practicable regime.

11. See Raz, Joseph, "Liberty and Trust," in *Natural Law, Liberalism, and Morality*. Oxford University Press, 1996. Raz rightly acknowledges that the "doctrine of liberty" which "limits the power of legislatures and executives and increases the power of the courts" is "an aspect of doctrines of balance of power among different organs of government, [which] far from being universally valid . . . is a parochial doctrine valid for its time and place" (p. 117). On the other hand, his subsequent discussion of "the politics of constitutional rights" (as opposed to "normal politics") seems to lack a sufficient concern for the danger of policy-making by unelected and relatively unaccountable judges.

12. For example, Robert Dahl's famous article "Decision-Making in a Democracy: The Supreme Court as a National Policy-Maker," 6 *Journal of Public Law* 279 (1957). More recently, Gerald Rosenberg has raised questions about the power of courts in *The Hollow Hope: Can Courts Bring About Social Change*. Chicago: University of Chicago, 1991. My own examination of the pro's and con's of modern judicial power is contained in *Judicial Activism*. Lanham, Md.: Roman and Littlefield, 1997.

13. 3 Dallas 386 (1798).

14. 3 Dallas, 387–88.

15. But see Ely, John, *Democracy and Distrust*. Cambridge: Harvard University Press, 1980), pp. 210–11, n. 41, which gives a revisionist view of Chase's opinion. I think Ely is wrong to infer from a general comment that Chase thought the specific law at issue contrary to principles of natural justice. Iredell's response to Chase seems to me to make it clear that Chase was asserting a judicial power to enforce principles of natural justice, apart from their embodiment in the Constitution.

Another interesting recent publication, Matthew Franck's *Against the Imperial Judiciary*. University Press of Kansas, 1996, also denies that Chase's *Calder* opinion stands for natural justice judicial review. While I agree fully with many of the limitations that Franck notes, I think that his thesis is not borne out by the text that he himself cites. His attempts to explain away Chase's remark about "certain vital principles in our free republican governments" as a reference only to specific constitutional prohibitions (including substantive due process, in the case of a legislative transfer of property from A to B) is unpersuasive. And, perhaps more importantly, his efforts to explain away Iredell's comments as misunderstandings of Chase are unsuccessful.

While Franck's book offers many useful insights into the limited understanding of judicial power in the founding, I do not think it succeeds in proving that only Justice William Johnson (and he, only in *Fletcher v. Peck*) exercised natural justice judicial review. If natural justice judicial review was decidedly outside the mainstream of the founding, I think it still must be admitted that it was a temptation that was flirted with for a while.

16. 3 Dallas, 399.

17. All the Founders thought that the right to property was a fundamental natural right, for example, but they all recognized limits on that right—and much of the common law was taken up with defining in detail the scope and limits of property rights. And while it is true that common law was "judge-made" law, it is also true that common law, clearly by the time of the American founding, was subject to legislative control.

18. See *The Rise of Modern Judicial Review*. New York: Basic Books, 1985, pp. 108–13.

19. Grey's argument is contained in a 1977 paper delivered at the American Political Science Association annual meeting: "Judicial Review and the Unwritten Constitution: the Original Understanding." It is well discussed in Jacobsohn, Gary, "E.T.: The Extra-Textual in Constitutional Interpretation," 1 *Constitutional Commentary* 21 (1984).

20. During the period 1789–1829, there were six Supreme Court opinions invoking principles of natural justice, as opposed to sixteen that used the more ordinary form of judicial review. See *Rise of Modern Judicial Review*, p. 112 and accompanying notes.

21. Ibid.

22. 6 Cranch 87 (1810).

23. 4 Wheat. 518 (1819).

24. 96 U.S. 97 (1877).

25. 87 U.S. 655 (1874).

26. Corwin, Edward, *Liberty Against Government*. Baton Rouge: Louisiana State University Press, 1948, pp. 63–64.

27. See *How to Read the Constitution*. Rowman and Littlefield, 1996, ch. 2, for an extensive discussion of the original intention of the due process clause. And see also Carey, George, *In Defense of the Constitution*. Cumberland, Va.: James River Press, 1989, ch. 6.

28. 4 Wheat. 518 (1819).

29. 13 N.Y. 378 (1856); Corwin, Edward, *Liberty Against Government*, pp. 101–10.

30. 19 Howard 393, 450 (1857).

31. 165 U.S. 578 (1897) and 198 U.S. 45 (1905).

32. For a discussion of this era, see *The Rise of Modern Judicial Review*, ch. 6.

33. Cited in Mason, A.T., Beaney, W.M., and Stephenson, D.G., Jr., *American Constitutional Law*, 11th ed. Upper Saddle River, N.J.: Prentice Hall, 1996, p. 336.

34. See, for example, *Mr. Justice Holmes*, ed. Felix Frankfurter. New York: Coward, McCann, 1931.

35. The Founders were, of course, very interested in protecting property rights. The contract clause and the prohibition of states making anything other than gold or silver legal tender is testimony to this, as is the general discussion of *Federalist* No. 10, for example. But the Founders, I think, recognized that property rights were subject to reasonable regulation, as they were in the common law, and did not generally view the due process clause as a catchall guarantee of property rights.

36. *The Rise of Modern Judicial Review*, pp. 223–30.

37. The Court did not itself explicitly justify its activism in this way—that would have been politically unacceptable. But what justices on the Supreme Court were unwilling to say, many of the legal scholars from whom they took their bearing were only too willing to say: namely, that the Court was rightly departing from an inadequate original intent. A good example of this is the work of Alexander Bickel, who argued in *The Least Dangerous Branch*. Indianapolis: Bobbs-Merrill, 1962 that *Marbury v. Madison* was an inadequate foundation for judicial review. His treatment of the original intent of the Fourteenth Amendment, relative to school segregation, also displays a recognition of the modern Court's departure from original intent, while trying to downplay that departure. See Berger, Raoul, *Government by Judiciary*. Cambridge, Mass.: Harvard University Press, 1977, ch. 6.

On the idea that the modern Court was employing its own version of natural law, see Hittinger, Russell, "Liberalism and the American Natural Law Tradition" 25 *Wake Forest Law Review* 429 (1990).

38. McCloskey, Robert, *The American Supreme Court*. Chicago: University of Chicago Press, 1960, ch. 5 and 6.

39. 28 L.Ed. 232 (1884), at 237.

40. 53 L.Ed. 109 (1908).

41. 287 U.S. 45 (1930), at 68.

42. 302 U.S. 325 (1937).

43. 302 U.S., 326.

44. 332 U.S. 46 (1947).

45. 342 U.S. 165 (1952).

46. 332 U.S., 69.

47. 332 U.S., 75.

48. 332 U.S., 90.

49. 332 U.S., 91–92.

50. 332 U.S., 65.

51. 332 U.S., 67.

52. 332 U.S., 68.

53. See his "Natural Law" in his *Collected Legal Papers*. New York: Harcourt Brace and Howe, 1920.

54. 163 U.S. 537 (1896).

55. Senate Judiciary Committee Confirmation Hearings on the Nomination of Clarence Thomas as Associate Justice of the Supreme Court of the United States, Part 1, p. 276–77.

56. Ibid., p. 277.

57. "Liberalism and the American Natural Law Tradition," 25 *Wake Forest Law Review* 429 (1990).

58. Ibid.

59. 381 U.S. 479. I say "pure" substantive due process, in the sense of its being used independently of the Bill of Rights. (The application of the First Amendment to the states, which was never called into question in the 1937 rejection of *economic* due process, assumes that the Fourteenth Amendment due process clause has a substantive dimension, insofar as it concerns First Amendment substantive concerns like speech and religion.) While Justice Douglas' opinion nominally relies on the Bill of Rights' penumbras, I think that a more intellectually honest statement of what the Court is doing can be found in Justice Harlan's concurrence, relying on his discussion of substantive due process earlier in *Poe v. Ullman*, 367 U.S. 497 (1961).

60. 405 U.S. 438 (1972).

61. 410 U.S. 113 (1973).

62. 476 U.S. 186 (1986).

63. 120 L.Ed.2d 698 (1992).

64. Hittinger, 25 *Wake Forest Law Review* 488.

65. The emphasis on moral realism differs not, of course, from Hittinger himself, who is a moral realist, but rather from the form of natural law (more loosely defined) embedded in contemporary constitutional law, as Hittinger describes it.

66. Moore, "Do We Have An Unwritten Constitution?" 63 *Southern California Law Review* 107 (1989), at 134, 135.

67. Moore, p. 135.

68. Ibid., p. 136.

69. He cites Stanley Brubaker as an example. I would fall in the same category, and we would both reject the label of skeptic.

70. Moore, p. 137.

71. *The Federalist Papers,* ed. Will. New York: Bantam, 1982, pp. 398–99.

72. Moore, p. 136.

73. Moore, p. 137.

74. I hedge my comments here with the qualifications "arguably" and "might" because, while I have not completely thought through the question of what might be called "political" rather than "judicial" constitutional interpretation, I suspect that even in the nonjudicial context I might find some of Moore's arguments too latitudinarian.

75. *Federalist,* No. 78, p. 394. For a discussion of legislative deference as a principle of moderate judicial review, see *The Rise of Modern Judicial Review*, chapter 4.

76. Bork, Robert H., "Natural Law and the Constitution," *First Things* (March 1992), pp. 16–20; Symposium "Natural Law and the Law: An Exchange," *First Things* (May 1992), with essays by Hadley Arkes (pp. 45–48), Russell Hittinger (pp. 48–50), William Bentley Ball (pp. 50–51), and a response by Bork (pp. 51–54). Subsequent citations will be by author's last name, page, and column (a or b).

77. Arkes, p. 46a.

78. Just to be clear, I should specify that "natural law-based judicial review" here means judicial review based on natural law *independent of the Constitution.*

79. Bork response, p. 52b.

80. Bork response, p. 53a.

81. Hittinger, "Natural Law in the Positive Laws: A Legislative or Adjudicative Issue?" 55 *Review of Politics* 5 (1993), at 29.

82. Bork response, p. 52b.

83. Bork response, p. 52b.

84. Bork response, p. 52b.

85. Bork, p. 17a. Hittinger makes the same point as Arkes, in his later *Review of Politics* article. After citing a remark of Bork's that seems to embrace emotivism, he notes: "If the argument from emotivism is taken seriously, the arguments which avail to that end undermine the moral basis for imposing the judicial discipline championed by Judge Bork himself. Surely, the basis for judicial discipline consists in something more than the rules of art imposed by a written text. If there is a good reason for imposing limits on the kind of moral argument available to the judge, that reason will be drawn from specifically moral considerations. . . ." "Natural Law in the Positive Laws," p. 29.

86. Hittinger, R., 25 *Wake Forest Law Review* 495. Note, however, that Hittinger begins the paragraph with the statement that, with Bork and others, "[w]e can jettison natural law as an *interpretive* device" (at 494, emphasis added).

Later in the same article, Hittinger also says that one test of any use of natural law is that "claims must be measured against the written Constitution [and if] they explicitly contradict the Constitution . . . then natural law is not being used to interpret, but rather to reconstruct the Constitution" (at 498). But this could hardly reassure Bork, since Hittinger goes on to suggest that Douglas' and Goldberg's reasoning in *Griswold* would pass this test! (This seems to imply that for Hittinger—at the time of this article—reading content into a very general constitutional phrase like "due process" would not constitute "explicitly contradicting" the Constitution.)

87. By classical natural law, I mean particularly the forms that are traceable to Thomas Aquinas and, further back, to Aristotle. I deliberately want to prescind at this time from contemporary debates between adherents of Aristotelian natural right, neoscholastic Thomistic natural law, and the new natural law theory of Germain Grisez, John Finnis, and Robert George. While there are some serious differences among these forms of natural law, and I do not want to deny their significance, I think that they have a great deal in common with each other, especially with respect to the task of providing the foundations of an American public philosophy.

88. Soterios Barber makes similar charges in his *On What the Constitution Means*. Johns Hopkins University Press, 1984; and *The Constitution of Judicial Power*. Johns Hopkins University Press, 1993, especially ch. 1.

89. *Summa Theologica*, I–II, Q. 94, Art. 4 resp.

90. 109 U.S. 3 (1883).

91. 4 Wheaton 518, 645.

92. Marshall, in *Cohens v. Virginia,* 6 Wheaton 264, 387 (1821).

93. See, for example, Olasky, M., *Abortion Rites*. Wheaton, Ill.: Crossways Books, 1992.

94. See my *The Rise of Modern Judicial Review*, revised ed. Rowman and Littlefield, 1994, Afterword.

PART FOUR

Natural Law and the Economy

Property, the Common Law, and John Locke

James R. Stoner, Jr.

It is no accident that property is—in America today, at any rate—the last thing one considers when reflecting on natural law. Part of the reason this is so is inherent in the subject. Natural law is concerned with universal principles and common good, but property is particular and private—indeed, it is the very idea of claiming something as one's own. Moreover, natural law is concerned with the timeless, with what belongs to man as man, but property is notoriously changeable, varying from society to society and from age to age. In Justinian, natural law is contrasted to civil law, the latter being the law of *meum et tuum*, of mine and yours, of property. When a philosopher like Plato wanted to describe the city most in accord with human nature, he thought it necessary to abolish property, at least among the better natures, and to confine it to the lesser classes and the flawed regimes.

Part of the reason is historical. In America, as Tocqueville noted, every significant political question tends to become a judicial question. Natural law and property were the subject of a great constitutional dispute earlier in this century that ended by discrediting them both, at least in the eyes of most constitutional commentators, for the battle against the growth of the regulatory state was waged in court in the name of natural law. When natural law has surfaced in American debates in the present generation, it has usually been on one or the other side in the so-called culture wars, where questions of property have been, if not entirely absent, at least ordinarily remote.

Times have changed since the "Constitutional Revolution" of 1937, of course. The economics then ascendant has suffered some embarrassment, and economic policies that restore a measure of laissez-faire have developed alongside the welfare state. The Supreme Court, which in 1937 renounced its scrutiny of economic legislation and its protection of economic rights, quickly found another arena for its enterprise, in subsuming under its wings various personal rights claimed against both the federal government and the states.

Without fully heeding the calls of those who advocate judicial enforcement of property rights, the Court has begun to show signs of reversing, if not the decisions of 1937 and its aftermath, at least some of the subsequent trends thought to rely on these, especially when the respective spheres of federal and state power are at issue.[1] Still, except for a few voices, conservatives especially have been reluctant to appeal to anything like natural law in developing a sober jurisprudence or, for that matter, a legislative program.[2] In short, property rights are a respectable subject of legal and political discussion again, but any account of them that makes much ado about natural law is bound to be viewed with circumspection.

In this essay, I argue that the American understanding of property, at least until the New Deal, was informed by a mixture of two distinct sources: the common law on one hand and liberal capitalism on the other. In turn, these two sources were indebted to two separate traditions of natural law: one exemplified by St. Thomas Aquinas, the other by John Locke.

The New Deal's reorientation of American thinking about property (though only partially effected in practice) came about in part because an imbalance had developed between the two historic traditions. It was thought that the dynamic set in motion by Lockean capitalism made return to earlier forms impossible. Today the pendulum has begun to swing back to embrace property rights partially on the Lockean model, even while the country holds tight to the welfare state, or at least to its entitlements. Attention is due to both traditions and to the need for a renewed understanding between them if we are to recover a robust sense of the complementary character of personal ownership and common good.

St. Thomas and St. German

Property According to St. Thomas

To say that property appears in the *Summa Theologica* only as an afterthought would be misleading, but in St. Thomas's account of natural law, it does not exactly have pride of place. In the celebrated Question 94 article two, where the basic precepts of natural law are sketched, property appears only by implication: "[W]hatever is a means of preserving human life and of warding off its obstacles belongs to the natural law."[3] In the fourth article, theft is condemned as "expressly contrary to the natural law," albeit in the context of explaining how, by the perversion of reason, some societies actually allowed it.

Finally in the fifth article, on whether natural law can be changed, the question of private possession is raised directly in an objection based on an authority who wrote that "the possession of all things in common and universal freedom are matters of natural law." St. Thomas replies that these things are as natural as nakedness is, but that does not mean that clothes are unnecessary. He explains: "[T]he distinction of possessions and slavery were not brought in by nature but devised by human reason for the benefit of human life." Property and slavery apparently belong not to natural law's "most general precepts that are known to all," but to "certain secondary and more detailed precepts which are, as it were, conclusions following closely from first principles."[4]

In St. Thomas' studied ambivalence or indirectness concerning property, one sees, perhaps, a reflection of Aristotle's complex account of money and moneymaking, which he treats as at once necessary and yet in a sense unnatural. Nonetheless, in contrast to what his medieval disciple would teach, Aristotle was unambiguous in his support for private possessions, most especially in his critique of the Platonic scheme, and of course he taught that some people are by nature slaves.[5]

St. Thomas's more thematic account of property occurs in his discussion of the virtue of justice, first in his discussion of right (*S.T.*, II–II, Quest. 57) and then in his discussion of theft (*S.T.*, II–II, Quest. 66). In the first passage, after establishing right as the object of justice, he distinguishes natural right from positive right and then natural right from the right of nations. Positive right depends upon agreement, either by the whole community or in the prince's decree. While positive right cannot override natural right, it is often needed, apparently because of man's changeable—that is to say, imperfect or corrupt—nature. The distinction between natural and positive right, of course, recalls the distinction between natural and human law.

Natural Right and Right of Nations The distinction between natural right and the right of nations is more subtle. Here St. Thomas writes that natural right involves what is commensurate with another person, and that this commensurability takes two forms: (1) absolute and (2) "according to something resultant from it." His examples of the first form are the commensurability of male and female in procreation and of parent and child in the matter of nourishment. The example of the second form is "the possession of property":

> For if a particular piece of land be considered absolutely, it contains no reason why it should belong to one man more than to another, but if it be considered in respect of its adaptability to cultivation, and the unmolested use of the land,

> it has a certain commensuration to be the property of one and not of another man, as the Philosopher shows (Polit. ii. 2). . . . [T]o consider a thing by comparing it with what results from it, is proper to reason, wherefore the same is natural to man in respect of natural reason which dictates it. Hence the jurist Gaius says (Digest 9): Whatever natural reason decrees among all men, is observed by all equally, and is called the right of nations.[6]

The right of nations (*jus gentium*) thus appears not as the opposite of natural right, but as one of its forms, and property seems rather to belong to it than to natural right, strictly speaking.

Private Property Curiously, it is in the discussion of theft that St. Thomas finally raises the questions, "Whether it is natural for man to possess external things?" and "Whether it is lawful for a man to possess a thing as his own?" He answers the first of these queries with a distinction: only God can possess the nature of things, as they obey His will, but "as regards their use, . . . man has a natural dominion over external things, because, by his reason and will, he is able to use them for his profit, as they were made on his account." He cites for this last point both Aristotle's *Politics* and *Genesis 1*.

The second query is also answered in the affirmative, and again with a distinction between power and use, but now to different effect. Human capacity "to procure and dispense [exterior things] . . . [means] it is lawful for man to possess property." There are three reasons this is so, all silently drawn from Aristotle's critique of the Republic: (1) Man is "more careful to procure what is for himself alone"; (2) "human affairs are conducted in more orderly fashion if each man is charged with taking care of some particular thing himself"; and (3) "a more peaceful state is ensured to man if each one is contented with his own."

But if ownership in the sense of the power to procure and dispense is to be private, use is to remain common, at least so far as to make a man ready to share with those in need, primarily himself and those in his care:

> Because each one must first of all look after himself and then after those over whom he has charge, and afterwards with what remains relieve the needs of others. Thus nature first, by its nutritive power, takes what it requires for the upkeep of one's own body, and afterwards yields the residue for the formation of another by the power of generation.[7]

In short, St. Thomas endorses the right of private property as an element of natural law only in a qualified way. It belongs to the secondary precepts of natural law, known as the *jus gentium*, which are not based immediately upon natural human inclinations but upon reflection on human experience, and which are devised for human benefit. Property is a right, in the language of one modern commentator, only to the private "administration" of things, not necessarily to their private "enjoyment," since private ownership is limited by the duty of sharing with the needy.[8] Not to all those in need, St. Thomas would insist, but to those in need closest to the giver, primarily himself.

Commerce and Usury In his brief consideration of commerce, in the questions under the general heading of justice concerned with cheating and usury (*S.T.*, II–II, QQ. 77–78), St. Thomas makes clear his adherence to the doctrine of the just price and his loyalty to the classical condemnation of usury. He cites in a critical passage both the *Politics* and the *Ethics* for the proposition that money was invented for the sake of exchange and so was meant for "consumption or alienation," not for "use" or hire, leaving usury "by its very nature unlawful."

Money remains in a sense unnatural for St. Thomas, as it was for Aristotle. The conclusions of human experience from which the rights of property derive are not, to his mind, like the findings of modern social science, subject to continuous amendment and likely to be reversed with each passing generation. Human laws can indeed be changed as human reason advances, according to St. Thomas. He does not say the same even for the secondary precepts of the natural law, however easily the latter "can be blotted out from the human heart either by evil persuasions . . . or by vicious customs and corrupt habits."[9] Above all, it should be remembered that for Thomas, as in a way even for Aristotle, the first source of all good things is nature or providence, even though the human contribution is acknowledged.

The question of property is thus a question of the distribution or exchange of goods that one finds ready to hand. In sum, St. Thomas views property not so much as a natural right, but as an essential right regulated by custom and legislation for the accomplishment of the requirements of natural law. It exists primarily to support one's own individual moral flourishing, for those in one's charge, and to give to others in need from one's superabundance or residue.

Property According to St. German

The Thomistic influence on American law begins not during the New Deal, but rather back in England, with the attempt to reconcile Thomistic natural law with common law, the most notable instance being the *Doctor and Student* dialogues of Christopher St. German.[10] Writing in the 1520s and 1530s, defending the common law through a consideration of the role of conscience and of equity in English jurisprudence, St. German produced a work that retained its authority well into the next century and beyond. It was cited with approval not only by Sir Edward Coke, the preceptor of early American lawyers, but also in the midnineteenth century by the dean of American common law in the early republic, James Kent.

St. German's work is a dialogue between a Doctor of Divinity and a Student of the laws of England, each querying the other on the matter of his own expertise in order to settle the question of conscience in relation to the common law. The Doctor responds first, laying out the forms of law in a manner that corresponds almost perfectly to St. Thomas's treatment: the law eternal, the law of nature (or law of reason), the law of God, and the law of man.[11] The account of these follows closely the reasoning in the *Summa*, except perhaps in an extended discussion of the relation of the temporal and spiritual power of the Church in relation to the law of God. (St. German was a lawyer who remained on good terms with King Henry VIII, though the first dialogue, referred to here, appeared in 1523, before the break with Rome.)

The Law of Reason The Doctor speaks of natural law as "the law of reason" in deference to the Student, since those "that be learned in the law of England" call it by this name. The Student then takes his turn relating the grounds of the laws of England, of which he finds six: the law of reason, the law of God, the "divers general customs of old time used through all the realm," principles or maxims "which have always been taken for law in this realm," particular customs of particular jurisdictions, and statutes made by the king, lords, and commons in Parliament.

The Student takes care to show the inner consistency of these grounds, announcing, for instance, that any general customs or statutes "directly against the law of God . . . were void" (although the example he gives characteristically saves a statute that seems to violate divine law but can be shown to observe its intent). He explains that statutes are made "in such cases where the law of reason, the law of God, customs, maxims, nor other grounds of the law of England seemed not to be sufficient to punish evil men and to reward good men."[12]

For our purposes, what is most striking about the Student's presentation is his treatment of the law of reason. This includes "the law of reason primary," which forbids murder, perjury, deceit, breaking of the peace, and the like, and "the law of reason secondary," which is in turn divided into two parts, the law of reason secondary general and the law of reason secondary particular, both of which are concerned with property. The law of reason secondary general

> is called the law or general custom of property because it is diffused throughout the whole world. . . . And this is called the law of secondary reason because it is founded not only upon reason, but also upon the aforesaid law or custom of property. For when the law of property says that a certain thing is the property of a certain man, then reason founded upon that law says that therefore that thing is not to be taken from him unjustly and without his will.[13]

This seems to correspond to St. Thomas's *jus gentium*, although St. German does not use the term. The law of reason secondary particular, by contrast, "is that law that is derived upon divers customs general and particular and of divers maxims and statutes ordained and held in this realm." The "secondary general" prohibits disseisin, trespass, theft, and the like, while the "secondary particular" articulates the consequences that derive from the customs and maxims of the common law and the statutes of the realm, consequences developed by judicial reason as it seeks to apply those customs, maxims, and statutes in the context of particular cases, so that "there is no need to have a written law on the point."[14]

Genius of the Common Law The six grounds of English law are interwoven, not hierarchical in all respects. The law of God and the law of reason can override a contrary custom or statute, and of course a statute can revise a custom. The basic genius of common law as St. German presents it is for reason to work upon not only its own first principles, but the whole array of divine commands, customs, maxims, and statutes to keep them all consistent with each other and to settle particular questions or controversies in accord with their logic.

Even the basic crimes forbidden by the law of reason primary and the law of reason secondary general depend for their "manner of punishing" upon the maxims and statutes of the realm.[15] Customs and conventions, therefore, combine with reason to determine one's rights in property, whereas pure reason (i.e., the law of reason primary) would determine one's rights in one's person or life.

Comparison of Summa *and* Dialogues

Does the account of English law given by St. German's student accord with the basic account of law in St. Thomas? The Doctor of Divinity seems to think so, for he even shores up the Student's confidence in the common law in an instance or two when the latter thinks its rules would go against conscience.[16] The key here is in St. Thomas's account of human law in his account of the law of nature.

Human law is derived from natural law, St. Thomas writes, but in two ways: first by way of drawing conclusions as from premises (here human law seems merely an extension of the secondary law of nature) and second by determining in one way or another matters left open by natural law.

Discretion and Statutory Law That St. Thomas means to leave room for human discretion is evident. It follows (1) from his discussion of the role of human law in training men away from evil and toward virtue; (2) from his constant reference to the common good in relation to law, which is naturally the good of a particular community, with "each man, in all that he is and has, belong[ing] to the community"; (3) from his reflections on the limited power of human law, which allows that human law can suppress "only the most grievous vices from which it is possible for the majority to abstain and chiefly those that are to the hurt of others," indeed going so far as to note that, while unjust laws do not bind in conscience, an exception is "perhaps in order to avoid scandal or disturbance, for which cause a man should yield even his right"; and (4) from his allowance, nay, endorsement of custom as valid law, as it declares "the inward movement of the will and concepts of reason," and among a people "free and able to make their own laws, the consent of the whole people expressed by custom counts far more in favor of a particular observance than the authority of the ruler, who has not the power to frame laws except as representing the people."[17]

Read by itself, St. Thomas's account of natural law seems to empower one who would, by legislation, reshape the world. Read in the context of the account of human law with which it is linked, it seems rather to show how basically just regimes can be shored up by finding the reason within their customs and laws, permitting resistance only in cases of extreme injustice.

Controlled Custom of the Courts This said, there does seem to be something specific about the scheme of human law in England as it appears in St. German, specific perhaps to the common law itself. In the first place, the emphasis is on judicial reason rather than legislative choice, evident throughout St. German's dialogue and even more dramatically in the works of such oracles of the common law as Coke. Statutes are not the paradigm of law here, as they are for us today and seem to be for St. Thomas; that role belongs to custom, especially the carefully controlled custom of the courts that goes by the name of precedent. For St. German and for Coke, statutes arise either to declare common law or to remedy specific mischiefs that have developed, and Parliament itself is styled a court, "high and most honourable."

In the second place, and in harmony with the priority of custom, distributive justice loses the sense of a political distribution of a society's goods that it retains in St. Thomas, from its roots in the political philosophy of the ancient polis. The origin of property—not of its rights per se, but its initial assignment to this or that individual—is lost in the mists of the immemorial to the classic common lawyer, like the origin of custom itself. When Coke discusses distributive justice, for example, he refers not to a fresh distribution of social goods but to the whole common law concerning tenures and descents. Here providence appears not only in its aspect as nature, but as having singled out individuals for its favors. Common use, meanwhile, is confined to certain circumscribed moments in the law, as the right to gather wood or hunt unreserved game, the right to graze the unenclosed common, or the duty to pay tithes.

That an emphasis on judging and on inherited right is the sort of determination permitted to human law by St. Thomas's scheme seems clear enough, provided the door be left open, as by statute it is, to legal change. But it does give common law a specific flavor that differs from the civil law tradition to which St. Thomas's writings, perhaps by historical accident rather than theological necessity, seem more especially linked.

Locke and the Original New Property

It was the genius of John Locke to introduce a new understanding of property and a new account of natural law in a way that seemed only slightly to shift emphasis in the traditional understanding, or at least seemed to resemble it sufficiently to assuage those who wanted to believe in its continuity. Locke's art is subtle enough to confuse contemporary commentators who, acquainted with the less abashed modernity descended from him and unfamiliar with the forebears he quietly abandoned, think his doctrine of property essentially the same as St. Thomas's.[18]

This view has the advantage of focusing attention on what Locke says about the public good, indeed on all those elements of his language which he derives from the natural law tradition, but it is important to concentrate as well on the differences, lest erudition blind common sense. First, in contrast to St. Thomas and the Aristotelian tradition, Locke distinguishes the grounds of slavery and property, treating slavery as against nature, except in punishment, and property as unmistakably natural; his redefinition of the end of government follows from this change. Second, Locke understands property to consist less in the distribution of what humans are given than in its creation from their labor and ingenuity. What for Aristotle and Aquinas was a concession to the intractable preference for self is to Locke the key to unlocking human potential.

Goods Reserved for Common Use

Locke's tactic of making concession to tradition even while developing a novel idea is exemplified by a passage in his *First Treatise* that is often cited to establish the traditional character of his ideas on property. Toward the end of the chapter on Filmer's claim that sovereignty originates in God's grant of dominion to Adam, in the context of an extended argument distinguishing private dominion or property from political rule, Locke admits that God has given one's "needy Brother a Right to the surplusage of his Goods; so that it cannot justly be denyed him, when his pressing Wants call for it," referring to this claim as a title given by charity.

This seems to be a reiteration of St. Thomas's requirement that goods be reserved for common use, even if assigned to private administrators. What is important to recall, however, is the context of Locke's passage. It does not seek to limit the right of property per se but to insist on the strict separation of the claim to own and the claim to rule, a separation that Locke intends rather to limit government than to disenfranchise property.

Indeed, in the next paragraph, he allows the "rich proprietor" to extract a contract of obedience from the needy in exchange for food, insisting only that the relationship should result from consent and not be seized as a matter of right, making clear that the title to charity might be pleaded, but might not be enforced.[19] Moreover, as has recently been argued, the claim to charity can be raised only by those without capacity to labor[20]—but to see this we must proceed to the *Second Treatise*, where Locke develops his theory of property and government in a positive rather than a critical frame.

State of Nature

Locke begins his *Second Treatise* with a definition of political power, which he develops by elaborating what he calls, like Thomas Hobbes, the state of nature. This "state of perfect freedom" and "also of equality" is a condition of people living together without government, that is, without a common judge. However, it is not a state of license, Locke insists, because they are under the law of nature: "And Reason, which is that Law, teaches all Mankind, who will but consult it, that being all equal and independent, no one ought to harm another in his Life, Health, Liberty, or Possessions."

Reason arrives at this conclusion by reflecting that human beings are "his Property, whose Workmanship they are," namely, that of "one Omnipotent, and infinitely wise Maker," and this yields each of them the duty "to preserve himself" and "as much as he can, to preserve the rest of Mankind," at least so far as "his own Preservation comes not in competition."[21] Except perhaps by the doubts that might be raised at the prospect of competition for survival, this beginning seems traditional enough. St. Thomas, after all, had followed the classical tradition in listing self-preservation as the first precept of natural law. Locke, however, does not proceed to the other precepts, and only occasionally does another ever appear in the *Second Treatise.*[22]

Instead, he introduces what he calls his "very strange Doctrine" that every man in the state of nature has the executive power of the law of nature. Although this makes each the judge of his own cause, where one is apt to prefer oneself, Lockean reason does not conclude that nature appoints people to live under a common judge or government. He quotes Richard Hooker, the Anglican Aquinas, for the traditional view that "to supply those Defects and Imperfections which are in us, as living singly and solely by our selves, we are naturally induced to seek Communion and Fellowship with others, this was the Cause of Mens uniting themselves, at first in Politick Societies," as if to highlight his departure. "But I moreover affirm, that all Men are naturally in that State [of nature], and remain so, till by their own Consents they make themselves Members of some Politick Society."[23]

Slavery

Six chapters or 108 sections ensue before Locke's men are ready to consent to "Politick Society." Although much of the intervening text has to do with the historical origins of government and with the family, Locke first considers, following Aristotle's order if not his theory, slavery and property. Aristotle distinguished the mastery of slaves from political rule, but the union of the naturally ruling and naturally ruled elements in slavery was indicative of the natural character of the household and so of the city.

As for Locke there is nothing natural about government, so slavery in the state of nature is narrowly confined. Captives in a just war may be enslaved by a victor who forebears killing them, but no one has a right to sell oneself into slavery. Locke repeats, now with some indirection and without mention of the Deity, that a man "cannot take away his own Life." Then, further undermining slavery and seeming to contradict the reason he just relied upon, Locke explains of the slave, without condemnation, that, "whenever he finds the hardship of his Slavery out-weigh the value of his Life, 'tis in his Power, by resisting the Will of his Master, to draw on himself the Death he desires."[24]

Property

Locke's account of property and its acquisition likewise departs from Aristotle's discussion of the art of household management and of acquisition as an ancillary art limited by need and use. Indeed, chapter five of the *Second Treatise*, "Of PROPERTY," is one of the most celebrated passages in the history of political theory.

The first thing to notice is that Locke treats property strictly in the context of the state of nature, that quasihistorical, quasitheoretical condition in which human beings are considered as free and equal individuals, subject only to natural law, living and judging for themselves alone. Now and again he "slips" and speaks as though property belongs to a family, but strictly speaking, the family is not introduced until the following chapter or two. Here Nature is "Mother," and what she offers belongs "equally to all her Children." Locke does begin with an acknowledgment that "God . . . hath given the World to Men in common," but He is quietly retired, for reasons we shall soon see, and the "spontaneous hand of Nature" takes His place.

The question with which Locke begins is how, out of this common world, "Men might come to have a property in several parts of that which God gave to mankind in common, and that without any express Compact of the Commoners." His answer is by his labor, which he wholly owns, since "every Man has a Property in his own Person."

The first indication of God's departure from the argument is Locke's silence on the question of how man can have property in something that he attributed a few chapters before to be God's property, namely, himself. James Tully suggested that this is unproblematic since a person's property in himself means only to exclude others and so can coincide with divine proprietorship.[25] This explanation is unsatisfactory, not only because Locke makes no such assertion, but also because it avoids the question of whether

God, who gave men the world in common, gave each sole ownership of himself, rather than, say, giving each to one another's care.

In any event, "the first gathering" is enough by way of labor to give each individual property in what he takes from the common, for it is enough to "exclude[] the common right of other Men." The only qualification is that this right to property in things taken from the common holds "at least where there is enough, and as good left in common for others," but soon Locke finds a way to neutralize even that.

Tully's assertion that "the fundamental argument of the *Two treatises*" is "that God gave the world to man as common property,"[26] is true only in the sense that most buildings have their foundation in the ground. You need the ground to build, but the ground does not determine the kind of structure, at least if the architect is clever. The burden of Locke's theory of property is to show how the common is parceled out, and its secret is that God in His wisdom did not give us very much of it.[27]

Now, the key to Locke's argument is understanding why the requirement that "enough and as good" remain is no serious obstacle to privatization. That the argument holds with air, at least outdoors in the absence of smoke, and usually with water, particularly when not in the midst of the desert or a drought or other scarcity, is self-evident and unproblematic; there is always plenty more. But land and its fruits seem otherwise and are often scarce enough to make Locke's case far less than universal in its application. Moreover, Locke adds that "Nothing was made by God for Man to spoil or destroy," suggesting a traditional limit on just acquisition, if also suggesting natural scarcity, against the presumption of "enough and as good." Then, with characteristic indirection, Locke writes, as if digressing: "To which let me add, that he who appropriates land to himself by his labour, does not lessen but increase the common stock of mankind." It is an elegant argument he makes: if cultivated land is ten times more productive than prairie, heath, or forest, to cultivate ten acres is to produce the natural yield of one hundred, so one "may truly be said, to give ninety acres to Mankind." Within the paragraph the ratio of productivity has grown to one against one hundred, and within a few pages it is one against a thousand. In the early days of economic development, as we would say, there was thus always "enough and as good," since enclosure was the seed of plenty. In more crowded modern times, land may not be so plentiful in the settled areas, but America is wide open, and Locke has even heard of land for the taking in Spain. Besides, he suggests, in a developed, or rather, continually developing economy, there are numerous profitable uses for human labor, even if land grows scarce. As he writes in one of his most celebrated sentences, contrasting the relative achievements of nature and human industry in providing human needs and wants, "a King of a large and fruitful Territory [in America] feeds, lodges, and is clad worse than a day Labourer in England."[28]

Money

What makes possible such development, of course, is the invention of money—that is, of a durable good that has its value from "the tacit Agreement of Men." Here, rather than in appropriation from the common, is the locus of consent in economic matters. It has the happy consequence not only of facilitating the complex exchanges upon which an industrious society depends, but also of solving the problem of spoilage, since durable money never rots. Introduced by consent, money is itself the product of labor and can be amassed without prejudice to anyone, according to Locke: "the exceeding of the bounds of his just Property not lying in the largeness of his Possession, but the perishing of any thing uselesly in it."[29]

While for St. Thomas and Aristotle, the essence of money was its usefulness in exchange, for Locke it is its durability. Locke does not call this "capital" yet, but he has clearly grasped its idea. One is not surprised to learn that, in his papers on interest, a sophisticated economics that anticipates the work of Adam Smith is in evidence.[30] Originating in tacit agreement, money, like real property, antedates government, even as it shares its basis in consent. Property, then, has a human origin, in labor or consent or some admixture of the two, but both issue naturally from the human personality prior to any authoritative structure of command.

Government and Law

Now Locke makes clear that, once governments are formed, property takes on a positive rather than a simply natural status. In his terms, individuals and nations "have, by positive agreement, settled a Property among themselves, in distinct Parts and parcels of the Earth." While the tacit agreement on valuing money insures "an inequality of private possessions" even without a fully formed civil society, "in Government the Laws regulate the right of property, and the possession of land is by positive constitutions." But natural law is not simply retired once government is formed, according to Locke. After all, it is the insecurity of property in the state of nature that helps give man the impetus to establish government in the first place. The end of government, Locke repeats again and again, is the preservation of property, understood to encompass life, liberty, and estate. If property has its origin in man's natural labor, it gains security in society when defined by "settled, standing rules" made by the legislature, rules that cannot be altered by absolute and arbitrary power.

That Locke is serious about the protection of property as the end of government becomes clear when he makes its violation a license for revolt. Private property is the common good of the new republicanism, not just for the pleasures it offers but also for the protection of liberty it affords.[31] The paradox apparent in this standard reflects the great discovery, or great hope, upon which the modern science of political economy was also based, namely, that by pursuing one's individual interest, a person might best contribute to the common wealth. In Locke this intimation does not take on the character of natural necessity, but it does reinforce natural law. Although the city does not exist by nature, the natural pursuit of one's own preservation and development, when channeled in the matrix of industry and rationality that is civil society, tends to raise the lot of all.

Common Law and Locke in American Constitutionalism

"In the beginning all the World was America, and more so than that is now," Locke wrote. It is hard for the commentator to resist spinning this sentence around into something of which Locke could only dream, that in America the Lockean world would have a fresh beginning. Still, not only good taste but the interests of accuracy compel us to resist this conclusion. In spite of Locke's influence on the Declaration of Independence and perhaps more generally on the thinking of the Revolution, American constitutionalism departs significantly from the Lockean mode, not least in the matters under consideration here.

In the first place, Locke's scheme for the separation of powers distinguished only the legislature and the executive, with the judiciary considered a mere branch of the latter. The American system has a coequal judiciary empowered to void legislative and executive acts in violation of a written Constitution. It eschews both the legislative supremacy and the executive prerogative Locke teaches, and it supposes that law has authority, or at least takes a form that transcends mere "settled, standing rules."[32]

In the second place, the law of property in America was not, at the time of the Revolution, entirely reconstituted on Lockean principles. Rather, each of the colonies-become-states declared the continuity of its common law foundation, excepting out only such elements of that law as were inconsistent with its circumstances or amended by its legislation. To be sure, the Revolution brought legislative changes in common law property. It typically abolished the rule of primogeniture in inheritance and any remaining feudal duties attached to estates, a move at once republican and Lockean. But these had been the exception rather than the rule already in America and had never been established, for instance, in New England.[33] In the Constitution of 1787 and the Bill of Rights that quickly followed, the American people included the right of property and the obligation of contract. It occurred in a context established as much by common law privileges and immunities as by Locke's theory of the state of nature and of property created by labor on a barren common. That property could be called, in the era of the Revolution, the "guardian of every other right" betrayed an attitude that Locke and the common law perfectly shared.[34]

Common Law Structure

Indeed, it was the genius of American constitutionalism on its original understanding to assimilate liberal reforms into a legal system that retained its common law structure. This was possible because the two worlds of thought shared a commitment to natural law—that is, to reason, however variously understood. The common law of property, in its American versions, proved supple enough to incorporate new principles into its ancient array without surrender to a regime of legislative omnipotence. There is no denying that the influence of Locke and his successors on the reforms was substantial.

As the country grew to the West, Locke's theory of economic development seemed especially apposite. Fresh settlement allowed as well for the carrying along of common law, without forcing the issue between the two approaches. This might have been unavoidable in an older land, where ancient use and modern projects were more apt to steadily conflict. The adjustment of common law doctrines in the direction of modern development was largely the business of state courts in the early nineteenth century. Now and again the issue came to the fore in federal constitutional law, most notably in the case of *Charles River Bridge v. Warren Bridge* in 1837. In this case, a majority of the Supreme Court joined Chief Justice Taney in supporting a newly enfranchised corporation and the legislative power that created it against an established corporation claiming an exclusive charter right. In the early republic most of the federal constitutional cases involving property rights that came to the Court arose under the Contract Clause. This was to be expected, as it was the only one of the chief property clauses that then applied to the states.[35]

Due Process Clause

The Fourteenth Amendment vastly expanded federal judicial competency by including a Due Process Clause protecting property against state infringement. How liberally the new amendment would be read by the Court was a question raised almost immediately in *The Slaughter-House Cases*. The majority settled on a cautious, restricted approach that would limit federal interference with state law under the Fourteenth Amendment to cases involving discrimination on account of race. But strong dissents in those cases by Justices Bradley and Field indicated a future course of decision which finally triumphed some twenty years later.

From our perspective, the remarkable thing about Field's *Slaughter-House* dissent was his reliance, in defense of butchers' constitutional right to be free from a state-imposed monopoly, on an amalgam of common law precedents and Lockean natural law claims. The liberty to follow "any lawful trade or employment," Field wrote, "is assumed to be the natural right of every Englishman." Since "[t]he common law of England is the basis of the jurisprudence of the United States," it ought to be protected in America, too.[36]

Following *Lochner v. New York*, up until the New Deal, the Court sat in judgment of regulations that governed property rights. It sometimes struck regulatory schemes that in its judgment infringed unreasonably on economic liberties protected by Due Process, but as often upheld them, frequently on common law grounds.[37] The model for the latter course was the 1877 case, *Munn v. Illinois*, where the Court sustained state regulation of grain elevators against a Due Process challenge on the grounds that it involved a business "affected with a public interest."[38] Usually the statute in question was defended as an exercise of the state "police power" to regulate the health, safety, and morals of its citizens and their trade strictly among themselves. This power seems not to have existed as such at common law, earning mention in Blackstone in only a limited sense[39] and no mention (that I know of) in the common law treatises of Coke. However, it was understood by the courts to include a number of matters open at common law to various forms of regulation and sometimes, as in the matter of nuisance, secured by the common law itself. While Justice Field in *Slaughter-House* would assimilate common law and natural rights, the pull in subsequent cases was often between a common law argument for moderate regulation and a Lockean-like natural right to economic liberty on the part of the individual. This last right usually featured a liberty to contract rather than Locke's right to appropriate. That liberty is really how the individuated right to labor and its fruits would appear in the context of an advanced commercial society rather than a primitive wilderness. Locke's treatment of property in fact presumes free contracts of barter and exchange. This liberty was allied, as in Locke, with tacit economic postulates friendly to laissez-faire. Still, it was in the first place a moral right of the individual to self-preservation and enjoyment of one's bounty, not an economic theory. It sought an economic game, like Locke's state of nature, with fair rules equally applied, not a specific outcome based on a presumption of collective ownership and free legislative choice.[40]

Constitutional Revolution

When the whole project of judicial protection of property rights or economic liberties was abandoned in the "Constitutional Revolution" of 1937, it was not by a shifting of the balance in favor of common law doctrines. These doctrines had never recommended judicial abdication, only a sensitivity to the complex duties involved in ownership and the occasional claims of the public in matters of private right. Rather, the Court adopted a new understanding of the judicial function that had the short-term effect of restraining judicial power and the long-term consequence of severing its bond to traditional law.

Central to the triumph of judicial realism—the public doctrine that courts are policy makers, albeit in the special circumstances of adjudication—was the rejection of natural law in its several forms. This is obvious on the simplest level in the treatment of questions of property rights as questions of economics, with collectivist trends overriding axioms of laissez-faire now thought defunct. One sees such an approach, for instance, in the opinions of Chief Justice Hughes, most notably in the *Minnesota Mortgage Moratorium Case*, but also in the 1937 opinions that signaled the "Revolution."[41]

Here, one must admit, the Lockean tradition was vulnerable. It grounded its right on a calculation of social utility and a promise of plenty, and it fell when the calculation stumbled and the promise faltered. But even more important, to my mind, was the reinterpretation of common law prepared in the writings of the enormously influential Oliver Wendell Holmes, Jr. He reconceptualized common law as judge-made law, treating change in judicial doctrine not as adjustment of enduring principles to changing circumstances but as historically conditioned policy experimentation, while he ridiculed natural law as the drunken folly of boastful men.[42]

Heralding the age of the economist in law and the role of the judge as self-conscious artisan of "profound interstitial change," Holmes taught at once an acquiescence in legislative will and a boldness in initiating social transformation. It should go without saying that anyone who could write the sentence in *Gitlow v. New York* that "the only meaning of free speech" is that "[i]f in the long run the beliefs expressed in proletarian dictatorship are destined to be accepted by the dominant forces of the community . . . they should be given their chance and have their way" was no more reliable a friend to the rights of property than he was to natural law, no matter how often his own urbane preference was with the well-to-do.[43]

Regulatory Takings and Property Rights

When in recent years the question of property rights has come before the Supreme Court, it has been with reference not to the buried "property" of Due Process, but to the Takings Clause of the Fifth Amendment. This clause has been held for a century now to be incorporated into the Fourteenth Amendment and thus binding on the states. Here the principle seems as likely to belong to natural law as any that acknowledges the right to private property: if the public takes your property for its purposes, it must pay you just compensation.[44] As with Due Process litigation in the past, the target is state regulation of property and economic exchange. This time the claim is not that unreasonable regulations are invalid but that, in diminishing an owner's "economically beneficial use" of his property, the state effects a "taking" of that property and owes the owner either just compensation or relief from the regulation in question.

Zoning

Unlike the old jurisprudence under Due Process or the even older jurisprudence of the Contract Clause, the issue here typically involves landed property—or as we still say in the common law idiom, real estate—and the land-use regulation in question is typically part of a zoning scheme. That land is frequently involved might suggest a common law analysis. As will become evident, there is a common law dimension, but the genius of the new Takings jurisprudence is that it understates the claim of a categorical right and emphasizes an economic calculation. Again, the challenge is not to the validity of the regulation in question, but to the private owner's having to bear its cost.

The constitutionality of zoning came before the Supreme Court in 1926. Interestingly, it received that court's approval in an opinion by Justice George Sutherland, ordinarily the intellectual power of the "Four Horsemen" who were to lead the defense of the old (Lockean) regime of property against the New Deal. Over the dissent (without opinion) of his three future companions, Justice Sutherland allowed that a regulatory scheme such as zoning might have been rejected by the Court "a century ago, or even half a century ago, . . . as arbitrary and oppressive," but he argued that it might be sustained "under the complex conditions of our day." He continued:

> And in this there is no inconsistency, for while the meaning of constitutional guaranties never varies, the scope of their application must expand or contract to meet the new and different conditions which are constantly coming within the field of their operation. In a changing world, it is impossible that it should be otherwise.[45]

Nuisance Legislation

With this traditional principle of common law adjustment to the Lockean world established, Sutherland turned for instruction in the definition of the scope of the police power to "the maxim *sic utere tuo ut alienum non laedas* [use your own property in such a manner as not to injure that of another], which lies at the foundation of so much of the common law of nuisance." He added that "the law of nuisances, likewise, may be consulted, not for the purpose of controlling but for the helpful aid of its analogies in the process of ascertaining the scope of the power."

Finding the definition of nuisance in modern industrial conditions a matter of degree, dependent on the local circumstances, Sutherland resisted the invitation to weigh the ordinance against a predicted course of "natural development." Instead, he deferred to the right of the municipality to govern itself in such matters. He found "the crux of the more recent zoning legislation" in the distinction of residential and commercial districts. Then he tested the restrictions to see whether they bear "a rational relation to the health and safety of the community." This procedure was consistent with his usual practice of finding an orderly way of meeting the claims of both private property and common good,[46] thus recalling the older balance between liberalism and the common law.

Justice Holmes silently joined Sutherland's opinion in the zoning case, but the new Takings jurisprudence turns not to this but to Holmes's opinion for the Court in a case a few years earlier. There he struck down a Pennsylvania law that would have banned a man from mining coal to which he owned the rights if this would endanger a separately owned surface structure. He wrote: "The general rule at least is, that while property may be regulated to a certain extent, if regulation goes too far it will be recognized as a taking."[47]

Classically Holmesian in its comfort with a question of degree reserved for judicial discretion, the rule has received new life in recent years. For several generations extensive latitude has been given land-use regulators, most notably in *Penn Central Transportation Company v. City of New York*. This decision upheld the city's power to restrict redevelopment of designated landmarks without the city's purchase of the property or an easement upon it.

Real Estate Development

Several recent cases indicate a trend that may have significant implications for natural law and America's treatment of property once again. Two cases involved the conditioning of building permits for development on the property owner's cession to the public of some right of passage, in one case across a beach, in another on a bikepath along a creek. Here the Court has established a test requiring a "rough proportionality" nexus between the permit sought and the condition imposed, to insure "that the required dedication is related both in nature and extent to the impact of the proposed development."[48]

The takings found in both cases are not merely regulatory but demands for physical rights of way. The cases are significant not for redefining the right of property but as evidence that the Court will again accord established property rights constitutional status by giving their regulation constitutional scrutiny. Yet the "rough proportionality" test has echoes in the common law treatment of property as a personal right, but one directed to the common good.

On the other hand, *Lucas v. South Carolina Coastal Council* seems to hearken back to a more Lockean conception of property rights, even though many libertarian commentators were disappointed in the reasoning. In *Lucas*, the Court found that the state's Beachfront Management Act, which forbade development in certain coastal zones, effected a taking of the petitioner's property in a couple of house lots in the midst of a coastal neighborhood once zoned for single-family residences, where further building was now disallowed.

Denying that Holmes's *Pennsylvania Coal v. Mahon* rule permitted the courts to engage in ad hoc inquiries, Justice Scalia found precedent for the scrutiny of regulatory takings in two instances: first, where a physical invasion of the property had taken place, as we have seen, and second, "where regulation denies all economically beneficial or productive use of the land." Finding the latter to apply to the circumstances here, and satisfied with a "categorical rule that total regulatory takings must be compensated," Scalia found that *Lucas* was owed for the lots he must keep vacant.

To the claim that the legislature in passing the act was preventing the environmental harm that further development would occasion, and that, as we saw, the common law right of property did not extend to its harmful use, he offered a complex response. On the one hand, he rejected the invitation to develop a legal distinction between regulations that prevent harmful use and those that confer public benefits. He held that the distinction between harm and benefit—for example, between preventing coastal erosion and providing a healthy coastal environment—is "often in the eye of the beholder." Thus it is "difficult, if not impossible, to discern on an objective, value-free basis." He treats the traditional "harmful or noxious use" analysis as simply a step in the emergence of the modern doctrine of "legitimate state interests." Thus, the fact that legislation claims to be preventing harm does not establish a license to regulate at will.

On the other hand, any newly legislated ban on all economically beneficial use of property must, if the state would avoid paying compensation, "inhere in the title itself, in the restrictions that background principles of the State's law of property and nuisance already place upon land ownership." Scalia's aim was to reinforce the prospectivity and generality of regulations that would be confiscatory if retrospective. In this sense at least, he sought Locke's world of "settled, standing rules," where the only harms and benefits that are objective are those that are economically harmful or beneficial. He insisted on the certainty of a categorical rule, but he abandoned the confident, categorical certainties of common law, where property had a purpose defined in the context of a common good.[49]

Justice Blackmun complained in his dissent in *Lucas* that the reliance on the common law of property and nuisance already in place in a state is misguided, since "state courts make exactly the decision that the Court finds so troubling when made by the South Carolina General Assembly."[50] Although Justice Scalia accepted the realist critique of distinctions such as those between harm and benefit, he rejected the realist assertion that there is no essential difference between the legislative and judicial function and so between the kind of findings each branch makes.

That the judicial role is especially concerned with the protection of property is not a historical accident. It is precisely the character of the judiciary that it determines law in the context of individual cases, where it is charged by its very structure with giving every person what is his or hers by right.

Property Rights Legislation

The qualified and limited character of the constitutional protection of property in the recent Takings cases might be contrasted with the recent efforts at legislation that would require property value impact statements from all who would establish new land-use regulations and would also authorize compensation when regulations cause land to lose between a third and a half or more of its value.[51] If the problem that the legislation seeks to remedy is bureaucratic obstruction of an individual's use of one's own property, the imposition of further bureaucratic regulation on bureaucracy itself seems as likely to entangle as to relieve.

In restoring some measure of constitutional protection for property rights, the Court may not have established a mechanism that can be generalized for the restoration of a balance between individual and public good. However, it did give authoritative recognition to the reborn Lockean concern with the individual as the author of material value. Whether this recognition can counteract the utilitarianism that governs economic thinking on both Left and Right will depend on whether the individual's economic initiative can again be understood as integral to, rather than competitive with, one's personal independence and responsibility in moral and political life.

The modern logic of a Takings defense against legislative and especially bureaucratic regulation has behind it the powerful movement of law and economics. This discipline, grounded in pragmatism, weighs the costs and benefits of social policies not only in the areas of property and commerce but, theoretically at least, in all matters of human concern.[52] This approach, dedicated to the use of the common law authority of judges and understanding common law in Holmesian terms, shapes the law in the name of economic rationality. To bring to bear upon this perspective a sturdy sense of right and wrong and of responsibility and freedom—indeed, the sturdy common sense that underlay the common law before Holmes's transformation—even in the midst of the worldly flux that Locke comprehended and economics tries to explain, would be no small contribution on the part of natural law today. Such an alliance of traditional natural law and a liberalism friendly to property rights might be difficult to effect in our postmodern intellectual milieu. Still, it has to recommend it the precedent of the common law constitutionalism under which America once thrived.

NOTES

1. See, e.g., *United States v. Lopez*, 115 S.Ct. 1624 (1995). The call for judicial protection of what are now called economic liberties has been raised by Siegan, Bernard, *Economic Liberties and the Constitution*. Chicago: University of Chicago Press, 1980; and Epstein, Richard, *Takings: Private Property and the Power of Eminent Domain*. Cambridge, Mass.: Harvard University Press, 1985. The Supreme Court's response to this call, especially the case of *Lucas v. South Carolina Coastal Council*, 505 U.S. 1003 (1992), will be discussed.

2. See Bork, Robert, *The Tempting of America: The Political Seduction of the Law*. New York: Free Press, 1990; Gingrich, Newt, *To Renew America*. New York: Harper Collins, 1995.

3. Fathers of the English Dominican Province, tr., *The "Summa Theologica" of St. Thomas Aquinas*. London: Burns, Oates & Washbourne, 1929 [also available on the internet at http://www.knight.org/advent/summa/summa.htm] I–II, Q. 94, art. 3.

4. *Ibid.*, I–II, Q. 94, art. 5–6. That St. Thomas consistently sees property and slavery as identical in status, citing Aristotle for both, appears in *ibid.*, II–II, Q. 57, art. 3.

5. *Politics* I (1257a–1259a) and II (1260b–1266a); and on slavery, I (1256b26).

6. *Summa Theologica*, II–II, Quest. 57, art. 2–3.

7. *Summa Theologica*, II–II, Quest. 32, art. 5.

8. See Broderick, Albert, O.P., "The Radical Middle: Natural Right of Property in Aquinas and the Popes," *The Solicitor Quarterly* 3 (1964): 127–59, at 129 ff. [Reprinted in John Finnis, ed., *Natural Law*. New York: New York University Press, 1991 I:155–87.]

9. *Summa Theologica*, I–II, Q. 97, art. 1; Q. 94, art. 6.

10. Plucknett, T.F.T., and J.L. Barton, ed., *St. German's Doctor and Student*. London: Selden Society [vol. 91], 1974. In the quotations that follow, I will modernize the spelling and punctuation of the English original and use Plucknett's and Barton's English translations of passages that originally appeared only in the Latin version of the text. St. German published, anonymously, Latin and English versions of *Doctor and Student*. For an intriguing, alternative account of St. Thomas's influence on modern law generally, see Gordley, James, *The Philosophical Origins of Modern Contract Doctrine*. Oxford: Clarendon Press, 1991.

11. *St. German's Doctor and Student*, First Dialogue, ch. 1–4.

12. *Ibid.*, ch. 5–11. The quotations in this sentence are from pp. 41 and 53.

13. *Ibid.*, pp. 34–35.

14. *Ibid.*, p. 133.

15. *Ibid.*, p. 33.

16. *Ibid.*, p. 133.

17. *Summa Theologica*, I–II, Q. 95, art. 2, 4; Q. 96, art. 4, 2; Q. 97, art. 3.

18. See Tully, James, *A Discourse on Property: John Locke and his adversaries*. Cambridge: Cambridge University Press, 1980; and his more recent *An Approach to Political Philosophy: Locke in Contexts*. Cambridge: Cambridge University Press, 1993, esp. ch. 3.

19. Locke, *Two Treatises of Government*, ed. Peter Laslett. Cambridge: Cambridge University Press, 1988, I.42–43.

20. See Sreenivasan, Gopal, *The Limits of Lockean Rights in Property.* Oxford: Oxford University Press, 1995, p. 102 ff.

21. *Two Treatises of Government*, II.6.

22. But see *ibid.*, II.56, where Locke says parents are "*under an obligation to preserve, nourish, and educate the Children,* they had begotten," qualified in I.65, where paternal power "so little belongs to the *Father* by any peculiar right of Nature, but only as he is Guardian of his Children, that when he quits his Care of them, he loses his power over them. . . ."

23. *Ibid.*, II.15.

24. *Ibid.*, II.23.

25. See Tully, *A Discourse of Property*, p. 105 ff.

26. *Ibid.*, p. 103.

27. The quotations in this paragraph are from *Two Treatises*, II.25–28.

28. *Ibid.*, II.31, 37, 43, 41.

29. *Ibid.*, II.36, 46, 34.

30. See Vaughn, Karen Iverson, "The Economic Background of Locke's *Two Treatises of Government*," in Edward J. Harpham, ed., *John Locke's* TWO TREATISES OF GOVERNMENT: *New Interpretations.* Lawrence: University Press of Kansas, 1992.

31. *Two Treatises*, II.45–46; cf. ch. 9 (esp. sect. 123), 11, and 19. See also Mansfield, Harvey C., Jr., "Responsibility versus Self-Expression," in Robert A. Licht, ed., *Old Rights and New.* Washington: AEI Press, 1993; and Pangle, Thomas L., *The Spirit of Modern Repubicanism.* Chicago: University of Chicago Press, 1988.

32. I discuss this matter more fully in my *Common Law and Liberal Theory: Coke, Hobbes, and the Origins of American Constitutionalism.* Lawrence: University Press of Kansas, 1992, esp. ch. 8.

33. See Ely, James W., Jr., *The Guardian of Every Other Right: A Constitutional History of Property Rights.* Oxford: Oxford University Press, 1992, esp. ch. 1–2.

34. Lee, Arthur, *An Appeal to the Justice and Interests of the People of Great Britain, in the Present Dispute with America*, 4th ed. New York, 1775, p. 14, quoted in Ely, *The Guardian of Every Other Right*, p. 26.

35. 11 Peters 420 (1837). See, generally, Horwitz, Morton, *The Transformation of American Law, 1780–1860.* Cambridge, Mass.: Harvard University Press, 1977. See McConnell, Michael, "Contract Rights and Property Rights: A Case Study in the Relationship Between Individual Liberties and Constitutional Structure," *California Law Review* 76 (1988): 267–95.

36. 16 Wallace 36 (1873), at 104. The citation for *Lochner* is 198 U.S. 45 (1905).

37. See McCloskey, Robert G., *The American Supreme Court.* Chicago: University of Chicago Press, 1960.

38. 94 U.S. 113 (1877).

39. Blackstone, William, *Commentaries on the Laws of England.* reprint ed. Chicago: University of Chicago Press, 1979, vol. IV, ch. 13, p. 162 ff.

40. On the moral basis of laissez-faire constitutionalism, see Benedict, Michael Les, "Laissez-Faire and Liberty: A Re-evaluation of the Meaning and Origins of Laissez-Faire Constitutionalism," *Law and History Review* 3 (1985): 293–331; and Arkes, Hadley, *The Return of George Sutherland: Restoring a Jurisprudence of Natural Rights.* Princeton, N.J.: Princeton University Press, 1994, p. 20 ff.

41. *Home Building and Loan Association v. Blaisdell*, 290 U.S. 398 (1934). Cf. *West Coast Hotel v. Parrish*, 300 U.S. 379 (1937) and *National Labor Relations Board v. Jones & Laughlin Steel Corporation*, 301 U.S. 1 (1937).

42. See Holmes, *The Common Law.* Boston: Little, Brown, 1881; and *Collected Legal Papers.* New York: Harcourt, Brace and Howe, 1920, esp. the final essay on natural law.

43. See *Collected Legal Papers*, p. 269; 208 U.S. 652, at 673.

44. See Kmiec, Douglas W.,"The Coherence of the Natural Law of Property," *Valparaiso University Law Review* 26 (1991): 367–84, esp. 380 ff.

45. *Village of Euclid v. Amber Realty Company*, 272 U.S. 365, at 387.

46. *Ibid.*, at 387, 390–91.

47. *Pennsylvania Coal Co. v. Mahon*, 260 U.S. 393 (1923), at 415.

48. The quotation is from *Dolan v. City of Tigard*, 114 S.Ct. 2309 (1994), at 2319–20. The first in the current line of cases is *Nollan v. California Coastal Commission*, 483 U.S. 825 (1987).

49. *Lucas v. South Carolina Coastal Council*, 505 U.S. 1003, at 1015, 1026, 1024, 1026, 1029. On the propriety of the distinction between preventing harm and conferring benefit as a matter of natural law, see Kmiec, "The Coherence of the Natural Law of Property," pp. 383–84. That constitutional protection of property rights has in all its forms aimed chiefly at the prevention of retrospective legislation, see Kainen, James L., "The Historical Framework for Reviving Constitutional Protection for Property and Contract Rights," *Cornell Law Review* 79 (1993): 87–142. That the insistence on prospectivity and generality in legislation is the characteristic mark of modern constitutionalism, see Wormuth, Francis D., *The Origins of Modern Constitutionalism.* New York: Harper and Brothers, 1949.

50. *Lucas v. South Carolina Coastal Council,* at 1054.

51. See 104th Congress, S. 605, "The Omnibus Property Rights Act of 1995," and S. 1954, the substitute bill proposed later in the second session of that congress; also the Report of the Senate Judiciary Committee on S. 605, Report 104–239.

52. See especially the work of Richard Posner, now a federal circuit judge and still a prolific author, e.g., *Economic Analysis of the Law*, 3rd ed. Boston: Little, Brown, 1986; and *Overcoming Law.* Cambridge, Mass.: Harvard University Press, 1995.

Taxation

John Mueller

I have been asked to elucidate the connection between the natural law and taxation. This is not the "piece of cake" I thought when I agreed to take the job. It was only when I sat down to my task that I realized, with growing horror, that tracing the connection would be more, not less, complicated than a much broader topic, like "the natural law and economics," or "the natural law and the meaning of life." At times it seemed the only more difficult topic would be "the natural law and cheese"; at least there are more kinds of cheese than taxes.

To conquer my subject, therefore, I have divided my paper, like (or with) Gaul, into three parts. First, I say something about the historical and logical connection between the natural law and economic theory. Second, I suggest what this implies for economic policy in general and taxation in particular. Finally, in light of recent developments in economic theory, I modestly suggest that the current plight of working families stems largely from the fact that nearly all existing tax codes violate the natural law. [1]

The Natural Law and Economic Theory

It is still customary, in discussing economic matters, for noneconomists to begin with Adam Smith.[2] This lamentable practice is due to the fact that noneconomists defer too much to economists on noneconomic matters. We economists, at least, have a reason for starting the discussion with Adam Smith, which one would think is readily apparent: we're half-wits! The division of labor has, on the thinking of the economist who ventures outside his specialty, the same effect Adam Smith described it having on the mental activity of the average labourer: "He naturally loses, therefore, the habit of such exertion, and generally becomes as stupid and ignorant as it is possible for a human creature to become."[3]

Until relatively recently, even historians of economic theory had a view of their subject much like the "New Yorker's-Eye View of the World"—the famous poster which depicts Manhattan's Seventh, Eighth, and Ninth avenues, right down to the fire hydrants, while the rest of the world consists of blank areas labeled "Jersey" and "Japan." For years, any textbook would detail the latest avenues of modern economics, right down to the fire hydrants, while in the hazy background were "Adam Smith" and "the Physiocrats."

The received view of Smith began to change radically in 1954, when Joseph Schumpeter's massive *History of Economic Analysis* was published.[4] In economics, according to Schumpeter, "much more than in physics have results been lost on the way or remained in abeyance for centuries. We shall meet with instances that are little short of appalling."[5] After carefully tracing the origins of the basic tools of modern economic analysis, Schumpeter concluded: "The fact is that the *Wealth of Nations* does not contain a single *analytic* idea, principle or method that was entirely new in 1776."[6] In fact, he said, Smith's theory of value was "a time- and labor-consuming detour" on the way to a workable price theory.

Schumpeter noted that even the theory most often identified with Smith (the division of labor) is taken directly from the ancient Greeks, whose contribution we know mostly through Plato's *Republic* and (especially) Aristotle's *Ethics* and *Politics*.[7] "This—presumably the extract from a large literature that has been lost—constitutes the Greek bequest, so far as economic theory is concerned."[8]

The Scholastics

It was the Scholastics in the Middle Ages, however, who played the chief role in developing scientific economic analysis, according to Schumpeter. In fact, Schumpeter says, St. Thomas Aquinas formulated the very method of "'modern' or 'empirical' or 'positive' science."[9] Building on Aristotle, the Schoolmen began using this method to work out the first truly scientific theories of prices, money, trade, interest, and profits.[10] "The 'pure' economics which they handed down to [their] laical successors was practically, in its entirety, their own creation. It is within their systems of moral theology and law that economics gained definite if not separate existence, and it is they who come nearer than does any other group to having been the 'founders' of scientific economics."[11]

Schumpeter then traces the descent to Smith of most of these scholastic tools—developed but not greatly modified—through intermediaries like Hugo Grotius, John Locke, and Samuel von Pufendorf.[12] However, the basic scholastic theory of value and prices was lost on the way, and rediscovered only after being laboriously reinvented in the late nineteenth century.

Smith's claim to the title of Founder of Economics, however, would not be seriously diminished by the mere fact that he had nothing both true and original to say about how markets work. The Founder of Economics must answer a much more fundamental question—namely, *why* markets work. Why is there order in markets, without apparent design, instead of chaos? Before this is answered, there cannot *be* a science of economics. Every science is built on first principles which come from beyond it. In the case of economics, the first principles come from philosophy.

Smith fit the main inherited tools of economic analysis, along with a vast amount of historical detail, into a simple and coherent philosophical framework. What was it? Schumpeter argues that Smith's "work was the channel through which eighteenth-century ideas about human nature reached economists."[13] But this last part of the history needs to be rewritten. It is more accurate to say that Smith's work was the channel through which third-century (B.C.) ideas about human nature reached economists. We can't make sense of Smith without recognizing, as the editors of his *Theory of Moral Sentiments* observe, that "Stoic philosophy is the primary influence on Smith's ethical thought. It also fundamentally affects his economic theory."[14]

Adam Smith

Smith's famous "invisible hand" is mentioned and presupposed, though never explained, in the *Wealth of Nations*.[15] But in his earlier *Theory of Moral Sentiments*, the "invisible hand" is explicitly based on the Stoic theory of Providence. "The ancient stoics were of the opinion," Smith says, "that as the world was governed by the all-ruling providence of a wise, powerful, and good God, every single event ought to be regarded, as making a necessary part of the plan of the universe, and as tending to promote the general order and happiness of the whole: that the vices and follies of mankind, therefore, make as necessary a part of this plan as their wisdom or their virtue; and by that eternal art which educes good from ill, were made to tend equally to the prosperity and perfection of the great system of nature."[16]

The *Theory of Moral Sentiments* includes an explanation of the "invisible hand" which is not only earlier than the better-known passage in the *Wealth of Nations*, but also more illuminating.[17] In it Smith ties the Stoic view of Providence to the nature of economic value and tries to explain how the order in markets comes about. The "real satisfaction" of wealth, according to Smith (speaking like a good Stoic), is "in the highest degree contemptible and trifling." Yet the pleasures of wealth and greatness "strike the imagination as something grand and beautiful and noble, of which the attainment is well worth all the toil and anxiety which we are so apt to bestow upon it. And it is well that nature imposes on us in this manner. It is this deception which rouses and keeps in continual motion the industry of mankind."[18] In Smith's view, then, economic order arises from an Author of Nature who engages in a "deception" about the true value of things, that leads men into the vice of selfishness—for their own good!

Some have dismissed Smith's explanation as "mystical," as if it were unscientific to trace economic order back to God. But here it is Smith's critics who are being unscientific. Smith was not a Christian (at least, not by the time he wrote the *Wealth of Nations*). He simply was not burdened by the strange modern notion that merely acknowledging God's existence is an act of faith. To put it bluntly, anyone who can't see that every effect has a cause (and so a First Cause) is not an unbeliever—he's a nitwit![19] Smith recognizes that it is impossible to say anything significant about the nature of man without saying something about the nature of God. To answer the questions, "What is man? How does he behave?" we must know the answers to the questions: "Is he God? Is he part of God? Is he a creature?" These answers determine our epistemology, our metaphysics, our psychology, and ultimately, our economics.

The trouble with Smith's explanation of the "invisible hand" is not *theo*logical, merely logical. God or no God, Smith never explains how the "general order and happiness of the whole" can result from a general *dis*order, "the vices and follies of mankind." The problem stems from a contradiction inherent in his Stoic worldview.

Stoicism has been described as "a low-grade metaphysics accompanied by high-grade moral ideals."[20] The Stoics firmly believed that all people are called to live in accord with right reason; but they never succeeded in explaining why. To the questions "Is man God? Is he part of God? Is he a creature?" the Stoic answers were "no," "yes," and "no." That is, the Stoics were pantheists. They conceived God as not a spirit, but a fiery form of intelligent matter (today we would say "energy"[21]) that made up the cosmos. The world was therefore not created; it was itself divine. Individual souls were material offshoots of the divine world-soul, into which they redissolved after this life.

Hence all evils and contradictions must be only apparent, ultimately resolved in the One. As Heraclitus, the originator of this cosmology, put it: "To God all things are fair and good and right, but men hold some things wrong and some things right." F.C. Copleston comments: "This is, of course, the inevitable conclusion of a pantheistic philosophy—that everything is justified *sub specie aeternitatis*."[22] Hence the Stoic difficulty in explaining why anyone should be virtuous: if right and wrong are all the same to God, why should it matter to us? The same difficulty leads, in Smith's case, to basing economic order on a systematic divine deception, and thus to a highly precarious defense of economic freedom. It amounts to saying that we may safely allow liberty in economic matters, precisely because people are not really free.

St. Augustine

Unfortunately, in the history of economic analysis, there is a large void where St. Augustine ought to be. Schumpeter says, inexplicably, that St. Augustine never "went into economic problems."[23] Yet, as a matter of historical fact, it was St. Augustine who first analyzed the apparent paradox of the "invisible hand." His ideas were worked out precisely in response to the Stoics' failure to reconcile man's free will with God's providence.[24]

St. Augustine's whole disagreement with the Stoics stems from his view that God is a creator and man a creature, radically contingent but morally free. There are, he says, three levels of reality (in descending order): God the Creator, created spirits, and created bodies; human beings are creatures composed of body and soul. St. Augustine agrees with the Stoics that the world is ordered by God's providence in "peace, the tranquility of order." Care of the body is ordained to the care of the soul; peace between body and soul is ordained to peace between man and his neighbor; and the peace of earthly society is ordained to peace between man and God. For human beings, therefore, the moral order naturally consists of four loves: love of God, love of one's own soul, love of one's neighbor's soul, and love of one's own body (in that order).[25]

The moral law governing these acts is expressed in the two Great Commandments: that one should love God above all else, and one's neighbor as oneself. These are not counsels of Christian perfection; they are the basic, universally binding moral precepts of the natural law—which, for added certainty, have received the sanction of Hebrew and Christian revelation.[26]

St. Thomas Aquinas cites St. Augustine to explain why there are four great loves, but only two Great Commandments: "As Augustine says (*De Doctr. Christ.* i. 23), *though four things are to be loved out of charity, there was no need of a precept as regards the second and the fourth*, i.e., love of oneself and love of one's own body. *For however much a man may stray from the truth, the love of himself and of his own body always remains in him*. And yet the mode of this love had to be prescribed to man, namely, that each person should love himself and his body in an ordinate manner, and this is done by loving God and his neighbor."[27]

Moral disorder is introduced by man's free choice, which is foreseen and allowed, but not caused, by God.[28] "Sin for man is a disorder and perversion: that is, a turning away from the most worthy Creator and a turning toward the inferior things he has created."[29] This disrupts the natural order between God and man, between man and man, and between body and soul.[30]

"And yet," St. Augustine says, "even what is perverted must of necessity be in harmony with, and in dependence on, and in some part of the order of things, for otherwise it would have no existence at all."[31] This is why there is a kind of order even among thieves: "For what thief will tolerate another thief stealing from him?"[32] Selfishness is not self-love, but *inordinate* self-love. "When it is said, 'Thou shalt love thy neighbor as thyself,' it at once becomes evident that our love for ourselves has not been overlooked."[33]

According to St. Augustine, the "law written in men's hearts, which not even wickedness can erase,"[34] explains not only social and political order,[35] but also specifically the order in markets: "This image or, as I said, trace of equity is stamped on the business transactions of men by the Supreme Equity."[36] In contrast to Smith, then, St. Augustine says the order in markets is entirely due to the natural inclination to good that remains in people despite—not because of—their vices. This order is real but imperfect; it can always be improved by increasing the degree of virtue; selfishness is never more "efficient" than virtue.[37]

The Stoic view of the moral order is different. For the Stoic, the highest virtue is not benevolence but "self-command," which is motivated by one's good opinion of himself. "It is not the love of our neighbor," Smith says pointedly, that makes a man "restrain his selfish and indulge his benevolent affections," but rather "a higher love, a more powerful affection": love "of the grandeur, and dignity, and superiority of our own characters."[38]

As a result, the Stoic (and Smithian) ethical system is "Ptolemaic" (everything revolves around the self), while the moral order described by St. Augustine is "Copernican" (the self, and everything else, revolve around God). This is not because the Stoics didn't believe in God, but because they believed that God does not transcend the world. A man must look outward to find his duty to his fellow humans, but could only look inward to find God. The Stoics' doctrine of the Inner Light accounted for "their dignity, their weariness, their sad external care for others, their incurable care for themselves," G.K. Chesterton incisively commented. "That Jones shall worship the God within him turns out ultimately to mean that Jones shall worship Jones."[39]

The view of Providence which understands God as a Creator and man as a morally free creature was necessary, both historically and logically, for the development of economics as a science. Because of it, St. Augustine gives a very different answer to the question Smith was to grapple with (unsuccessfully) fourteen centuries later: why don't market prices reflect the natural order of things?

Utility as a Criterion of Value

In the natural order, St. Augustine says, living things obviously rank above inanimate objects. "But there is another gradation which employs utility as the criterion of value," he says. "For instance, would not anyone prefer to have food in his house, rather than mice, or money rather than fleas? There is nothing surprising in this; for we find the same criterion operating in the value we place on human beings, for all the undoubted worth of a human creature. A higher price is often paid for a horse than for a slave, for a jewel than for a maidservant."[40] Utility, St. Augustine observes, is the value of things, not in themselves, but considered as means to some other end. Since external goods are necessary for human life and virtue, their economic value must be based on utility, not intrinsic worth, for saints and sinners alike. The City of God uses temporal goods toward the end of eternal happiness, while members of the Earthly City aim only at temporal happiness.

Alejandro Chafuen notes that this key passage in the *City of God* "served as the starting point for Scholastic investigation" of market prices.[41] In fact, from St. Augustine's theory of value we can proceed directly to modern price theory. Modern price theory takes three things as given: first, that each economic agent has a ranking of economic goods by utility; second, that each makes rational choices to maximize the utility of his or her wealth[42]; and third, that each begins with a certain endowment of wealth. From these data, the economist is able to construct the supply and demand curves that are the starting point of economic analysis and prediction.

In arguing that the scholastics have the best claim to being the 'founders' of scientific economics, Schumpeter goes on: "And not only that: it will appear, even, that the bases they laid for a serviceable and well-integrated body of analytic tools and propositions were sounder than was much subsequent work, in the sense that a considerable part of the economics of the later nineteenth century might have been developed from these bases more quickly and with less trouble than it actually cost to develop it, and that some of that subsequent work was therefore in the nature of a time- and labor-consuming detour."[43]

What he means, specifically, is that while the scholastic theory of value and prices is essentially the same as current economic theory,[44] Smith's effort to derive prices from intrinsic value finally had to be abandoned, and then only after many decades of confusion (spawning Karl Marx as a by-product). The theory of value based on utility, once mislaid, could not occur to Smith, because of his Stoic worldview. Smith could not assume that most people behave rationally, and so he had to search elsewhere for the origin of economic value.

If Schumpeter is correct in saying that the scholastics have a better claim than any other group to being the "founders" of "scientific" economics, then St. Augustine is their Adam Smith. Like a modern skyscraper built over a solid but hidden Roman foundation, the whole structure of modern economic theory depends on St. Augustine's—not Adam Smith's—"invisible hand."

The Natural Law and Economic Policy

To proceed from economic theory to economic policy, we need also to know what the natural law has to say about government and society. The order in society and markets, St. Augustine showed, is due to the reason and virtue that remain even in bad people.[45] The problem of government is essentially how to increase this order, or at least to reduce the amount of disorder.

Scale of Values

The analysis means that there are basically two ways to get people to change their behavior. One is to correct the scale of values in light of which they act (through education in virtue); the other is to alter the consequences of acting upon their existing scale of values (through incentives and punishments). St. Thomas Aquinas calls these "mediate" and "immediate," or indirect and direct, policies.[46]

To simplify analysis, economic theory typically takes the scale of values of an economic agent as given. But in fact the scale of values is not given in other disciplines, much less in human life. Yet how can a person's scale of values be altered? The French economist Jacques Rueff observes:

> Coercion would be the only instrument for governing men, if their scales of preference, that is to say, their fundamental characters, were strictly unchangeable. It would be a serious mistake, however, to forget that certain states of love are able profoundly to alter the hierarchy of values, in light of which each individual considers the acts he is able to do, and chooses those he will perform. Love, in all its forms—love of God, love of country, love of parents—is able to substitute for his own scale the one which the authority he reveres commands him to adopt. It is then without constraint, in the ardent desire to obey or to serve, that he does the actions which otherwise would not be the most desirable for him. "If ye are led by the Spirit, ye are no longer under the law" (Gal. 5:18). But for someone led by the Spirit, everything is as if love or faith had actually changed his nature, to the point of desiring that which his beloved or his God desires for him.[47]

Obviously, virtue is preferable to coercion, since it governs both internal and external acts, while incentives and punishments govern only external acts. But to say this is also to describe the policy maker's difficulty. Few people love the government. The most effective ministers of virtue are the "little platoons" of society—family, church, neighbors, coworkers, teachers, and other institutions of a "human scale." These are effective because they are personal; they can recognize and treat each person as unique, with special needs, strengths, and weaknesses, and provide relationships through which love can alter a person's scale of values. The law teaches, and the presidency is a "bully pulpit"; but the "mediate" or indirect policies of government are largely subsidiary—that is, helpful—to the more primary institutions. Most government policy is immediate or direct, and therefore impersonal. It must of its nature rely on a one-size-fits-all approach using incentives and disincentives (supported if necessary by coercion).

The range of mediating institutions can be simple or incredibly diverse, depending on the kind of society. But all have one thing in common: their function and authority is derived from the household. Aristotle, in his *Politics*, explains that the household is the basic unit of society—because the household, not the individual, is the smallest unit capable of reproducing and sustaining itself.[48]

The prevalence of the household implies that private ownership of most, though not all, wealth is natural.[49] The household is not fully self-sufficient, and this is why villages and other associations and, at the highest level, the *polis*, are necessary. Such a commonwealth requires some common wealth to provide for the common defense, justice, and worship, and to ensure the adequate production and distribution of private wealth.[50]

Governmental Policies

The government's policies regarding wealth can be divided into regulatory and fiscal methods.[51] Regulation leaves wealth in private hands, but restricts how it shall be used. With fiscal policy, the government itself becomes an agent in the market, acquiring and disposing of common wealth.[52] The regulatory and fiscal methods can be used separately or in concert.[53] For example, suppose the government wants to reduce cigarette smoking. It may resort to indirect methods, such as education campaigns to persuade people to stop smoking (or not to start); or to direct methods, which may include both regulation (establishing smoke-free zones, prohibiting sales to minors) and fiscal measures (raising taxes on cigarettes or cutting tobacco subsidies).

The fiscal approach can be further analyzed in terms of the sources and uses of common wealth. The sources of funds are income from wealth already owned by the government, taxes on private wealth,[54] borrowing, and token-money creation.[55] The uses of funds are government purchases of goods and services,[56] transfer payments, and debt service.

The forms and relative importance of taxation depend not only on the kind of government and the goals of the social order, but also on the economic development of the society.[57] When we speak of taxation today, more often than not we mean the income tax. But for most of history, government revenues meant the income from the ruler's personal estates, and taxes were not clearly distinguished from land rents.[58]

The income tax is a fairly recent development. As Sir John Hicks notes, labor income cannot be taxed or even measured until there exists a class of salaried public officials or corporate workers who are paid cash wages.[59] Property income is difficult to measure or tax before there exists a market which values assets, legal definition and enforcement of contracts, and the corporation. Therefore, income, profits, and payroll taxes are late developments associated with a mercantile economy.[60]

Does natural law have anything to say about "progressive" as opposed to "flat" tax rates?[61] The question assumes that the tax base is the same in both cases. But the choice of tax base will give a widely different result under either tax-rate system. As we will see, the biggest current issues in fiscal policy concern the tax base, not the tax rates.

Current Issues in Tax Reform

To understand the current debate over fiscal policy, we must start from an earlier point. In real life, and therefore in the natural law, the household, not the individual, is the basic unit of society. Likewise, in economic theory, the basic economic agents are ordinarily not the individual worker and the individual entrepreneur, but rather the household and (its more specialized offshoot) the firm.

Aristotle divides the economic resources that sustain the household into two categories: people and things. Or rather, wealth consists of the "useful" part of the people and things at the disposal of the household. The "useless" parts of people and things are, of course, more important than the useful parts. Babies, for example, are almost entirely useless; they are useless because they are ends in themselves and not to be used for some other purpose. Worship is completely useless; that is its peculiar value. It is almost the definition of modernity to reverse the priority of the useful and the useless—coupling an advanced civilization with a backward culture.

Human Capital

Adam Smith, following Aristotle, counted as saving[62] not only the accumulation of things (machines and buildings), but also of people (child-rearing, education, and the maintenance of workers).[63] Nevertheless, it was only about thirty-five years ago that economists began to explore, generalize, and apply the latter insight. In between was a long detour.

Education and Longevity The later classical economists followed Thomas Malthus, who focused on the size of the population but ignored changes in human capital per person, such as education and training. But just as he was writing, the relative importance of education was beginning a tremendous growth. The main reason, which is often overlooked, is the unprecedented decline in mortality that began in the eighteenth century.

Formal education is a poor investment when average life expectancy is only thirty years. But as mortality from disease declines, average life expectancy rises to approximate the biblical three-score years and ten. As this happens, the return on investment in formal education rises sharply, because the returns can be expected to accrue for many more years. Also, as mortality declines, the birthrate does not have to be as high in order to achieve a certain number of surviving offspring. Hence the decline in mortality is followed by a decline in fertility. The result of declining mortality, then, is a sharp rise in the relative importance of formal education as a share of "human capital."

Unfortunately, the neoclassical school did not recognize these changes any better than Malthus. Neoclassical economists reacted against the failure of Malthus's predictions by (as it were) throwing out the babies with the bilgewater. They assumed that both fertility *and* human capital per person are given, so that all growth comes from the stock of nonhuman capital per worker.[64] The neoclassical theory, like that of Malthus, was disproved by events—especially after it was unable to predict the postwar recoveries of Germany and Japan, or to explain where most U.S. economic growth comes from (as a vast body of research now attests.)[65]

So, in the past few decades, some economists have again focused on the importance of "human capital" to explain the "missing" growth. Gary Becker, who won the Nobel Prize for his work in this field, notes: "Particularly in developed nations but perhaps in most, there is sufficient investment in education, training, informal learning and just plain child-rearing that the earnings *un*related to investment in human capital are a small part of the total. Indeed, in the developmental approaches to child rearing, *all* the earnings of a person are ultimately attributed to different kinds of investment made in him."[66] In short, much of what is classified as "consumption" in the neoclassical life-cycle theory is in fact a form of investment.[67]

Becker's theory has two levels, one of which goes beyond economics to make some dubious philosophical claims (modeled in fact on Adam Smith's); these I consider in Appendix II. Here I am concerned with Becker's specifically economic theory, which is valid and useful.

Economists call the useful part of people "human capital," and the useful part of things "nonhuman capital." A parent's ability to provide for the family is a kind of "human capital." The family car's ability to provide transportation services is a kind of "nonhuman capital." A share in a company, which provides income to purchase such services, is another kind of "nonhuman capital."

Family Wealth For most families, human capital is by far the most important kind of wealth;[68] the investment of time and money in child-rearing and education is the most important form of saving; and wages (the return on this investment) are the most important kind of income.

There is a good reason for this. For most households, the return on child-rearing and education, in terms of increased future earnings, puts the stock market in the shade. The economic return on the first year of caring for a child is astronomical—because the return in all future years depends on it. The return on the first year of formal education is almost as high. But with each additional year, the added return gets a little smaller. Eventually the return on, say, the cost of one more year of college is less than the return you could get by putting the same money into the stock market. At that point—but not before—it pays to put savings into the stock market.

This is why lower- and middle-income households save mostly in the form of human capital and receive most of their income in wages. It is also why ownership of businesses and other property makes up a much larger share of the wealth and income of upper-income households.[69]

When we take all American households together, we find that just under two-thirds of gross national income is labor compensation earned from earlier investment in human capital, and just over a third is earned by property owners as a return on investment in nonhuman capital. These pretax income shares have remained remarkably constant for over a century—because workers consistently contribute about two-thirds, and property owners about one-third, to increases in total output.[70]

Transfer Payments

The constant income shares mean that gross labor compensation has kept pace almost exactly with the rest of national income. However, part of this labor and property income is taxed and distributed as transfer payments to persons who do not contribute to current output.[71] If we estimate the distribution of net national income after all taxes and transfer payments, a different picture emerges. Since World War II, the wedge of national income devoted to transfer payments has risen by about sixteen percentage points—shrinking net property income by about six percentage points and take-home pay by about ten percentage points.

This, in my view, is the main reason for the "middle-class squeeze" on working families. Rising welfare and Medicaid payments increase the cost of labor, reducing property's share of income and raising unemployment; while increased Medicare and Social Security outlays reduce workers' take-home pay.[72]

In Europe, there has been a similar rise in transfer payments as a share of income. But this has generally been accompanied by a much sharper rise in unemployment and a smaller decline in take-home pay than in the United States. The mix of benefits in Europe has been more heavily skewed toward the unemployed, while the benefit increases in the United States have gone more to persons outside the labor force.[73]

Tax Reform

Since transfer payments drive the level of tax rates over time, meaningful tax reform cannot be undertaken without reforming benefits at the same time.[74] However, peculiarities in the tax code are responsible for the fact that the rising tax burden has fallen almost entirely on lower- and middle-income working families. At the United States federal level, this concerns primarily the income tax (which is used for general purposes) and the payroll tax (which is earmarked for Social Security, disability, and Medicare benefits).

Income Tax Since the income tax is used for general purposes, both equity and efficiency suggest that it should fall in equal proportion upon all kinds of income. Yet it is still true, as Theodore W. Schultz said in 1961, that "Our tax laws everywhere discriminate against human capital" and "in favor of nonhuman capital."[75] For example, a bread-making company, before calculating its gross income, deducts the cost of operating its bread-making machines; and before calculating taxable income, deducts the cost of acquiring the machines. But the worker who operates the machine may not write off the cash cost of acquiring those skills (or of investing in his children's skills). Standard deductions and exemptions fail to cover even the "maintenance cost" of keeping body and soul together, let alone maintaining health and skills.

The result is that, while workers consistently produce about two-thirds of all income, they pay more than three-quarters of all federal taxes. And the burden has been steadily rising.[76]

Tax Base The current crop of tax-reform proposals, despite many attractive features, would worsen this disparity. This is because all rely on the archaic definitions of income, consumption, and investment found in neoclassical theory. All would increase the write-off for machines and buildings, but allow no such deduction for investment in human capital; all would also get rid of some or all tax deductions or credits for "human maintenance" costs. Workers' share of the federal income tax burden would rise from over three-quarters to nearly 100 percent.[77]

In economic terms, such a tax base would worsen the allocation of resources, and therefore lower rather than raise total output and real income. The neoclassical model assumes that any tax on nonhuman capital will be shifted entirely to labor, but that a tax on labor cannot be shifted to nonhuman capital.[78] As Becker points out, this does not hold unless the population is fixed.[79] He says, "even a modest tax on births can have a large negative effect on the number of children."[80] Shifting to a so-called "consumption tax" would lower the birthrate, reduce investment in education, and ultimately reduce the size of the workforce and the economy. Since the return on investment in human capital for most people is higher than on nonhuman capital, even the smaller population would have lower incomes than without the reform.

In political terms, this approach is a nonstarter because it would mean a tax increase on the majority of middle-class households, whose income is mostly from investment in human capital. At the very bottom of the income scale, over half of family income comes from government benefits, while at the very top, over half comes from property income; but in the middle, most family income is labor income. Hence a flat tax rate combined with a tax base that exempts property income (and most government benefits) is a "lumpy" tax, not a flat tax. It would shift virtually the entire tax burden onto workers in each income class, and onto the middle class as a group. I have shown that all this is true, even when the extra growth which could be expected from flatter marginal tax rates is taken into account.[81]

The key to a solution is to adopt the principle that human capital must be treated no worse than nonhuman capital. Though many different solutions are imaginable,[82] my own suggestion[83] has been to allow a deduction for the costs of *maintaining* human and nonhuman capital—as we now do for physical capital. Wages below the poverty level—a minimum standard of human maintenance—would be exempt from federal income and payroll taxes. But, as is already the case for human capital, there would be no separate deduction for the costs of *acquiring* such capital—no deduction for "expensing" or "depreciating" the cost of an asset.[84] This seems to me the best approach because it is the simplest,[85] would have the most neutral treatment of human and nonhuman capital,[86] the most efficient allocation of resources, and (by bringing most of the economy into the tax base) the lowest revenue-neutral marginal income tax rate: as low as 16 or 17 percent.

The same analysis applies not only to the United States, but to tax codes in all other industrial countries of which I am aware. The universal trend in recent decades has been away from income taxes and toward payroll and consumption taxes—a move which, in my view, is away from both efficiency and equity in taxation.

Social Security The debate over reform of the Social Security system follows a similar logic. Theorists using neoclassical assumptions have argued that pay-as-you-go Social Security reduces national saving by substituting for private provision for retirement.[87] All the "neoclassical" reform proposals amount to replacing pay-as-you-go Social Security with claims on nonhuman capital. However, the analysis and the proposed cure are flawed in the same way as the neoclassical proposals for income tax reform.

The neoclassical critique implicitly assumes that fertility is given, so that the provision of retirement benefits encouraged people to increase their "consumption" at the expense of "saving." But if fertility is not fixed, then pay-as-you-go Social Security, by the same logic, should have been partly responsible for the Baby Boom—because young workers, able to count on retirement benefits in excess of contributions, responded by raising more children.[88]

Ending pay-as-you-go Social Security involves a transition problem which is the mirror image of the start-up. Just as the first generation received more in benefits than it contributed, the last generation would receive less. If the transition is done within one generation, that generation will have to "pay twice" for retirement—paying for its parents' benefits while also providing for its own retirement.[89]

Forcing people to save in the form of claims on nonhuman capital means they will be less able to acquire wealth in the form of human capital. Because fertility is not given, this means that increased investment in nonhuman capital will come at the expense of lower investment in human capital—that is, the birthrate would fall further. And (as mentioned) because, for most people, the return on investment in human capital is higher than on nonhuman capital, even the smaller population will have lower per capita incomes than without the reform.

Rather than abolishing pay-as-you-go Social Security, therefore, a better method is to fund it at a reasonable level, combining current reductions in the payroll tax with commensurate reductions in future benefits. This would not only permit working families to keep more income now, to invest in human or nonhuman capital; it would also mean that, even if the birthrate does not increase, payroll tax rates would not have to be raised above current levels.[90]

Moreover, such a reform would keep in place protections for survivors and dependents which would be stripped away under any privatization scheme. Social Security is one of the last institutions in American public life that treats the household rather than the individual (in accord with the natural law) as the basic unit of society.[91]

Conclusion

The life of the poet Petrarch overlapped that of Dante Alighieri. But while Dante's art is an expression of the high Middle Ages, Petrarch is already a figure of the Renaissance and the modern era. Few did more than Petrarch to kindle the Renaissance love for the freshly rediscovered poets and philosophers of antiquity.

The Loss of Values

But late in life, Petrarch revealed that he lived between two sorrows. "The first sorrow was that his beloved Cicero lived too early to have been a Christian. . . . Would that he had lived a little later so that his noble mind which was on its way to affirming monotheism, the divine providence and the creation of the world would have found peace in the truths that Christianity expressed so clearly and that Cicero himself wanted so much."

Petrarch's second, and deeper, sorrow was that "his contemporaries . . . were philosophizing as if Christianity did not exist. Here they were, these young and supposedly learned Aristotelians, proclaiming every error that Aristotle had ever committed and proclaiming it as though it were philosophical truth. At least Cicero did not know better; they did, and their guilt was all the greater and the sorrow of Petrarch more acute."[92]

Petrarch was not sad because his contemporaries were learning to reason better, but, unfortunately, as pagans; he was sad because they were starting to forget the answers that Christianity had astonishingly supplied to riddles that had stumped the best of the ancients—and were beginning to reason more stupidly.

As the Second World War was ending and the Cold War beginning, Christopher Dawson described the cultural problem in exactly the same terms. "The present plight of Western culture is due," Dawson wrote, "to the fact that the real values that we are defending against the totalitarian state are values that have been divorced from their religious and metaphysical foundations, and are insofar indefensible, but which remain the highest values which we possess."[93] Since the end of the Cold War and its external threat, this internal problem has expressed itself with increasing force.

The debate over economic policy is merely one facet of this modern tragedy. We ought to feel Petrarch's sorrow for today's libertarians, who proclaim every error that Adam Smith ever committed and proclaim it as though it were philosophical truth. In my experience, most are driven by a genuine religious impulse. Honest-to-God atheists are always rare. It simply requires too many exhausting mental gymnastics to maintain that every single thing has a cause, but everything together does not.

Pantheism and Monotheism

Pantheism, not atheism, has always been the main rival to monotheism. It still is. What else could possibly unite Marxists, secular libertarians, and one brand of supply-siders—who share nothing else but a religious zeal about economic matters—in their peculiar affinity for Adam Smith? It's the mating call of pantheism; philosophically, they differ only about which particular collective—the proletariat, the free market, or the "global electorate"—best expresses the mind of God.

It is highly tempting, therefore, to draw a line between the pantheists and skeptics on the one hand—including Stoics, Epicureans, and most modern philosophers—and all monotheists on the other—bringing under this head Plato and Aristotle together with orthodox Christian, Jewish, and Islamic philosophers, as well as Descartes, Kant, and all the Enlightenment Deists. The distinction would presumably consist in the fact that the Stoic–Epicurean–modern view confines reality to the world of sensual experience, while monotheism considers other-worldly realities a part of this life. If so, the common language of monotheism might seem to be the natural law, since nature logically presupposes some kind of god.

But, as the case of Adam Smith shows, not just any god or any version of natural law will do. And the problem is not unique to the Stoic version. The real logical divide is not between atheism and theism, or between pantheism and monotheism. It is between a created world and an uncreated world; between a God who is a Creator and a god who is not. A Creator creates by free choice: a created world adds nothing to God, is radically contingent, and is therefore not the best or even the only possible world. But a god who must create to prove his goodness, or who must create the best of all possible worlds, is not a creator at all. Such a god is himself ruled by necessity, and so is the uncreated world with which he coexists. Yet such is the god of all the Greek and Arabic (and modern) philosophers, monotheist and pantheist.[94] All of them entail the same logical contradiction found in Adam Smith's stoicism.

That is the curious thing: the idea of creation can be explained in purely philosophical terms; it is logically and historically the basis of modern science; yet it does not exist anywhere outside of Christian (and perhaps Jewish) philosophy.[95]

Who but a devout Christian or Jew—someone who accepts God's self-chosen biblical name to be simply, "I Am"—would think up a philosophy of pure being which is the very basis for the scientific method? What could lead Joule to formulate the fundamental principle of thermodynamics, except a firm conviction that to assume that anything in the universe, even a particle of energy, could be lost would be contrary to the dignity of its Creator? What astronomer would dream up a thesis known as the "Big Bang," except a Belgian priest who had no fear that scientific experiment could ever disprove that "In the beginning, God made the heavens and the earth?" And who would be the first to state the theory of economic value—except the fifth-century bishop of Hippo, who detected the telltale order of a Creator even in the headstrong, dishonest haggling of grubby North African bazaars?

Each of these examples resulted in a scientific, testable proposition, which, as such, might have occurred to anyone; only it didn't. Each started in fact from an intuition based on accepting the nontestable authority of God's revelation as true.[96]

Natural Law Applied

I hope to have shown in the first part of this paper that, as Schumpeter put it, "social science discovered itself in the concept of natural law;"[97] and that the first (and only) coherent explanation of the order in markets comes from St. Augustine. In the rest of the paper, I hope to have shown that the plight of workers and their families stems directly from the fact that all tax codes in the industrial world today violate the natural law; and that most of the supposed solutions (such as consumption taxes and privatizing Social Security) would worsen the problem.

The potential consequences are not merely economic. Aristotle, after elaborating the various kinds of political constitution (monarchy, oligarchy, democracy, and so on), quickly amends his own classification. The real difference, he says, is not whether government is by one, the few, or the many—but rather, whether it is run by the property owners (who are usually, but not necessarily, few) or by those without property (who are usually, but not necessarily, the many). The most stable constitution, he observes, requires a large middle class.[98] Today's squeeze on working families, therefore, concerns not only the economic basis of the household, but also the long-term stability of our social and political system, which we usually take for granted.

Distributists

I think there is a growing need for some kind of political and social movement in the same spirit—though not along exactly the same lines—as the "Distributists" of seventy or eighty years ago. It clearly isn't going to happen through today's libertarians, either of the left or the right. Their philosophy prevents them from even seeing the problem; in fact, it *is* the problem.

It is customary to poke fun at the distributists, like Chesterton and Belloc, who sought to broaden the distribution of property, because they preached a "back to the land" movement while being for the most part inexorably drawn to the city. As a result, they are generally dismissed as irrelevant romantic agrarians.

I disagree. What the Distributists grasped very clearly—as many modern defenders of the market economy do not—is that in economics, a broad distribution of wealth is technically a prior condition, not the inevitable outcome, of a properly functioning market economy. As Chesterton put it, "It is the negation of private property that the Duke of Sutherland should have all the farms in one estate; just as it would be the negation of marriage if he had all our wives in one harem."[99]

The Distributists had a three-part program which addressed all three basic economic prerequisites under the natural law: first, a defense of religious, political, and economic freedoms; second, a personal conversion of values; and third, a broader distribution of wealth.

The Distributists were also ahead of their time—even ahead of their own theories—because they were all living examples of how a broader distribution of property can be brought about by means of a broader distribution of human capital. Chesterton purchased Top Meadow, and Belloc his King's Land farm, with money earned from their writing. It made perfect sense: both were much better writers than farmers, and neither would ever have been able to "get back to the land"—meaning owning the land—as a thrifty tenant farmer. This shows why removing the artificially high tax burden on labor would broaden rather than narrow the distribution of property.

Economic policy is too important to be left to the economists. Every analytical tool, every scientific theory, every economic policy, is necessarily, logically, and historically rooted in a worldview. The unique value of the natural law is to make that worldview explicit—and true.

APPENDIX I

The Two Great Commandments: Precepts of Natural Law, Not Counsels of Perfection

German scholars have long discussed *"das Adam Smith Problem"*: namely, how could the same person be the author of the *Theory of Moral Sentiments* and the *Wealth of Nations*? Perhaps the most frequently cited passage in the *Wealth of Nations* says, "It is not from the benevolence of the butcher, the brewer, or the baker, that we expect our dinner, but from their regard to their own self-interest. We address ourselves, not to their humanity but to their self-love, and never talk to them of our own necessities but of their advantages."[100] The most frequently cited passage in the *Theory of Moral Sentiments* says: "And hence it is, that to feel much for others, and little for ourselves, that to restrain our selfish, and indulge our benevolent affections, constitutes the perfection of human nature."[101] The so-called "*Umschwungstheorie*"—that Smith simply changed his mind—doesn't make sense, because Smith published a revised version of *The Theory of Moral Sentiments* in 1789, long after The *Wealth of Nations* was published in 1776.

That this should be considered a problem proves that there is still such a thing as Western civilization, and that it is not Stoic. Smith is not inconsistent, but rather consistently Stoic.

The gist of the *Theory of Moral Sentiments* is not accurately conveyed by the passage referring to benevolence. For Smith immediately goes on to say: "As to love our neighbor as we love ourselves is the great law of Christianity, so it is the great precept of nature to love ourselves only as we love our neighbour, or what comes to the same thing, as our neighbor is capable of loving us."[102]

Far from identifying Christianity with the natural law, Smith is contrasting the Stoic with what he takes to be the Christian ethic. In the Stoic view, to love your neighbor as yourself goes beyond the dictates of nature.[103] Instead of increasing love of neighbor to match love of self, Smith's ethic calls for conscientiously curbing selfish impulses and exciting oneself to observe the duties to one's neighbor to some middle ground, as might an intimately informed but totally impartial observer.

For Adam Smith, exactly as for the Stoic Cleanthes, the highest virtue is not benevolence but "self-command," which is motivated by a man's good opinion of himself: what Smith calls the "man within the breast." Smith says pointedly: "It is not the love of our neighbor, it is not the love of mankind, which upon many occasions prompts us to the practice of those divine virtues. It is a stronger love, a more powerful affection, which generally takes place upon such occasions; the love of what is honourable and noble, of the grandeur, and dignity, and superiority of our own characters."[104] For Smith, what makes a man "restrain his selfish, and indulge his benevolent affections" is the love of "the grandeur, and dignity, and superiority of our own characters."

Natural Law and Love

The real contrast here is not between natural law and Christian charity. It begins with a disagreement among the Greeks about the nature of virtue and of the natural law—between the Stoics and the Peripatetic philosophers (mostly Plato and Aristotle), whose philosophical tools the Christian theologians adopted.[105]

The difference can be seen by asking what it means to "love your neighbor as yourself." Smith grounds his own ethical theory by saying,

> Every man, as the Stoics used to say, is first and principally recommended to his own care; and every man is certainly, in every respect, fitter and abler to take care of himself than of any other person. Every man feels his own pleasures and his own pains more sensibly than those of other people. The former are the original sensations; the latter the reflected or sympathetic images of those sensations. The former may be said to be the substance; the latter the shadow.

> After himself, the members of his own family, those who usually live in the same house with him, his parents, his children, his brothers and sisters are naturally the objects of his warmest affections. They are naturally and usually the persons upon whose happiness or misery his conduct must have the greatest influence.[106]

St. Augustine grants this principle of Stoic ethics: "They say, and say truly that it is as it were the first and strongest demand of nature that a man cherish himself, and naturally therefore avoid death, and should so stand his own friend as to wish and vehemently aim at continuing to exist as a living creature, and subsisting in this union of soul and body."[107]

He and St. Thomas also grant its application: "We ought out of charity to love those who are more closely united to us more, both because our love for them is more intense, and because there are more reasons for loving them."[108]

But St. Thomas Aquinas and St. Augustine draw a crucial distinction: "Love can be unequal in two ways: first on the part of the good we wish our friend. In this respect we love all men equally out of charity: because we wish them all one same generic good, namely, everlasting happiness. Secondly love is said to be greater through its action being more intense: and in this way we ought not to love all equally." In other words, "As regards beneficence we are bound to observe this inequality, because we cannot do good to all: but as regards benevolence, love ought not to be thus unequal."[109]

Therefore, benevolence toward God and one's neighbor are not counsels of Christian perfection, but the two basic moral precepts of natural law—which are also given the force of Jewish and Christian revelation.[110]

St. Thomas Aquinas notes, "the love of God and our neighbor is not commanded according to a measure, so that what is in excess of the measure be a matter of counsel." We are commanded to love God "with our whole heart" and our neighbor "as ourself."[111]

"Perfection for man consists in the love of God and of neighbor," St. Thomas Aquinas says. "For a man to love thus, he must do two things, namely, avoid evil and do good. Certain of the commandments [the Third and Fourth] prescribe good acts, while others forbid evil deeds. And we must know that to avoid evil is in our power; but we are incapable of doing good to everyone. Thus, St. Augustine says that we should love all, but we are not bound to do good to all. But among those to whom we are bound to do good are those in some way united to us."[112]

Love of Neighbor

St. Thomas amplifies the point about beneficence elsewhere. After noting that the word "neighbor" denotes the reason for loving—"because they are nigh to us, both as to the natural image of God, and as to the capacity for glory"—St. Thomas says, "The mode of love is indicated in the words '*as thyself.*' This does not mean that a man must love his neighbor equally as himself, but in like manner as himself."[113]

Smith does not clearly distinguish between the dictates of reason and "moral sentiments" and "affections." St. Thomas carefully notes the distinction. "Some have said that we ought, out of charity, to love all our neighbors equally, as regards our affection, but not as regards the outward effect. They held that the order of love is to be understood as applying to outward favors, which we ought to confer on those who are connected with us in preference to those who are unconnected, and not to the inward affection, which ought to be given equally to all including our enemies. But this is unreasonable."

He explains: "Even as regards the affections, we ought to love one neighbor more than another. The reason is that, since the principle of love is God, and the person who loves, it must needs be that the affection of love increases in proportion to the nearness to one or another of those principles."

According to St. Thomas, then, the affections are naturally bipolar: the intensity of one's affections is naturally increased not only by proximity of the beloved to oneself, but also by proximity to God. We naturally love another person more intensely when either we or the other person is closer to God.

Smith, however, has a thoroughly unipolar view of the moral world: each individual is guided by sentiment to love those who are closest to him first; those more remote less; and so on.[114] In practice, Smith's system is Ptolemaic, in that everything revolves around the self; while the other is Copernican, in that the self revolves around God. The reason is not that Smith doesn't believe in God, but that in the Stoic view God does not transcend the world. A man must look outward for his duty to his fellow man, but he can only look inward to find God.

All this is a good illustration of the fact that one's metaphysics necessarily determines one's psychology. It brings to mind Chesterton's incisive comment about the Stoics: "Marcus Aurelius is the most intolerable of human types. He is an unselfish egoist. An unselfish egoist is a man who has pride without the excuse of passion. Of all conceivable forms of enlightenment the worst is what these people call the Inner Light. Of all horrible religions the most horrible is the worship of the god within. Any one who knows any body knows how it would work; any one who knows any one from the Higher Thought Centre knows how it does work. That Jones shall worship the god within him turns out ultimately to mean that Jones shall worship Jones."[115]

Since the Stoic governing principle of self-command is ultimately based on an inordinate love of self, St. Augustine regards it not as a virtue, but a "splendid vice;" that is to say, "though a vice, it counts as a virtue because it checks greater vices."[116] St. Augustine compares the Stoics favorably with the Epicureans, because the Stoics place the highest human good in virtue rather than pleasure. But he adds, "And yet men must not think themselves free from this degradation by posing as despisers of glory and paying no heed to the opinions of others, while they esteem themselves as wise men and win their own approval. For their virtue, if it exists, is dependent on the praise of man in another kind of way."[117]

APPENDIX II

The Philosophical Assumptions of "Human Capital" Theory

The debate over tax reform contains a strong philosophical aspect. But economists tend to disguise their worldviews in a discussion of economic theory. This almost always happens by way of assumption; nearly all academic crimes are committed in the footnotes. (I would state it as a general law that anyone who discusses Adam Smith nowadays is really discussing his own worldview.) What is so fascinating about "human capital" is that the issue exposes worldviews that normally remain hidden.

Each economic theory is devised to address a certain set of problems, like the Great Depression, inflation, or the effect of federal debt or pay-as-you-go social security systems. The "best" theory is usually the simplest one needed adequately to explain the problem at hand. However, when an economist habitually uses the same theory for a wide variety of applications—including those where it is inappropriate—this tends to reveal that person's philosophy in noneconomic matters.

For example, it was often suggested by his neoclassical critics that Keynes' short-run focus ("In the long run we are all dead.") corresponded to a hedonistic set of principles.

But it is no less true that the neoclassical life cycle theory corresponds rather neatly to a libertarian philosophy, in which society is made up not of households but of mythical self-sufficient individuals whose origins and destiny beyond this life are ignored. Children, estates, and bequests are inexplicable. A decision to have children is equated with the purchase of a consumer durable, which returns "psychic income" to its "owners"—the parents. Ignored is the fact that the decision results in future taxpayers, let alone people good in themselves. (I take a perverse pleasure in pointing out to earnest libertarians sporting Adam Smith ties that Smith regarded children as an investment; it drives them nuts.)

Implications of Human Capital Theory

However, there is a similar philosophical problem with the theory of human capital. The term "human capital" was coined by Theodore Schultz, who won the Nobel Prize for showing (in his words) that "investment in human capital accounts for most of the impressive rise in the real earnings per worker."[118] Schultz used the term apologetically, because he recognized its ambiguity—the danger of reducing people to the level of machines. I have felt justified in using this analysis against the neoclassical tax reformers because it is couched in terms they can understand, so long as the main current policy issue is whether to *raise* people to the level of machines.

But later theorists of human capital have used the term unapologetically. As I mentioned earlier, preserving the dignity of human beings by outlawing slavery has the side effect of producing underinvestment in human capital, which is reflected in the fact that human capital receives a higher rate of return than nonhuman capital. Once you accept the notion of human capital uncritically, the natural tendency among economists is to figure out ways to "cure" this "market imperfection"—that is, to restore slavery.

Milton Friedman has long proposed encouraging investors "to 'buy' a share in an individual's earnings prospects; to advance him the funds needed to finance his training on condition that he agree to pay the lender a specified fraction of his future earnings."[119] Friedman notes: "There seems no legal obstacle to private contracts of this kind, even though they are economically equivalent to the purchase of a share in an individual's earning capacity and thus to partial slavery." Rather than pausing here, he goes on to examine how this might be accomplished. I recently met some entrepreneurs in the process of establishing a family of Wall Street "human capital mutual funds" based on Friedman's proposal. Their main concern at the moment is to change a number of state laws to clarify the legal nature of such claims.

Gary Becker

The state-of-the-art theory about human capital is that of Nobel laureate Gary Becker.[120] But it is important to distinguish two different levels in Becker's theory. The economic part of Becker's theory is primarily "confined to the material aspects of family life, to incomes and spending patterns."[121] It represents a significant advance on the neoclassical assumptions, not only in economic but also in philosophical realism. Economic theory of this kind, as we have seen, must take as given the findings of other disciplines.

But in *The Economic Approach to Human Behavior* and his more recent *Treatise on the Family*, Becker has gone further, to try to apply the same methods outside the market: "My intent is more ambitious: to analyze marriage, births, divorce, division of labor in households, prestige and other nonmaterial behavior with the tools and framework for material behavior."[122] "Indeed," he continues, "I have come to the position that the economic approach is a comprehensive one that is applicable to all human behavior."[123]

Becker asks his lay audience "not to be put off by the terminology and techniques, for their participation is required to achieve a full development and evaluation of the rational approach to the family. I say this because many economists are hostile to this application of the approach, whereas increasing numbers of sociologists, anthropologists, lawyers, biologists, psychologists, and historians are using a rational choice approach or related methods to analyze the family. My 'treatise' is intended for an interdisciplinary audience—for sceptics as well as advocates."[124]

If we accept Becker's invitation, the first question we must ask is why his invitation is not extended to philosophers, or better still, to theologians. Becker is engaged in what is first of all not a work of economics or sociology or anthropology or jurisprudence, but rather moral philosophy; in fact, moral theology.[125] The real difficulty with his approach is not that it applies the method of rational choice to nonmarket decisions—man is, after all, a rational animal—but rather the assumptions he makes about human good: the end to which one chooses the means.

Becker says his theory is intended to be "relevant to behavior—to consumption and production choices—rather than giving a philosophical discussion of what 'really' motivates people."[126] But this is inadmissible. To say that "the economic approach is a comprehensive one that is applicable to all human behavior" is precisely to "give a philosophical discussion of what 'really' motivates people."

Gary Becker often credits Adam Smith with the idea of human capital[127] and describes his own work in this respect as a return to "classical" economic theory. But, as Schumpeter points out, Smith's analysis of human capital comes directly from Aristotle.

Household Relationships

When we read Aristotle's account of the household, our first instinct is to put it aside.[128] Aristotle speaks of the household as based on three fundamental natural relationships: man–woman, parent–child, and master–slave. The man rules in all three.

With not too much effort, we can get past the first two. In contrast to Plato, Aristotle does not view these as three versions of a single power relation. To Aristotle, neither the wife nor the child is a man's property.[129]

The child is subordinate only as long as his reason is still undeveloped. And although Aristotle assumes the wife will be ruled by her husband,[130] marriage for Aristotle is a love of friendship, which requires equality and not utility.[131] He notes (with disapproval) that in certain radical democracies, wives do not even take a subordinate role.[132]

No, our real difficulty is with the master–slave relationship, which is despotic (that is, for the benefit of the master). Aristotle notes that, besides land, "the wealth may consist also of slaves, cattle, coined money, and all that is generally called moveable property."[133] "The worker in a craft is, from the point of view of the craft, one of its tools"; the slave is a "tool worth many tools."[134] And for Aristotle, the worker is a quasislave,[135] who should not be a citizen unless he first qualifies by acquiring property.[136] Rather than saying that a slave is treated like a beast, Aristotle says that the ox is "the poor man's slave."[137]

Why, then, didn't Christian philosophers adopt stoic rather than Aristotelian philosophy? The Stoics were closer to Christianity than was Aristotle on many points—for example, that slavery is not natural, that all people are equally human, and that all are governed by a universal law of nature grounded in a divine reason or Logos.

Priority of Leisure

If we correct his error about slavery, Aristotle is maintaining a point about human nature that is absolutely fundamental for Western culture (yet left out of the Stoic scheme). The key is his insistence on the priority of leisure over work.

Aristotle says that the end of economics is wealth.[138] Wealth is what can be measured by money,[139] which in turn measures *chreia* (variously translated as "need," "utility," or "demand").[140] Wealth is not useful in itself, but only for the sake of something else. "Life is action, not production," he says.[141] And: "We are busy [lit.: unleisurely] in order to have leisure."[142] But what Aristotle means by leisure is nearly the opposite of today's notion, especially among economists.

Josef Pieper expresses the idea this way: "Culture depends for its very existence on leisure, and leisure, in its turn, is not possible unless it has a durable and consequently living link with the *cultus*, with divine worship."[143] Far from meaning idleness or amusement or time off from work—which essentially means time off *for* work, to become better workers[144]—leisure means above all contemplation, a primal wonder at reality.[145] Plato, Aristotle, and all Christian thinkers agree that the happiness of a rational being consists in the contemplation of God (even when they disagree on the nature of God). In classical and Christian philosophy, man is first of all a "knower," not a "thinker."[146] While man actively uses discursive reason in preparation for understanding, the act of understanding itself is passive: it is receptive to reality. In philosophy, as in Scripture, it is true that "man being without understanding is like the beasts that perish."

The contrast with Becker's philosophy of economics becomes clear if we insert the term "human capital" wherever Aristotle uses the term "slave." "Human capital," as we saw, is the wealth a person has in his own useful abilities, just as "nonhuman capital" or property is the wealth a person has in his external goods. The relation between a person and his own "human capital" is indeed fundamental to the household. And, exactly like the master–slave relationship, and unlike the relation between husband and wife or between parent and child, this relation is "despotic"—that is, for the sake of the ruler.[147] The free man is free, Aristotle says, precisely because he is "master of himself."[148] That is, he is free only if what is "useful" (his "human capital") is only a part of his person, and is in fact subordinated to serve the "useless" part of his person—because useful things are done for the sake of something else; but things done for their own sake are strictly "useless." Every person, as it were, is a combined Mary and Martha, and Mary has not only chosen, but *is*, the better part.[149] If a person is only a Martha, if his life consists only of the "useful," he is no longer free but has become a slave to utility.[150]

Totalitarianism

On this point, the Smithian view puts itself outside of the mainstream of Western culture. Smith has little patience with contemplation as opposed to practical knowledge: "The most sublime speculation of the contemplative philosopher," he says, "can scarce compensate the neglect of the smallest active duty."[151] In Smith's system of "natural liberty," utility takes over life; contemplation is useless, so not worth doing. For the mainstream of Western civilization, contemplation is "use-less" precisely because it *is* worth doing, for its own sake and not for the sake of something else.

Becker's views of human nature closely follow Smith's. Among Becker's most important basic assumptions, I would list three: First, that all human behavior (not just economic behavior) is based on utility—including the behavior of "altruists." Second, that altruism does not apply to persons outside one's own "dynasty"—that is, beyond one's relatives. Third, that economic agents do not act in view of a personal existence after death.

First, Becker's economic theory begins with the assumption that all time is employed in the production or consumption of utility. "Time and goods are inputs into the production of 'commodities,' which directly provide utility. These commodities can be produced as well as consumed by households using market purchases, own time, and various environmental inputs. These commodities include children, prestige and esteem, health, altruism, envy, and pleasures of the senses, and are much smaller in number than the goods consumed."[152] In a footnote, Becker refers the reader to Bentham's list of pleasures and pains.[153]

In Becker's theory, the value of time is ultimately measured in goods. Moreover, all time is devoted to work, nonmarket production and consumption of "commodities," or "maintenance of capital."[154] Becker's theory literally leaves no time for contemplative activity. And by referring all behavior to "psychic income," he does not allow that market or nonmarket "work" may have a contemplative component. This is a (rather radical) philsophical presupposition, not a necessary tenet of economic analysis.

Becker does allow that the value of different uses of time can vary because of "productive consumption."[155] But this carries us still further away from the nature of contemplation. Consumption may indeed be efficient, but true celebration, on the contrary, always contains an element of sacrifice—that is, sheer waste of utility. This was captured by Keynes' ironic phrase, "Two pyramids, two masses for the dead are twice as good as one; but not so two railways from London to York."[156] A sacred person, object, or place is precisely one which is not *used*, but rather vacated of utility.

The market value of leisure, of its nature, cannot even in theory be measured or even estimated. Time spent praying, or dancing, or reading poetry, or hearing Mozart, or witnessing Shakespeare, or even in strenuous child-rearing, is not prayer or poetry or music or Shakespeare or child-rearing at all if an economic taxi meter is always running in the background, ticking off a supposed price measured as the cost in foregone earnings. Things done for their own sake may indeed have an implicit cost in this life, but not a price, because they have no marginal utility or economic value. The opposite assumption leads to what might be called "totalutilitarianism": a totalitarianism of utility.

Limits of Taxation

These philosophical presuppositions appear to underlie Becker's position that the nonmarket time of students and parents should be considered as "expensed" for tax purposes—while at the same time holding that cash outlays for human "maintenance" costs should not be expensed for tax purposes.[157] But under this reasoning, there can be no objection (apart from practicality) to taxing the imputed value of all nonmarket time.

The natural law, however, suggests going in the opposite direction; rather than adding more and more dubiously imputed items to the national income and product accounts, we should omit them as far as possible. We should tax only stocks of wealth or flows of income that have a market price (and of course prohibit from sale certain things which might have a price—such as human beings or sex). At that point, they are fair game for the tax collector—but not before. And, as I suggested in the main text, we should exclude from the domestic product human maintenance costs, which are really intermediate inputs that do not add to the final product. Such an approach to taxation would have the added utility of being much simpler.

Value of Love

Becker's second and third assumptions are basically implications of the first. We saw earlier that Smith refers all human loves to "a stronger love, a more powerful affection, which generally takes place upon such occasions; the love of what is honourable and noble, of the grandeur, and dignity, and superiority of our own characters."[158] This is exactly the case with Becker's "altruism" within the family, which he justifies with a quotation from Adam Smith.[159]

One of the most interesting features of Becker's theory is that it posits two important features of human nature: first, that the economic actions of an individual will have results beyond his own natural life; and second, that such decisions are motivated by love—or, since this is a word that embarrasses economists, by "altruism."

The good part about this development is that love is recognized as basic to economic life and modeled as an identification of the self with the beloved. The bad part is that, in Becker's theory, all love is based on utility. St. Thomas, following Aristotle, distinguishes two kinds of love—love of concupiscence and love of friendship. The love of concupiscence is a love of utility (love for the sake of something else), while the love of friendship is for its own sake. I "love" vanilla ice cream—because I love myself: the first is a love of utility, the second a love of friendship.[160]

The way Becker and others model love (altruism) is to say that the happiness (utility) of a spouse or descendant enters into the rational decision making (utility function) of the economic agent. Thus altruism may or may not actually increase the utility of the other person (depending on how well we know what they desire and are able to deliver it); but altruism always provides utility to the agent, in the form of "psychic income."

This definition accounts for some of the peculiar features of Becker's altruism. The theory tries to explain certain behavior which will reap results beyond an individual's lifetime and is motivated by love; but it ignores such behavior if it is motivated by love for anyone but one's own relatives—for example, one's next-door neighbor or God. Also, each person is assumed to take into account the well-being of all relatives and descendants, not only today, but long after one's own natural death, to the remotest generation; but the same person does not consider his own personal state after this life.

This assumption corresponds to the Stoic–Epicurean worldview.[161] But as a matter of descriptive realism, it obviously cannot apply to a large share of the economic behavior of a large share of the world's population, which believes—whether from reason, inclination, or religious faith—in the persistence of the personal self beyond this life.

Selfishness and Altruism

It might seem that these problems could be solved with a few simple adjustments. There is, after all, something unnecessarily labored in the whole modeling of selfishness and altruism. It is customary to define selfish behavior as taking only one's own utility into account, and altruistic behavior as taking someone else's utility into account (usually weighted by some fraction between 0 and 1, to stand for one's degree of altruism). But surely the loving person takes his own utility into account, while the utility of others enters into the calculation of even the most selfish person. What distinguishes a selfish person from a loving person is the relative ranking of the other person's good in one's own scale of values.

We might therefore modify Becker's assumptions slightly and admit altruistic behavior toward those outside the family dynasty. If there is no afterlife, we must of course explain, say, the voluntary poverty and service of Mother Teresa as the production of "psychic income" which must necessarily be "consumed" in the present. But if we recognize the belief in personal existence after death, then Mother Teresa can be seen as making an "investment" which will reap future returns—a literal storing of "treasure in heaven." Under this aspect, Mother Teresa (who could easily have been another Bill Gates because of her media skills and worldwide organizational ability) might be described as the Bill Gates of heaven.

Such adjustments might temper Becker's systematic tendency to view economic factors as taking precedence over religious factors.[162] For example, he holds that the change in divorce and contraceptive practices in Catholic Ireland occurred because of economic factors.[163] Giving due weight to economic factors, the more obvious explanation (certainly to anyone who has viewed many Irish films of the past twenty years) is that the change in religious views preceded the change in behavior.

Such modifications to Becker's theory would raise a number of interesting but complicated questions. For example, if we model love by including the beloved's utility in the lover's utility function, how does our love of God increase God's utility? Perhaps we might admit that it can't ("Do I eat the flesh of strong bulls?" Ps 50:13; "The Lord's are the earth and its fullness." Ps 24:1; "Sacrifice or oblation you wished not." Ps 40:7); but observe that He tells us that if we love Him, we should take our neighbor's utility into account ("What does the Lord require of you but to do justice, love goodness, and walk humbly with your God?" Mi 6:8; "When you do anything for the least of my brethren, you do it for me." Mt 25:40).

But that raises a different question: how much marginal utility is necessary to be admitted to paradise? There would seem to be a sort of sliding scale: "Of those to whom much is given, much is demanded." Lk 12:48. The widow's mite in the temple treasury is "worth more than all the rest." Lk 21:3. "If I give away all I have to the poor and have not love, I am nothing." 1 Cor 13:3.

All this would be a fascinating exercise. But it would not remove the main problem: it is impossible to construct a philosophy that purports to explain all human behavior in terms of utility, without specifying the ends things are to be used *for*. Becker's underlying assumptions about human nature are essentially stoic; but Becker has not explained why such a theory should be based on stoic assumptions rather than on some other (less contradictory) philosophy.

As we saw, Aristotle, Plato, and St. Thomas Aquinas all agree that human happiness consists in contemplation not of the excellence of one's own character, but of the highest good: God.[164] It is therefore clear that a person cannot be perfectly happy in this life—precisely because the demands of utility keep pressing in. In fact, a little thought reveals that perfect happiness even in the next life must exceed our unaided natural powers.[165] How can anyone understand God, except through God's action?

Therefore, any version of the natural law which is closed rather than open to revelation is objectionable, purely in human terms. Smith's and Becker's philosophy is a closed system. The ancient Stoics were not wrong to react against Aristotle's view that human beings are unequal by nature, so that only some people can be free and others cannot. The Stoics rightly insisted in response that every human being is equal by nature. But in the modern version of the Stoic philosophy, no one is free; all are equally slaves to utility.

I should emphasize (if it is not already sufficiently obvious) that Gary Becker is an economist whose sandal I am unworthy to unlatch. He also strikes me as a humane and humorous man, a gentle man. One of the best parts of Becker's books is the footnotes, where he is always generous in acknowledging the source of an inspiration or a change in his own earlier view—and best of all, likely to illustrate a point from Dickens or The Forsythe Saga or St. Paul or Dondi or the Wizard of Id.

But the basic assumptions, and the philosophy which animates the whole, do not come from Dickens or St. Paul or the Wizard of Id; they come from Zeno of Citium, by way of Adam Smith. Precisely because Becker's influence is so great, I fear that unless Becker himself corrects the philosophical errors, the promising theory of human capital will undergo decades of unnecessary confusion, exactly like the nineteenth-century controversy over the nature of value.

BIBLIOGRAPHY

Adams, Charles, *For Good and Evil: The Impact of Taxes in the Course of Civilization.* New York: Madison Books, 1993.

Albright, William Foxwell, *From the Stone Age to Christianity: Monotheism and the Historical Process.* Garden City, N.Y.: Doubleday, 1957.

Aquinas, St. Thomas, *Summa Theologica,* Westminster MD: Christian Classics, 1981. [*S.T.*]

———, *Summa Contra Gentiles.* Notre Dame, IN: University of Notre Dame Press, 1975. [*S.C.G.*]

———, Anderson, James F., ed., *An Introduction to the Metaphysics of St. Thomas Aquinas.* Washington, D.C.: Regnery Gateway, 1989.

———, Bigongiari, Dino, ed., *The Political Ideas of St. Thomas Aquinas.* New York: Hafner Press, 1953.

———, Vernon J. Bourke, ed., *The Pocket Aquinas.* New York: Washington Square Press, 1976.

———, Mary T. Clark, ed., *An Aquinas Reader: Selections from the Writings of Thomas Aquinas.* Garden City, N.Y.: Image Books, 1972.

———, Dawson, J.G., *Aquinas: Selected Political Writings.* Oxford: Basil Blackwell, 1959.

———, Pegis, Anton C., ed., *Introduction to St. Thomas Aquinas*, St. Thomas, *The Catechetical Instructions of St. Thomas Aquinas*, Jospeh F. Wagner, Inc., New York 1939. New York: Modern Library, 1948.

Aristotle, *The Nichomachean Ethics*. Sir David Ross, ed., London: Oxford University Press, 1963.

———, *The Politics*. Baltimore: Penguin Books, 1972.

———, Ackrill, J.L., ed., *A New Aristotle Reader*. Princeton N.J.: Princeton University Press, 1987.

———, *The Student's Oxford Aristotle*, Vol. III. Ross, W.D., ed. London: Oxford University Press, 1942.

Augustine of Hippo, *City of God*. New York: Penguin Books, 1984.

———, *Confessions*. New York: Penguin Books, 1973.

———, Vernon J. Bourke, ed., *The Essential Augustine*. New York: Mentor–Omega Books, 1964.

———, Henry Paolucci, ed., *St. Augustine: The Political Writings*. Chicago: Gateway Editions, 1985.

Barro, Robert J., "Are Government Bonds Net Wealth?" *Journal of Political Economy* 82 (1974) 1095–1117.

Becker, Gary S., *The Economic Approach to Human Behavior*. Chicago: University of Chicago Press, 1976.

———, *A Treatise on the Family*. Cambridge: Harvard University Press, 1994a.

———, *Human Capital*, 3rd ed. Chicago: University of Chicago Press, 1994b.

Belloc, Hilaire, *The Servile State*. Indianapolis: Liberty Classics, 1977.

Bentham, Jeremy, "*Principles of Morals and Legislation*," in *The Utilitarians*. Garden City, N.Y.: Dolphin Books, 1961.

Blaug, Mark, *Economic Theory in Retrospect*, 3d ed. Cambridge: Cambridge University Press, 1978.

Bourke, Vernon J., *St. Thomas and the Greek Moralists*. The Aquinas Lecture, 1947, Marquette University Press.

Bouwsma, William J., *John Calvin: A Sixteenth Century Portrait*. London: Oxford University Press, 1988.

Carlson, Allan, "Social Security, Dependency and the Family," paper presented to a Cato Institute conference on Social Security, Washington, D.C., December 10–12, 1986.

Chafuen, Alejandro A., *Christians for Freedom: Late-Scholastic Economics*. San Francisco: Ignatius Press, 1986.

Chesterton, G.K., *Orthodoxy*. London: The Bodley Head, 1909.

———, *What's Wrong With the World*. New York: Dodd, Mead & Co., 1910.

Copleston, F.C., *A History of Philosophy*, Vol. 1. Norwich: Burns Oates & Washbourne Ltd., 1946; other Vols: Image Books, 1962–1964.

———, *Aquinas*. New York: Penguin, 1991.

Dawson, Christopher, *A Selection from the Works of Christopher Dawson*, James Oliver and Christinia Scott, eds., Image Books, Garden City, New York(1975)

Deane, Herbert A., *The Political and Social Ideas of St. Augustine*. New York: Columbia University Press, 1963.

Denison, Edward F., *Accounting for United States Economic Growth, 1929–1969*. Washington, D.C.: Brookings Institution, 1974.

Douglas, Paul H., *The Theory of Wages*. New York: Augustus M. Kelley, 1964.

Eisner, Robert, *The Total Incomes System of Accounts*. Chicago: University of Chicago Press, 1989.

Encyclopedia Brittanica (EB), 15th ed.
Epictetus, "Encheiridion," in *Classics of Western Philosophy*, 3rd edition. Steven M. Cahn, ed. Indianapolis: Hackett Publishing, 1990.
Feldstein, Martin S., "Social security, induced retirement, and aggregate capital accumulation," *Journal of Political Economy* (September–October 1974) 905–26.
Friedman, Milton, *Capitalism and Freedom*. Chicago: University of Chicago Press, 1962.
Gilson, Etienne, *History of Christian Philosophy in the Middle Ages*. New York: Random House, 1955.
———, *Thomist Realism & the Critique of Knowledge*. San Francisco: Ignatius Press, 1986.
Hartshorne, Charles, & William R. Reese, *Philosophers Speak of God*. Chicago: University of Chicago Press, 1953.
Heller, Agnes, *Renaissance Man*. New York: Schocken Books, 1981.
Hicks, Sir John, *A Theory of Economic History*. London: Oxford University Press, 1969.
Horton, John, and Susan Mendus, eds., *After MacIntyre: Critical Perspectives on the Work of Alasdair MacIntyre*. Notre Dame IN: University of Notre Dame Press, 1994.
Kendrick, John W., *The Formation and Stocks of Total Capital*, New York: Columbia University Press, 1976.
Keynes, John Maynard, *The General Theory of Employment, Interest and Money*, Harbinger (Harcourt Brace & World), New York, 1965.
Komonchak, Joseph A., "Theology and Culture at Mid-Century: The Example of Henri de Lubac," in *Theological Studies* 51 (1990) 578–602.
———, "The Encounter Between Catholicism and Liberalism," in *Catholicism and Liberalism*, R. Bruce Douglass and David Hollenbach, eds. Cambridge: Cambridge University Press, 1994, 76–99.
Maddison, Angus, *Monitoring the World Economy, 1820–1992*. Paris: OECD, 1995.
Mill, John Stuart, "Utilitarianism," in *The Utilitarians*. Garden City, N.Y.: Dolphin Books, 1961.
Mueller, John, "Virtue, Incentive and Economic Policy," *Crisis*, (November 1985) 19–24.
———, "A Subsidy for Motherhood: Why I Now Support Social Security," *Policy Review* (Fall 1987) 46–48.
———, "How Can Wages Fall While Unemployment Rises?" March 11, Lehrman, Bell, Mueller, & Cannon, Inc., Arlington, VA, 1994a.
———, "A Challenge to Conventional Labor-Market Wisdom," May, *LBMC, Inc.*, Arlington, VA, 1994b.
———, Testimony and papers submitted as an adviser to the National Commission on Economic Growth and Tax Reform.
"The Tax Treatment of Human and Nonhuman Capital," June 21, 1995a.
"Curing Workers' Biggest Headache," June 21, 1995b.
"The Distribution of a Federal 'Consumption' Tax," August 10, 1995c.
"The LBMC Plan for Tax Reform," September 26, 1995d.
Myrdal, Gunnar, *Population: A Problem for Democracy*. Cambridge: Harvard University Press, 1940.

Novak, Michael, *The Spirit of Democratic Capitalism.* New York: AEI/Simon & Schuster, 1982.

Pegis, Anton C., *St. Thomas and the Greeks.* The Aquinas Lecture, 1939, Marquette University Press.

———, *St. Thomas and Philosophy.* The Aquinas Lecture, 1964, Marquette University Press.

Pieper, Josef, *Leisure the Basis of Culture.* New York: Pantheon Books, 1964.

Plato, *The Republic of Plato*, Translated by Francis MacDonald Cornford, Oxford University Press, New York and London, 1945.

Reynolds, Susan, *Fiefs and Vassals: The Medieval Evidence Reinterpreted.* London: Oxford University Press, 1994.

Roepke, Wilhelm, *A Humane Economy: The Social Framework of the Free Market.* South Bend: Gateway Editions, 1977.

Rothbard, Murray, *An Austrian Perspective on the History of Economic Thought*, Hants, England: Aldershot, 1995.

Rueff, Jacques, *L'Ordre Social.* Paris: Editions Genin, 1967.

Schindler, David L., "Economics and the Civilization of Love," *The Chesterton Review* (May–August 1994) 189–212.

Schultz, Theodore W., "Investment in Human Capital," *The American Economic Review* (March 1961) 1–17.

Schumpeter, Joseph A., *History of Economic Analysis.* New York: Oxford University Press, 1954.

Smith, Adam, *An Inquiry into the Nature and Causes of the Wealth of Nations.* New York: Augustus M. Kelley, 1966.

———, *The Theory of Moral Sentiments.* D.D. Raphael & A.L. Macfie, eds. Indianapolis: Liberty Classics, 1984. [*TMS*]

Smith, T.V., ed., *From Aristotle to Plotinus.* Chicago: University of Chicago Press, 1959.

Spiegel, William Henry, *The Growth of Economic Thought.* Duke University Press, 1971.

Taylor, Charles, *Philosophical Arguments.* Cambridge: Harvard University Press, 1995.

———, *Philosophy and the Human Sciences.* Cambridge: Cambridge University Press, 1985.

Tomes, Nigel, "The Family, Inheritance, and the Intergenerational Transmission of Inequality," *Journal of Political Economy* 89 (5) (1981) 928–958.

Trevor-Roper, H.R., *The European Witch Craze of the Sixteenth and Seventeenth Centuries and Other Essays.* New York: Harper & Row, 1969.

Weaver, Warren, *Lady Luck: The Theory of Probability.* Garden City, New York: Anchor Books, 1963.

NOTES

1. I would like to acknowledge the valuable advice of Lewis Lehrman (especially on the nature of value), Jeffrey Bell (especially on historical and current

political applications), and Frank Cannon (for his immense common sense, particularly in the simple presentation of complex subjects). It is rare to have business partners who are such original (and published) thinkers. I would also like to express my thanks for the very helpful insights of G.A. Mackenzie of the I.M.F. (especially on the relation between economics and philosophy) and Justin Mundy, consultant to the World Bank (especially on recent developments in philosophy)—both of whom happen to be my neighbors, but for whose opinions it would be worth traveling much farther than across the alley.

2. For example, when theologian Michael Novak wishes to defend what is defensible in "democratic capitalism," he writes a book in which Adam Smith plays the central role. And when theologian David Schindler takes issue with Novak's views on the economy and culture, he begins his attack under cover of a barrage upon Smith's "invisible hand;" Novak (1982) and Schindler (1994). I choose this example because it is timely and interesting, and I have had a peripheral connection with it. I am grateful to both Michael Novak and David Schindler for their generous assistance in exploring the background of the controversy, and to Fr. Joseph Komonchak for helping me to making sense of the theological issues involved; see Komonchak (1990) and Komonchak (1994).

3. Smith (1966), Vol. 2, 366. Book V, Chapter 1.

4. Schumpeter (1954). Parts of Schumpeter's thesis were criticized. (For that matter, I will criticize parts of it.) But the *Encyclopedia Brittanica* refers to Schumpeter's *History of Economic Analysis* as the "definitive work" on the history of value and price theory.

Schumpeter's impact on historians of economic theory can be roughly gauged by comparing two standard textbooks: Marc Blaug's *Economic Theory in Retrospect*, first published in 1962, and Henry William Spiegel's *The Growth of Economic Thought*, which appeared in 1971. Blaug's text, even in its third edition, devotes a slim opening chapter to "Pre-Adamite economics," entirely concerning eighteenth-century ideas (except for a two-page "afterthought" on scholastic influences, in reaction to Schumpeter). Nine years later, Spiegel's book devotes fully *one-third* of its text to the "pre-Adamites"—almost exactly the same proportion as did Schumpeter.

5. Schumpeter (1954), 6.

6. Schumpeter (1954), 184. According to Schumpeter, Smith represents the transition from moral philosopher as part-time economist to economist as full-time specialist. "It is highly significant that A. Smith found it impossible to do what Hutcheson had done as a matter of course, namely, to produce a complete system of moral philosophy at one throw." Schumpeter (1954), 141.

But if the tools of economic analysis had long been available, why didn't an Adam Smith appear much sooner? Schumpeter doesn't say, but the answer, I believe, is that as long as society is basically agricultural, most economic activity occurs outside the market. In such conditions, economics remains what the name implies—the science of "household management," not the study of markets.

It is only with the rise of industrialism that the bulk of economic activity occurs through the market. This change began in the United Kingdom around the eighteenth century—sooner than in other nations. For example, by 1820, 70 percent of the population was employed in agriculture in the United States and only 15 percent in industry, while in the United Kingdom only 38 percent of the population was employed in agriculture and 33 percent in industry (the remainder comprising services). Maddison (1995), 253. This development requires an expositor like Adam Smith (whose theory, as he himself observes, is valid only for a mercantile economy).

7. The two major theories of money (money as token and money as commodity) can be traced to Plato and Aristotle, respectively, both of whom were closer to mankind's first coinage of money than we are to the American Revolution. Coinage was introduced in Lydia in the seventh century B.C., and in Greece in the sixth, only about 150 years before Plato and Aristotle analyzed the nature of money.

In Plato's *Republic* we find the first analysis of the division of labor, including its effect in raising productivity. *Republic*, Chapters VI and VII. Hicks comments, "We have become so accustomed, ever since Adam Smith, to the association of the division of labour with market development that it comes with something of a shock when one realizes that this was not its origin. The first development of skill is independent of the market." Hicks (1969), 23.

Aristotle analyzes the logic of this division of labor, along with economic utility and exchange value, private property, and monopoly. He draws distinctions between what economists now call human and nonhuman capital, and between producer and consumer goods. Along the way he outlines a theory of economic history that proceeds from self-sufficient households to barter to money, like an economics textbook. For summaries, see Schumpeter (1954), 57–65, and Spiegel (1971), 24–34.

8. Schumpeter (1954), 60.

9. Schumpeter (1954), 8. "As a landmark we choose the *Summa Theologica* of St. Thomas Aquinas, which excludes revelation from the *philosophicae disciplinae*, that is, from all sciences except supernatural theology (*sacra doctrina*; natural theology is one of the *philosophicae disciplinae*). This was the earliest and most important step in methodological criticism taken in Europe after the breakdown of the Graeco–Roman world. It will be shown below how exclusion of revelation from all sciences except the *sacra doctrina* was coupled by St. Thomas with the exclusion from them of appeal to authority as a *scientific* method" (8n).

"Aristotle defined each science by its subject. But St. Thomas realized that different sciences often deal with the same things (*de eisdem rebus*) and that it is not the subject but the cognitive process (*ratio cognoscibilis*) which identifies a science" (83n).

"St. Thomas himself became, for many people, simply the man who had succeeded in harnessing Aristotle for the service of the Church. This misconception of the revolution of the thirteenth century and, in particular, of St. Thomas' performance was not corrected but, on the contrary, fostered by the scientific practice of the next 300 years. For Aristotle's work continued to provide the systematic frame for the growing scientific material and to supply the need for nicely pedestrian texts; everything, therefore, continued to be cast in the Aristotelian mold—nothing so completely as scholastic economics, which also illustrates the way in which, by this convenient practice, the scholastic doctors were likely to lose the credit for their original contributions" (89).

10. In the scholastics, all of the earlier Greek elements are preserved and developed into scientific theories of money and prices (including a theory of competitive equilibrium), though the Greek attitude toward work and commerce is transformed. On St. Thomas Aquinas' contributions to the justification of private property and the "redemption of business," see Spiegel, 57–68.

Following a suggestion from St. Thomas that profits are "a kind of wage" for a social service, the later Schoolmen developed the first theory of profits and interest, explaining what had puzzled Aristotle: "the fundamental factor that raises interest above zero is the prevalence of business profits." Schumpeter (1954), 105.

11. Schumpeter (1954), 97. The main motive of the Scholastic "economists" was not speculative but pastoral. "They wrote for many purposes but principally for the instruction of confessors" Ibid., 102. A council of 1215 had greatly stimulated the demand for such analysis by establishing the (still current) church law that everyone confess his or her sins to a parish priest at least once a year.

12. Schumpeter traces the path through the "Protestant scholastics" of the sixteenth and seventeenth centuries ("The laics of the seventeenth century continued rather than destroyed scholastic work." Ibid., 81); then the natural law philosophers of the eighteenth century. Ibid., 117–18, 229.

13. Schumpeter (1954), 186.

14. Smith (1984), Introduction by Raphael and Macfie, eds., 5.

Smith's stoicism must be the best-kept open secret in economics. The influence is obvious to the editors of the *Theory of Moral Sentiments*; but I have never heard or seen it referred to by any economist or historian of economic analysis.

Economic historians have searched in vain for sources of inspiration of the "invisible hand" among Smith's contemporaries and immediate predecessors. Was it Mandeville, or Ferguson, or Shaftesbury, or his teacher Hutcheson, or his friend David Hume? Spiegel (1971), 226–28. Or did it come more circuitously, via Grotius and Pufendorf, along with the tools Schumpeter proved to be inherited from the scholastic tradition? Blaug (1978), 30. Or was it a product of Smith's supposed "dour Calvinism"? Rothbard (1995), vol. I, 457 (Rothbard cites Emil Kauder and Paul Douglas to support this position).

None of the explanations has proven satisfactory. Careful study has shown that the influence on Smith of moral philosophers of his time is "remarkably small." Smith (1984), Introduction, 10. Blaug's explanation cannot account for the remarkable Smithian "detour" from the scholastic theory of value. Rothbard's does not square with Smith's letters and other writings, which indicate that by the time he wrote the *Wealth of Nations*, he was not a Christian, much less a Calvinist. Smith (1984), Appendix II.

Smith's contemporaries and immediate predecessors provided him the problems to work on and solutions to react against; but he was far more likely to quote from Zeno, Cleanthes, Cicero, Seneca, Epictetus, or Marcus Aurelius (and more accurately, too!). These were his intellectual contemporaries, with whom he was likely communing during his legendary bouts of absentmindedness. Smith is said to have stumbled into a tanning pit during some earnest discussion with a friend, and was known for stepping into his garden in a dressing gown and waking up to find himself fifteen miles away. Smith's front porch was the *Stoa poikile*.

I believe that a careful analysis of Smith's conception of God would indicate that it is not just logically but consciously pantheistic. Smith's characteristic description of God is not the Creator but "the great Conductor of the Universe" (*TMS* VI.ii.3.4)—a conductor who is very much part of the orchestra. Smith speaks (paraphrasing Marcus Aurelius) of God as "that divine Being, whose benevolence and wisdom have, from all eternity, contrived and conducted the immense machine of this universe, so as at all times to produce the greatest possible quantity of happiness" (*TMS*, VI.ii.3.5)—implying that God is coeternal with the universe.

The same conclusion is suggested by Smith's psychology (see Appendix I) and by the guarded and ambiguous nature of Smith's comments on an afterlife and on the (in)efficacy of divine sanctions (*TMS*, III.2.12, III.2.33; *WN*, vol. 2, 354–55, Book V Chapter I). The ancient Stoics "taught that human souls were offshoots of the world-soul, to which they returned after death." Albright (1957), 352. Some believed in a temporary existence of the soul after death, at least for the wise man, but only until being resolved into the fiery principle in the final conflagration.

In a letter dated August 14, 1776, Smith writes: "Poor David Hume is dying very fast, but with great chearfulness and good humour and with more real resignation to the necessary course of things, than any Whining Christian ever dyed with pretended resignation to the Will of God." Smith (1984), 19. Smith is paraphrasing Marcus Aurelius' reaction upon witnessing the death of Christian martyrs: "What a soul is that which is ready to be released from the body at any requisite moment, and be quenched or dissipated or hold together! But the readiness must spring from a man's inner judgment, and not result from mere opposition (as is the case with the Christians). It must be associated with deliberation and dignity and, if others too are to be convinced, with nothing like stage-heroics." Quoted in Gilson (1955), 16. (Gilson notes dryly, "Marcus Aurelius forgets that the stage had not been set by the Christians themselves.") This episode was a rather literal example of the view of Poseidonius of Apamea, a first-century Stoic historian, who "taught that the Stoic takes a position above the rest of mankind, looking down on their struggles as on a spectacle" *EB* 14:255, "History of Western Philosophy."

I don't think it fanciful to suggest that Smith took seriously the doctrine of Epictetus that the ideal teacher would be unmarried so as to be calm and free (Discourses III, 22). It is curious that, in listing the many kinds of natural human affection (parents, children, brother and sister, etc.), Smith omits to mention the affection between husband and wife. *TMS*, VI.ii.1.1.

There is indeed a strong affinity between Smith's explicitly Stoic view of Providence and Calvin's theory of predestination. Calvin's asides on the nature of economic value are also much like Smith's theory of a helpful divine deception: "Does he [God] not, in short, render many things attractive to us, apart from their utility?" Bouwsma (1988), 135. But there is no evidence of direct influence upon Smith from Calvin's writings of which I am aware.

Rather, both Calvin and Smith drank directly from Stoic sources. Calvin's theory of "double predestination" is strikingly similar to a famous passage of the Renaissance Stoic Lorenzo Valla, whom Calvin studied carefully (Bouwsma [1988], 13): "Jupiter, as he created the wolf fierce, the hare timid, the lion brave, the ass stupid, the dog savage, the sheep mild, so he fashioned some men hard of heart, others soft, he generated one given to evil, the other to virtue, and, further, he gave a capacity to reform to one and made another incorrigible. To you, indeed, he assigned an evil soul with no resource for reform. And so both you, for your inborn character, will do evil, and Jupiter, on account of your actions and their evil effects, will punish sternly." Quoted in Heller (1981), 434.

Moreover, while Smith's Stoicism is thorough and consistent (as befits an eighteenth-century thinker), Calvin is eclectically semiStoic, adopting the Stoic position in some cases, but disagreeing sharply in others. "A systematic Calvin would be an anachronism; there are no 'systematic' thinkers of any significance in the sixteenth century." Bouwsma (1988), 5.

15. In the *Wealth of Nations* Smith says that every individual "intends only his own gain, and he is in this, as in many other cases, led by an invisible hand to promote an end which was no part of his intention. Nor is it always the worse for the society that it was no part of it. By pursuing his own interest he frequently promotes that of the society more effectually than when he really intends to promote it." Smith (1966), II, 35. Book IV, Chapter II.

In this passage, Smith identifies the "public interest" or "public good" with what today we would call national income ("the annual revenue of society") or its counterpart, domestic product ("the exchangeable value of the whole annual produce of its industry").

16. Smith (1984), 36. TMS I.i.3.4.

17. "The rich only select from the heap what is mot precious and agreeable. They consume little more [food] than the poor, and in spite of their selfishness and rapacity, though they mean only their own conveniency, though the sole end which they propose from the labour of all the thousands whom they employ, be the gratification of their own vain and insatiable desires, they divide with the poor the produce of all their improvements. They are led by an invisible hand to make nearly the same distribution of the necessaries of life, which would have been made, had the earth been divided into equal portions among its inhabitants, and thus without intending it, without knowing it, advance the interest of the society, and afford means to the multiplication of the species." Smith (1984), 183–84. TMS IV.1.10.

18. "If we consider the real satisfaction which all these things are capable of affording, by itself and separated from the beauty of that arrangement which is fitted to promote it, it will always appear in the highest degree contemptible and trifling. But we rarely view it in this abstract and philosophical light. . . . The pleasures of wealth and greatness, when considered in this complex view, strike the imagination as something grand and beautiful and noble, of which the attainment is well worth all the toil and anxiety which we are so apt to bestow upon it.

"And it is well that nature imposes on us in this manner. It is this deception which rouses and keeps in continual motion the industry of mankind." Smith (1984), 183. TMS IV.1.9,10.

19. Or, put more politely: "Some truths about God exceed all the ability of the human reason. Such is the truth that God is triune. But there are some truths which the natural reason is also able to reach. Such are that God exists, that He is one, and the like. In fact, such truths about God have been proved demonstratively by the philosophers, guided by the light of natural reason." *Summa Contra Gentiles*, Book I Chapter 3 Section 1.

The probabilities always overwhelmingly favor the "argument from design." The odds of proverbial monkeys pecking away at typewriters and producing *Hamlet* are about 1 in $10^{41,600}$. Arthur Eddington estimated that the total number of atomic particles in the universe—protons and electrons—is on the order of 10^{79}. Weaver (1963), 236–37. At these odds, even a dogmatic skeptic has to be a fool not to accept Pascal's Wager.

This is as good a place as any to reveal my cheerful ignorance of modern philosophy, which seems to me mostly about what engineers call a "Scotch tape problem"—that is, a problem which is no problem at all. When Scotch tape was invented, it promised to revolutionize packaging; but an incredible amount of effort went into solving the problem of how to keep Scotch tape from sticking to itself before use: should it be sold in sheets with a peel-off backing? and so on. Finally, some genius figured out that Scotch tape *should* stick to itself before use. And so it was sold in rolls.

The problem of "critical" philosophy, I take it, is how we can be sure the world exists. I'm an inveterate Johnsonian on this point. When Samuel Johnson heard about Bishop Berkeley's doubts about the external world, he remarked, "I refute him thus," and kicked a large boulder. If you can't accept it as certain that "there is an is," you have one of two choices: meaning without a world (Descartes) or a world without meaning (the empiricists, positivists, and utilitarians). As Etienne Gilson pointed out, this peculiarly modern problem seems to afflict even some "Thomists." Gilson (1986).

Yet nobody lives according to such a philosophy, least of all the philosophers who espouse it. As Hume observed: "I dine, I play a game of backgammon, I converse and am merry with my friends; and when after three or four hours' amusement, I would return to these speculations, they appear so cold and strained and ridiculous that I cannot find in my heart to enter into them any further. Here then I find myself absolutely and necessarily determined to live and talk and act like other people in the common affairs of life." Cited in Copleston's *History of Philosophy*, Vol. 5, 119.

20. "Though the Greek Stoics are materialistic, naturalistic and pantheistic in their concepts of divinity, at least they conceived of a deity which could be an immutable guide for moral action. It is a case of a low-grade metaphysics accompanied by high-grade moral ideals. Their right reason is one of the high points in Greek ethics." Bourke (1947), 27–28.

21. If the worldview sounds too bizarre to be credible or popular, simply imagine a pantheist modern astronomer, like the late Carl Sagan or Stephen Hawking.

22. Heraclitus, Frag. 102. Copleston (1946), I, 42–43.

23. Schumpeter (1954), 72. Spiegel's text, following this lead, assigns St. Augustine a peripheral role.

24. The earlier Stoics had argued that everything is fated by God; but this made it difficult to explain why anyone should practice virtue, as they also maintained. (Cicero, in order to preserve free will, later asserted that God does not have foreknowledge—in effect, that there is no God.)

25. The proper order, according to natural law, is this: we love God above all things, next our own soul in God, third our neighbor's soul in God, and finally our own body because of its connection with our soul. On why this hierarchy is consistent with "loving one's neighbor as oneself," see Appendix I.

26. Dt 6:5, Lv 19:18; Mt 22:34–40; Mk 12:28–31; Lk 10:25–28.

27. *Summa Theologica* II–II Q44 A3 ad1.

28. St. Augustine insists on both man's free will and God's foreknowledge: "The fact that God foreknew that a man would sin does not make him sin." *City of God*, Book V, Chapter 10.

29. Bourke, ed., 45. *Questions for Simplicianus*, I.2.18. As a reformed manichee, St. Augustine is quite clear that evil is not a thing or principle, but rather the privation of good.

30. "The soul of fallen man, in a 'reach of arrogance utterly intolerable,' perversely seeks to ape God by aspiring 'to lord it over even those who are by nature equals—that is, its fellow man.'" Deane, ed., 49. Fallen man also finds it difficult to practice virtue, because his passions no longer readily obey his reason.

31. St. Augustine, *City of God*, Book XIX, Chapter 12. Paolucci, ed., 142.

32. St. Augustine, *Confessions*, II.IV.9. Deane's translation.

33. Deane (1963), 88.

34. St. Augustine, *Confessions*, II.IV.9. Deane's translation.

35. "And so, justice removed, what are kingdoms but great robber bands? And what are robber bands but little kingdoms?" *City of God*, IV.4. There is even a kind of magnificence to the vices of ancient Rome, in which lesser vices were suppressed in favor of human glory. But the order which results from a properly ordered love is always, necessarily greater than that which results from a disordered love.

36. *Questions for Simplicianus*, I.II.16, quoted in Deane (1963), 97.

37. Some difficulties arise because St. Augustine uses current neo-Platonist language to express an idea which has no counterpart in Greek philosophy: creation. But the difference between the philosophical and theological methods does not become a "problem" until the thirteenth century.

St. Thomas Aquinas's metaphysics of being radically recast (and improved) St. Augustine's philosophical description of the nature of God, both in Himself and in relation to His creatures. (For St. Augustine, God is immutable, but apparently not outside of time; Boethius' definition of eternity came only a century later.)

St. Thomas also corrected St. Augustine's Platonic tendency to describe human nature as "a soul using a body." (The phrase occurs in *On the Moral Behavior of the Catholic Church*, I, 27, 52, cited in Bourke, ed., 67.) St. Thomas' psychology is, on the one hand, more "empirical" than that of the Stoics, who believed that ideas originate in sense impressions, but also believed in innate ideas; yet it is also more rational.

But all this only had the effect of putting St. Augustine's social and political theory on a firmer philosophical foundation. On all questions of order—the nature of evil (S.T. I–I Q18 A1; Q48 A4; Q49 A1; Q49 A2 ad2; I–II Q92 A1; Q93 A6); God's providence (*Summa Theologica* I–I Q22 A2-A4); the ineradicability of natural law from human nature (*Summa Theologica* I–II Q94 A6); the real but imperfect order in human society (S.T. I–II Q91 A4; *Summa Contra Gentiles*, III, XX)—St. Thomas follows St. Augustine closely.

The distinction between Augustinians and Thomists, so useful in theology or philosophy, does not apply to economics—because in this field St. Thomas is thoroughly Augustinian. "What he did was to express Augustinianism in terms of Aristotelian philosophy." Copleston (1991), 33.

38. Smith (1984), 137. TMS, III.3.4. For a more detailed discussion of this point, see Appendix I.

39. Chesterton (1909), 136.

40. *City of God*, Book XI, Chapter 16.

41. Chafuen (1986), 94. Chafuen traces the development of the scholastic analytical tools through the later Scholastics (fourteenth–fifteenth century) and Hispanic Scholastics (sixteenth–seventeenth century).

According to Schumpeter, "the Aristotelian distinction between value in use and value in exchange was deepened and developed into a fragmentary but genuine subjective utility theory of exchange value or price for which there was no analogue in either Aristotle or St. Thomas, though there was in both what we may describe as a pointer." (Schumpeter [1954], 98)

In fact, as we have seen, this "pointer" is really a road map, and it comes straight from St. Augustine. The passage cited in the text comes from a chapter in the *City of God* titled, "The distinction among created things; and their different ranking by the scales of utility and logic."

St. Augustine says: "Now among those things which exist in any mode of being, and are distinct from God who made them, living things are ranked above inanimate objects. . . . This is the scale according to the order of nature; but there is another gradation which employs utility as the criterion of value. . . . For instance, would not anyone prefer to have food in his house, rather than mice, or money rather than fleas? There is nothing surprising in this; for we find the same criterion operating in the value we place on human beings, for all the undoubted worth of a human creature. A higher price is often paid for a horse than for a slave, for a jewel than for a maidservant.

"Thus there is a very wide difference between a rational consideration, in its free judgement, and the constraint of need, or the attraction of desire. Rational consideration decides on the position of each thing in the scale of importance, on its own merits, whereas need thinks only of its own interests. Reason looks for the truth as it is revealed to enlightened intelligence; desire has an eye for what allures by the promise of sensual enjoyments." (*City of God*, Book XI, Chapter 16)

St. Augustine is making not one but three important distinctions: between utility and goodness; between need and desire as the sources of utility; and between value in exchange and value in use.

First, economic value, St. Augustine says, is based on utility—not intrinsic worth—both for the City of God and the Earthly City. The end of economics is wealth, but wealth is not useful in itself, only for the sake of something else. Usefulness pertains to the means; goodness pertains to the end. Rational choice concerns the means; intention refers to the final good. Therefore, even members of the City of God will make rational economic choices based on utility. And even an evil person prefers real or apparent "goods," not "bads." In important ways, they will have a different priority in their scale of utility than members of the Earthly City.

However, one's ranking of absolute goods cannot easily be deduced even from perfect knowledge of that person's "utility function," precisely because the "utility function" includes only intermediate means, not those to whose love they are ordered. St. Augustine refuses to identify the City of God with the visible Catholic Church; in heaven there will be many found inside who were apparently outside, and vice versa. St. Augustine's economic and political theories might be regarded as an extended meditation on the parable of the wheat and the tares.

Second, St. Augustine also distinguishes between two different aspects of utility: "the constraint of need and the attraction of desire." The "attraction of desire" is what economists would call "subjective utility"; a simple ranking, for whatever reason, in the desirability of one good over another.

The "constraint of need," however, originates in the nature of things. Certain needs must be satisfied, and to gratify our desires in the market, we must give up something of equal value as considered by others. The principle implied here is that, although prices will be determined by subjective utility, this price will be regulated over time by the cost of production—a principle worked out later by Duns Scotus.

The one route leads to a pure "subjective" theory of utility; the other, taken by itself, leads to a "cost-of-production" theory of value. But the only complete theory is to take the two together.

Third, an economist might also recognize in this passage a statement of the "paradox of value"—the fact that things which are more useful may nevertheless have a lower price or exchange value. The reason is that value in exchange depends not on total but on marginal utility—the value of one more unit. The total usefulness of air is vastly greater than the total usefulness of diamonds; but one more pound of air is cheaper than one more pound of diamonds because air is more abundant.

42. This condition is satisfied when each agent adjusts his holdings of wealth until the ratio of marginal utility and market price is equal for each good.

43. Schumpeter (1954), 97.

44. "The elements for such a theory were all there and the technical apparatus of schedules and of marginal concepts that developed during the nineteenth century is really all that had to be added to them." Schumpeter (1954), 98.

45. St. Augustine distinguishes two methods for maintaining order, whether in the soul ruling the body, human government ruling society, or God governing man: education and coercion. But in practice, he identifies human government with coercion. He notes that, although desiring earthly goods for their own sake is perverted, this very perversion inherently chooses its own punishment, both in this life and in the next.

St. Augustine observes: "You see also that there would be no punishment inflicted on men either by injury done them or by legal sentence if they did not love the things that can be taken from them against their will." (Deane, 140. *On Free Will*, I.XV.32.111). "So long as they fear to lose these earthly goods, they observe in using them a certain moderation suited to maintain in being a city such as can be composed of such men. The sin of loving these things is not punished [by human law]; what is punished is the wrong done to others when their rights are infringed." Ibid.

However, those who place their happiness solely in earthly goods also choose their own terrible eternal punishment: when life is over, "They have received their reward"—and they can't take it with them. In the next life, there is only God, whom they will not have attained; this is the essence of eternal punishment. The members of the City of God, on the other hand, use their temporal goods not as ends, but as means necessary in this life for practicing virtue, which is ordained to God; they are happy, imperfectly in this life, but perfectly in the next. Those who seek first the kingdom of heaven receive all else besides.

46. St. Thomas adopts St. Augustine's analysis of human government but integrates it into a broader view. To Aristotle, man is a "political animal," so the state is not only "natural," but the most perfect human society (*Politics*, 28. Book I

Chapter 2). But to St. Augustine, man is a "social animal," so that society is "natural"; but human government is "remedial"—a result of the Fall of Man (*City of God*, Book XII Chapters 9, 22). To St. Thomas, man is a "social and political animal" (*Summa Theologica* I–II Q72 A4.). Human government is "natural" in the sense that some government would be necessary even without sin; but in that case, government would consist essentially of education for the sake of order, not coercion (*Summa Theologica* I–II Q91 A6, Q96 A4).

St. Thomas therefore distinguishes not between education and coercion, but between "mediate" and "immediate" government policies. "The human law," he says, "does not prescribe all the acts of all the virtues, but only those that may be directed toward the common good—either immediately (when some things are done directly for the sake of the common good) or mediately (as when the legislator enacts certain provisions relative to good discipline, through which citizens are educated and accustomed to respect the common good of justice and of peace" (S.T. I–II, Q96 A3).

There is a similar difference in emphasis in their treatment of private property. St. Augustine considers private property, like government, to be entirely "remedial"; like many other Fathers of the Church, he argues that without sin, all ownership would be in common. St. Thomas considers private property, as he puts it, a device no more opposed to nature than the wearing of clothes. However, of St. Thomas's three arguments justifying private property, two (productivity and peace) are at least partly "remedial" and only one (order) is not (*Summa Theologica* II–II Q66 A2).

We recall that Smith says the individual pursuing his own interest "frequently promotes that of society more effectually than when he really intends to promote it." Smith (1966), II, 35. Book IV Chapter II. If by saying this, Smith meant only that individuals pursuing their own scales of values can achieve these better by free market transactions than they could if those transactions were directed by the government, he would be correct according to natural law. But if (as appears to be the case) he means that market transactions are always more efficient than government, then he is confusing distributive and commutative justice.

Government has a comparative advantage in legal or distributive justice—justice between each person and the public good—while private parties have a comparative advantage in pursuing commutative justice—justice between private persons. In the *Theory of Moral Sentiments*, Smith restricts justice to commutative justice.

St. Thomas notes: "Now the relations of one man with another are twofold: some are effected under the guidance of those in authority: others are effected by the will of private individuals. And since whatever is subject to the power of an individual can be disposed of according to his will, hence it is that the decision of matters between one man and another, and the punishment of evildoers, depend on the direction of those in authority, to whom men are subject. On the other hand, the power of private persons is exercised over the things they possess: and consequently their dealings with one another, as regards such things, depend on their own will, for instance in buying, selling, giving and so forth." *S.T.* I–II Q105 A2.

47. Rueff (1967), 496, (my translation).

48. *Politics*, 26. Book I Chapter 2. "Man is naturally inclined to form couples—even more than to form cities, inasmuch as the household is earlier and more necessary than the city." (*Ethics*, 214. Book VIII Chapter 12.)

49. According to Aristotle, within the household, wealth is shared; among households, wealth is exchanged (*Politics*, Book I Chapter 9). Rueff says somewhere that the reason the family is more efficiently ordered on "communist" principles (from each according to his ability; to each according to his need) is that the father and mother know the scale of values of the children better than do the children. The reason the price mechanism is required outside the household is that such intimate knowledge seldom exists beyond the household. St. Thomas Aquinas follows Aristotle, against Plato, in justifying private ownership of property on the grounds of productivity, order, and peace. *Summa Theologica* II–II, Q66 A2.

50. Aristotle lists the necessary functions within the state as those of the food producer, the artisan, the soldier, the priest, the property owner, and the judge (*Politics*, 272. Book VII Chapter 8). He says that while justice is the most essential, religion is the most excellent of the necessary functions within the state:

"We must also ask how many are those things without which there can be no city. . . . Let us therefore make a count of all the things and actions needed, for that will show the answer. They are (1) food, (2) handicrafts and their tools, (3) arms. Arms are included because members of the constitution must carry them even among themselves, both for internal government in the event of civil disobedience and to repel external aggression. (4) Wealth too is required for war and for all the internal needs. Then (5) the needs of religion (this might have been put first) and (6) (most essential of all) a method of arriving at decisions, both about policy and about matters of right and wrong as between one person and another." *Ibid.*

Though the list does not specifically include commercial activity, the artisan, as Hicks notes, is not essentially different from a trader, because his craft consists of buying goods, adding value with his labor, and selling them.

These functions are ordered to the common good by laws. The wealthy person is necessary, Aristotle says, because without wealth (roughly speaking, taxes) you can't have a state. *Politics,* 129. Book III Chapter 12. The person with wealth is not necessarily a separate person, though in Aristotle's ideal scheme, only the property owner is a citizen.

According to Aristotle, public wealth is collected and distributed, not according to each one's contribution (as in the market), but according to each one's worth. *Ethics*, 111. Book V Chapter 2.

Aristotle favors providing for the needy, but is against "welfare" payments. He would prefer providing enough property to permit the poor man to support his household by his own efforts—a kind of "workfare"; of course, this presumes that the poor person is able-bodied.

While justifying private property, St. Thomas Aquinas nevertheless insists that its fundamental purpose is to sustain life. If someone is in need, and if the needy person is able to work, he is obliged to do so. But if not, as a matter of justice, other individuals should provide voluntarily out of their own wealth. If this too fails, the needy person must be taken care of out of the public funds. If the need is dire enough and cannot be satisfied any other way, it is not against the natural law for the needy person to take what he needs. *Summa Theologica* II–II Q66 A7.

This, at least, is the principle. But who actually decides how the common stock of public wealth is to be collected and distributed? The government. But government may be ruled by one, the few, or the many; and it may be run for the common good or in the sole interest of the rulers. If the government is run by one for the common good, it is a monarchy; if for the ruler's own sake, a tyranny. If it is run by the few for the common good, it is an aristocracy; if for the sake of the few, an oligarchy. When government is run by the many for the common good, we have a "polity"; if for the sake of the majority, we have a democracy. *Politics*, 116, 117. Book III Chapter 8.

51. Rueff calls these the "authoritarian" and "liberal" methods. Rueff (1967), 527 ff.

52. For example, a volunteer army represents the fiscal approach, and the draft a regulatory approach, to national defense—a diversion of "human capital" from private to public use.

53. As a rough generalization, regulation is more appropriate when dealing with human beings (child labor laws are better than the government's purchasing children and ordering them not to work); and the fiscal approach is more appropriate when dealing with things (e.g., subsidizing public housing is more efficient than controlling rents).

54. Broadly defined to include customs, tolls, fines, and fees.

55. Monetary policy has both a regulatory and a fiscal aspect: establishing the monetary standard is regulatory, but issuing token money is "fiscal," because it benefits the treasury or fisc.

56. Whether for investment or consumption; this includes monetary reserves.

57. The following section is indebted to Sir John Hicks's *A Theory of Economic History* (1969).

58. For most of mankind, through most of history, government and economic functions were not clearly separated, but rather intertwined, if not in a "master–slave" relation, then in a "lord–peasant" arrangement (Hicks, 101 ff.). The lord provided protection, while the peasant provided food. In this case, the peasant's land rents were not clearly distinguished from taxes.

With the rise of the market, the two functions became separable. However, at this point, the landowner/lords more often than not took advantage of their roles as judges and constables to appropriate wealth that in justice belonged partly to the peasants.

Belloc notes that the industrial revolution in England might have had an entirely different character if the distribution of property had not been concentrated in this way at the start (Belloc [1977], 85–106). This skewed distribution of property had nothing to do with the working of a free market; as we have seen, economic theory must take the initial distribution of wealth as given. (The United States was, in the beginning, more fortunate in this respect.)

During the "lord–peasant" stage, the "budget receipts" of the central government (when there was one) consisted largely of the income of the ruler's own estates. "If there is one thing in general about [kings], which we seem to learn from history books, it is that more often than not they were hard up. Of course it is only since they began to use money that they were short of money; but since that time this does seem to have been their general condition." "The 'tax base' was narrow; collection was inefficient, and (just because it was inefficient, falling on those whose liability was easy to assess, and letting others escape) it was inequitable; and the inequity of the system was one of the reasons why the revenue was so inelastic."

59. Even here, compliance largely depends on a system of withholding—typically instituted as a "temporary" wartime measure.

60. Sales taxes, property taxes, customs, and tolls have existed for at least 3,000 years [Adams (1993), 13], but have been a relatively minor source of revenue, precisely because during most of that time, market transactions have been a relatively minor part of daily life.

Similarly, public borrowing is a relatively recent phenomenon. Kings generally had poor credit, because they were so likely to default. The credit rating of governments becomes good enough to make public borrowing feasible only under republics. The short-term Treasury bill dates only from the nineteenth century.

Taxation is also related to the monetary system. A metallic standard (such as Aristotle advocated, against Plato's token money) implies that all expenditures will be paid for with taxation; if expenditures cannot be paid for by token-money creation, borrowing only rearranges the timing of the tax. Put another way, the "supply without a demand" imposed by taxation will be exactly offset by the "demand without supply" of purchases by the government or by recipients of transfer payments. Debasement and monetary expansion through the purchase of government debt are forms of taxation. (An interesting and novel feature of twentieth-century "reserve currency" systems is that the tax involved with token money can be levied partly on foreign holders of money.)

However, during the "lord–peasant" stage, resort to debasement would often shrink the king's tax base in real terms, because taxes were largely "specific" rather than "ad valorem"–for example, so many cents per pound, rather than some proportion of the total price. Aristotle says that taxes should be adjusted for changes in the value of money—what we now call "indexing" (*Politics,* 210. Book V Chapter 8). But the reason he gives is exactly the opposite from the modern purpose. Where taxes are levied in money terms, a rise in prices means a fall in revenue in "real" or price-adjusted terms. But with incomes taxed at progressive rates, a rise in prices means a "real" rise in revenues. In the first case, indexing is necessary to keep tax revenues from shrinking; in the second, it is necessary to prevent a tax increase.

61. Aristotle, however, is against redistributive taxation. *Politics*, 212–13; Book V Chapter 8.

62. Economists have come to understand wealth generically as a stock of productive assets, and income as the flow of goods and services it produces. The stock of wealth is worth the present value (adjusted by the interest rate) of the income it is expeced to produce over its remaining useful life. Part of the goods and services is used up within the period under consideration (typically a year); this is the portion of income devoted to consumption. The remainder of the flow forms a net addition to the stock of wealth; this is the income devoted to saving or investment.

63. "The outstanding feature of classical population theory is that it treats the production of children not as a means of spending income on 'consumer goods' for the sake of psychic satisfaction in the present, but as a means of investing in 'capital goods' for the sake of a future return" (Blaug (1977), 78).

64. Becker (1994b), 324. To be sure, there were important differences among neoclassical economists. When Keynes set out to explain the volume of consumption in a given year, he explained it as a function of income in that year. Later economists objected to this short-run focus as unrealistic and likely to bias economic policy in undesirable ways. In the 1940s and 1950s, they developed a "life-cycle" theory, in which consumption in any year depends on one's "permanent" or lifetime, not annual, income. A person consumes more than his or her income in early life, less than income in midlife, and finally consumes beyond income again until death, when all wealth is used up.

Though more realistic, the life-cycle theory could not explain why there is any net accumulation of human or nonhuman capital from one generation to the next—that is, why there is any economic growth, why people raise children or leave bequests, or how behavior may be affected by programs that treat one generation differently from another. Because it still assumes that the population and its skills are given, the neoclassical theory literally means that if 260 million Cannibal Islanders took over the United States tomorrow, output would be unchanged, because the size of the labor force and the capital-to-labor ratio would be the same.

65. "The income of the United States has been increasing at a much faster rate than the combined amount of land, man-hours worked, and the stock of reproducible capital used to produce the income. . . . To call this discrepancy a measure of 'resource productivity' gives a name to our ignorance but does not dispel it." Schultz (1961), 5. "The growth of physical capital, at least as conventionally measured, explains a relatively small part of the growth in income in most countries." Becker (1994b), 11. See also Kendrick (1976) and Denison (1974).

66. Becker (1994b), 111.

67. All costs of child-rearing, education, and training that increase future labor income can be considered "investment in human capital." In Becker's theory, each person seeks to maximize not economic welfare during his own life, but the welfare of his "dynasty," including all descendants, and neither the stock of nonhuman capital, nor the population, nor human capital per person, is assumed fixed. Becker (1994a), Chapters 7 and 8.

68. This wealth produces goods and services. The goods and services are sold, and the proceeds received as income, by the owners of these "factors of production." Therefore, total spending on investment and consumption (gross national product) is equal to total labor plus property income (gross national income). In a competitive market, the incomes are distributed according to the relative contribution of each factor to increasing output.

69. Becker suggests that the distribution of different kinds of wealth, and hence sources of income, by income class is due to the different nature of human and nonhuman capital. Becker (1994b), 145–48. Because we do not allow slavery on moral grounds, there is no market for human beings as there is for property. But this also causes the market to underinvest in human capital, which is reflected in the fact that the return on human capital is higher than on other kinds of capital.

70. Douglas 1964; Mueller (1994a).

71. As a result, there are three kinds of family income: take-home pay, net property income, and government benefits—each measured net of all taxes paid and benefits received. Benefits may be based on a criterion such as need (e.g., welfare benefits, Medicaid), or for having paid earlier contributions (e.g., Civil Service retirement benefits), or based on some combination of the two (e.g., Social Security benefits).

72. In economic terms, we can think of benefits received as purchases of labor services by the government, which are withheld from the market. The effect of these benefits will depend on the conditions for receiving benefits.

Benefits available to the unemployed (such as unemployment insurance, welfare; and Medicaid) have the same effect as a minimum wage: they increase the relative share of national income going to workers (including unemployed workers). However, raising labor's income share is the same as raising the real price of labor. This causes employers to cut back their hiring until the contribution of the last worker hired is equal to his net addition to output. As a result, for each one percentage point rise in labor's share of national income, national income falls about two percentage points—so that real labor income actually shrinks by one percentage point in absolute terms.

However, benefits to persons outside the labor force have a different result. Because most workers cannot qualify for, say, Social Security or Medicare benefits, employed workers are unable to demand a larger income share. The pretax share of income received by labor remains the same, and the benefits are paid for by a reduction in take-home pay. National output remains the same, except insofar as workers leave the labor force; but the loss of income may actually force more working-age persons to seek work in order to make ends meet.

73. Mueller (1994b).

74. A comprehensive solution to the problem requires reforms on both the tax and benefit sides. (In fact, a comprehensive analysis would include not only federal spending, but also state and local policies.)

Perhaps the single most important federal reform would alter benefit formulae. Mueller (1995b). As we saw, workers' pretax compensation grows in line with productivity, measured at the selling price of the goods produced. Benefits, however, are generally "indexed" for inflation by a different formula. For example, Social Security benefits are indexed by the Consumer Price Index, which has risen more rapidly than output prices. And the fastest-growing benefits have been medical benefits, which have a sort of "gold clause"—that is, medical benefits are generally provided as a bundle of services, regardless of dollar cost. Both kinds of benefits, therefore, have grown, not only because of expanded eligibility, but also because of explicit or *de facto* indexing.

75. Schultz (1961), 13, 15.

76. Although federal revenues of all kinds have absorbed a nearly constant share (about 19 percent) of gross domestic product since World War II, the average federal tax on property income has fallen from about 30 percent to about 15 percent, while the average federal tax on labor has risen from about 17 percent to about 23 percent. Mueller (1995a).

77. I have shown that the revenue-neutral flat tax rate would have to be about 27 percent when such a plan is fully phased in, and would be levied almost entirely on workers' incomes. Mueller (1995c).

78. In tax theory, the incidence of a tax and the burden of a tax are not necessarily the same. That is, the person upon whom the tax initially falls may not be the person who ultimately bears the burden. The burden depends on a number of factors, especially on how easy it is to find substitutes for the good that is taxed. The proponents of such tax-reform plans are all adherents of the old neoclassical model

which, as we saw, assumes that the population is given but the stock of physical capital is not.

79. "The neoclassical conclusion about tax incidence, that in the long run a tax on capital is fully shifted to other factors, no longer holds when fertility is endogenous." Becker (1994a), 18.

80. Becker (1994b), 23.

81. Mueller (1995d).

82. We could, for example, write off all cash costs of investment for both human and nonhuman capital, as well as all maintenance costs. But, practically speaking, this would remove most of the economy from the tax base, requiring a flat income tax rate of at least 40 percent on top of the payroll tax. It involves complexities of definition (to what extent is a liberal arts education, or a company Mercedes, saving or current consumption for tax purposes?).

83. Mueller (1995d).

84. Becker has argued, against Schultz, that although cash outlays for human capital are treated worse than investment in property for tax purposes, certain noncash costs are "expensed," because the foregone earnings of parents and of students are not taxed.

"Tax laws are said to discriminate against education and other kinds of human capital because depreciation can be deducted only from the taxable income of physical capital. Unquestionably, a more symmetrical tax treatment of these two classes of capital would be desirable. However, one should be aware that a good deal of depreciation on human capital occurs unknowingly. Thus, as pointed out elsewhere, part of the costs of human capital are 'written off' immediately because foregone earnings are, in effect, deducted from accrued taxable income." Becker (1994b), 240–41.

That is, the effect is the same, according to Becker, as if parents and students earned a wage for child-rearing and going to school, but were allowed to deduct this wage as an investment in human capital. Therefore he suggests that the tax treatment of human capital, taken as a whole, is not really so bad as it may seem.

However, as Kendrick points out, if such an imputed addition is made to labor income, human maintenance costs should first be subtracted (Kendrick [1976], 6–7). Human maintenance costs, by Kendrick's measure, are about twice the size of the imputed value of nonmarket time invested in human capital (Kendrick [1976], 31). Therefore, if anything, the tax burden on workers is probably somewhat higher, not lower, than the figures in the text (which are based on the conventional national income accounts) would suggest.

85. We could, of course, have a partial deduction, but this involves all the complexities of a full deduction and raises the marginal tax rate accordingly.

86. It is often argued that there is a trade-off between equity and efficiency; for example, that a flat tax rate would increase output but be regressive in its distribution, while a progressive tax-rate structure would be "fair" but reduce real incomes. But this is a false dilemma. Progressive tax rates and multiple taxation of some property income are a rough offset to the fact that most property income never shows up in the tax base. If all gross income were included in the tax base, a flat tax rate would be about as progressive as the current tax code, because most of the missing income accrues to upper-bracket families.

87. Beginning with Feldstein (1974).

88. Mueller (1987). Some critics have argued that Social Security reduces fertility by breaking the link between having children and supporting oneself in retirement (Carlson [1986]). But this argument, which originates with the Swedish socialist economist, Gunnar Myrdal, pertained to fully funded government pensions as well as private saving for retirement—not pay-as-you-go pensions. Myrdal attributes the decline in fertility to industrial development and concludes that to restore the agrarian *status quo ante*, "The burden of supporting the aged must be laid effectively upon the individual young families (by abolishing the whole structure of social policy enacted to support old and needy persons—and, do not forget, by actually denying them the right to live on their own savings)." Myrdal (1939), 200–01. The argument therefore cannot be used to favor privatizing Social Security.

89. The transition cost cannot be overcome by a supposedly higher return on private retirement accounts invested in physical capital, for three reasons. First, comparisons made by privatizers never adjust for the higher level of risk of loss in the stock market. Social security is almost unique in providing a high return relative to its (low) volatility. The risk-adjusted return on physical capital does not appear to be any higher than on a mature pay-as-you-go retirement system. Second, as long as the current system pays benefits to current retirees, the government must finance the transition to a fully funded system by either borrowing or taxing several trillions of dollars more than under a pay-as-you-go system; these funds are therefore not available to invest, even if a higher return were available. Third, the forced saving in claims on physical capital would squeeze investment in human capital, which offers a higher, not a lower, return than physical capital.

90. Under current projections, payroll tax rates will have to double because, just as the Baby Boom was nearly twice the size of its parents' generation, the generation following the Baby Boom is only half as large. To fund benefits at existing levels would therefore require a near-doubling of payroll taxes. One way to solve this problem would be to cut payroll tax rates (in the context of, and if necessary paid for by, income tax reform). For example, if the payroll tax is cut by, say, 20 percent, there would be a prorated reduction in future benefits. Assuming a fifty-year working career, a worker one year from retirement would have benefits reduced by 0.4 percent as a result of paying the 20 percent lower taxes for only one-fiftieth of his contributions; but a worker benefiting from lower tax rates for a full fifty years would have benefits reduced a full 20 percent from currently promised levels. Because of growth in the economy, benefits would still rise in real terms by about 60 percent over the next seventy-five years, instead of a projected doubling beyond adjustments for inflation. Such a plan is outlined in Mueller (1995d).

91. Contributions are the same for all workers, and benefits are linked (progressively) with contributions; but a couple in which one spouse foregoes market earnings to raise children (that is, future taxpayers who will support even single retirees) receives an additional 50 percent upon retirement. The survivor's benefit is 100 percent of the basic benefit. Such insurance based on the household is not available in the private market.

92. Pegis (1939), 85–86. Pegis cites Petrarch, *De Sui Ipsius et Multorum Stultitia*, IV (ed. L.M. Capelli, Paris: Librairie H. Champion, 1906).

93. Dawson (1975) 295–96. Dawson begins the passage: "In the past,

Western civilization was based on the assumption that man had an immortal soul, and however much the state demanded, it admitted, at least in theory, that the destiny of every human being reached beyond the extreme limits of political society, so that human conduct was ultimately governed and judged by supersocial laws. The secularization of Western society did not immediately destroy the consequences of this belief. On the contrary, the more men lost their faith in God, the more desperately did they cling to the belief in the liberty and value of human personality which was the fruit of a thousand years of Christian culture."

94. Pegis (1939). To exhaust the logical possibilities, one should include "panentheism," a curious modern attempt to fuse monotheism and pantheism, described in Hartshorne and Reese (1953). Reese lobbies for it in "Pantheism and Panentheism," *EB* 13:948–54.

95. Josef Pieper calls this the "contrapuntal relationship" between theology and philosophy. Many would argue that the term "Christian philosophy" is an oxymoron, on the grounds that if it is really Christian it ceases to be philosophy, and if it is really philosophy it ceases to be Christian. But Pieper, a philosopher, is of a different opinion:

"The philosopher who reflects upon the things of this world in the light of the revealed doctrine of the Logos, will attain to knowledge that would otherwise remain hidden from him, though the knowledge he gains will not be theological knowledge but demonstrable knowledge, philosophical knowledge of things in themselves." Pieper (1964), 116.

"The point of these theological truths about the world as a whole, and the meaning of human existence," Pieper says, "is that it should hinder and resist the natural craving of the human spirit for a clear, transparent and definite system." Pieper (1964), 123.

The current tax code, not only in the United States, but in all industrial countries, is urgently in need of reform. But in some versions, the cure could be worse than the disease. Neoclassical economic theory is a "clear, transparent, and definite system"; but tax-reform proposals based on it would worsen the current squeeze on working families. The theory of human capital is also a "clear, transparent, and definite system"; but as I show in Appendix II, in some forms it goes beyond economic analysis to make some philosophical claims that can reasonably be interpreted as reducing all of human nature to human capital.

As Chesterton observes, "The real trouble with this world of ours is not that it is an unreasonable world, nor even that it is a reasonable one. The commonest kind of trouble is that it is nearly reasonable, but not quite. Life is not an illogicality; yet it is a trap for logicians. It looks just a little more mathematical and regular than it is; its exactitude is obvious, but its inexactitude is hidden; its wildness lies in wait." Chesterton (1909), 146.

96. This point is recognized but minimized by Schumpeter, when he argues that scientists like Joule and Euler "simply co-ordinated their methods and results with their live Christian belief as they would co-ordinate it with everything else they did. They put their scientific work in a theological garb. But, so far as the content of this work is concerned, the garb was removable." Schumpeter (1954), 31. This is true of the scientific content, but cannot explain the fact of the intuition that led to it.

97. Schumpeter (1954), 112.

98. But he considers this only a theoretical possibility. *Politics* 192. Book V Chapter 1.

99. Chesterton (1910), 60.

100. Smith (1966), 119.

101. Smith (1984), 25. TMS I.i.5.5.

102. Smith (1984), 25. TMS I.i.5.5.

103. Smith also tends to reduce the dictates of nature to instinct or inclination, without clearly distinguishing between what is natural to humans in common with other animals and what is unique to human nature: reason.

104. Smith (1984), 137. TMS, III.3.4.

105. St. Thomas Aquinas observes: "The Stoics said that the wise man is free from all passions; even more, they maintained that true virtue consisted in quiet of soul. The Peripatetics, on the other hand, held that the wise man is subject to anger, but in a moderate degree. This is the more accurate opinion." He argues that this "is proved from reason. If all the passions were opposed to virtue, then there would be some powers of the soul without good purpose." *Catechetical Instructions*, 112–13.

106. Smith (1984) TMS VI.ii.1.1–2.

107. Augustine; Paolucci, ed., 131–32.

108. *Summa Theologica*, II–II Q26 A8. Also: "In as much as the friendship of comrades originates through their own choice, love of this kind takes precedence of the love of kindred in matters where we are free to do as we choose, for instance in matters of action. Yet the friendship of kindred is more stable, since it is more natural, and preponderates over others in matters touching nature: consequently we are more beholden to them in the providing of necessaries." Ibid.

109. *Summa Theologica*, II–II Q26 A6.

110. "Divine law is offered to man as an aid to natural law. Now, it is natural to all men to love each other. The mark of this is the fact that a man, by some natural prompting, comes to the aid of any man in need, even if he does not know him." *Summa Contra Gentiles*, Book III Chapter 117 Section 6.

111. *Summa Theologica*, II–II Q184 A3. St. Thomas explains this with reference to Aristotle: "The end is not subject to a measure, but only such things as are directed to the end, as the Philosopher observes (*Polit.* i. 3); thus a physician does not measure [that is, moderate] the amount of his healing, but how much medicine or diet he shall employ for the purpose of healing." Choice concerns the means, but not the end; and our intent is to achieve the whole end, not just part of it.

112. *Catechetical Instructions,* 101.

113. He explains: "and this in three ways. First, as regards the end, namely, that he should love his neighbor for God's sake, even as he loves himself for God's sake, so that his love for his neighbor is a *holy* love. Secondly, as regards the rule of love, namely, that a man should not give way to his neighbor in evil, but only in good things, even as he ought to gratify his will in good things alone, so that his love for his neighbor may be a *righteous* love. Thirdly, as regards the reason for loving, namely, that a man should love his neighbor, not for his own profit, or pleasure, but in the sense of wishing this neighbor well, so that his love for his neighbor is a true love: since when a man loves his neighbor for his own profit or pleasure, he does not love his neighbor truly, but loves himself." *Summa Theologica* II–II Q44 A7.

114. One of Smith's contemporaries who attended his lectures described Smith's ethical system as a kind of moral Newtonianism, and noted that it was recognized at the time as a departure: "His Theory of Moral Sentiment founded on sympathy, a very ingenious attempt to account for the principal phenomena in the moral world from this one principle, like that of gravity in the natural world, did not please Hutcheson's scholars so well as that to which they had been accustomed." *Theory of Moral Sentiments*, Introduction by Raphael and Macfie, 3.

115. Chesterton (1909), 136. Chesterton's comparison of Christianity with stoicism is worth quoting at length:

> It is commonly loose and latitudinarian Christians who pay quite indefensible compliments to Christianity. They talk as if there had never been any piety or pity until Christianity came, a point on which any medieval would have been eager to correct them. They represent that the remarkable thing about Christianity was that it was the first to preach simplicity or self-restraint, or inwardness and sincerity. They will think me very narrow (whatever that means) if I say that the remarkable thing about Christianity was that it was the first to preach Christianity. Its peculiarity was that it was peculiar, and simplicity and sincerity are not peculiar, but obvious ideals for all mankind. Christianity was the answer to a riddle, not the last truism uttered after a long talk. Only the other day I saw in an excellent weekly paper of Puritan tone make this remark, that Christianity when stripped of its armour of dogma (as who should speak of a man stripped of his armour of bones), turned out to be nothing but the Quaker doctrine of the Inner Light. Now, if I were to say that Christianity came into the world basically to destroy the doctrine of the Inner Light, that would be an exaggeration. But it would be very much nearer the truth. The last Stoics, like Marcus Aurelius, were exactly the people who did believe in the Inner Light. Their dignity, their weariness, their sad external care for others, their incurable care for themselves, were all due to the Inner Light, and existed only by that dismal illumination. Notice that Marcus Aurelius insists, as such introspective moralists always do, upon small things done or undone; it is because he does not hate or love enough to make a moral revolution. He gets up early in the morning, just as our own aristocrats living the Simple Life get up early in the morning; because such altruism is much easier than stopping the games of the amphitheatre or giving the English people back their land. Marcus Aurelius is the most intolerable of human types. He is an unselfish egoist. An unselfish egoist is a man who has pride without the excuse of passion. Of all conceivable forms of enlightenment the worst is what these people call the Inner Light. Of all horrible religious the most horrible is the worship of the god within. Any one who knows any body knows how it would work; any one who knows any one from the Higher Thought Centre knows how it does work. That Jones shall worship the god within him turns out ultimately to mean that Jones shall worship Jones. Let Jones worship the sun or moon, anything rather than the inner light; let Jones worship cats or crocodiles, if he can find any in his street, but not the god within. Christianity came into the world firstly in order to assert with violence that a man had not only to look inwards, but to look outwards, to behold with

astonishment and enthusiasm a divine company and a divine captain. The only fun of being a Christian was that a man was not left alone with the Inner Light, but definitely recognized an outer light, fair as the sun, clear as the moon, terrible as an army with banners. Ibid., 134–37.

116. *City of God,* Book V, Chapter 13.
117. *City of God,* Book V, Chapter 20.
118. Schultz (1961), 1.
119. Friedman (1962), 103.
120. Partly in collaboration with others, notably Robert Barro and Nigel Tomes.
121. Becker (1994a), *ix*.
122. Ibid.
123. Becker (1976), 8.
124. Becker (1994a), *x*.
125. Becker's ambition is nothing less than "to present a comprehensive analysis that is applicable, at least in part, to families in the past as well as in the present, in primitive as well as modern societies, and in Eastern as well as Western cultures." Becker (1994a), 3.
126. Becker (1994a), 279.
127. Becker (1994b), 120, 197n, 299.
128. *Politics* 30. Book I Chapter 3.
129. Ethics, 123. Book V Chapter 6.
130. He calls marriage an "aristocracy" (that is, a rule of the best, by consent of the governed, for the common good).
131. *Ethics*, 214. Book VIII Chapter 12.
132. *Ethics*, 244. Book VI Chapter 4.
133. *Politics*, 77. Book II Chapter 7.
134. Ibid.
135. *Politics*, 53. Book I Chapter 13.
136. *Politics*, 109, 111. Book III Chapters 4, 5.
137. *Politics*, 27. Book I Chapter 2.

One is reminded of St. Thomas' argument that, despite the existence of natural law, revelation is necessary because by reason alone we arrive at the truth about natural things only after much effort and with the admixture of error. If even Aristotle can get it wrong, reason alone would seem a fairly shaky reed to lean on. Aristotle's argument for slavery as "natural" was unconvincing even to many of his contemporaries; he cites, without adequately answering, the cogent objection (probably of the proto-stoics) that slavery is unnatural. *Politics*, 31. Book I Chapter 3.

138. *Ethics*, 1. Book 1 Chapter 1.
139. *Ethics*, 79. Book IV Chapter 1.
140. *Ethics*, 119. Book V Chapter 5.
141. *Politics*, 32. Book I Chapter 4.
142. *Ethics*, 290. Book VII Chapter 15.
143. Pieper (1964), *xix*.
144. Contemplation is not the same as play. "Play has its uses, but they belong rather to the sphere of work; for he who works hard needs rest, and play is

a way of resting, while work is inseparable from stress and strain." *Politics*, 302. Book VIII Chapter 3.

145. Pieper notes that in the Septuagint, "Be still, and know that I am God" is translated "Have leisure . . . "

146. Modern philosophers like Immanuel Kant, Pieper observes, reduce the human intellect to pure reason (man is not a "knower," just a "thinker"); so that the scholar—the Greek for leisure is *schole*—is no longer a man of leisure, but rather an "intellectual worker," a "doer." "The simple vision of the *intellectus*, however, contemplation, is not work," as Pieper observes. "If to know is to work, then knowledge is the fruit of our own unaided effort and activity; then knowledge includes nothing which is not due to the effort of man, and there is nothing gratuitous about it, nothing 'in-spired,' nothing given about it." Pieper (1964) 12, 13.

147. *Ethics*, 210. Book VIII Chapter 10.

148. *Politics* Book I Chapter 2.

149. Luke 10:38–42.

150. "As the proverb says, the slave has no leisure." *Ethics*, 290. Book VII, Chapter 15.

151. Smith (1984), 237. TMS, VI.ii.3.6.

152. Becker (1994a), 24.

153. Utilitarianism more closely resembles epicureanism than stoicism, but as Heller points out, at the Renaissance, "stoicism and epicureanism finally merged." Heller (1981), 105. "It is conduct that predominates in both." Ibid., 102. "Man is born into a world given by nature, a world without purpose which offers one neither an individual end nor any overall meaning." Ibid., 104.

To Bentham, as to the Epicureans, all happiness is based on pleasure (of the mind or of the body). In theory, Bentham has no scale of values, because all pleasures are equal: "Quantum of pleasure being equal, pushpin [a children's game] is as good as poetry"—a doctrine at which even J.S. Mill jibbed. Mill accepts, against Bentham, that "some *kinds* of pleasure are more desirable and more valuable than others;" and he says that the quality of two pleasures can be judged only by "those who are equally acquainted with, and equally capable of appreciating and enjoying, both." Mill, 408–09. But to anyone but a dogmatic materialist, this is an argument for the necessity of divine revelation: who is competent to judge the relative merits of earthly and heavenly pleasures, except "one who came down from heaven"?

154. Becker (1994a), 22f.

155. Becker (1994a), 22n.

156. Keynes (1965), 131.

157. See discussion in the "Current Issues" Section; esp. note 84.

158. Smith (1984), 137. TMS III.3.4.

159. Becker (1994b), 277–78. Cited above: TMS VI.ii.1.1.

160. *Summa Theologica* I-II Q27 A1. Ignoring the distinction between love of friendship and love of utility can lead to rather odd juxtapositions, like the bumper-sticker slogan "Pro-Child, Pro-Choice"; which is like saying, "Pro-Pig, Pro-Pork."

161. Pomponazzi was the first to argue that "The question of the immortality of the soul is a neutral problem"; that is, "it is unnecessary—indeed, it is to be rejected—from the standpoint of ethical conduct." Heller (1981), 110. Despite its roots in stoicism and epicureanism, the view itself is peculiarly modern: "it was foreign to the spirit of antiquity to draw this kind of distinction between thought and deed." Ibid., 144.

162. "The decline [of polygyny] has been attributed to the spread of Christianity and the growth of women's rights, but I am skeptical of these explanations. Doctrines encouraging monogamy are attractive only when the demand for polygyny is weak." Becker (1994a), 81.

163. Becker (1994a), 17.

164. In his earlier *Eudemian Ethics*, Aristotle says that the end of man is "to serve and contemplate God." Ethics, xxiv.

165. *Summa Theologica* I-II Q5 A5; *Summa Contra Gentiles* III, XXXVII.

Welfare

R. George Wright

The mainstream American attitude toward many forms of welfare rights normally ranges between ambivalence and dismissal. But such an attitude does not, to put it mildly, draw unequivocal support from the natural law tradition. Consider, for example, the striking claim by Thomas Aquinas that the imperatives of vital need can rewrite familiar property rules. Aquinas concludes that

> if the need be so manifest and urgent that it is evident that the present need must be remedied by whatever means be at hand, then it is lawful for a man to succor his own need by means of another's property, by taking it either openly or secretly, nor is this properly speaking theft or robbery.[1]

Taken in isolation, however, this formulation is as incomplete as it is bracing.

Every theory of welfare rights must encompass five separate elements. *First* is that of the subject, holder, or beneficiary of the right. Who does or should bear or benefit from the welfare right? *Second* is that of the formal character or nature of the welfare right at stake. Welfare rights could, for example, be moral rights, legally enforceable rights, or both. If legally enforceable, they might be held as merely statutory rights or, more fundamentally, as constitutional rights. *Third* is that of the substantive nature or content of the welfare right. Are there welfare rights to food, housing, income, education, training or employment, health care, or physical safety, and if so, to what degree of substantive fulfillment? If a particular kind of substantive welfare right is at stake, what degree of social effort or actual successful provision of a benefit is required? There is a difference in social cost between a welfare right to a pertussis shot and a welfare right to a kidney transplant. *Fourth* is the range of respecters or providers of the welfare right in question. A legal right to welfare might, for example, be binding and enforceable against either the state, the federal government, or both, or against some set of private actors.

The *fifth* and final element of any welfare rights theory refers to the one or more goals, purposes, or values underlying the right and its exercise. This element is closely linked with any attempt to ground or justify the right in question. There will of course be any number of possible grounds or justifications for any possible welfare right. In the passage from the *Summa Theologica* just quoted, Aquinas seems to suggest that desperate need not only triggers what might in our century be thought of as some sort of right to welfare, but also constitutes, negatively, a point or purpose of the right. If the passage in question does recognize some sort of right to welfare, the point seems to be roughly to relieve manifest and urgent need, however else we might characterize the underlying point of the right. Of course, there may be deeper explanations of why we ought to relieve needs or at least not interfere with their relief. The right in any event certainly seems practical, and not merely symbolic.

In the quoted passage, Aquinas may not be propounding any principle of welfare rights or any principle that he would himself recognize as translatable into welfare rights. Certainly, he is not attempting to deploy, even schematically, all five of the necessary elements of a complete welfare rights theory. Still, at least the rough idea of meeting vital needs is clearly present.

For many purposes, the focus on staving off disaster will suffice. Theorists still talk in terms of meeting needs,[2] and it is certainly common to think of welfare rights as avoiding some undesirable state of affairs. Thus, one hears welfare rights defended in terms of protection against vulnerability,[3] protection against hazards,[4] relief of suffering or distress,[5] or of preventing the exploitation of social dependencies.[6]

All these formulations are, on their face, in some sense negative in emphasis, focus, and tone. Attention is on averting or relieving some undesirable state of affairs, such as starvation, hunger, or poverty more broadly. We may suppose that this negative focus conveys directly the urgency and immediacy of the case for welfare rights. Relieving distress seems more compelling than, say, making even happier an already modestly contented person. But there is no reason why a negative focus cannot be complemented with and completed by a more affirmative, positive focus. On such an approach, welfare rights still exist to, say, relieve grinding poverty, but also for the further sake of some more affirmative vision that requires, as a means, that poverty be relieved.

More affirmative visions of welfare rights may take a variety of forms congenial to various sorts of natural lawyers. We shall cursorily sketch one form of such an affirmative vision of welfare rights. In a way that is rudimentally traceable at least to Aristotle, we shall focus on welfare rights not only as "negatively" relieving suffering, but as conducing to the realization of "positive" human capacities as well. This positive vision thus emphasizes what might be called human functioning, or human development and flourishing in its many and richly varied possible forms.

Now, if one's task is to persuade the public to recognize some form of welfare right, the most effective tactic may well involve a merely negative focus on human suffering and its relief. This is a complex empirical question. But in any event, natural lawyers should, if for no other reason than theoretical completeness, be interested in complementing the negative focus on relieving suffering with a more affirmative vision of welfare rights as promotive of human flourishing. Different natural lawyers, including Aquinas, present different affirmative visions. We shall focus here on a vision that obviously owes much to Aristotle, while setting aside unacceptable elements of the Aristotelian account.

An Aristotelian Vision

It is fair to interpret Aristotle as offering an affirmative theory of human functioning and development within the natural law tradition.[7] Virtually every significant element of Aristotle's theory, admittedly, is contested as to interpretation[8] or degree of persuasiveness.[9] But we can get the discussion off the ground by assuming that Aristotle believes that for humans, functioning well involves what is in some sense a particular form of life, namely, activity in accordance with rational principle, or reason well-exercised.[10]

Aristotle seems to assume that humans as such have a characteristic activity[11] or function[12] linked to the exercise of reason.[13] Our function is a matter of human nature, or of what we collectively are uniquely[14] suited to do.[15] At a minimum, we may think of what makes sense of our capacities and potentials,[16] however those capacities and potentials may have come to be what they are.[17] The exercise of reason in accordance with the virtues or excellences pertaining to reasoning is thus a matter of human development[18] or human actualization,[19] by analogy to the way in which an acorn flourishes and realizes its natural capacity by developing into an oak tree.[20]

Thus, on Sir Ernest Barker's reading of Aristotle, human functioning involves a life in which the "complex powers of nutrition, sensation, and reason all come into play."[21] And the form of reason involved is "not indeed pure reason (that is for higher beings than man), but reason permeating and controlling the physical elements to which it is tied."[22]

There are again any number of grounds upon which to object to Aristotle's account.[23] One obvious, and on its own terms overwhelming, objection can, however, for our purposes be set aside. Aristotle may or may not have intended to exalt one particular lifestyle above all others.[24] To many of us, it is simply implausible to say, within a very broad range of lifestyles, tastes, pursuits, and plans of life, that one or more are intrinsically superior to others. Instead we recognize a very wide range of forms of human flourishing not susceptible of objective hierarchical ranking. An illustrious tenor and a philosopher may indeed vary in the degree to which the conscious exercise of reason and principle inform their activity, but we certainly need not rank their lives hierarchically on that basis.

Freedom, Reason, and Human Flourishing

In fact, many of us would rank liberty or autonomy in the choice of lifestyle so highly that even the otherwise allegedly highest and most exalted lifestyle would not involve genuine human flourishing if it is compelled, or otherwise not freely chosen. The lesson of John Stuart Mill is that objective human development is inseparable from extensive freedom in the realms of thought, speech, action, and style of life.[25]

Whatever Aristotle would say, we thus cannot say that Bertrand Russell flourishes more fully than the illustrious tenor, even if Russell exercises reason more variedly and more excellently than the tenor. Or suppose we have a brilliant composer, perhaps a distant relative of Mozart, who has studied some musical theory but whose compositions seem to flow more from inspiration and the play of the intuitive, subconscious mind than from reason. Why not view such a composer as, all else equal, as fully realized as any scientist?

Such a modern critique of Aristotle's theory of functioning well thus does several things. It first suggests the very wide potential range of forms of human flourishing. And second, it rejects any possible implication that styles of life can be objectively and generally hierarchically ranked as to their worth by the degree to which they involve the excellent use of reason.

For our purposes, though, it is crucial to notice what this modern critique of Aristotle is not committed to. The modern critique does not imply that every condition of life, no matter how abject or constrained, involves human development and flourishing to an equal degree or even that no two conditions of life can be objectively compared. If freedom is commonly necessary for human flourishing, we may doubt that reason without freedom, if that is possible, invariably amounts to the most fully realized way of living. We may also conclude that a freely chosen lifestyle involving somewhat less reason or principle might involve greater flourishing than an imposed lifestyle of contemplation. But the very importance of freedom to human flourishing tends to show that a lifestyle that is unfreely chosen or imposed may well rank lower in terms of human flourishing than other, more freely chosen lifestyles.[26] Thus we certainly have no grounds for inferring that all lives, no matter how miserable, should be thought of as equal or even merely unrankable in terms of human flourishing.

In fact, the modern critique of Aristotle does not imply that the ability to reason with some efficacy cannot be a crucial criterion in assessing whether a way of living promotes substantial human flourishing. Admittedly, the philosopher and the illustrious tenor might flourish equally even if the former reasons or contemplates in work, and about life, far more than the latter. Let us simply assume that the tenor does not in the same sense lead a life of reason, but still genuinely flourishes.

Material and Social Prerequisites

From the example of the illustrious tenor, however, we cannot infer that in other cases, denying persons the material and social prerequisites to reasoning at least moderately well with regard to their basic interests is irrelevant to their ability to flourish. Many people who cannot become illustrious tenors also cannot otherwise achieve self-realization without a genuine opportunity to develop minimally sufficient capacities to reason about relevant matters. Denying or failing affirmatively to provide an opportunity to develop those dimensions of reasoning means, in practice, that such persons cannot reasonably well fulfill their potential.

When access to the material and social requisites to human fulfillment is unavailable, the justification offered by a society for the absence of such opportunities is in a sense irrelevant. A society may believe that it has a moral right, or a good practical reason, for failing to provide some persons with such social and material prerequisites. Regardless, those persons adversely affected cannot, on our assumption, achieve human fulfillment, whether the broader society bears them any malice or not. This is clearly true, at a minimum, of familiar post-subsistence-level economies.

This does not mean that a society should attempt legally to require human fulfillment even of genuinely and freely uncooperative subjects. To some extent, compelled human fulfillment is a logical impossibility, given the linkages between freedom and fulfillment. But even if human fulfillment could somehow be imposed upon those who prefer to retain a generally acorn-like status, a society may have more pressing priorities. And persons who have been deprived of the material and social bases of the capacity to reason well in the first place can hardly be said to have freely and knowledgeably consented to, or ratified, that deprivation. To be denied the opportunity to reason at least moderately well on potentially significant matters is to be denied the capacity freely and rationally to waive any claim one might make to be afforded that opportunity. One cannot freely and knowledgeably consent to being deprived of any opportunity to ever be able to have freely consented.

The Social Bases of Reasoning Well

The material and social requisites to developing the ability to reason well may vary historically. So even if, for example, John Locke subscribes to an Aristotelian view linking functioning well with the ability to reason,[27] Locke's belief may in his time have different practical consequences than does Aristotle's. A public school system may be economically practical, even if unpopular, in one historical era but not in another. What a person needs to know, and what a person needs to be able mentally to do, in order to be capable of reasoning well may also vary from era to era.

There may well also be common historical elements to the capacity to reason well. It would be rather odd, for example, for a natural lawyer of any era to be indifferent to whether people have had sufficient educational opportunity to understand the basic elements and implications of the natural law itself. A natural law that is not taught or understood[28] may still be in some sense a promulgated natural law, but not a natural law that is respected or that contributes as such to the life of a person or a community. As well, persons of any era need some capacity to detect bias or propaganda from political leaders.

Thus the social and material requisites to functioning well will involve both historical continuities[29] and innovations.[30] There is certainly no guarantee that all persons and all societies will recognize, let alone promote, all of the minimally necessary social and material bases of human flourishing.[31] There will unavoidably be at least narrow disputes about the real elements of human flourishing, and then about what constitutes the minimally sufficient social and material bases for those elements. But the basic elements of human flourishing and lack of flourishing, at least in extreme cases, should be reasonably clear. And at least in extreme cases, it may also be quite clear that some social or material requisite to flourishing is lacking. On such a basis, it is possible to sketch some portions of an affirmatively-toned natural law defense of welfare rights.

We will of course not attempt herein a deep explanation of how human flourishing should be understood. We will not attempt an exhaustive inventory of the various possible elements of human flourishing. Nor will we even attempt to explain why those particular elements upon which we do focus really contribute crucially to human flourishing. Instead, our main interest is merely in linking one or more apparent elements of human flourishing to welfare rights claims.

Opportunity to Acquire Knowledge

It would not be difficult to build a case for the view that some degree of sheer physical safety and security[32] or of the opportunity to acquire relevant knowledge,[33] for example, are commonly prerequisite to substantial human flourishing. We will herein focus in particular on linking the opportunity to acquire knowledge, as a presumed element of human flourishing, to welfare rights.

The linkage of knowledge to functioning well can be illuminated by the work of, for example, the contemporary epistemologist Alvin Plantinga. Plantinga ascribes epistemic value to "having epistemic faculties that function properly,"[34] as opposed to cases of cognitive malfunction.[35] He assumes that most of us have at least some rough, intuitive idea of what proper functioning in general involves—a bird's wing that is broken and thus incapable of contributing to flight is in that respect not functioning well.[36] More particularly, we recognize that in many contexts, rapid ingestion of large quantities of alcohol temporarily impairs proper cognitive functioning in a number of respects.[37]

Plantinga develops his theory of epistemic warrant far more richly than we need take note of. For our purposes, it suffices merely to assume, unnecessary complications aside, that a person's beliefs lack epistemic warrant unless that person's cognitive equipment, including the capacities to form, maintain, recall, test, and otherwise process beliefs, is functioning properly.[38]

Admittedly, proper cognitive functioning is often a matter of degree.[39] No rights are violated if society does not even try to provide everyone with the material and social requisites of becoming an Aristotle. And we cannot always determine what proper cognitive functioning involves merely by noticing what happens, locally, to be the most statistically common pattern.[40] Myopic vision is not properly functioning vision, even if a majority of persons surveyed are myopic. The example of eyeglasses also shows that it is at best of only secondary importance whether proper functioning can be achieved without external assistance.[41] A society cannot pretend that eyeglasses have nothing to do with seeing well because they are external and artificial.

Among the inferences we may draw at this point are these: first, we cannot say that a person's epistemic faculties are functioning well merely because they are functioning no worse than those with whom that person compares him- or herself. Relatedly, we cannot say that a person's epistemic faculties are functioning well merely because that person is contented with how they are functioning. As well, whether a person's epistemic faculties are functioning well is not merely a matter of what that person can somehow achieve unaided, in the absence of some particular form of social assistance. Even if someone insists on saying that a person's visual system itself functions no better with appropriate prescription lenses than without them, we clearly want to be able to judge whether a person is functioning well cognitively on the basis of actual and potential external assistance, including state-provided education of a particular quality. It is hardly an abuse of language to ask whether a person would be in a position to function well cognitively if given realistic access to a particular form or degree of education.

Education, Information, and Knowledge

There are any number of ways in which an educational system can fail to contribute to the student's functioning reasonably well cognitively, or to the acquisition of crucially relevant knowledge. As Jonathan Kozol has eloquently observed over a period of years, such schooling as is realistically available may, for some persons, be utterly inadequate, and even physically unsafe.[42] But there is a subtler point to be made about the relationship between education and knowledge as a dimension of human functioning. Even if all persons had access to nonmisleading, nonpropagandistic educations, this would not ensure the opportunity to acquire genuine knowledge. Consider the observation of the epistemologist Keith Lehrer:

> If you tell me something and I believe you, even though I have no idea whether you are a source of true and correct information about the subject or a propagator of falsehood and deception, I may, if I am fortunate, acquire information when you happen to be informed and honest. This is not, however, knowledge in the sense that concerns us; it is merely the possession of information.[43]

This is no idle, abstract distinction. We may happen to acquire true beliefs as a result of looking at a clock that happened, unknown to us, to stop exactly twelve hours ago. But we do not thereby acquire genuine knowledge.[44] Staring at clocks that have stopped functioning is not ordinarily a reliable way to acquire knowledge or even true information about the current time. Even in cases in which we thereby happen to acquire true beliefs, we remain crucially ignorant about the utterly coincidental, arbitrary, and unreliable nature of our true belief.

Nor is the distinction, more broadly, between knowledge and merely true belief irrelevant to cognitively functioning well. If there were some high-tech way of immediately implanting many true beliefs directly into the cerebra of persons otherwise subjected to inadequate educational opportunities, those persons would in some obvious sense be educationally better off. But they would have been denied, crucially, the opportunity to develop minimal skills of fact gathering, investigation, hypothesis formulation and testing, critical thinking, and the drawing of sound inferences. Without fair opportunity to develop these skills, functioning well cognitively is precluded.

Of course, inadequate education does not currently take this particular form. But often, even when true information is conveyed, it is instilled as a mere conclusion, as a finished product. It is to be absorbed rather than reasoned to or critically tested. Doubtless some more or less rote absorption of masses of facts is essential. Sometimes, even this much is missing from persons' educations. But the mere inculcation of even the best preordained conclusions fails to promote cognitively functioning well in crucial ways. And this unfortunate result obtains whether or not we ascribe good faith and benevolence to those funding and operating such school systems.

Cognitive Bias

There are of course any number of ways in which one's information base, or one's reasoning skills, may be misdirected or left unnurtured. We will not attempt a full census. But even where people disagree as to the best substantive outcomes of a debate, they can often recognize some of the general forms in which even very subtle biases, informal fallacies, and other sorts of cognitive malfunctioning may arise.[45]

Consider, for example, the following recognizable cognitive biases:

> (1) the "vividness bias," under which the decision maker tends "to place more weight on concrete, emotionally interesting information than on more probative abstract data;" (2) the "availability bias," under which people "judge the probability of an event not by the actual likelihood of its happening, but by the ease with which they can recall particular instances of the event's occur-

> rence;" and (3) the "saliency bias," which is the tendency of "colorful, dynamic, or other distinctive stimuli [to] disproportionately engage attention and accordingly affect judgment."[46]

Similarly, it has been found that "data and scenarios that are instantiated, vivid, and concrete will normally be more salient than data and scenarios that are general, pallid, and abstract, such as statistical findings and generalized probabilities."[47] As well, "[a]nother widespread and stubborn illusion is the belief that others share one's attitudes and behaviors to a greater extent than they really do."[48]

Of course, these cognitive biases affect us all. They are in that sense universal, and in a further sense ineradicable. As well, their strength and impact doubtless vary according to the particular decision-making circumstances. But all this is fully compatible with these cognitive biases having a disproportionate impact on those denied minimally sufficient educational opportunities. Let us briefly speculate on how these sorts of biases, if not controlled through one's educational opportunity, might adversely impact the lives of the poor.

Education and the Taxpayer

Consider in particular the vividness bias, in which we attach more weight or significance than is fully rational, in light of our deepest goals, to concrete as opposed to abstract sorts of information. We may thus overly rely on merely personal experience or on what we have sensorally witnessed as opposed to the best established broad statistical evidence. To determine whether smoking is dangerous, we consider our own case, or those of our acquaintances, and not the newspaper reports of scientific studies.

Again, we are all vulnerable to this bias to some degree, regardless of level of education. But it is difficult to believe that a reasonably serious education, aimed at cognitively functioning well and at developing the capacity to reason effectively, would have no tendency to counteract this bias. Someone denied a reasonably serious educational opportunity will, almost as a matter of definition, tend to rely more on the concrete, as opposed to the abstract, than better-educated persons. This point surely does not rely on some sophisticated theory of maturation, cognitive development, or the psychology of learning. Learning the power and limitations of abstract reasoning and evidence is ordinarily possible only through education.

We need not decide how this bias will actually play out among the educationally deprived in political practice. A bias in favor of concrete experience might lead to ultimately irrational passivity on the part of the educationally deprived. Such persons might, for example, tend to assume that their own focus on monthly economic and even physical survival is normal,[49] and that most persons therefore genuinely understand and empathize with one's own struggles but are somehow prevented from actually improving one's situation. The actual, concrete, vivid social experience of poor people is, after all, mainly of other persons roughly as poor as themselves.

This cognitive bias is thus related to the bias already noted[50] in favor of assuming that other people share one's attitudes and behaviors. Here again, we need not establish the net political implications of this cognitive bias within the poor or uneducated. But this bias may undermine the basic interests of the poor. If, for example, poor persons see their employment opportunities as limited for reasons largely beyond their control, they may not view their poverty as their own fault. If, however, the poor are cognitively biased in favor of assuming that other persons understand their straits and also do not blame the poor for their own poverty, their reading of broader American popular opinion may be dangerously inaccurate.[51] The poor might thus tend excessively to assume that the nonpoor believe the poor morally deserving of assistance, but that the nonpoor simply lack the means to help more than they actually do.[52]

Susceptibility to these sorts of cognitive biases, and to the dangers these biases pose, could to some degree be diminished with enhanced educational opportunity. A societal failure to reduce the severity of these biases through educational opportunity is thus a societal failure, to that extent, to encourage the development of a capacity for sound decision making within those particularly adversely affected. In that respect, such a society thereby fails to promote the cognitive dimension of human flourishing. At what precise point such a societal failure, for whatever reason, rises to the level of a natural rights violation will again be indeterminate and historically variable. But it is difficult to match up the actual conditions of our least-effective contemporary public schools against the scale of social resources potentially available to ameliorate such conditions without finding a prima facie case for a natural rights violation.

It is fair to say that each year the taxpayers devote quite substantial resources to public schools that, blamelessly or otherwise, do not invariably provide all that is necessary to close the gap between the child's current capacities and those minimally necessary for the sorts of cognitive flourishing we have been discussing. There is certainly a legitimate taxpayer interest in wringing unnecessary inefficiencies, unnecessary failure, and sheer avoidable waste out of the system. This may involve redesign of the public and private educational system; welfare and child care services mechanism; community policing and security; and the delivery of child, infant, and prenatal health care. In general, whatever enhances the range of practical options genuinely available to poor parents will tend to contribute to the flourishing of their children. Devolution, decentralization, and local control can be valuable in reducing waste and inefficiency and for other reasons. Let us remember, though, that the ability to compose a coherent paragraph is important in all jurisdictions.

Issues of waste, efficiency, and means are, however, rarely basic. The deeper objection raised by taxpayers is not really one of waste or inefficiency in providing opportunities for cognitive flourishing, but of having to pay the necessary price, or indeed any price at all, so that children can be afforded a path to the sort of cognitive competence we have described. This objection can, of course, be battled out along the lines of priorities among liberties, levels of autonomy, arbitrariness and moral luck, the meanings of equality, and the equal and absolute dignity of each human person.

We can add little here, beyond noting what is at stake. We have argued for the moral incumbency of providing to all persons the social bases of the genuine opportunity to develop certain minimal cognitive abilities and, to this extent, to flourish as persons. Those taxpayers who object on principle to contributing such genuine opportunities typically do not argue that exacting their contribution seriously threatens such material or economic harm, personally, that the taxpayers will, ironically, be thereby deprived of the necessary material basis for their own minimally adequate levels of cognitive competency. Nor could taxpayers typically make any such argument, given our enormous, if quite oddly directed, collective economic surplus.

We have thus cursorily linked welfare rights to education with the capacity to function well cognitively and to epistemic well-being. Let us conclude the argument by noting that educational welfare rights can also be linked to the profoundly important idea of the conditions of bearing moral responsibility. Lloyd Weinreb has rightly argued that for effective agency,

> one has to perceive accurately a situation calling for action and understand the consequences of actions that one might take. This perception and understanding depend upon having general information as well as a capacity to reflect, abstractly and concretely. Repeated failure to accomplish what one intends may reasonably prompt a conclusion that it is pointless to try. Every person has a right to education conducive to effective agency.[53]

One might also directly link educational opportunity with human dignity. The depths of the linkages between genuine knowledge, reason, and various forms of human freedom are also remarkable. Suffice it to say that educational rights have multiple links to some of the deepest and most powerful currents of moral argument.

Conclusion

It is certainly possible to respond to all of this by pointing to current inclinations to depreciate any robust conceptions of, among other notions, freedom, knowledge, and reason. Such depreciation does admittedly tend to weaken the case for human rights, among other consequences. But since the case for such a depreciation has been widely debated, we have simply assumed for purposes of this essay that familiar ideas of rights, traceable back at least to Aristotle, remain viable.

Quite realistically, Aristotle observes that "happiness seems to require a modicum of external prosperity. . . ."[54] Happiness thus requires that one be "adequately furnished with external goods. . . ."[55] Aristotle concludes that "those are clearly right who . . . maintain the necessity to a happy life of an addition in the form of material goods."[56]

It is easy to underappreciate the moral and political implications of Aristotle's argument. Aristotle himself seems to steer the argument away from some significant possible implications. He observes, for example, that "[i]t is difficult, if not impossible, to engage in noble enterprises without money to spend on them; many can only be performed through friends, or wealth, or political influence."[57]

Now, if this is the direction in which we pursue Aristotle's argument, its implications will not seem particularly egalitarian, redistributionist, or broadly rights-generative. As a matter of practicality, if not of logic, we cannot all be in a position to perform noble deeds in Aristotle's sense. We similarly cannot all be distinctively influential on political matters. To deny this would come perilously close to supposing that most of us can have the best house on the block, or the best view of the ocean, or that the typical public school can be better than average.

Thus on this reading of Aristotle, the rights-implications of his argument seem limited. What we cannot all do, as a matter of logic or practicality, we cannot all have an enforceable legal right to do.

Let us note, though, that we have not argued herein for anything like a right to engage in noble activities, or even for a right to the material prerequisites of noble activity. Similarly, we have not argued for a universal right to be more persuasive than average, or even for the material prerequisites thereto. Instead, we have argued, less self-defeatingly, for a right to the material prerequisites of generally functioning well, particularly in the realms of knowledge and cognition. This is largely a matter of a genuinely meaningful education, and of what is socially and materially prerequisite to such an education. Here, the necessary resources are not, as a matter of practicalities or logic, so scarce or costly as to undermine the case for general and legally enforceable rights claims.

Pursuit of Happiness

But this is not the only way in which Aristotle's development of his own basic principles can tend to trivialize their rights implications. We may also, given our contemporary understanding of the idea of happiness, be in this respect misled by Aristotle's use of the term we translate as happiness.[58] There can of course be no general, legally enforceable right to happiness itself. The happiness of A and B might well depend crucially upon their exclusively marrying the same person C, or winning the same laurel wreath in the same event. So A and B cannot, irreconcilably, both have a right to happiness itself.

This basic insight has not been lost on our own rights-laden American tradition. Thus the Declaration of Independence refers not to a right to happiness, which would for any number of reasons lie beyond the power of any government to fulfill, but to a right to the pursuit of happiness. Arguably, the mere pursuit of happiness does not require much, if any, affirmative government provision. Each person's pursuit of happiness may thus be successful or unsuccessful, without anyone's rights being violated.

Plainly, a general legal right to happiness itself would be futile, if not incoherent. To the extent that we assume that Aristotle was concerned simply about happiness as we normally understand the term, we will not see his discussion as interestingly rights-generative. But our focus herein has not been on happiness in the current sense, or even on the material prerequisites of such happiness.

Reasoning Well

Instead, we have focused on ideas such as the material bases for reasoning well, recognizing and articulating one's basic interests, making a useful economic contribution, limiting the practical influence of cognitive biases, and obtaining knowledge. None of this is a matter of inherent, inevitable scarcity. Of course, in our society, providing the material bases for achieving these ends and capacities to some reasonable degree of fulfillment would be expensive. Some redistribution of resources across class lines would be involved. These latter considerations may well explain why our society does not legally recognize the rights in question. But lack of legal recognition and political unpopularity hardly undermine the moral logic of an otherwise tenable claim of right. Rather, they provide the proper occasion for the invocation and defense of such a right.

NOTES

1. SAINT THOMAS AQUINAS, ON LAW, MORALITY, AND POLITICS 186 (William P. Baumgarth & Richard J. Regan eds., 1988) (SUMMA THEOLOGICA II-II, question 66, article 7). *See also id.* at 187 (reply to objection 2)("[i]t is not theft, properly speaking, to take secretly and use another's property in case of extreme need because that which a man takes for the support of his life becomes his own property by reason of that need"). Let us not, however, oversimplify Aquinas' approach; possible issues of the desirability of non-violence, public reimbursement, and penance may come into play.

2. *See, e.g.*, DAVID BRAYBROOKE, MEETING NEEDS (1987).

3. *See* ROBERT E. GOODIN, PROTECTING THE VULNERABLE: A REANALYSIS OF OUR SOCIAL RESPONSIBILITIES 145 (1985).

4. *See* ROBERT E. GOODIN, REASONS FOR WELFARE: THE POLITICAL THEORY OF THE WELFARE STATE 16 (1988).

5. *See id.* at 19.

6. *See id.* at 21.

7. *Cf.* Elizabeth Anscombe's remark that "it is a bit much to swallow that a man in pain and hunger and poor and friendless is 'flourishing,' as Aristotle himself admitted." *G.E.M. Anscombe, Modern Moral Philosophy*, in ETHICS 186, 209 (JUDITH J. THOMSON & GERALD DWORKIN eds., 1968) (reprinting 33 Phil. 1–19 (1958)).

8. *See, e.g., Marcus Hester, Aristotle On the Function of Man in Relation to Eudaimonia*, 8 HIST. PHIL. Q. 3, 4, 12 (1991)(querying the extent to which Aristotle's view of eudaimonia really depends upon a biological concept of human functioning, and whether eudaimonia depends simply upon reflection itself, or upon reflection on one's virtuous acts, experiences, and (other) reflections); *Richard Kraut, The Peculiar Function of Human Beings*, 9 CAN. J. PHIL. 467, 467, 477 (1979)(querying whether or in what sense contemplation or reasoning is distinctive of or peculiar to human beings, as opposed to the gods).

9. *See, e.g., Richard Kraut, supra* note 8, at 467; *Christine M. Korsgaard, Aristotle On Function and Virtue*, 3 HIST. PHIL. Q. 259, 259 (1986)(referring to critiques of Aristotle's allegedly illicit teleological reasoning; the existence of some

(distinctive) human function in the first place; the inference from a human function to a human good; the choice of rational activity in some fashion as that function; and the linkages among rational activity, moral virtue, and happiness).

10. *See* ARISTOTLE, THE ETHICS OF ARISTOTLE book I, ch. 7 at 38–39 (J.A.K. THOMSON trans., 1955) (translation of the Nicomachean Ethics).

11. *See, e.g.*, NANCY SHERMAN, THE FABRIC OF CHARACTER: ARISTOTLE'S THEORY OF VIRTUE 117 (1989).

12. *See, e.g., Kyron Huigens, Virtue and Inculpation*, 108 HARV. L. REV. 1423, 1449–50 (1995).

13. *See, e.g.*, TERENCE IRWIN, ARISTOTLE'S FIRST PRINCIPLES 364 (1988).

14. Query whether Aristotle's theory requires revision if we discover that Vulcans are neither higher beings nor humans, but are better at exercising and applying reason in contemplation, intellectual discovery, or practical problem solving.

15. *See, e.g., Stephen Clark, The Use of 'Man's Function' in Aristotle*, 82 ETHICS 269, 274 (1972).

16. *See id.*

17. *See id.*

18. *See, e.g.*, HENRY B. VEATCH, ARISTOTLE: A CONTEMPORARY APPRECIATION 104 (1974).

19. See, e.g., TERENCE IRWIN, *supra* note 13, at 364.

20. See, e.g., HENRY B. VEATCH, *supra* note 18, at 104.

21. ERNEST BARKER, THE POLITICAL THOUGHT OF PLATO AND ARISTOTLE 243 (1959).

22. *Id.*

23. *See supra* notes 8–9 and accompanying text.

24. *See, e.g., Marcus Hester*, supra note 8, at 12.

25. *See generally* JOHN STUART MILL, ON LIBERTY (DAVID SPITZ ed., 1975).

26. There is certainly a difference between a lifestyle that is freely chosen, initially or on a continuing basis, but which may not involve great substantive freedom in living, and a lifestyle that is coercively imposed or otherwise unavoidable, but which in the subsequent actual living involves great freedom. But this difference does not appear to affect our argument.

27. *See Bruce N. Morton, John Locke, Robert Bork, Natural Rights and the Interpretation of the Constitution*, 22 SETON HALL L. REV. 709, 723 (1992)("Locke determines that Aristotle rightly concludes that the proper function of man is acting in accordance with reason . . . .").

28. *Cf.* Thomas Aquinas' discussion of the failure of the Germans of Julius Caesar's time to recognize the general wrongfulness of theft, in the SUMMA THEOLOGICA, I-II, question 94, article 4.

29. *Cf. Michael S. Moore, Law as a Functional Kind*, in NATURAL LAW THEORY: CONTEMPORARY ESSAYS 188, 210 (ROBERT P. GEORGE ed., 1992)(the human heart as functioning so as to promote the evident overall goal of physical health).

30. *Cf.* MICHAEL J. PERRY, MORALITY, POLITICS, AND LAW: A BICENTENNIAL ESSAY 20 (1988)("[G]iven our commitment to flourishing, we have an interest in the personal capacities and social and political conditions that are prerequisites to flourishing, including capacities and conditions we may not presently understand to be prerequisites").

31. *See id.*

32. Governmental provision for personal safety and security is strongly emphasized in a remarkable range of modern political theorists. *See, e.g.*, THOMAS HOBBES, LEVIATHAN 100 (M. OAKSHOTT ed., 1962); BENEDICT SPINOZA, A THEOLOGICO-POLITICAL TREATISE 258–59 (R. ELWES trans., 1951)("the ultimate aim of government is . . . to free every man from fear, that he may live in all possible security"); *James Harrington, The Commonwealth of Oceana*, in THE POLITICAL WRITINGS OF JAMES HARRINGTON 70 (C. BLITZER ed., 1955); JOHN LOCKE, TWO TREATISES OF GOVERNMENT 368 (PETER LASLETT rev. ed., 1963); DAVID HUME, DAVID HUME'S POLITICAL ESSAYS 39 (CHARLES HENDEL ed., 1953); CONDORCET: SELECTED WRITINGS 73 (KEITH BAKER ed., 1976); JEAN-JACQUES ROUSSEAU, THE SOCIAL CONTRACT book I, ch. VI, at 17 (LESTER CROCKER ed., 1967).

33. *See, e.g.*, JOHN FINNIS, NATURAL LAW AND NATURAL RIGHTS 61 (1980)(referring to "the well-informed and clear-headed person as, to that extent, well-off (and not only for the profitable use he can make of his knowledge")). Of course, not all forms of knowledge tend equally to conduce to well-being. *See id.* at 62. Context importantly affects the value of knowledge. *See id.* And sometimes, knowledge is an important disvalue, as when knowledge involves tactless disclosure, the over-analysis of a personal relationship or of a golf swing, or sapping the ultimately vital motivation and confidence of a person facing long odds. Entire cultures may not value broad areas of possible knowledge. But all of this is a long way from undermining the claim that knowledge is, commonly, a crucial requisite to a person's generally functioning well.

34. ALVIN PLANTINGA, WARRANT AND PROPER FUNCTION 4 (1993).

35. *See id.*

36. *See id.* at 5.

37. *See id.*

38. *See id.* at 4. It would be fair to say that much of the remainder of Plantinga's entire text involves the development of, refinement, qualification, and defense of this rough basic claim.

39. *See id.* at 10.

40. *See id.* at 9.

41. *See id.* at 10.

42. *See, e.g.*, JONATHAN KOZOL, SAVAGE INEQUALITIES: CHILDREN IN AMERICA'S SCHOOLS (1991); JONATHAN KOZOL, DEATH AT AN EARLY AGE (1986). For discussion of the constitutional dimensions of this situation, see, e.g., *Susan H. Bitensky, Theoretical Foundations for a Right to Education Under the U.S. Constitution: A Beginning to the End of the National Education Crisis, 86* NW. U.L. REV. 550 (1992); *R. George Wright, The Place of Public School Education in the Constitutional Scheme*, 13 S. ILL. U. L.J. 53 (1988).

43. KEITH LEHRER, THEORY OF KNOWLEDGE 4 (1990).

44. *See id.* See ALSO ALVIN I. GOLDMAN, EPISTEMOLOGY AND COGNITION 42 (1986)("[W]hether a true belief is knowledge depends on why the belief is held, on the psychological processes that cause the belief or sustain it in the mind").

45. *See, e.g.*, SUSAN L. HURLEY, NATURAL REASONS: PERSONALITY AND POL-

ITY 326 (1989)(endorsing the design of social and political institutions in such a way as to minimize, e.g., deceit, prejudice, and propaganda); RICHARD B. BRANDT, A THEORY OF THE GOOD AND THE RIGHT 115 et seq. (1979)(non-exhaustively cataloguing a number of sorts of mistake-based desires); JUDGMENT UNDER UNCERTAINTY: HEURISTICS AND BIASES (DANIEL KAHNEMAN, PAUL SLOVIC, & AMOS TVERSKY eds., 1982).

46. *Donald P. Judges, Of Rocks and Hard Places: The Value of Risk Choice*, 42 EMORY L.J. 1, 81 n.265 (1993)(citing the jury decisionmaking studies of Harry Gerla, who in turn quotes SHELLEY E. TAYLOR, THE AVAILABILITY BIAS IN SOCIAL PERCEPTION AND INTERACTION, IN JUDGMENT UNDER UNCERTAINTY: HEURISTICS AND BIASES, *supra* note 45, at 190, 192).

47. *Melvin A. Eisenberg, The Limits of Cognition and the Limits of Contract*, 47 STAN. L. REV. 211, 221 (1995).

48. *Donald Langevoort, Ego, Human Behavior, and Law*, 81 VA. L. REV. 853, 859 (1993).

49. To some extent, this conclusion may be weakened by what one sees on popular commercial television programs, where the poor and educationally deprived are hardly overrepresented as characters or subjects. But while popular television programs may not promote abstract or statistical reason, they may not entirely count as concrete experience either. Television's implicit lesson that most Americans are not poor may be blurred somewhat if television is assumed to present a mixture of concrete reality and sheer fantasy. There may be some tendency on the part of the poor to assume that popular entertainment programs may sacrifice realism for entertainment.

50. *See supra* text accompanying note 48.

51. This is not to suggest that the chronically unemployed, and to a degree even the working poor, do not sense any tendency within non-poor groups to ascribe responsibility for their poverty to the poor themselves. Clearly, a cognitive bias can have untoward effects even if one is in possession of evidence tending, accurately, to counteract the bias.

52. Doubtless the attitude of the non-poor toward the poor is not uniformly one of blame and lack of sympathy. But the non-poor presumably will sacrifice or work to overcome the practical and technical problems of poverty with some reference to the degree to which the poor are believed to deserve their fate, and the poor may tend to misperceive the attitudes of the non-poor in this respect.

53. LLOYD L. WEINREB, OEDIPUS AT FENWAY PARK: WHAT RIGHTS ARE AND WHY THERE ARE ANY 119 (1994). *See also id.* at 117.

54. ARISTOTLE, *supra* note 10, at book one, ch. 8.

55. *Id.* at ch. 10.

56. *Id.* at ch. 8.

57. *Id.*

58. *See id.* at chs. 7, 8.

Tort Reform

Patrick J. Kelley

The public debate over tort reform has degenerated into a shouting match between two special-interest groups—manufacturers and doctors on the one side versus plaintiff personal injury lawyers on the other. In all the hullabaloo, the real purpose of tort liability—to redress private wrongs—has been obscured and its continued achievement has been threatened. A natural law analysis that insists on the primacy of that purpose may shed some disinterested light on this vital issue and help us to identify the real solutions to the real problems in the tort liability system.

Tort reform seems to have become a perennial issue in our politics. The Republican Contract with America contained a tort reform provision, and Bob Dole made tort reform an issue in his 1996 presidential campaign. President Clinton's reelection has for now darkened the prospects of tort reform at the federal level, but the issue is still alive and well at the state level: major tort reform bills were enacted in 1995 in Texas and Illinois, and tort reform bills continue to be introduced in state legislatures, even though the Illinois act was voided by that state's highest court.

The continuing public debate over tort reform has taken a nasty turn, with both sides resorting to name calling, horror stories, and partisan appeals. The ordinary voter, observing such heated debate over such seemingly complicated questions of law and the judicial system, may be confused. What is all the fuss about? What is at stake? Why is the debate so heated and so partisan? What is the right thing to do?

In the following pages, I shall try to answer these questions. I begin by examining the current debate over tort reform and isolating the unanswered question underlying that debate: What is the purpose of tort liability? Modern natural law analysis may help us to discover an objective, defensible answer to that question: John Finnis's focal case methodology applied to the tort liability system provides an answer that will then enable us to identify the real problems with our tort liability system and the real solutions to those problems. This analysis suggests that both sides in the current partisan debate over tort reform are wrong: the antireformers are wrong to oppose all significant reforms, and most of the particular reforms urged by the reformers would make things worse.

Tort Law and the Current Debate over Tort Reform

The law of torts determines when one who caused injury to another will be ordered to compensate the injured plaintiff for the harm done. A "tort" is the wrongful conduct causing injury for which the courts order compensation to be paid. Torts come in many different flavors: if I punch you in the nose, that's a tort; if I slander your good name and damage your reputation, that's a tort; if I negligently drive my car and run you down, that's a tort.

For most torts, one may obtain insurance that will pay off all or part of any liability one may subsequently incur. The sale of liability insurance for torts causing personal physical injury is big business. Spurred in large part by common concerns about the high cost of liability insurance, a coalition of businesses, doctors and doctors' associations, public agencies, and trade associations formed the American Tort Reform Association [ATRA]. The ATRA, together with its spin-off state tort reform associations, has been a strong lobbying group for tort reforms intended to lower the costs of the tort liability system.

Leading the fight against tort reform has been the American Trial Lawyers' Association (ATLA), a professional association of plaintiffs' attorneys. Together with individual plaintiffs' attorneys and some consumer groups, the ATLA has steadfastly lobbied against tort reform at both the state and federal levels.

Politics and Tort Reform

The individuals involved in any particular accidental injury leading to a tort claim, both plaintiff and defendant, are ever-changing and unlikely to have had any prior experience with the tort liability system. ATRA and ATLA, the two major combatants in the tort reform debate, however, represent repeat players with special financial interests in the operation of the tort liability system. These two opposing interest groups have enlisted their natural political allies in the fight. The issue has become highly partisan, with Republicans, by and large, supporting tort reform and Democrats, by and large, opposing it. This highly-charged partisanship was the reason a harsh reform bill was enacted in Illinois immediately after the Republicans gained control of both houses of the legislature in 1994. The bill was a payback for plaintiffs' attorneys' massive support for Democrats and a thank-you for doctors' and business support of Republicans.

Since the issue has slipped out of the genteel debates of the academy and into the tougher arena of politics, the arguments on both sides have become less and less subtle.

American Tort Reform Association

The American Tort Reform Association claims as its "Bible" a book by Peter Huber called *Liability: The Legal Revolution and Its Consequences*.[1] Huber has a doctorate in mechanical engineering from M.I.T. and a law degree from Harvard. The form of many of his arguments is that of a mathematical proof. His writing style, however, is populist and polemical. Reading Huber is like reading Descartes reincarnated as P.J. O'Rourke. Huber argues that the tort liability system has been transformed over the last thirty years by the adoption of more and more plaintiff-favoring substantive and procedural rules. The new rules were embraced by judges influenced by the theories of the academic "founders" of modern tort liability, who saw the tort liability system as a means to promote safety, compensate the injured, and spread catastrophic individual losses over a large group dissipating the large loss by passing it on in the form of tiny individual costs to each member of the group. The mechanisms for spreading losses were liability insurance and the market.

This proplaintiff system, Huber argues, has resulted in a litigation explosion that in fact imposes a huge tort liability "tax" on all of us in increased costs of goods and services. He says that tort liability costs $80 billion each year in direct costs and an additional $300 billion in indirect liability-avoidance costs for things like unnecessary medical tests ordered only to protect physicians from potential liabilities.

Huber argues that the changes are self-defeating. Ironically, the tort liability system decreases safety by imposing heavy costs and risks on those (such as emergency room doctors) charged with helping us avoid harm and by discouraging innovations that might lead to safer products or services. Ironically, too, the tort liability system is dreadfully poor at spreading losses. For one thing, the tort liability tax is unfairly regressive, as everyone pays about the same but the injured rich recover more in damage awards for lost wages than the injured poor; for another, it is grossly inefficient, with less than 50 percent of the total amount paid into the system going to compensate the injured.

Along the way, Huber tells horror story after horror story of tort liability imposed by misguided juries when the defendant was not at fault or the plaintiff's own foolishness was the cause of the harm.

The ATRA's literature is also awash in horror stories. The older woman who "recovered millions when she burned herself with hot McDonald's coffee" has become the poster child of the tort reform movement.

The American Tort Reform Association's primary goal seems to be to reduce the costs of the tort liability system. It proposes a six-point reform agenda:

1. Abolish joint liability
2. Abolish the collateral source rule
3. Limit punitive damages
4. Cap or otherwise limit recovery for noneconomic losses
5. Reform the substantive law of product liability so that the standards are clear and compliance possible.
6. Reform medical liability law to include caps on noneconomic damages, limits on attorneys' contingency fees, periodic payment of future costs and elimination of the collateral source rule.

All except the fifth proposal are aimed directly at reducing the overall costs of the tort liability system.

American Trial Lawyers Association

Plaintiffs' attorneys, through the American Trial Lawyers Association, have fought back. They attack the factual assumptions underlying the tort reform movement. There is no litigation explosion, they argue. Further, they contend that the costs of the tort liability system are wildly overstated by the tort reformers. And they argue that the jury is the common-sense, common-people bulwark of our civil liberties. They point out that jurors are just ordinary people; they are not the overly compassionate boobs the tort reformers make them out to be.

The plaintiffs' attorneys argue positively that the tort liability system as it is now achieves two important social goals. First, it achieves justice by holding wrongdoers accountable for their wrongs and by providing compensation for those they have wronged. Second, it prevents injuries by forcing wrongdoers to change their dangerous behavior. This twofold positive argument for the tort liability system was adopted by ATLA after focus groups, polls, and consultants showed them that these were the most effective positive arguments for the tort liability system.

The ATLA, too, has its horror stories, of innocent victims, horribly injured by grossly negligent defendants, who cannot obtain full compensation for their injuries because of harsh limitations on tort recovery, adopted by compliant legislatures urged on by the tort reform lobby. A favorite story of theirs is the tort reform lobbyist in Indiana who helped persuade the Indiana legislature to impose a stringent cap on recovery for total damages in medical malpractice cases. He was subsequently the victim of medical malpractice himself and was barred from adequate recovery for his loss by the very limit he had previously lobbied for. He now rues the day he argued for tort reform.

Of course, each side in this public debate has noticed that the other side has a special economic interest in the outcome. "Greedy-plaintiffs-attorneys" is one word in the tort reformers' dictionary. The trial lawyers, on the other hand, continually point out that tort reform is the project of rich doctors and manufacturers, or, as they sometimes call them, "organized tortfeasors," or "the Wrongdoers of America, Inc."

The Underlying Question: What is the Practical Point of Tort Liability?

The Question

As men and women of good will, intent on identifying and promoting the common good, what are we to make of this debate? Is there some objective, independent ground on which to stand that will enable us to evaluate the arguments on both sides? I believe there is, but in order to reach that ground we must first identify the underlying question at issue here.

As a preliminary matter, it may be helpful to focus on the primary goal of the tort reformers: to reduce the costs of the tort liability system, which they say are excessive. One might ask, "Why not abolish tort liability altogether? That would reduce the costs of the system to zero." The answer to that question, of course, is that by eliminating tort liability completely we would lose completely the benefits—the contribution to the common good—that tort liability provides. That answer leads us to other questions: What is the purpose or practical point of tort liability, how does the achievement of that purpose affect the common good, and is it worth the cost?

We can put the same question another way. Arguments about excessive costs and unacceptable consequences can be judged only from the standpoint of the practical point or purpose of the tort liability system and its relative importance compared to other shared social purposes. If the purpose of tort liability is to spread the costs of accidents, increased claims frequency and consequent increased overall costs of the system may not in itself be a problem, since greater use of the system to spread the costs of injuries would be seen as desirable. The real problem then would be the system's inefficiency as a loss-spreading mechanism. Alternatively, if the purpose of tort liability is to hold wrongdoers accountable by forcing them to compensate those they have wronged, the system's inefficiency as a loss-spreading mechanism is irrelevant.

The basic theoretical problem, then, is to determine the practical point or basic purpose of tort liability. And here we find that the purpose of tort liability is a hotly contested question in the academy and in the courts. A number of competing answers have been given:

- Some say the purpose is to impose the costs of injuries on the enterprise inevitably causing those injuries.
- Some say the purpose is to spread large losses over a broad base so that everyone pays a little bit and no one has to bear a huge loss alone.
- Some say the purpose is to encourage the efficient allocation of resources to accident prevention.
- Some say the purpose is to deter dangerous conduct.
- Some say the purpose is to redress wrongs.
- Some, taking refuge in eclecticism, say the purpose is to do a number of different things, including all or most of the things others say it is to do.

How can we hope to answer this question when the experts themselves do not agree on the answers and give such a bewildering variety of answers?

The Natural Law Answer

It is precisely here that natural law theory may be of help, in the form of the social science methodology elaborated by John Finnis in his book *Natural Law and Natural Rights*.[2] Finnis argues that we are privy to inside information about human institutions and practices. To determine the practical point of human institutions and practices, we should take the internal point of view of one concerned to act within that institution.

The descriptive theory developed from that point of view will contain an irreducibly normative component because a reasonable person talking about human institutions, practices, and interactions cannot leave out their most important parts, which are human purposes, goals, and judgments of practical reasonableness. Once one includes these, any coherent description must include a critical evaluation. The better the evaluation, the better the description.

An analogy proposed by Lon Fuller[3] may be helpful. Any coherent description of a boy trying to open a clam must include several evaluative judgments, including the judgment that he is trying to open a clam, a judgment about whether the method he is using is a good way of opening claims, and a judgment about whether he has succeeded. In describing the boy's conduct, one who is good at opening clams and who has talked to the boy will have a decided advantage, for that skill and that experience make it more likely that one will make correctly the evaluative judgments called for by the descriptive enterprise.

The Practical Purpose of Tort Liability To determine the practical point or purpose of tort liability, then, we should take the internal point of view of one with a view to acting within the tort liability system, employ basic principles of practical reasonableness, focus on the fundamental realities of the system, and take into account recurring explanations of its purpose by those whose actions and practices constitute it.[4]

The first bedrock fact that any tort theory must take into account is the ordinary form of tort liability—a judicial judgment ordering the defendant to pay the plaintiff a specified amount of money, which is called the award of "damages" or "money damages." The amount awarded is determined by measuring the loss or harm to the plaintiff caused by defendant's conduct. The announced aim of the damage award is to "make the plaintiff whole"—to have the defendant pay what will restore the plaintiff to the position he was in before the tort. Judges have repeatedly justified this measure of damages by explaining that it is called for by the purpose of compensatory damages. That purpose, they say, is to redress the wrong that the defendant has done to the plaintiff.

The recurrent explanation that the purpose of the ordinary tort remedy is to redress a wrong is consistent with the bedrock terminology of torts as well. "Trespass," the name of the earliest tort form of action at common law, originally meant simply "a wrong." The word "tort" itself originally meant crooked, twisted—wrong. Courts and commentators often use the term "injury" as an element in all torts in the sense of the Latin "*injuria*," which originally meant a *wrong* or *wrongful*.

One final bedrock fact about the operation of the tort liability system is consistent with this recurring explanation. Tort actions are brought by one private individual against another private individual for a remedy that transfers money just between them. The government provides only the method of adjudicating the claim and the means of enforcing the remedy. This is a more limited role than the government's role in criminal actions, which are brought by the government and seek fines paid to the government or imprisonment in government-run jails. The more limited governmental involvement in tort cases tends to confirm the private nature of the wrongs redressed by tort actions.

The ordinary tort remedy of compensatory damages, its traditional justification, and the terminology and operation of the tort liability system, then, all suggest that the practical point of tort liability, from the internal point of view, is to redress private wrongs. It remains to be seen whether this hypothesized purpose can pass the test of practical reasonableness, and whether it is still the practical point of tort liability or merely a historical curio.

Practical Reasonableness To apply the test of practical reasonableness, one must first ask why the political community would want to provide a mechanism for redressing private wrongs, which seem to concern only two private individuals within the community. To answer that question, one must discover the practical point of the political community itself. John Finnis has argued that the purpose of a political community is to achieve the "common good," understood as "a set of material and other conditions [including forms of collaboration and coordination] which enables the members of a community to attain for themselves reasonable objectives. . . ."[5] If we accept that as the goal of a political community, we can see the tort liability system as one of those conditions that comprise or promote the common good. The following analysis of the relationship between tort liability and the common good tends to bear this out.

In any community, individuals coordinate their activities with the activities of others according to established patterns of behavior. These patterns of coordination enable members of the community to pursue their goals without interference by other members pursuing theirs. The coordinating behavior may be positive (action) or negative (refraining from action). For example, we drive on the right-hand side of the street, and we refrain from hunting animals in town with rifles. These patterns may have developed through governmental edict, custom, or moral teaching. Once a pattern of coordination is accepted, members of the community rely on it in determining their own conduct, and they expect other members of the community with whom they come in contact to follow the pattern as well.

If Alice coordinates her activities with Joe in accordance with these expectations, and Joe acts contrary to those expectations in a way that injures Alice, Alice feels wronged. Joe drives on the left-hand side of the street, for example, and crashes into Alice. Joe hunts squirrels in town with a high-powered rifle, for another example, and accidentally shoots Alice.

Why does Alice feel wronged? At the most basic level, the answer is simple. Alice acted as she did in the expectation that Joe and others like him would follow the accepted pattern. She acted according to patterns of conduct that would coordinate with his if he acted in accordance with that expectation. At a deeper level, we can say that Alice feels wronged because Joe has not respected her claim that, in his decision making and activity, he should give due consideration to her interest in the pursuit of her own concerns. He has failed to recognize her standing claim to respect for her personal worth and dignity. One has dignity not as an abstract, universal human being but as a particular person with a unique identity, formed in part by historical and social conditions. So respecting Alice's dignity means respecting the choices she makes in accordance with her expectations about the conduct of others in light of their community's accepted patterns of coordination.

When Alice brings to court her claim that Joe wronged her, then, we can see that the claim contains both intensely personal and broadly social components. It is personal because Alice claims Joe wronged her by failing to respect her standing claim to respect for *her* personal dignity, in a way that resulted in serious personal harm to *her*. It is broadly social because the way Joe injured Alice was by ignoring a *social rule* she had relied on in coordinating her conduct with others in the *community*. In light of the personal and social components in a plaintiff's claim to have been wronged, we can see a number of reasons why a community would provide a mechanism for adjudicating and redressing claims of private injustice.

First, if we look on the judicial judgment as a response to Alice's claim of a personal wrong, we can see that the judicial judgment that Joe wronged Alice and must now redress the wrong vindicates Alice's claim to respect for her personal dignity. It reaffirms her worth as a respected member of the community. Moreover, that judgment provides Alice with a good that she could not obtain on her own: justice in the form of a court order, backed by the power of the state, requiring Joe to act justly toward her now by restoring what he has unfairly deprived her of.

Second, if we look at the relationship between the judicial judgment and the social component in Alice's claim, we can see that the community, in redressing the wrong to Alice, also promotes the common good by reaffirming the social convention that Alice relied on. If the formal representative of the political community refused to redress this claimed wrong, Alice and others in the community might place less reliance on this pattern of coordination in the future, thereby limiting the range of activities that could be coordinated effectively. Alice and others like her might limit their reliance on this pattern of coordination to exchanges with people they know for sure accept this practice. Granting redress reaffirms both the community itself and the community standards shared by Joe and Alice.

A political community's failure to redress serious private injustice could rupture that community. Alice might band together with others to enforce her claim against Joe for redress of a wrong. Thus, if Alice belonged to the Red group, and Joe to the Green group, she might complain to the Reds of Joe's action. They might then proceed to exact retribution or coerced compensation from Joe or his group. A political community's refusal to recognize and redress claims of private injustice may thus threaten the continued existence of the political community itself.

The purely personal and the broadly social components of Alice's claim of wrong combine to point to additional reasons why the community should provide a method of adjudicating and redressing claims of private injustice. The community may thereby provide a satisfactory resolution to a dispute. It will be satisfactory insofar as the court has considered the plaintiff's claim of wrong seriously, as a claim of personal injustice, and has authoritatively determined the merits of that claim on its own terms, as a claim that the defendant wronged the plaintiff by breaching a social convention that the plaintiff rightfully relied on in coordinating her conduct with the defendant's.

Moreover, in resolving disputes in this way, the courts will be "doing justice." Judicial action on behalf of the community will vindicate those innocent of a wrong and require those guilty of a wrong to act justly to redress it. The community thus both promotes and achieves justice through its judicial institutions. It thereby demonstrates the community's commitment to justice and reaffirms a vision of community in which people treat each other justly.

The hypothesized practical point of tort liability therefore seems to pass the test of practical reasonableness.

This explanation of tort liability in terms of corrective justice described the common law of torts almost perfectly until the system was redescribed in consequentialist public policy terms by various theorists, beginning in 1881 with Oliver Wendell Holmes in his *The Common Law*.[6] Although the core of tort law can still be understood in corrective justice terms, courts influenced by the newer consequentialist theories have adopted some rules and procedures that are neither justified nor justifiable in corrective justice terms. This, of course, is now blurred by the plaintiffs' lawyers represented by ATLA, who now seek to defend all of current tort law by appeals to corrective justice principles, but were happy to urge the adoption of strict liability rules based on the trendy modern consequentialist theories of loss spreading or optimal cost avoidance back in the heyday of liability expansion.

Other Answers are Inadequate

The mixed status of current tort law, however, raises a difficult question. In exploring possible changes in tort liability, why should we privilege the corrective justice purpose over other purposes currently embodied in parts of tort law? The answer, I think, is this. The basic elements of the tort liability system [*private individual sues another private individual seeking money damages fully compensating harm done by wrongdoing defendant*] seem to have been developed specifically to redress private wrongs. The system as a whole is well-suited to achieving that purpose. Not surprisingly, then, it is not well-suited to achieving other purposes that it was not originally developed to accomplish. Ironically, consequentialist redescriptions of the tort liability system will therefore fail the practical reasonableness test of efficiency in achieving the end sought. We can see this, I believe, by examining the two most prominent consequentialist theories—loss spreading and deterrence—to see how efficiently the tort liability system achieves those goals.

Loss Spreading Turning to the loss-spreading purpose first, I ask you to imagine what you would say to someone you had charged with designing a system for spreading the losses from injuries over a broad base, who came up with the tort liability system. The exchange might well remind you of a George Burns–Gracie Allen routine.

> George: *Let me get this straight—you propose to spread the burden of injury from the individual to a large number of people, who each contribute small amounts, by requiring each injured individual to bring a law suit against the person whose faulty conduct caused his injury?*

Gracie: *That's right.*
George: *But wouldn't that just shift the loss to the other individual, not spread the loss?*
Gracie: *It would, though, if defendants have liability insurance.*
George: *But what if they don't?*
Gracie: *We'll make them.*
George: *Even so, it can't effectively shift losses because everyone injured by someone else doesn't sue.*
Gracie: *They should.*
George: *And, anyway, there are a lot of injuries where there will be no one to sue—like if someone slips in their own bathtub.*
Gracie: *I hadn't thought of that. Maybe they could sue the bathtub maker.*
George: *And if this is a loss-spreading system, how come the injured rich get to spread more loss than the injured poor? If they each own a car, their liability premiums will be the same, but the rich guy gets to recover his lost earnings of $250,000 a year, while the poor guy gets only his $10,000 a year.*
Gracie: *I hadn't thought of that.*
George: *And why should we spread noneconomic losses at all? This will send insurance costs up, and accentuate the difference between those who are lucky enough to be hurt by someone else's faulty conduct and those who can't blame someone else.*
Gracie: *I hadn't thought of that, either. Let's limit or abolish noneconomic damages.*
George: *And, if we're just trying to spread losses, why require that the defendant have been at fault at all? As long as his conduct caused the harm and he's likely to be insured, he ought to pay.*
Gracie: *That's a good idea. Let's change the liability rules so that "strict liability" applies—if an insured defendant causes plaintiff harm, let's impose liability. Why, maybe we could change the rules so the only thing that counts is that the defendant is insured. Maybe we shouldn't insist that he caused plaintiff's harm at all?*
George: *Aren't you going a little too far? Wouldn't this be done better by government social insurance against all injuries?*
Gracie: *That would smack of socialism. And the people of this country won't vote for something that looks like socialism.*
George: *Is that why you've tried to hijack the tort liability system—to turn it into a socialized injury system, limited as that system might be?*
Gracie: *Now, let's not get personal.*
George: *Say "good night," Gracie.*

Deterrence Your response might be less harsh to one you had charged with designing a system for deterring dangerous conduct who came up with the tort liability system. That is so because the coordination–reinforcement rationale for correcting wrongs can, by squinting just a little, be seen as a *deterrent* purpose. There is a significant difference, however, in that the safety rule is not a judicial rule, but a social convention. It is followed by people in the community *not* primarily because of the threat of legal sanction for violation, but out of a general commitment to social safety mechanisms and a desire to avoid harm, do the right thing, and avoid social opprobrium. Nevertheless, there is a series of harsh questions you would undoubtedly ask.

> Q. *How can the threat of tort liability deter dangerous conduct when it is not imposed every time one acts dangerously, but only* if *someone is injured by that conduct and* if *the injured person decides to sue?*
>
> A. *There is deterrence here because any one can foresee that if a person acts dangerously and harm follows, he will be held liable if the plaintiff sues.*
>
> Q. *That would work only if the law clearly defines ahead of time what conduct will and what conduct will not lead to liability. But liability standards (particularly negligence standards) are not that fixed, definite, and certain.*
>
> A. *The law, to become more effective in its deterrence function, should always be transforming itself into fixed, definite, and certain rules. This is what Holmes called the process of specification.*
>
> Q. *But why isn't the criminal law much more effective as a deterrent? In the criminal law, punishment doesn't depend on actual harm and the choice of the injured party to sue. Why fiddle around with a system that can never be as fully effective a deterrent as another existing system?*
>
> A. *I hadn't thought of that.*

The same kind of efficiency argument could be made against each of the other currently popular consequentialist purposes—enterprise liability and optimal cost avoider. That would still leave us with the following question. What's the matter with the "eclectic purposes" answer? We seem to have a set of purposes for tort liability, including correcting wrongs, spreading losses, and deterring dangerous conduct, which all mutually limit each other. The courts attempt to pursue purpose *X* up to the point where that pursuit clashes with the pursuit of purpose *Y*, where the existence and extent of a conflict significant enough to limit the pursuit of *X* is partly a matter of fact and partly a matter of judgment. That seems, after all, to be what courts do throughout the common law. The common law can be seen as a series of judicial decisions over time made on the basis of a set of mutually limiting principles and policies. For example, courts enforce the freely chosen, mutual obligations of contract except when to do so would be to reward a wrongdoer.

To answer this question, we need to look more carefully at the working of the common law. The mutually limiting principles of the common law are different than the proposed mutually limiting purposes in tort law because traditional common law reasoning was based on an understood basic purpose; the competing, limiting principles were harmonized and made coherent by deference to that basic purpose. In the example given, the principle of contract enforcement is reconciled with the limiting principle that "the wrongdoer should not profit from his own wrongdoing" by the fundamental purpose to redress private wrongs. Courts ordinarily require the party breaching a contract to compensate the contracting party wronged by the breach, but when the party who claims to have been wronged has also done wrong and would be rewarded for it if courts allowed him to recover in a breach of contract action, the basic principle of corrective justice requires the courts to bar recovery.

Why can't we do the same thing with the competing consequentialist policy goals of tort law? Couldn't we resolve the conflicts by reference to an overarching principle? Unfortunately, this resolution is impossible. The clashes between separate intermediate policies cannot be reconciled by reference to the overarching general principle because that overarching principle is incoherent. One cannot simply "maximize desirable consequences" because there are a number of separate and distinct desirable goods for human beings, which are incommensurable. The problem is compounded, not resolved, if one throws in as an intermediate, mutually limiting principle, among a set of purely consequentialist policy goals, the previously overarching one of providing redress for wrongs. The problem is this: Once you assume that it, too, is just a consequences-based justification, then the incommensurability problem kicks in for it as well.

Criteria for Tort Reform

The analysis so far seems to support the following conclusions.

- *There are sound reasons to retain a tort liability system aimed at redressing private injustices understood as injurious breaches of the community's safety coordination norms.*

- *Attempts to modify the tort liability system to achieve consequentialist goals are unsupportable. The basic features of the tort liability system make its use to achieve these other purposes inefficient. Moreover, use of the tort liability system to achieve consequentialist goals threatens positive injustice in two ways. To achieve a consequentialist goal, the courts may use the tort liability system, which was designed to redress wrongs, to impose liability on one who has done no wrong. Conversely, courts bent on achieving consequentialist goals may refuse to redress a private injustice or refuse to redress it fully within a system whose basic understood purpose is to redress wrongs.*

With these conclusions in mind, we can look at the current tort liability system to see what needs reforming, using this composite criterion. *What rules and processes threaten positive injustice either by imposing liability where there is no wrongdoing or by refusing to redress or refusing to redress fully a private injustice?*

If we look at the horror stories each side tells in the debate aimed at the popular audience, this criterion is confirmed. The tort reformers tell stories of cases where liability is imposed although there is no wrongdoing. Antireformers tell stories of cases where there is clearly a wrong and the tort reform rules preclude the courts from righting that wrong or righting it fully.

Through their horror stories, both sides appeal to the public's understanding of the basic corrective justice purpose of the tort liability system. The tort reformers tell stories about defendants held liable who have done no wrong because we all believe that tort liability should be imposed only to redress a private injustice. One who has done no wrong, but has innocently caused harm, can therefore legitimately expect to be free from liability. To impose liability anyway violates that legitimate expectation and constitutes a positive injustice to the innocent defendant. The antireformers tell stories of seriously injured victims of wrongdoing who are precluded from adequate compensation for their injuries by harsh tort reform rules because we all believe that tort liability should fully redress a private injustice. One who has been seriously wronged can legitimately expect to obtain adequate redress for the wrong through the courts. To deny full compensation for the wrong, on consequentialist grounds unrelated to any corrective justice principle, violates that legitimate expectation and constitutes a positive injustice to the seriously wronged plaintiff.

The twofold criterion, confirmed by the horror stories of both sides in the debate, simply asks to what extent our tort liability system deviates from its original corrective justice purpose either positively, by imposing tort liability where there was no wrong to redress, or negatively, by failing to adequately redress a serious wrong. An alternative way of identifying the substantive rules, procedural rules, and outcomes that violate one or the other parts of the twofold test is to identify those rules, procedures, and outcomes that implement one of the proposed consequentialist purposes of tort liability at the expense of the original corrective justice purpose.

The Real Problems with Tort Liability: Rules that May Impose Tort Liability on One Who Has Done No Wrong

It makes sense to start, then, with the modern substantive law of personal injury torts. Since the consequentialist theories have had little influence on the branch of tort law dealing with intentional infliction of physical harm, we may focus on the two categories of unintended torts—negligent infliction of personal injury and "strict liability" torts.

Cost–benefit Tests of Negligence

The standard for determining whether a defendant was negligent is whether he failed to act as an ordinary reasonable person would have acted under the circumstances. This standard, ordinarily applied by the community-representing jury, was, at the beginning of the development of negligence law, a good way to invoke and apply the community's accepted safety conventions in determining whether the defendant wronged the plaintiff. The standard was not explicit in its invocation of preexisting community safety conventions, however, and its vagueness on that question provided room for a consequentialist redescription of the standard in purely cost–benefit terms. This was done first by Henry Taylor Terry in 1915[7] and most famously by Judge Learned Hand in the famous *Carroll Towing Co.* case.[8] Hand said that a defendant was negligent if the burden of taking precautions against a foreseeable risk of harm from the defendant's conduct was less than the foreseeable probability of harm multiplied by the foreseeable gravity of the harm threatened by the defendant's conduct [$B<P\times L$].

The *Carroll Towing Co.* test leaves out preexisting community conventions and their related expectations altogether. It seems to authorize the court to hold a defendant liable who complied with all the community's prevailing safety conventions, based on a determination that the defendant should have acted differently because the judge, after the fact, determines that the burden of taking precautions was less than the foreseeable probability multiplied by the foreseeable gravity of harm. The *Carroll Towing Co.* test thus seems to be a standing invitation to courts to commit a positive injustice by imposing tort liability, on consequentialist grounds, on one who had not wronged the plaintiff.

In most negligence cases, the question of negligence is decided by the jury under instructions that state the negligence standard in terms of the conduct of the ordinary reasonable person. On occasion, however, the *Carroll Towing Co.* test has led courts to declare that conduct consistent with the prevailing community conventions was nevertheless negligent because it failed the court's retroactive risk–benefit test. These cases are admittedly rare, but the *Carroll Towing Co.* test is undesirable nonetheless because it serves as a continuing temptation to judges to legislate retroactively applicable safety standards not previously adopted by the community.

Comparative Negligence

The horror stories told by the tort reformers point us toward the most problematic rule in modern negligence law. Over and over, the tort reformers tell stories of plaintiffs who foolishly endangered their own safety, but were nevertheless allowed to recover millions of dollars for the harm they brought on themselves. The McDonald's hot coffee case leads their list, but they cite many, many more.

Under the old common law rules, the plaintiffs in most of these cases would have been barred from recovering anything for their injuries because they were contributorily negligent. The plaintiffs in the tort reformers' horror stories were allowed to recover, however, because the plaintiff's contributory negligence is no longer a complete defense under modern negligence law; the plaintiff's negligence merely reduces the recoverable damages by the percentage the plaintiff's negligence bears to the total fault of all those whose wrongful conduct contributed to cause the plaintiff's injury. The plaintiff's contributory negligence is thus "compared" to the defendants' negligence, and the new rule is called "comparative negligence" or "comparative fault."

Lawyers, law professors, and judges are virtually unanimous in preferring the comparative negligence rule to the old contributory negligence rule. Almost every state has changed from the old contributory negligence rule to some form of comparative negligence. Could they be wrong? An analysis of the history of comparative negligence theory and a reexamination of the old contributory negligence rule[9] suggests that the tort reformers' horror stories are in fact pointing to a serious flaw in the comparative negligence rule.

Contributory Negligence

Contributory negligence is the failure of the plaintiff to act as an ordinary reasonable person would have acted to avoid harm to oneself, when that failure contributes to cause that harm concurrently with the defendant's negligence. Under traditional negligence law, contributory negligence was a complete defense to a plaintiff's claim. The original utilitarian deterrence theorists explained the contributory negligence defense in a chillingly simple way: Since the purpose of tort law is to prevent harm by deterring dangerous behavior, the contributory negligence rule was justified as a means of deterring the plaintiff from engaging in conduct posing foreseeable danger to oneself. From the standpoint of tort law's deterrent purpose, then, the negligent defendant and the contributorily negligent plaintiff were equally "at fault," because the conduct of each threatened foreseeable harm, even though the ultimate harm threatened by the plaintiff's conduct was to no one but himself.

The deterrence rationale for contributory negligence was undercut from two directions. First, common sense kept intervening to suggest that in the circumstances posited by the utilitarian view, the defendant has wronged the plaintiff, but the plaintiff has wronged no one. Only the most rigidly ideological utilitarian can maintain that the plaintiff's conduct was just as bad as the defendant's, or that they were even comparable.

Second, the deterrence rationale itself was called into question. It was argued that, in order for the contributory negligence rule to have any deterrent effect on the plaintiff's conduct, the plaintiff would have to foresee the risk of harm to himself from such conduct and a subsequent inability to recover damages from the defendant for that harm. But since one must foresee the risk of injury before one can foresee the inability to recover for injury, the legal inability to recover damages would seem to add little additional deterrent. The foreseen threat of actual physical harm should be sufficient deterrence.

Under straight or modified deterrence theories, then, contributory negligence became an unwelcome defense. Under a straight deterrence theory, the possible defense of contributory negligence reduced the threat of liability for the defendant's negligence' and hence reduced the deterrent effect of primary negligence liability. In more sophisticated optimal cost avoider theories, the contributory negligence defense was unwelcome because it haphazardly interfered with the allocation of accident costs to the optimal cost avoider. And, of course, under modern utilitarian theories based not on deterrence but on maximizing utility by spreading the cost of accidents through the optimum insurer, the contributory negligence defense is anathema as well, for it necessarily impairs the desired allocation of costs to insured defendants.

All the attacks on the contributory negligence defense assumed its only possible purpose was deterrence, as the early utilitarian deterrence theorists had said. An analysis of the early development of contributory negligence before the utilitarian redescription, however, may serve to rehabilitate the much-maligned defense by showing its real point, which had little to do with deterrence.

One of the first cases in the development of the contributory negligence defense was *Proctor v Harris*,[10] an 1830 case decided by a jury upon instructions by Chief Justice Tindal of the Court of Common Pleas. In that case, a pubkeeper had opened the flap door in the sidewalk over his cellar to let in a butt of beer, at night, with only the street lamps to light the opening. The plaintiff, a pedestrian, fell in and was injured. In instructing the jury, Chief Justice Tindal said:

> The question is, whether a proper degree of caution was used by the defendant. He was not bound to resort to every mode of security that could be surmised, but he was bound to use such a degree of care as would prevent a reasonable person, acting with an ordinary degree of care, from receiving any injury. The public have a right to walk along these footpaths with ordinary security.[11]

Reciprocity Chief Justice Tindal's formulation captures an important feature of most community patterns of coordination—their reciprocity. We act in certain ways to coordinate our conduct with that of others based on what we expect them to do. They, in turn, act based on what they expect us to do. Ordinarily, then, if we act in a way that would not cause harm to others acting as we can expect them to act, we have acted properly. The contributory negligence formula in *Proctor* focused the jury's attention generally on the reciprocal expectations that had to be taken into account in determining whether the pubkeeper wronged the pedestrian. The jury would have to apply that general formula to the reciprocal expectations associated with the accepted patterns of conduct in that community. A finding of contributory negligence could be seen as one way of finding that defendant did not wrong the plaintiff in the first place, given the reciprocal expectations about each other's conduct derived from the generally established patterns of coordination in that community.

This assumes, of course, that the content of the defendant's duty to those using the sidewalk is to protect from physical harm those using the sidewalk in the normal, expected way. Some social rules, however, are intended to protect even those acting abnormally. One would conclude from this analysis that in cases in which that kind of rule is breached the contributory negligence rule would not apply, since the content of the defendant's duty would not depend on the expectation that people in the plaintiff's position would act normally. The second leading case on contributory negligence from the early nineteenth century supports this conclusion.

In *Davies v Mann*,[12] decided in 1842 by the Court of the Exchequer, the plaintiff owned a donkey, which he turned out into the public highway with its forefeet fettered. It was grazing by the side of the road when the defendant's wagon came down a slight rise at a fast pace, knocked the donkey down, and ran over it, causing its death. At trial in an action in case for negligence, the trial court instructed the jury:

> that though the act of the plaintiff, in leaving the donkey on the highway so fettered as to prevent his getting out of the way of carriages travelling along it, might be illegal, still, if the proximate cause of the injury was attributable to the want of proper conduct on the part of the driver of the wagon, the action was maintainable against the defendant . . . .[13]

Baron Parke of the Exchequer upheld the jury instruction here and found no inconsistency with the contributory negligence rule, stating "for, although the ass may have been wrongfully there, still the defendant was bound to go along the road at such a pace as would be likely to prevent mischief."

How are we to understand *Davies v Mann*? In *Davies*, the plaintiff claimed that the defendant's servant was driving too fast to stop within the assured clear distance ahead. That conduct breached a general community rule of the road intended to protect all who venture on the highway, however they get there. The rule protects those there illegally, as well as those who through negligence are unable to get out of the road quickly. Since the defendant breached a social rule intended to protect the plaintiff even if the plaintiff acted negligently, the defendant's general wrongful conduct was also a specific wrong to the plaintiff.

A theoretical explanation of the contributory negligence defense consistent with its original thrust, then, would understand contributory negligence as one method of determining whether the defendant had wronged the plaintiff in the first place. If the defendant acted in a way that would not harm those following the generally-expected course of conduct, and the defendant did not breach a social rule intended to protect those acting abnormally, the plaintiff's failure to follow the generally-expected course is deemed "contributory negligence." The contributory negligence label means just that the defendant did not wrong the plaintiff in those cases where the specific content of the defendant's duty to the plaintiff is defined by reference to the plaintiff's expected conduct. When the defendant is expected only to act so as to avoid harm to others in the plaintiff's position acting normally, the plaintiff's abnormal behavior is contributory negligence.

As *Davies v Mann* so clearly illustrates, however, contributory negligence as a defense should be strictly limited to those instances in which the social rule the defendant is accused of breaking defines the specific content of the defendant's duty by reference to the plaintiff's expected conduct. When the defendant breaches a social rule whose content is not fixed by reciprocal expectations, the contributory negligence defense should not apply if careless folks like the plaintiff are within the class the fixed rule was intended to protect.

Fact-Specific Judgment The proper application of the original contributory negligence rule, therefore, depended on a subtle judgment about the content and purpose of the coordinating conventions at stake. And that judgment is very fact-specific.

Ironically, the facts that most people don't know about the McDonald's hot coffee case may well take that case outside the scope of the original contributory negligence rule. The initial response of most of us to the *McDonald's* case is to assume it was not McDonald's fault because everyone knows it's the responsibility of the consumer to make sure she doesn't spill hot coffee on herself. That's our community's applicable coordination norm. But people follow that norm in light of a background understanding that the risk of carelessness in handling a cup of hot coffee from a fast-food place is the minor discomfort of wet clothes and the minor sting of moderately hot water.

The evidence in the *McDonald's* case, though, showed that McDonald's deliberately decided to serve its coffee at scalding hot temperatures between 180 and 190 degrees, while other fast-food outlets served their coffee at temperatures between 150 and 160 degrees.[14] Testimony at trial established that it takes less than three seconds to produce a third-degree burn at 190 degrees, and about twenty seconds at 160 degrees. The eighty-one-year-old plaintiff in the case suffered severe third degree burns on her groin and buttocks when she spilled the coffee. McDonald's had been warned repeatedly before this injury that its coffee caused third-degree burns, but it kept its standard coffee temperature at between 180 and 190 degrees nonetheless.

A reasonable jury deliberating on these facts could conclude that the ordinary coordination norm was a trap for the unwary, who would have no idea of the significant, unusual danger posed by McDonald's coffee, and that McDonald's should not be able to hide behind a coordination norm developed for cooler coffee, which most of us would agree is not applicable here.

Consequentialist Developments in Strict Liability for Defective Products

The modern law of strict liability for harm caused by defective products began in a sensible enough way. In cases where a defendant who was in the business of selling products of a certain kind sold a plaintiff one of those products, the courts had long recognized that the plaintiff–buyer relied on the seller to provide a product that was fit for its ordinary intended use and that was, therefore, reasonably safe for its intended use. If the product was not reasonably safe for its intended use, and it caused harm to the plaintiff–purchaser, the defendant–seller had wronged the plaintiff–purchaser. The courts allowed the plaintiff–purchaser to recover damages in such cases, on the technical legal theory that the defendant–seller had breached an implied warranty of merchantability.

The courts gradually came to recognize that, in our modern mass-marketing economy, the purchaser often relies more on the manufacturer of the product than on his immediate seller. If you buy a Buick or a Maytag, you rely on Buick or Maytag to make sure that the product is reasonably safe for its intended use. Furthermore, the ultimate user of the product may not even have bought it herself, but, just as much as any purchaser, may also have relied on the manufacturer to make a reasonably safe product.

For a while, courts thought of allowing contractual claims against the manufacturer for breach of an implied warranty of merchantability to the ultimate purchaser or the ultimate user, even though there was no direct contract between the ultimate purchaser or the ultimate user and the manufacturer. Justice Traynor of the California Supreme Court and Professor William Prosser, leading tort gurus of the twentieth century, recommended that it would be simpler and cleaner to treat these claims as tort claims rather than contract claims.

Voila, the modern tort of strict liability for harm caused by a defective product was born. A manufacturer would be held strictly liable for the resulting physical harm if it sold a product in a defective condition unreasonably dangerous to the ultimate user or consumer. Consistent with the implied warranty history of this cause of action and the reliance theory on which the claim of wrong was based, the proposed test to determine whether a product was in a defective condition was whether it was as safe as the ordinary consumer reasonably expected it to be.

Alternative Tests for Product Liability

Influenced by the alternative consequentialist justifications for strict product liability, like enterprise liability, loss spreading, and optimal cost avoider theories, however, some courts elaborated alternative tests for determining whether a product was in a defective condition unreasonably dangerous to the user or consumer. Some said the test was whether a reasonably prudent manufacturer, with constructive knowledge of the particular danger posed by the design of the product, would nevertheless have manufactured and sold the product as designed.

Within this group of courts, some said the manufacturer should be held to the knowledge of the danger available at the time the product was sold; others said the manufacturer should be held to the knowledge of the danger available at the time of trial. Both sets of courts assumed that the ordinary reasonable manufacturer would make a cost–benefit analysis *à la Carroll Towing Co.* to determine whether to sell a product whose design posed a particular kind of risk of harm.

Other courts would dispense with the hypothetical ordinary reasonable manufacturer altogether, and simply ask whether the risk of harm posed by the product as designed outweighed the benefits from the product as designed.

All these alternatives to the consumer expectation test of defect threaten to impose liability on manufacturers who have done no wrong because they manufactured and sold a product that was as safe as users and consumers reasonably expected it to be. Just like the *Carroll Towing Co.* test for negligence, these tests are an open invitation to courts or juries to impose liability in cases where they determine, after the fact, that the product as designed should never have been sold because in their judgment the retroactively determined risks outweighed the benefits. So, courts have held that a product may be held to be defective even though it was a useful product with no alternative feasible safer design. And one court has even held that a manufacturer had a duty to warn users, at the time of sale, of a subsequently discovered danger that the manufacturer could not possibly have known about at the time it sold the product.

Some courts have abolished or undermined other doctrines originally associated with the implied-warranty basis for strict liability for defective products. Thus, consumer misuse of a product early on in the strict liability development would preclude liability, because a reasonable consumer would not expect the product to be safe for a use it was not intended for. For example, everyone should know that plastic-handled screwdrivers are not intended for use as chisels. Someone using a screwdriver to pry two nailed boards apart by hammering on the plastic handle, therefore, could not reasonably expect the screwdriver to be safe for that use. If he is hurt when the plastic handle breaks and a sliver of plastic lodges in his eye, he has not been wronged by the manufacturer. Courts influenced by consequentialist theories, however, have said that consumer misuse does not bar the consumer's claim if the misuse was reasonably foreseeable. A manufacturer may be liable if its product was not reasonably safe for a foreseeable misuse.

Similarly, courts have refused to apply the traditional defense of implied assumption of risk in strict product liability cases. A user, knowing the specific danger posed by the product, who voluntarily proceeds to use the product anyway may still recover for harm caused by the known danger because many courts just fold implied assumption of risk into the comparative fault mix and apply the comparative fault rule to strict product liability.

Applying the comparative fault rule to strict product liability cases creates two other problems. Consistent with the consumer expectations standard, Professor William Prosser and his influential Restatement (Second) of Torts argued that the plaintiff's failure to take steps to discover or guard against a defect in the product should not bar the plaintiff's strict liability claim.[15] This is sensible under the reliance rationale for strict tort liability. If the consumer can rely on the product to be reasonably safe for its intended use, a reasonable consumer would not take steps to test the safety of the product or to take precautions against potential dangers the product might pose. By treating all contributory negligence as comparative fault, however, recent strict liability cases run the risk that the plaintiff's failure to test for product dangers or to guard against potential product dangers may reduce the plaintiff's recovery in a case in which the product failed to meet the consumer's reasonable expectations of safety. Second, clearly unreasonable conduct on the part of the plaintiff may not bar the plaintiff's recovery, even though the manufacturer could reasonably expect that no one would act that way while using its product and the plaintiff could not reasonably expect the product to be safe while he was acting in that way.

The Real Problems with Tort Liability: Inequalities in Jury Awards

There seem to be at least two significant problems with juries as triers of fact in tort cases. First, juries consistently award more money to plaintiffs who sue impersonal "deep pocket" defendants such as corporations or government entities. Second, when a lawsuit is brought in state court, it is filed in the state court for a particular county. The case is then tried to a jury composed of residents of that county. The juries in a few counties in this country—including Madison and St. Clair counties in Illinois, and Lowndes County, Alabama—are notoriously friendly to plaintiffs' claims and are thought to be more likely than juries in other counties to impose liability on defendants and to return large damage awards. Consequently, tort claims that one might assume should have been brought in another county wind up in those "plaintiff's heavens" because of liberal venue rules that allow plaintiffs to sue business defendants in any county in which they do business.

Deep Pockets Effect

The Rand Corporation study of jury verdicts in Chicago[16] provided solid statistical evidence of the existence of the first problem. For the period from 1960 through 1979, the Rand team studied over 9,000 reported jury verdicts. They determined the level of injury in each case, ranking injuries on a scale from slight to very serious. The "deep pockets" effect was persistent over moderate and very serious injuries, but the effect was greater for very serious injury cases. A very seriously injured plaintiff could expect to receive almost three times as much against a government defendant as against an individual defendant. Against corporate defendants, the very seriously injured plaintiff collected awards that ran an astounding four times higher than awards against individual defendants. At less severe injury levels, the "deep pockets" effect was not this large. Even the moderately injured plaintiff received a larger award when he sued a "deep pockets" defendant, however, with awards running as much as 50 percent higher.

Plaintiffs' Heaven

As far as I know, there have not been comparable scientific studies comparing awards in counties that all trial lawyers perceive as "plaintiffs' heavens." The anecdotal evidence, however, is persuasive, as is the size and efficiency of the plaintiffs' personal injury practices of the leading trial lawyers in those counties. The following excerpt from John A. Jenkins' book, *The Litigators: Inside the Powerful World of America's High-Stakes Trial Lawyers*,[17] explains how Madison and St. Clair counties in Illinois came to be known as plaintiffs' heavens:

> Fortuities of law, geography and commerce long ago made the area, in [a leading local attorney's] words, "just an ideal place to have lawsuits," and in [a leading Chicago attorney's words], "a mecca for litigation in the Midwest."
>
> Federal statutes enacted in 1910 and 1915 gave injured rail and barge workers the right to file suit anywhere the defendant railroad or barge company did business. Because both counties were major rail and barge centers—more than a dozen railroads had lines there, and the Illinois and Missouri rivers joined the Mississippi nearby—and because there was a high concentration of unionized blue-collar workers from whom to draw potentially proplaintiff jurors, the area's courts routinely produced huge verdicts for injured rail and barge workers.
>
> "If you're hurt in California and that railroad passes through here, this is where you can file suit," [a leading local plaintiff's attorney] gleefully explained. "Railroading is hazardous work, so the types of injuries are always bad—legs off, arms off, deaths. A good lawyer, big defendants and sympathetic, working-man-type juries—all that laid the foundation for this area."
>
> In 1982, the St. Louis *Post-Dispatch* reported that more than a thousand rail and barge lawsuits had been filed in the two counties during the prior two years alone and that, on the basis of a random sample of those cases, 80 percent involved accidents that had occurred elsewhere. Business was so good in the two counties that four hometown lawyers . . . were members of the trial lawyers' most elite million-dollar club, the Inner Circle of Advocates.
>
> [Cases from all over the Middle West are funneled into the courts in Madison and St. Clair counties. For example, a local attorney] who represented the barge workers' National Maritime Union, got injury cases from up and down the Mississippi as well as from all the rivers flowing into it. By making [the] local courts the venue of choice for virtually all of their important cases, [the local plaintiffs' lawyers] were "forum shopping," a perfectly legal practice as long as the court allowed it.[18]

The Real Problems with Tort Liability: Tort Reforms that Preclude Full Compensation for Serious Wrongs

One of the aims of the organized tort reformers is to reduce the overall costs of the tort liability system—in their words, to lower the "tort liability tax" imposed on all of us. Some of the cost-reducing reforms they support, however, would impair the ability of the courts to require a wrongdoer to compensate fully one who was seriously injured by the wrong. The two planks in their national platform that most seriously threaten this kind of injustice are their proposal to cap recovery for noneconomic losses and their proposal to abolish joint liability of joint tortfeasors.

Caps on Damages for Noneconomic Loss

The early common law of tort allowed recovery of money damages for the physical injury itself and all its harmful consequences. The physical injury included the physical harm itself (a broken hip, say, and the limp caused by the broken hip), pain and suffering, and physical disfigurement. All these could be proved at trial based on a general pleading of physical injury, so they were called "general damages." A plaintiff could recover for the economic consequences of these physical injuries, including lost wages while recovering from the broken hip, medical expenses in treating the broken hip, and lost future wages predicted because of the broken hip. Those consequent economic losses had to be specially pleaded in order to be compensated. Hence, consequent economic losses were called "special damages." The primacy given to the physical injury by the traditional distinction between general and special damages reflected the common-law courts' understanding that the primary wrong the defendant's wrongful conduct had done was the physical injury itself.

Pain and Suffering Modern writers who elaborated economic utilitarian theories of tort liability like loss spreading, enterprise liability, or optimal cost avoidance necessarily inverted the implicit ordering of the common law. Under the loss-spreading theory, there was little reason to spread noneconomic losses, and compensating for pain and suffering could not be supported in the enterprise liability or optimal cost avoider theories. The academic tort reformers seeking to remake tort law along consequentialist, utilitarian principles almost unanimously recommended abolition or reduction of damages for noneconomic losses.

Ironically, the current tort reformers, who oppose extension of tort liability without fault under those consequentialist reforms, have adopted some of the arguments against damages for noneconomic losses that were originally developed by those earlier reformers. Pain and suffering cannot be translated accurately into dollars and cents, they say. Jurors have no objective guidelines, so verdicts involving large dollar amounts for pain and suffering may simply reflect jurors' emotional reactions to the plaintiff's injury, they say. An injured plaintiff who recovers all of his economic losses is fully compensated, they say. Large awards for noneconomic losses inflate the cost of the tort liability system unnecessarily and increase the tort liability tax unnecessarily, they say.

The most effective counterarguments start by directing our attention to a very seriously injured plaintiff. Imagine a young child, seriously burned in a fire caused by a defendant's negligence. Assume she has third-degree burns over 60 percent of her body. After she is compensated for the economic consequences of this terrible injury—lost earning capacity, past and future medical expenses—is she fully compensated for the wrong? What about the terrible, recurring pain and suffering, the horrible disfigurement, the permanent physical impairments? Is $250,000 or $500,000 sufficient compensation for a lifetime of pain, suffering, disfigurement, and disability visited on this young girl by the defendant's negligence? Of course not.

This argument reminds us in a dramatic way that pain and suffering, disfigurement, and physical disability are real losses, affecting the plaintiff's well-being in important ways, which are not just reducible to their economic consequences. When these real losses are caused by a defendant's wrongdoing, the wrong cannot be adequately redressed unless the defendant pays for these losses, too. The fact that a jury cannot refer to any markets to translate the pain and suffering, disfigurement, and disability into dollars and cents does not mean that these are not real losses that should be compensated as fully as we can by an award of money damages.

The Problems with Damages Caps The tort reformers ordinarily do not argue for total abolition of noneconomic damages; they support caps on recoverable noneconomic losses—usually $250,000, at times $500,000. Caps on damages for noneconomic losses are peculiarly unfair ways to reduce the overall costs of tort liability, for the cap applies only to the most seriously injured plaintiff—to those like the horribly burned little girl we have been thinking about, whose noneconomic losses would exceed the arbitrary cap. Caps say that the less seriously injured plaintiffs can recover fully for all their losses, but the most seriously injured cannot. Caps tell the courts that, because we want to reduce the overall costs of tort liability, they can fully redress less serious wrongs but they cannot fully redress the most serious wrongs. It would be like telling doctors that, because we want to reduce the overall costs of medical care, they cannot treat their most seriously ill patients.

Elimination of Joint Liability

At common law, joint tortfeasors were "jointly and severally" liable for their joint torts. What does this mean? Think of the following example.

Alice drives her car at 70 miles per hour south toward an intersection and fails to keep a careful lookout ahead of her. Barney, headed north, is stopped at the intersection, waiting to turn left. Just after the car ahead of Alice's car passes him, Barney pulls left, directly in front of Alice, although there was not a safe interval to do so. The cars crash because Alice was driving too fast and failed to keep a proper lookout, and because Barney turned left in front of Alice's car when there was not enough room to safely make the turn in front of oncoming traffic. Carmen, a passenger asleep in the passenger seat beside Barney, is seriously injured in the crash.

Under traditional tort law, Alice and Barney are joint tortfeasors because each was negligent and the negligence of each was a cause of the indivisible injury to Carmen. They were therefore "jointly" liable to Carmen. Carmen may join them as defendants in a single tort action against them both and recover a judgment against both of them jointly. But each is also "severally" liable for the entire amount. Carmen could enforce the joint judgment against just Alice, or against just Barney, although she could recover the full amount only once. Because each tortfeasor is both jointly and severally liable, moreover, Carmen could sue just one of them and recover fully against just one of them.

Contribution among Joint Tortfeasors Besides the joint and several liability of joint tortfeasors, the second important common-law rule was that there was no contribution among joint tortfeasors. If Carmen obtained a judgment against Alice and Barney jointly but recovered the full amount of the judgment from Alice alone, Alice could not force Barney to reimburse her for any of the amount she had to pay. Similarly, if Carmen sued Alice only and obtained a judgment against Alice, Alice could not then force Barney to reimburse her for any of the amount she paid to Carmen.

In almost all states, the old common-law rule prohibiting contribution among joint tortfeasors has been changed. A joint tortfeasor required to pay all of a judgment may now claim contribution from a joint tortfeasor. The amount of contribution differs in different states. Some states require contribution based on equal shares; other states require contribution based on the jury's determination of the joint tortfeasors' comparative fault. In the equal-shares states, Alice could force Barney to pay her half the amount she paid to Carmen. In comparative fault contribution states, the jury would be called on to determine the percentage of total fault contributed by each defendant. In this case, let's assume the jury determined that Alice's negligence was 60 percent of the total fault and Barney's negligence was 40 percent of the total fault. If Carmen enforced the entire judgment against

Alice, Alice could then force Barney to reimburse her for 40 percent of the total judgment, based on the comparative fault contribution rule.

Proportionate Fault The tort reformers now argue that it makes no sense to retain joint liability after adoption of comparative fault contribution rules. Each defendant should be liable only for the amount of liability equal to that defendant's proportionate fault. That is only fair, they argue; one defendant should not have to pay for the liability that is proportionately attributable to another defendant. Stated more simply, and misleadingly, the tort reformers argue that this violates the principle of proportionate liability embodied in the comparative fault contribution rule, which they say is "the concept that a party is responsible only for the damages caused by his own negligence."[19] Moreover, the reformers argue, retention of joint liability after the adoption of comparative fault contribution leads to unfair results. An ATRA "Issues Brief" argues as follows:

> A Wisconsin case illustrates the rule's unfairness. An uninsured driver of a car with faulty brakes struck and killed a six year old boy at a school crossing, despite a stop sign and a crossing guard. Plaintiff argued that the accident might have been avoided if the crossing guard, instead of signaling the car to stop, had attempted to get the child out of the car's path. The city, as the crossing guard's employer, was found to be simply one percent at fault. Yet because it was the only solvent party, the city had to pay 100%, the full amount of damages. (*Zimmer v. City of Milwaukee*)[20]

The argument by the ATRA here loads the deck in favor of their conclusion. Given the limited facts they give, the obvious conclusion of the reader is that the city was not negligent at all and that no reasonable jury could conclude that the city was negligent. If that is so, the problem in the case is not the joint liability rule but the failure of the trial court to direct a verdict in favor of the city. Even if the reader assumes the city was negligent, the statement of the case says that the jury found the city's negligence was only 1 percent of the total fault, so it seems unfair for the city to be stuck with the whole judgment.

But this assumes that the jury's allocation of percentages of total fault relates to some objective reality. A moment's reflection, however, suggests that that is not true. If there was evidence from which the jury could find that the crossing guard failed to act reasonably to protect the six-year-old boy (such as motioning the child to cross in the face of an oncoming car that had not stopped), then the guard wronged the poor child, who had relied on him to protect him at the crossing. The jury's 1 percent–99 percent allocation as between the driver and the city does not have any relevance to the question of whether the city should have to pay the whole amount on the insolvency of the driver. If the guard was really negligent and really wronged the child, why should the child's survivors, harmed by the child's death, have to bear the risk of insolvency of the *other* tortfeasor?

Furthermore, the ATRA's statement of the "proportionate liability" principle is deliberately inaccurate. At common law, tortfeasors were jointly liable only if the wrongdoing of each was a cause of an indivisible injury to the plaintiff. You can see this in the Alice–Barney–Carmen hypothetical, where Carmen's entire injury was caused by Alice's negligence, as well as by Barney's. The proportionate liability principle embodied in the comparative fault contribution rule is not based on responsibility proportionate to the percentage of the harm actually caused, but on the percentage that one defendant's "fault" bears to the "total fault of all defendants" after it is determined that each defendant's fault caused all the harm.

The ATRA example works polemically because the reader is given no facts from which to conclude that the city was at fault at all. A better test to determine whether the ATRA's proposed rule of "several liability only" is fair is the Alice–Barney–Carmen hypothetical. Assume again that the jury determines that Alice's negligence was 60 percent of the total fault and that Barney's negligence was 40 percent of the total fault.

Assume further that Alice is insolvent. Under the "several-liability-only" rule, Carmen could recover only 40 percent of her damages, against Barney. Put another way, the "several-liability-only" rule puts the risk of a defendant's insolvency on the injured plaintiff and removes that risk from the other wrongdoing defendant, where the common law had placed it. This does not seem fair. The "several-liability-only" rule protects a wrongdoer from the responsibility to compensate fully for all the harm his wrong has caused; it precludes the courts from fully redressing a private injustice.

Conclusion: An Alternative Tort Reform Agenda

The preceding survey of tort law using the criteria derived from an analysis of the practical point of tort liability suggests that there are real problems with our tort liability system. The horror stories used by each side in the current nasty debate over tort liability point to the real possibilities for injustice in our tort liability system: the imposition of tort liability on one who has not wronged the plaintiff, and the inability of courts fully to redress a real and grievous wrong because of misguided tort reforms.

The analysis of the real problems in our tort liability system leads to the following alternative tort reform agenda.

1. We should root out cost–benefit tests from our understanding of the negligence standard and explicitly adopt a test that refers to the community's previously adopted safety conventions.
2. We should eliminate the modern comparative negligence rules and return to an earlier contributory negligence rule that sensibly barred a plaintiff's recovery when the safety convention applicable to a defendant's conduct required him to act in a way that would prevent harm to those themselves acting as he could expect them to act.
3. We should root out cost–benefit tests of defect in strict liability for defective products and return to the original implied warranty model to determine whether a manufacturer wronged a user or consumer by manufacturing a product that was not as safe for its intended use as one could reasonably expect.
4. We should delimit and reinvigorate the role of the jury in tort cases:
    (a) We should develop jury instructions that clearly tell jurors what we want them to decide in negligence, contributory negligence, and strict product liability cases. These instructions should tell them how these questions relate to facts about existing social coordination conventions and their correlative individual expectations.
    (b) We should attempt to equalize damage awards in similar cases to eliminate the inequalities based on the defendant's identity. This could be done by enacting a schedule of recoverable damages for specific injuries or by making damage questions legal issues to be decided by the judge or by instituting a system of itemized damage verdicts, reported by a jury verdict reporter system, that could be used by judges in ruling on remittitur and additur motions.
    (c) We should cut down on outside business in "Plaintiffs' heavens" by tightening up venue rules.
    (d) We should tighten judicial control over jury decision making by more rigorous use of summary judgment and directed verdict procedures. This should be possible once we have eliminated some of the confusion invited by the current uninformative formulations of tort standards.

This tort reform agenda would clarify and preserve the original purpose of tort law, which was to redress private wrongs. Incidentally, this reform agenda responds to the horror stories told by both sides in the current debate over tort reform. This is not surprising. Those horror stories are told to get ordinary people on your side, and the common sense of ordinary people coincides with the truly perennial philosophy of natural law.

NOTES

1. PETER HUBER, LIABILITY: THE LEGAL REVOLUTION AND ITS CONSEQUENCES (1988).

2. JOHN FINNIS, NATURAL LAW AND NATURAL RIGHTS (1980).

3. *Lon Fuller, Human Purpose and Natural Law*, 3 NAT.L. FORUM 68 (1958).

4. The following analysis is taken from *Patrick J. Kelley, Who Decides? Community Safety Conventions at the Heart of Tort Liability*, 38 CLEVE. ST. L. REV. 315 at 323–26 (1990). reprinted with permission.

5. JOHN FINNIS, NATURAL LAW AND NATURAL RIGHTS at 155.

6. OLIVER WENDELL HOLMES, JR., THE COMMON LAW, LECTURES II & IV (1881); *see generally, Patrick J. Kelley, A Critical Analysis of Holmes's Theory of Torts*, 6l WASH. U.L.Q. 681 (1983).

7. *Henry Taylor Terry, Negligence*, 29 HARV. L. REV. 40 (1915).

8. *United States v. Carroll Towing Co.*, 159 F. 2d 169 (2d Cir. 1947).

9. The following analysis is taken from *Patrick J. Kelley, Who Decides? Community Safety Conventions at the Heart of Tort Liability*, 38 CLEVE. ST. L. REV. 315 at 365–71 (1990), reprinted with permission.

10. 4 C. & P. 377, 172 Eng. Rep. 729 (N.P. 1830).

11. *Id.* At 337, 172 Eng. Rep. At 730.

12. 10 M. & W. 546, 152 Eng. Rep. 588 (Ex. 1842).

13. Id. At 547, 152 Eng. Rep. At 589.

14. *See Andrea Gerlin, A Matter of Degree: How a Jury Decided That a Coffee Spill is Worth $2.9 Million*, WALL ST. J., Sept. 1, 1994.

15. 2 Restatement of the Law of Torts 2d, Sec 402a, comment n, at 356 (1965).

16. A. Chin & M. Peterson, DEEP POCKETS, EMPTY POCKETS: WHO WINS IN COOK COUNTY JURY TRIALS (Rand Corp. Institute for Civil Justice, 1985).

17. JOHN A. JENKINS, THE LITIGATORS: INSIDE THE POWERFUL WORLD OF AMERICA'S HIGH-STAKES TRIAL Lawyers (1989).

18. *Id.* At 375–76

19. ATRA, Issue, Brief, *Joint and Several Liability Reform* (undated).

20. *Id.*

Part Five

Natural Law and Foreign Policy

Just War and Defense Policy

JOHN P. HITTINGER

> *"Multo autem magis est conservanda salus reipublicae, per quam impediuntur occisiones plurimorum et innumera mala et temporalia et spiritualia, quam salus corporalis unius hominis."*[1]

It may seem odd that a modern nation's citizens and its leaders should resort to the writings of a thirteenth-century friar for clarification of policy pertaining to issues of war and peace. Of any dimension of human affairs, surely the conduct of war has changed most significantly in the modern era.[2] Yet, policy involves concrete possibilities and moral principle. As John C. Murray once stated,

> Policy is the hand of the practical reason set firmly upon the course of events. Policy is what a nation does in this or that given situation. In the concreteness of policy therefore the assertion of the possibility of limited war is finally made and made good. Policy is the meeting place of the world of power and the world of morality, in which there takes place the concrete reconciliation of the duty of success that rests upon the statesman and the duty of justice that rests upon the civilized nation that he serves.[3]

So long as a nation considers itself civilized, so long as a nation strives to meet the duties of justice and does not proscribe the world of morality, then the great contributions of prior civilizations that feed our own streams of ethics and principle will avail us.

The issue of the right use of military force leads inevitably to natural law. The natural law approach to the issue has continued to dominate the academy, the public forum, and the military profession. The constellation of questions, principles, and traditions known as the "just war theory" represents today's best understanding of the problem. Its rivals, realism and pacifism, find it necessary either to attack the just war framework or to couch their arguments in its terms. During the Gulf War, major periodicals devoted space to the issue of just war, with sidebars on Augustine and the terminology of the doctrine.[4] If now the Gulf War is forgotten, new issues concerning the right use of force have emerged, such as humanitarian intervention in places like Haiti and Bosnia.[5]

The just war problematic continues to provide a forum for the debate. In 1996, the Carnegie Institute hosted a small conference celebrating the twentieth anniversary of the publication of Michael Walzer's book, *Just and Unjust Wars*. A classic in the field, this work displays the fruitfulness of the just war approach. Although it also shows that not all just war approaches are natural law ones, natural law approaches are full partners in the ongoing explorations of its meaning and the debates over its applications.[6]

Indeed, the just war approach always recalls its origins.[7] Its long history finds seed in classical Greek and Roman philosophy, and its mature fruition in the Christian philosophy of Augustine and Thomas Aquinas. In the middle ages, it was added to by canonists and lived out in codes of chivalry. In the modern era, it served as the basis for international law. In the latter part of the twentieth century, the just war theory has been refined and developed by a number of American theorists, including Paul Ramsey and John Courtney Murray. It remains the official teaching on war of many mainstream Christian churches. The just war theory is an important part of the ethics curriculum of West Point, Annapolis, and the Air Force Academy.[8] Thus, if we wish to find the continued relevance of natural law to policy and to appreciate its basic strategies of moral reasoning, the problem of war and peace is an appropriate place to look[9] for the just war tradition is a major carrier of the natural law approach to ethical–political thinking.

In addition to appreciating the use of natural law in framing political and policy issues pertaining to war, we must also allow the current to reverse itself: issues pertaining to war and peace raise significant foundational and methodological questions about natural law. The debates about war and peace bring into play important principles regarding the nature of politics, the conditions of justice, the nature of God's kingdom, the presence of sin, the role of authority, and the prospects for progress, to name but a few. John Courtney Murray has said that the threat of war and political disorder has an "unparalleled vertical dimension; it goes to the heart of the very roots of order and disorder in the world—the nature of man, his destiny, and the meaning of human history."[10]

How the just war precepts are grounded is central to determining their application to a given problem. One just war/natural law approach led to a call for a stand-down from nuclear deterrence for all men and women of good conscience; while it led others to assert the conditional acceptance of deterrence.[11] The listing and ordering of human goods, the conception of practical reasoning, the role of virtues, the nature of the political common good—these important backdrop issues must come to foreground when dealing with issues of war and peace. Although public interest in the policy question will ebb and flow, the perennial questions of metaphysics and ethics remain as an invitation to reflection and academic disputation.

Here I wish to explore the following four aspects of the natural law approach to war and peace: (1) key distinctions for understanding natural law; (2) the natural law rationale for limited war as formulated by Thomas Aquinas; (3) the challenge of limiting modern war, and (4) application to contemporary policy issues: the Smithsonian Hiroshima Exhibit, Humanitarian Intervention, and the policy of future use of armed forces for situations other than war.

Key Distinctions for Understanding Natural Law: Ontological and Epistemological Elements

According to Thomas Aquinas, law is a rule and measure, and eternal law is a rule or measure embedded in nature by which things derive their "respective inclinations to their proper acts and ends."[12] Natural law is the manner in which human beings, as rational creatures, "participate" in eternal law; by using their reflective capacity they can come to know their proper acts and ends, and by the capacity of free will to so order their lives accordingly.

Aquinas states that human beings are ordered not simply to their "proper" act and end, but to their "due" or "obligatory" acts and end.[13] Thus, the natural law is an order in nature, and it primarily designates an "ontological" element, or a way of being. As Jacques Maritain explains,

> Possessed of a nature, or an ontological structure which is the locus of intelligible necessities, man possesses ends which necessarily correspond to his essential constitution and which are the same for all. . . . This means that there is, by the very virtue of human nature, an order or a disposition which human reason can discover and according to which the human will must act in order to attune itself to the essential and necessary ends of the human being. The unwritten law, or natural law, is nothing more than that. . . . Let us say, then, that in its ontological aspect, natural law is an ideal order relating to human actions, a divide between the suitable and the unsuitable, the proper and the improper, which depends upon human nature or essence and the unchangeable necessities rooted in it.[14]

The ontological structure of natural law is to be distinguished from the epistemological aspect: how it is known, who knows it, or how well it is known. Not surprisingly, the epistemological issues have come to predominate in the debates about natural law. The ontological framework for natural law, some variation of "Aristotelian nature," is problematic scientifically and philosophically. Nevertheless, many natural law thinkers have made efforts to explain the ways in which such a view of nature can be defended, recovered, and adapted to the present state of scientific knowledge.[15]

Other proponents of natural law skirt the issue by relying more directly on the unique dimensions of practical reasoning, although even in their case a certain view of human nature is implied by or lies at the foundation of the natural law account.[16] Natural law first of all refers to an order in nature that gives substantive content to the notion of human flourishing. Natural law is derived from some concept of the perfection of human nature. It is teleological in character. Thus, the problem of ends, purpose, telos in nature has a direct relevance to natural law theory. The scientific elimination of teleological thinking poses a special problematic for natural law, but the purposeful striving of human beings is equally problematic for mechanistic science.

What is the content of human flourishing? Elaborating on Aristotle, Aquinas argues that human flourishing requires developing the virtues, and the highest virtues at that; but it also requires goods of the body, external equipment, and so on.[17] How to develop the list of basic or fundamental goods is a point of dispute among contemporary natural law theorists. One school has developed a list of seven basic goods: life, knowledge, play, religion, aesthetic experience, friendship, and practical reasonableness.[18] Others use the well-known passage in Aquinas in which he uses a gradation of goods as based on various perfections of human nature.[19] The flourishing of human nature includes perfections of life and health; association of a man and woman in marriage and stability for the rearing and educating of children; association in other forms of community, especially and essentially political community whereby justice is brought forth; and finally, the quest for knowledge and truth.[20]

Following his mentor, St. Augustine, Aquinas further posits the relationship to God as the highest perfection and fulfillment of human nature. Intellect and will, and the orientation to truth and the good, perfected by knowledge and love, inevitably seek an absolute. These ends may seem arbitrary in a moral schema emphasizing personal choice, but their naturalness is conveyed in both city and humanity: in the city by institutional commitments to hospitals, families, political constitutions, schools, and churches; in human beings by the poetic and literary explorations of these great themes of human existence.

The natural law approach encompasses a wide range of psychological, sociological, and political concerns to promote the whole or integral human good and to maintain the conditions for its continued practice, development, and perfection. Accordingly, moral precepts are derived to promote and protect, and even to constitute human flourishing. "Do good and avoid evil"—this is the form or basis for natural law.

Such a general form must issue in specific rules as well as specific habits for human flourishing; that is, it must encompass rules and virtues. Specific precepts for actions are intelligible in the pursuit of these goods; that is, human beings ought to do whatever promotes the full human good and to avoid that which detracts from it. Murder, lying, and infidelity, for example, are clear violations of the human good and are therefore prohibited. In addition to such laws, personal virtues are encouraged to live out life to its fullest. McInerny says, "The moral order is protected on its borders by negative precepts, but in the interior positive precepts suggest the inexhaustible openness of the human good."[21] In this light, virtue must have priority over rule.

How human beings come to know these things, the scope of moral knowledge, and the conditions for moral knowledge pertain to the epistemological aspects of natural law. First of all, it must be said that the notion of natural law does not require a universal assent of mankind. John Locke is an example of a thinker who made the prospects for natural law (as innate knowledge) turn on the condition of universal assent, a test which it must inevitably fail. Human cultures are various and promote or reject various aspects of human flourishing.[22] As Maritain argues, "This proves nothing against natural law, any more than a mistake in addition proves anything against arithmetic."[23]

Thomas suggests that human beings come to know natural law gradually, over time, piecemeal, and with error (much like knowledge of God "by very few, after a very long time, and admixed with many errors").[24] Thomas appeals to human inclination–by experience and reflection, human beings can better grasp intellectually the end in view of their various inclinations. We come to see that we are not random creatures, acting for the point of personal pleasure or whim, but for greater purpose as found in natural structures and embedded in social structures designed to further those ends.

Further, as Aristotle pointed out, although man is political by nature, he must nonetheless found political associations; conventions must assist human nature to achieve its ends well and consistently; good habits need to be established and maintained. Good practice is a condition for the experience of knowing the proper ends in view of inclination. Passion and bad habit can obscure the ends of human striving.

In addition, faith suggests that there are effects of original sin such as a darkened mind and a weak will, militating against conditions for knowing the natural law. Grace and revelation are therefore often necessary for knowing and doing what is right. Thus, avoiding an extreme of pessimism concerning human corruption and the extreme of Pelagian optimism concerning human perfectibility, natural law approaches usually combine the possibility of rational assent to moral truth with a limited expectation about its achievement.[25]

Precept and Justification

Assuming then that natural law contains a list of precepts pertaining to human flourishing (modeled on the form of "do good and avoid evil"), we must realize that the notion of human flourishing requires an extensive rationale and justification. It must lead up to some ultimate conception of human life, meaning, and purpose. To quote Murray again, our thinking must go "to the heart of the very roots of order and disorder in the world—the nature of man, his destiny, and the meaning of human history."[26]

Surely this is what differentiates Aristotle and Athenian gentlemen from Aquinas and third-order Dominicans; or an Augustinian from a Lockean; or a follower of D.A.J. Richards from a Calvinist.[27] How else do we account for apparent agreement concerning a precept for action, but such divergence in application and interpretation of its meaning? It is for this reason that we cannot see natural law merely as a list of precepts; the precepts come from a rationale for human existence which justifies them. But the precepts must take on some ordering, a priority; to leave this to intuition is to beg the question.

At the time of application, the rationale looms large. Metaphysics and theology cannot be kept at bay forever, especially when it comes to the issue of the use of military force. Paul Ramsey claims that the just war theory is derived from the parable of the good Samaritan and not as a precept of "natural justice."[28] He means that the just war precepts were not simply derived from axioms of fundamental good, but elaborated in light of fundamental purpose and images of the good life.

Principle and Prudence

Natural law does provide a set of precepts—rules for action and models for character. Yet there is often an unreal expectation for moral science when it comes to natural law approaches to ethics and politics, especially with respect to just war theory.[29] There seems to be an expectation that the theory is an algorithm that will provide a certain answer at the end. But it can only provide a general or rough outline; the rest is left for good judgment.[30] Debate about war policy must combine empirical and historical judgments, as well as reference to moral principle.

The just war theory provides a principled framework for analysis and discussion, but disagreements about policy may often turn on differing assessments of empirical fact and historical context. For example, a principle states that wars of domination and subjugation of another people are unjust. Was American involvement in Vietnam such a war, or the Soviet fighting in Afghanistan? People of good will can sincerely disagree on these matters.

The just war theory framework allows both parties to be clear as to the nature of the disagreement. The U.S. Bishops' letter *Challenge of Peace* adopts the just war theory framework. The bishops explain that moral principles are universally binding, but a particular application of the principles is not binding because judgment depends upon "circumstances which can change or be interpreted differently by people of good will." Thus, "the church expects a diversity of views even though all hold the same universal moral principles."[31] For this reason they call for civility and charity in discussion, confident in the unity of belief in principle.

The just war theory provides this basis for unity and diversity in discussion. Natural law can provide some general guidelines and help to establish a certain habit of thought and frame of reference, but the actual judgment or recommendation for decision requires knowledge of military and political affairs. The principles are not at all a matter for rationalizing war, but for critical thinking about it.

Persuasion: ad intra *and* ad extra

The fourth and final distinction that serves a key role in interpreting natural law and applying it to the problem of force is the matter of persuasion and the various audiences of moral reasoning. This is related to the issue of universal assent. It is often expected that natural law will demand a universal consent because it appeals to reason and to men and women of good will. Its audience is potentially all.

James Turner Johnson, for example, dismisses the Paul Ramsey approach because it is too embedded in a Christian tradition; he desires a global philosophy which will incorporate Buddhists and Hindus and Moslems.[32] I suspect that Johnson has accepted too uncritically the enlightenment demand for a cosmopolitan point of view demanding an unencumbered self. First of all, this demand forgets the vital importance of persuasion *ad intra*—that is, the maintaining of a tradition which finds the natural law, specifically restraints on war, intelligible and valuable.

The religious traditions which have accepted and develop the just war tradition represent a large part of Western society. Perhaps their numbers or influence are diminishing, but they keep alive the discourse and the ideal. So, too, military professionals draw upon these terms to understand their mission, the limits of the use of force, and to ground their rules of engagement and sense of integrity. Surely this is an important task.

Johnson is right to point out the need for further development and global dialogue on these important matters. But the maintaining of community discourse is a very important matter also. Cadets often ask about the restraints on war—what if the other side does not accept them? If there is a state of war, then by definition, the prospects for persuasion are very limited.

The just war standard defines who we are, as a nation and as a military organization, and sets out criteria for professional and moral performance. The issue of whether limits or restraints on war render our side weak brings us up to the proper issue at hand: the rationale for limited war. We must come to terms with the "Machiavellian lies" that a political community is made weak by justice and that evildoing may contribute to political success.[33]

Aquinas and the Natural Law Rationale for Limited War

The use of military force, deadly in its application, requires some kind of moral justification, since it can be destructive of the fundamental goods of flourishing and leads to gross violations of many known and accepted standards of right conduct. For example, Lincoln spoke as eloquently as Erasmus of the evils of war and admitted that the American Revolution "breathed forth famine, swam in blood and rode on fire; and long after, the orphan's cry and the widow's wail continued to break the sad silence that ensued."[34]

We often think of the evil of war as killing. This is rightly so, but from a natural law perspective, we must also be reminded of the obvious—war destroys families and produces the widow and orphan. (Lincoln in his second Inaugural speaks of binding up the wounds of war, especially taking care of widows and orphans.) In addition, truth is often a casualty of war (the "first casualty"), and war very often brings to a collapse any decent form of political association as it unleashes suspension of civil liberties and the temptation to dictatorship. Indeed, it is a corruption of those who fight, indulging, as Augustine observed, in "the cruel thirst for vengeance, the unpacific and relentless spirit, the fever of revolt, and the lust for power."[35] A whole range of human goods are destroyed and fundamental moral precepts are often abandoned. It is no wonder then that Thomas Aquinas in his classic treatment of the issue of war queries "whether it is always sinful to wage war?" No more war, war never again, is surely the cry of any man or woman of conscience who has seen or lived its devastations.

So why not pacifism? As we noted at the outset, Aquinas forms a reasoned judment that the very goods of flourishing are at stake, perhaps requiring the sacrifice: "*Multo autem magis est conservanda salus reipublicae, per quam impediuntur occisiones plurimorum et innumera mala et temporalia et spiritualia, quam salus corporalis unius hominis.*"[36]

Criteria for Use of Armed Force

Aquinas proposes three basic criteria for the moral use of armed force: proper authority, just cause, and right intention. Each criterion contains important philosophical content. Together they implicitly contain the more elaborate sets of criteria for just war that have been developed over the centuries.[37] These criteria are fairly well-known, but for simplicity and clarity, we shall comment on the core threefold criteria articulated by Thomas Aquinas.

Proper Authority First, war must be an act by "the authority of a sovereign by whose command the war is to be waged. . . ." Thomas views strife as an opportunity for indulging "private feelings of anger or hatred" (II–II 41.1.ad 3). It is incumbent upon political leadership to follow reason, a public reason devoted to a measured good and a measured action. Competent authority is the criterion that prohibits the waging of private wars for personal ambition with anarchic results.

In the American context, it may entail further questions about the separation of powers and congressional war powers. The Civil War saw the anarchy of private armies and bushwhacking across Missouri and Kansas. It is not for private individuals to assemble or summon the people. On Aquinas' account, authority is necessary for a community to act with unity;

authority must make formal consideration about what is to the common good. Private individuals must act for individual or partial goods. The magistrate has "care for the common good" and a duty to "watch over the common weal." There is a profound political teaching contained in this requirement for proper authority.

The nature and purpose of the political community are the terms which set the issue of war in perspective. Just war and proper authority are not first of all a matter of legalism, but rather a condition for political legitimacy.[38] Paul Ramsey is often quoted to the effect that the use of armed force is part of the larger issue of the right use of force; force is part of the *bene esse* or well-being of political life.[39] This first principle distinguishes natural law just war teaching from pacifism and realism.

Aquinas states that the magistrate must use the "sword" to defend against internal disturbances, as well as against external enemies. A judgment is made that the order of justice, to be established and maintained, may require the use of force or the threat of its use. And further, such use of force is morally required if the commitment to a just peace is serious. This is the heart of the issue distinguishing absolute pacifism from the just war theory.[40] There is an empirical/historical claim that order requires force and that such force be in the hands of the authority.

There is also a moral judgment that there are goods worth the risk of war and that "peace at any price" is unacceptable. So indeed if war is *prima facie* evil because it destroys a large range of human goods and flourishing, so too must a magistrate protect such goods from destruction by others. War is therefore a political act, a deliberate act by a political authority for a political good. The pacifist misses this complex reality of the possibility and political conditions for human flourishing. By the same token, the political good sets a limit on what kinds of wars may be waged. The realist approach, by which the conduct of war is bound by no moral limit, undermines the very moral and political legitimacy of the regime.

Just Cause Aquinas' second criterion follows as the next obvious point: a just cause is required, "namely that those who are attacked should be attacked because they deserve it on account of some fault." The judgment is left in general terms, referring to an underlying assumption of culpability or moral regard. For specifics, Aquinas cites Augustine justifying force "when a nation or state . . . refuses to make amends for the wrongs inflicted by its subjects or to restore what is unjustly seized." Aquinas makes no distinction between offensive or defensive wars, as later just war thinkers do; he simply points to an order of justice and acknowledges the possibility of wrongful harm and unjust seizure.

Such a response may be defined as inherently defensive insofar as it is a response to a wrong or a seizure. This notion must not be initially interpreted in a legal sense, but morally and politically in the realm of human flourishing. Thus, the right of war is not simply the self-defense of physical life, although that is part of it; it is a defense of the very order of justice. As Aquinas stated in the opening citation, it involves guarding against "innumerable evils both temporal and spiritual." There is implicit here a judgment of proportionality and last resort.

Lincoln stated in his Second Inaugural Address, "Both parties deprecated war; but one of them would make war rather than let the nation survive; and the other would accept war rather than let it perish." Both sides attempted to gauge certain values, certain claims to justice, at stake in the conflict, and both saw war as a proportionate and last resort. Are there things truly worth the risk of human life? Jacques Maritain states that true civilization "knows the price of human life . . . but it does not fear death, it confronts death, it accepts risk, it requires self-sacrifice—but for aims which are worthy of human life."[41] Such goods are justice, honor, truth, and brotherly love. Given the presumption against war, and given the precious value of human life, one may yet judge that force of arms is a risk necessary to engage for human aims. Proportionality is at work here; it refers to the relation of the achievement of success to the overall cost and loss imposed upon both sides. It is the final declaration or judgment that the war was worth it.

Lincoln refers to the Revolutionary War as a success because it achieved so much with a minimum of bloodshed and loss: "If the relative grandeur of revolutions shall be estimated by the great amount of human misery they alleviate, and the small amount they inflict, then, will this be the grandest the world shall have ever seen." It seems too hard to make a simple claim for the Civil War, with its enormity of death, waste, and destruction. Lincoln's Gettysburg Address is an attempt to establish the worth of the struggle: the dead shall not have died in vain if there is a rebirth of freedom. Lincoln can but briefly mention the land as consecrated by the dead, as if to avert any crass calculation of cost and benefit.

The judgment of proportionality is the hardest to make because of the unknown consequences and magnitude of the human undertaking of war. Yet political justice is not a good to be abandoned to the terrible maw of might. In the Vatican II document, "Gaudium et Spes," statesmen are warned to "conduct such grave matters soberly." It is finally a matter of prudential judgment. Prudence is used here in the expanded sense of the term, which includes a judgment of justice as an end, and selection of the appropriate means to that end.[42]

Right Intention Prudence is deeply affected by the dispositions of the agent. So war is also about character—of the leaders and the people of the nation. Aquinas next lays down a third criterion to ensure that such risk is not taken lightly or with rash spirit: rightful intention. The rightful intention is the advancement of good—ultimately, it is peace.[43] Again citing Augustine, Aquinas excludes the intention of aggrandizement and cruelty: "The passion for inflicting harm, the cruel thirst for vengeance, and unpacific and relentless spirit, lust of power" are "rightly condemned in war."[44]

This demand for right intention not only establishes the proper disposition or frame of mind for conducting such "grave matters soberly," but it also shapes other criteria as well. The goal of a just peace is the proper intention of a magistrate in charge of a commmonweal. It would be a contradiction to intend in the name of justice an unjust goal, an excessive revenge, or desire to dominate others.

The nation itself is in some way part of a larger community of nations. Lincoln rightly mentions in his Second Inaugural the desire for peace in the nation and with all nations. The good of peace for itself, as well as the conditions of flourishing, are goods for all human beings and for all nations. Although the magistrate does not have direct responsibility for the conditions of flourishing in another nation or community, he can will it as a good for all and seek to do no harm to that other.

These three criteria—rightful authority, just cause, and right intention—form the core principles of the just war theory. The three can be unpacked into the longer list of the "*jus ad bellum*," but the simplicity of the three recommends them to our use. With them we are less likely to lose the political and moral origins of the just war effort, and we can better avoid a checklist and casuist mentality.

Right Conduct in War

Where in the traditional three criteria is the obligation of the right *conduct* in war, the "*jus in bello*"? John Finnis is probably correct to say that the distinction between *jus ad bellum* and *jus in bello* is very misleading and "scarcely part of the tradition."[45] It suggests that a just war may posit an end which then comes into conflict with the means. The realist exploits this very distinction, as we shall see. For Aquinas, the limit on conduct follows from the very criteria for the *jus ad bellum.*

Aquinas does not allow a double morality, one for the magistrate and another for the private citizen. The magistrate in care for the commonweal is bound by natural law and so is limited in the taking of life—innocent life may never be taken. In fact, in his treatment of homicide, Aquinas allows the taking of the life of an aggressor in self-defense only as a matter of double effect.[46] Aquinas sees lethal force strictly as a counterforce measure; the humanity of the other is always acknowledged. Thus, it is implied that a soldier who is wounded or who has surrendered is no longer a wielder of force and not an object for attack. Capital punishment may be directed against the noninnocent—those noxious to the community. The noncombatant is not a noxious element to be removed or halted by use of force.

The second criterion of just cause would also place some limitation on conduct of war. The presumed moral warrant for taking up arms for the order of justice is undermined by unjust conduct in war. As Paul Ramsey argues, the modern violations of noncombatant immunity are reflections of a totalitarian political principle that reduces "everyone without discrimination and everyone to the whole extent of his being to a mere means of achieving political and military goals."[47]

The third criterion of intention also touches on the question of means. So often the attack on civilians is simply a matter of "cruel thirst for vengeance" or lust for power. Is there a true necessity to do so, one free of vengeance and *libido dominandi*? Here we get down to the nub of policy, and I turn to a further amplification in light of modern war. For although it cannot be said that earlier magistrates and armies were not tempted and did not act to slaughter the innocent, it must be said that such temptations were more easily resisted in the premodern age. It is now urged that the conditions of modern war require the violation of fundamental moral norms in the conduct of war. We shall challenge this notion in light of the three criteria outlined by Thomas Aquinas.

The Policy Challenge: The Nature of Modern War

The military is limited in the purpose and in the means of what it is assigned to achieve. The basic focus of the natural law approach, of the just war, is that of limited versus total war. This is the issue to be taken up with the realist position. For the realist, the very idea of limits on war seems absurd. Reason of state and military necessity require a total effort.

Total war looms for both political and technical reasons. The political reasons have to do with the spirit of nationalism and the mobilization of a vast population. This entails a tremendous degree of control over the population and a domination of resources for the purposes of the state. It is further intensified by the rise of totalitarian ideology, which makes a moral claim over the total life of society and the population. On the technical front, modern scientific weapons open up the possibility of indiscriminate and mass destruction of populations and territory. John Courtney Murray says that war must be limited as a moral mandate. Is this a credible position?

Doubtless there are powerful trends against the limitation of warfare, as this century has so sadly observed. Michael Howard agrees that the trend toward totality in warfare is due to political and technical factors. The political factor is also present in the development of mass democracy and government control of communications, allowing total alienation of belligerent societies and the mutual perception of figures as evil.

The second, more obvious, factor is the development of modes of destruction of an indiscriminate kind, both technically and strategically.[48] Howard points out that British jurists came to favor the blockade and viewed the entire population as a factor in warfare. From John Seldon onward, he claims, "British jurists argued that the economic activities of civilians, in so far as they made possible the belligerent acts of governments, were a perfectly legitimate target for military activity."[49] Advocates of air war, especially Douhet, simply expanded on this notion that the entire population was a legitimate object of attack.[50]

Military Necessity

Despite these historic trends, the American military forces are not at all committed to overturning the fundamental concepts of the just war. The terms used to explain the laws of war binding on American military personnel are a good indication of the commitments and tensions in the contemporary military. On the one hand, "military necessity" is

> the principle which justifies measures of regulated force not forbidden by international law which are indispensable for securing the prompt submission of the enemy, with the least possible expenditures of economic and human resources. This concept has four basic elements: (*i*) that the force used is capable of being and is in fact regulated by the user; (*ii*) that the use of force is necessary to achieve as quickly as possible the partial or complete submission of the adversary; (*iii*) that the force used is no greater in effect on the

> enemy's personnel or property than needed to achieve his prompt submission (economy of force); and (*iv*) that the force used is not otherwise prohibited.[51]

But as a counterbalance to the principle of necessity, the document makes an unequivocal affirmation of the "principle of humanity":

> [This principle] forbids the infliction of suffering, injury, or destruction not actually necessary for the accomplishment of legitimate military purposes. This principle of humanity results in a specific prohibition against unnecessary suffering, a requirement of proportionality, and a variety of more specific rules examined later. The principle of humanity confirms the basic immunity of civilian populations and civilians from being objects of attack during armed conflict. This immunity of the civilian population does not preclude the unavoidable incidental civilian casualties which may occur during the course of attacks against military objectives, and which are not excessive in relation to the concrete and direct military advantage anticipated.[52]

Noncombatants

One notices the principle of double effect; thus, we may assume a fundamental precept against the killing of noncombatants. Of course, the corresponding principle of military necessity does seem to contain an ambiguity and an escape clause. The realist would point to that gap. Thus, Robert Tucker claims that there is a "significant conflict between the necessities of state and the demands of *bellum justum*. The general nature of conflict must make it clear enough. Whereas reasons of state must reject the claim that there are any inherent limits on the means that may be threatened or employed to preserve the state, *bellum justum* must insist that there are such limits and that whatever the circumstances they may never be transgressed."[53] Dean Acheson's recollections on the Cuban Crisis of 1962 express this view. He recalls that moral considerations were irrelevant to their discussion: "moral talk did not bear on the problem." They only weighed the need for decisive and effective action.[54]

Men of military and political affairs such as Sir John Winthrop Hackett and Michael Howard do not always share this sentiment.[55] The prospect for total war undermines the very rationale of the armed services. The notion of total war is first of all inimical to military professionalism as such. The activity of war is limited by the sheer functional necessity of command and control. Yet, as Michael Howard claims, the military criteria do not always coincide with "the dictates of humanity."[56] Control and limit are possible, but can there be control and limit "derived from criteria other than those inherent in sound strategy and the requirement for good order?" Howard assumes here that the moral is outside of the military–political.

It seems to me that Murray's point is precisely that policy must be in place to make certain things possible. Military planning requires a commitment to principles of natural law and just war theory. The problem with military or political necessity taken by itself is its proneness to a false necessity, but any necessity that is always dependent upon certain ends, purposes, and possibilities. And such ends, purposes, and possibilities are also contingent affairs involving human planning and commitment.

How should military planners define political purpose and construct a policy with appropriate means? The gap between end and means can always be exploited by the realist position. If the goal of quick submission dictates "necessity," then the direct killing of the noncombatant may be necessary. This remains the great question, stemming back to Sherman and the deliberate attempt to punish the civilian population because it would bring the war to a quicker end and ironically be more merciful to do so. Yet the troubling question remains from the natural law approach. Paul Ramsey stated the issue most eloquently:

> At stake in preserving this distinction is not only whether warfare can be kept barely civilized, but whether civilization can be kept from barbarism. Can civilization survive in the sense that we can continue in political and military affairs to *act civilized*, or must we accept total war on grounds that clearly indicate that we have already become *totalitarian*—by reducing everyone without discrimination and everyone to the whole extent of his being to a mere means of achieving political and military goals? Even if an enemy government says that is all its people are, a Christian or any truly just man cannot agree to this.[57]

There is a strong political reason to deliberate, plan, and act within the constraints of the *justum bellum*. To do otherwise commits us to abandoning our reason for being—and fighting to begin with.

Prudence

Thus we come back to an appeal to prudence. Avoiding false necessity, we can strive to remain civilized in our national policies. As John Courtney Murray urged decades ago, the principle of limited war is a moral imperative that demands that the possibility be created as a work of "intelligence and the development of manifold action on a whole series of policy levels with the important inclusion of public opinion and public education."

The realist position begs the question, for policy is precisely the "meeting place of the world of power and the world of morality, in which there takes place the concrete reconciliation of the duty of success that rests upon the statesman and the duty of justice that rests upon the civilized nation that he serves."[58] All bear the full weight of these duties: the political authorities, the citizens who elect them to power, and the military personnel who must implement such policies.

Specific Policy Issues

The Smithsonian Enola Gay Exhibit and the Use of Nuclear Weapons

The fiftieth anniversary of the atomic bombing of Japanese cities passed with great media fanfare and, unfortunately, more show than substance. Perhaps it should not be surprising that a very important issue was obscured by politics, excess rhetoric, and the sound bite. The furor erupted over the Smithsonian's planned exhibit of the Enola Gay, the bomber used in the raid on Hiroshima. The exhibit, dominated by the anti-cold-war, revisionist history of U.S. diplomacy, also included some important accounts of the actual effects of the bomb and some challenges to the moral acceptability of its use.

Because of the strong revisionist themes, the American Legion and the Air Force Association challenged the appropriateness of the exhibit. The American Legion called for its cancellation.[59] On January 30, 1995, the planned exhibit was eliminated, and only the fuselage of the Enola Gay remained for exhibit. The instrument for the most problematic and disturbing act of war is presented without context or discussion. It is a shame that this event was commemorated without the discussion or debate it deserves. The natural law approach surely provides us with the intellectual framework to do so in a fruitful way, and the writers in this tradition have provided the best account of it.

Revisionists and Apocalyptic Accounts

The revisionist and apocalyptic accounts have their footing in the fact that the bombing clearly crossed the line of international law and the deep principles of *jus in bello*. It is often countered that aerial bombing had already crossed the line in the European theater and in the Tokyo firebombings. This of course does not justify either type of bombing and is a very weak defense. It is one of the few weak arguments mustered by Donald Kagin.[60] Although Kagan admits the bombings were "terrible acts against unarmed civilians," he claims that condemnation will not avoid such acts and that they were the lesser of two evils.

Thus, it is hard to separate the moral issue—was this an act of indiscriminate bombing?—and the proportionality issue—was this act necessary? The revisionist weighs in on the latter; the moralist on the former. The two are of course interconnected, but it was not always the case that we would clearly admit the indiscriminate nature of the act. In his announcement after the event, Truman said in his opening line: "Sixteen hours ago an American airplane dropped one bomb on Hiroshima, an important Japanese Army base."

So too, during the Nuremberg trials, in response to the absurd Nazi defense that indiscriminate attacks on Jews were legitimate if American indiscriminate attacks on Japanese cities were so, the American tribunal responded with the following counterargument:

> A city is bombed for tactical purposes; communications are to be destroyed, railroads wrecked, ammunition plants demolished, factories razed, all for the purposes of impeding the military. In these operations it inevitably happens that nonmilitary persons are killed. This is an incident, a grave incident to be sure, but an unavoidable corollary of battle action. The civilians are not individualized. The bomb falls, it is aimed at the railroad yards, houses along the track are hit and many of their occupants killed. But that is entirely different both in fact and in law, from an armed force marching up to these same railroad tracks, entering those houses abutting thereon, dragging out the men, women, and children and shooting them. It was agreed in behalf of the defendants that there was no moral distinction between shooting civilians with rifles and killing them by means of atomic bombs. There is no doubt that the invention of the atomic bomb, when used, was not aimed at noncombatants. Like any other aerial bomb employed during the war, it was dropped to overcome military resistance.[61]

There is an evasive line in this statement was not an accurate description in the initial statements by our leaders. More honest accounts would admit that the shift in our approach to war demanded an abandonment of the distinction, or at least that it be so broadly construed such that all members of the enemy society are de facto combatants, and it is fitting that they be punished or at least included in the scope of legitimate targeting.[62] I am not qualified to comment upon the question of the necessity of its use. I am persuaded by the antirevisionist accounts of the decision-making process. I can appreciate the prudential context for the decision, and the veterans' feelings of appreciation for being spared the mission of an attack on the Japanese mainland. But I can only say that something of great importance was lost when the fateful decision was made: a moral concern for humanity.

Balanced Approach

It can only lead me to believe with Father Murray that the possibility for its nonuse must be constructed by the work of policy makers. Natural law provides the most balanced approach. Writing in *Orbis* almost fifteen years ago, just war theorist James E. Dougherty, in reviewing the newly published works by William O'Brien and James T. Johnson, made the following wise remarks:

> If the saturation bombings of Dresden, Leipzig, and Tokyo must be judged indiscriminate, the atomic bombing of Japan must be regarded an even more gross violation of discrimination by any standard of allowable collateral damage. . . . Neither Johnson nor O'Brien wants to imply a moral condonation of the atomic bombings of Hiroshima any more than I. One should remember though that in the chaos of war policymakers have to make decisions on partial and imperfect knowledge. . . . We should be slow to levy blame against President Truman and his advisors. . . . No policymaker had ever seen an atomic bomb detonated. . . . But neither should we try, even while recognizing the arguments from proportionality, to throw a mantle of moral approval over the A-bombing of Japan. Such a tragedy does not deserve to be exploited for purposes of political criticism, as it often is. Just war moralists who are concerned about the possibility of future nuclear war are quite correct in trying to understand the tragedy of Hiroshima and Nagasaki in context without bestowing their moral approval.[63]

Thus, within the just war framework, a fairly balanced discussion of the issue has been carried on. Perhaps the Smithsonian should ask these authors to draft a new text for a new exhibit.

Now that we have the real truth as a matter of record, a utilitarian or pragmatic justification for the use of atomic weapons can have a corrosive effect on our attitudes toward war and the tactics employed. I believe that this is where the full-blown or thick natural law approach is needed to convey the basis for noncombatant immunity.

In the classroom many cadets are inclined to the pragmatic or utilitarian approach to justify the indiscriminate attacks. The antinomy with respect to laws of war makes no difference. To cite a Kantian principle of respect for all humanity or an ideal kingdom of ends gets nowhere. An intuitive grasp of the good of life does not carry the day either, especially when more lives may be saved by the effort or if it is the saving of American lives in time of war. Proportionalism is too attractive. What does seem to make an impact are statements from Paul Ramsey or from Solzhenitsyn about the sacred quality of life and inviolability of moral order. Jeffrie Murphy, in a Kantian attempt to use the notion of human dignity to shore up noncombatant immunity, ultimately must invoke the Bible for support.[64]

Do we want it both ways? George Grant approvingly quotes Nietzsche to the effect that "Kant is the great delayer."[65] Is it forward to Nietzsche, or back to premodern grounding of human dignity, moral restraint, and Aristotelian prudence? I believe that the just war principles must find their root in the natural law, with its metaphysics of human nature, creation, and the good. For proper commemoration and for planning for the future, a natural law basis for the *justum bellum* invites embrace.

Humanitarian Intervention

Since the end of the cold war, the United States military finds itself being put to new uses, including humanitarian intervention. Somalia, Kurdish areas of Iraq, Haiti, and Bosnia have engaged national troops in missions other than warmaking. Peacekeeping and humanitarian relief are now the considerations for the use of military force.

The just war theory has been helpful in providing the basic categories for inquiry.[66] Ironically, the humanitarian intervention cases bring on a shift in philosophical adherents. The hawks who would invoke just war doctrine for intervention in favor of national interests now find themselves balking at the notion. The liberals or doves who strenuously objected to American intervention and the very idea of just war are readily latching on to intervention for humanitarian purposes. Walzer states, "Old and well-earned suspicions of American power must give way now to a wary recognition of its necessity."[67] While I agree that the impulse for humanitarian intervention is consistent with the just war theory and its natural law approach, I believe that its fundamental political, ethical, and even theological premises would serve to place some important qualifications to it.

Criteria for Intervention A look at Aquinas' threefold criteria focuses the issues. The right intention is central. Intervention is often a pretense for national aggrandizement or special interests, but in these cases, the humanitarian factor rises above the more selfish intentions. The international cooperation entailed by such operations has an elevating effect, for in these cases the *jus ad bellum* does not involve a direct appeal to national defense. It involves rather an appeal to justice or the duty to prevent injustice or to do good for the life, health, and security of others. The national interest factors in only indirectly, through the appeal to international stability or order.

Nevertheless, the case is not quite so simple, as we shall see. Lacking the ballast of national interest, the sail of humanitarian concern may well push a nation (or nations) well beyond what it may realistically sustain and accomplish. The principle of intervention clearly and consistently follows from the natural law approach, but prudence may well dictate significant qualifications.[68]

The very status of the nation-state is one of the most important issues brought on by the call for humanitarian intervention. The principle of nonintervention as an international policy has served for centuries as the assumed or default position. Questioning the very idea of statehood or state sovereignty, Kenneth Himes points out that national integrity is being pressured from above and below: from above through the agency of international organizations such as transnational corporations and international rights organizations; from below by ethnic and local demands for greater autonomy or control. From a moral point of view, Himes argues war has lost a rational justification, whereas intervention now possesses it. On the other hand, Hehir realizes that intervention threatens the order of states, while war confirms the right of states ultimately to decide when their vital interests are at stake.[69] The nation-state is the form of political association that has some measure of Aristotelian "sufficiency" and therefore is a morally rightful object of defense and loyalty. The political standing of the common good in the nation-state is one of the most important issues for political philosophy today.[70] For the present, however, I should just like to point out a few dilemmas brought up by the humanitarian intervention cases in light of the just war framework.

Dilemmas of Intervention The first dilemma, simply put, is this: Today an international body or even a multinational front is a new source of rightful authority in determining the appropriateness of intervention. A justification for the new authority is to overcome selfishness or national domination. Some writers have even used the Kantian notion of universalizability as a check on selfishness or particular interest.

Yet, to the degree that a particular nation does not recognize its own vital interest at stake, it will not be inclined to intervene or have the popular support to do so. Perhaps humanitarian sentiment kept aflame by news coverage could sustain interest, but it would surely be for a short period of time (and until another concern emerges elsewhere) and of shallow commitment.[71] This situation would imply that such interventions could succeed only with the barest of casualties. The deeper question here is on what grounds a nation could ask its young men and women to die in such a mission if a more direct connection to national interests or honor is not clear. As we get closer to vital national interests and honor, the quality of disinterested intervention weakens. Perhaps these interventions may require a new set of volunteer forces, whose mission will combine the peace corps with the national guard. Many military professionals have questioned the wisdom of attempts at redefinition of the military mission to focus on drug interdiction, civil order, and humanitarian aid.[72]

One argument in favor of the special status of nation-states is the sheer fact that no other higher association is yet seriously able to form or field a combat army. The loyalties are simply too precarious. A cosmopolitan army may be a contradiction in terms. We are brushing up against some of deeper questions concerning human nature—the love of one's own, the conditions for spiritedness, and the mediation of the universal through particular communities and traditions.[73]

An additional qualification concerns the probability for success. Although advocates of intervention are attentive to the issue, perhaps they are not attentive enough to the political and ethical requirements for success. The presence of civil war and the failure of a nation-state are political in nature. The success of a mission requires political rebuilding. It is a long process, involving self-interest and partisanship, yet humanitarian intervention demands a degree of nonpartisanship and neutrality.

Eventually, the occupying force will be pulled to one side or another, or it will enter only because of a successful defeat or military setback to one of the parties. Intervention in Iraq for the Kurds was made possible by the military defeat of Hussein by allied forces. In Somalia, the warlords came to view the United States as a hostile force. The Bosnia peace established by NATO inflicted setbacks on Serbian forces, yet America wishes to appear as a neutral peacekeeper. But as the interventionists seek to prosecute Serbian war criminals and evict Serbian populations from previously held areas, one can only hope that the fragile peace or cloak of neutrality remains in place so that the Serbian forces do not attempt to make war on the peacekeepers as they have in the past.

Perhaps I can end on a note made by Paul Ramsey many years ago—the greatest obstacles to peace on earth are the different conceptions of peace. So, too, the warrant of humanitarian intervention, especially when done in the name of human rights, may well be an imposing of one understanding of rights on another. It is for this reason, I believe, that the dominant view is still attracted to the principle of nonintervention as the safer guide. But American political purpose and its military means must be connected to the natural law basis for the regime. As Arkes wisely observed concerning American debate over our intervention in Vietnam, "The claims of 'prudence' should not furnish a crude license for evading duties borne of principle when it becomes inexpedient to honor them."[74]

Conclusion

To close, I wish to return to the opening issue concerning the function of the natural law approach to appeal to all men and women of good will and reason. The discovery of natural law principles as they pertain to the use of military force has been a long and gradual process. It has been primarily focused in Western society and now has become embodied in international law.

James T. Johnson is right to point out how this is a "culture-conditioned conception of natural law." Further, he says that we must "reach beyond the de facto acceptance of the international law of war to discover whether it is possible to identify underlying this phenomenon a global consensus as to justice in war."[75]

I admire Johnson's ambition to strive for the global consensus. But I believe our first task, and the more urgent one, is the "persuasion *ad intra*"—to encourage our intellectual and religious traditions to carry on the natural law inquiry into human affairs; to seek to educate and cooperate with our policy makers and military professionals concerning the truth of the natural law approach, which is the tradition of the promotion of human flourishing in political association and the need to have military force prepared for limited war in its defense. Then we must turn our attention to "persuasion *ad extra*," to other religious traditions and ideological trends, to engage the work of reason to advance the cause of justice as best we can.

NOTES

1. Thomas Aquinas, *Summa Theologia* I–II, q. 40, a. 4: "There is much more reason for guarding the common weal (whereby many are saved from being slain, and innumerable evils both temporal and spiritual prevented), than the bodily

safety of an individual." (Fathers of the English Dominician Province, trans. New York: Benziger, 1947.) This passage shows that there is more at stake than simple survival or physical injury; cf. Arkes, Hadley, *First Things: An Inquiry into the First Principles of Morals and Justice*. Princeton: Princeton University Press, 1986, pp. 15ff, 204–31.

2. See Brodie, Bernard and Fawn M., *From Crossbow to H-Bomb*. Bloomington: Indiana Univ. Press, 1973; Nef, John U., *War and Human Progress: An Essay on The Rise of Industrial Civilization*. Cambridge: Harvard Univ. Press, 1950; Fuller, J. F. C., *The Conduct of War*, 1789–1961: Minerva Press, 1961.

3. Murray, John Courtney, S.J., *Morality and Modern War*. New York: Council on Religion and International Affairs, 1959, p. 19.

4. Walsh, Kenneth T., "Bush's 'Just War' Doctrine," *U.S. News and World Report*, 4 February 1991, 52–53; Sheler, Jeffrey et al., "Holy War Doctrines," *U.S. News and World Report*, 11 February 1991, 55–56; Woodward, Kenneth L., "Ancient Theory and Modern War," *Newsweek*, 11 February 1991, 47; Walzer, Michael, "Moral Ambiguities in the Gulf Crisis," *The New Republic*, 28 January 1991, 13–15.

5. See Himes, Kenneth, "Just War, Pacifism and Humanitarian Intervention," *America*, August 14, 1993, 10–15, 28–31; Roberts, Adam, "The Road to Hell: Humanitarian Intervention," *Harvard International Review*, Fall 1993, 10–13, 63; Walzer, Michael, "The Politics of Rescue," *Dissent*, Winter 1995, 35–41; Phillips, Robert L., and Duane L. Cady, *Humanitarian Intervention: Just War vs. Pacifism*. Lanham, Md.: Rowman & Littlefield, 1996.

6. Thus Joseph Boyle, a prominent representative of the Grisez - type natural law approach, contributed "Natural Law and International Ethics" to the useful survey in Nardin, Terry, and David R. Maple, *Traditions of International Ethics*. New York: Cambridge University Press, 1992; see also Boyle, Joseph, "*Just and Unjust Wars*: Casuistry and the Boundaries of Moral Discourse," in *Ethics and International Affairs* 11(1997): 83–96; see also the contributions by John Finnis and Joseph Boyle in Nardin, Terry, *The Ethics of War and Peace*. Princeton: Princeton University Press, 1996. Paul Ramsey's work in this area is seminal: Ramsey, Paul, *War and the Christian Conscience*. Duke: Durham, 1960; *The Just War: Force and Political Responsibility*. New York: Scribner's, 1968; see also, Ramsey, Paul, and Stan Hauerwas, *Speak Up for Just War or Pacifism*. University Park: Pennsylvania State University Press, 1988.

7. See Johnson, James Turner, "Historic Roots and Sources of the Just War Tradition in Western Culture," in *Just War and Jihad*, edited by John Kelsay and James Turner Johnson. New York: Greenwood Press, 1991: 3–30. See also Johnson, James T., "The Just War Idea and the Ethics of Intervention," The Joseph A. Reich, Sr., Distinguished Lecture on War, Morality, and the Military Profession, number 6, 17 November 1993, United States Air Force Academy, CO.

8. Christopher, Paul, *The Ethics of War and Peace: An Introduction to the Legal and Moral Issues*. New York: Prentice Hall, 1994; and Hartle, Anthony, *Morality and Military Decision Making*. Lawrence: Univ. of Kansas Press, 1988 (both are West Point instructors); Wakin, Malham, *War, Morality and the Military Profession*, 2nd edition. Boulder: Westview Press, 1990 (Air Force author); Johnson, David Eugene, Roush, Paul E., and Sills, Clarence Frank, Jr., *Readings in Philosophy and Ethics for Naval Leaders*. New York: American Heritage Press, 1995 (Annapolis instructors).

9. In the contemporary debate, the just war theory has been declared dead, bankrupt; or irrelevant by a number of prominent philosophers and theologians. Their reasons include the development of nuclear and other weapons of mass destruction, the dysfunctional nature of nations and states in a time of globalism, the rediscovery of authentic Christian pacifism, and the tendency to rationalize self-interest. I wish to thank Loras College for the opportunity to discuss the viability of the just war categories ("Just War Theory: Rationalization or Restraint?" unpublished lecture delivered at Loras College, Dubuque Iowa, 1992).

10. Murray, John Courtney, *We Hold These Truths*. New York: Sheed and Ward, 1960, p. 253.

11. Compare Finnis, John, Joseph Boyle, and Germain Grisez, *Nuclear Deterrence, Morality and Realism*. Oxford: Oxford Univ. Press, 1987; and Novak, Michael, *Moral Clarity in the Nuclear Age*. Nashville: Thomas Nelson, 1983.

12. "*Manifestum est quod omnia participant aliqualiter legem aeternum, inquantum scilicet ex impressione eius habent inclinationes in proprios actus et fines*." *Summa Theologiae* I–II q. 91, a. 2.

13. "*Unde et in ipsa participant ratio aterna, perquam habet naturalem inclinationem ad debitum actum et finem*." Ibid.

14. Maritain, Jacques, *Man and the State*. Chicago: Univ. of Chicago Press, 1951, pp. 86–88.

15. See Simon, Yves R., *Practical Knowledge*. New York: Fordham Press, 1991, pp. 115–36; also Simon, Yves R., *The Great Dialogue of Nature and Space*. New York: Magi Press, 1970; also DeKoninck, Charles, *The Hollow Universe*. London: Oxford Univ. Press, 1960.

16. Finnis, John, *Natural Law and Natural Rights*. Oxford: Clarendon Press, 1980; see also George, Robert, *Natural Law*. Oxford: Oxford Univ. Press, 1990.

17. Aquinas, Thomas, *Summa Theologiae*, I–II, qq. 1–5. Cf. Aristotle's *Nicomachean Ethics*, Bk. I. Cf. Sullivan, Roger, *Morality and the Good Life*. Memphis: Memphis State Univ. Press, 1977; and Cooper, John M., *Reason and Human Good in Aristotle*. Cambridge: Harvard Univ. Press, 1975; Maritain, Jaques, *Moral Philosophy*. New York: Scribners, 1964, ch. 3.

18. Finnis, John, *Natural Law and Natural Rights*, pp. 85–90; see also by Finnis, *Fundamentals of Ethics*. Washington D.C.: Georgetown Univ. Press, 1983. Cf. Hittinger, Russell, "Varieties of Minimalist Natural Law Theory," in *The American Journal of Jurisprudence* 34 (1989): 133–70.

19. McInerny, Ralph, *Ethica Thomistica: The Moral Philosophy of Thomas Aquinas*. Washington, D.C.: CUA Press, 1982, pp. 44 ff. Also his *St. Thomas Aquinas*. Notre Dame: Univ. of Notre Dame Press, 1977, pp. 63–67. Rice, Charles, *50 Questions on the Natural Law*. San Francisco: Ignatius Press, 1993, pp. 44 ff. Simon, Yves R., *The Tradition of Natural Law*. New York: Fordham Univ. Press, 1965, pp. 122–25.

20. See *Summa Theologiae* I–II, q. 94, a. 2.

21. McInerny, *Ethica Thomistica*, p. 48.

22. See Benedict, Ruth, *Patterns of Culture*. Boston: Houghton Mifflin, 2d ed., 1959.

23. Maritain, *Man and the State*, p. 90.

24. Aquinas, Thomas, *Summa Theologiae*, I.1.1 and I–II.91.4; see the article by Hittinger, Russell, "Natural Law and Catholic Moral Theology," in *A Preserving Grace: Protestants, Catholics, and Natural Law*, Michael Cromartie, ed. Grand Rapids: Ethics and Public Policy Center–Eerdmans, 1997.

25. On the limits of communicability and certitude of moral truth, see the discussion by Yves R. Simon in *Practical Knowledge*. New York: Fordham Press, 1991, pp. 71–76.

26. Murray, John Courtney, *We Hold These Truths*. New York: Sheed and Ward, 1960, p. 253.

27. See my "Three Philosophies of Human Rights: Locke, Richards, and Maritain," in *In Search of a National Morality*, William Ball, ed. Grand Rapids: Baker Press, 1992, pp. 246–57.

28. Ramsey, Paul, *Just War*, p. 142.

29. See Wallace, William, "The Atom Bomb: A Moral Dilemma," in *From a Realist Point of View*. Washington: University Press of America, 1979, pp. 247–62.

30. "For a number of years we have been witnessing a tendency, in teachers and preachers, to assume that natural law decides, with the universality proper to the necessity of essences, incomparably more issues than it is actually able to decide. There is a tendency to treat in terms of natural law questions which call for treatment in terms of prudence. It should be clear that any concession to this tendency is bound promptly to cause disappointment and skepticism." Simon, Yves R., *The Tradition of Natural Law: A Philosopher's Reflections*, ed. Vukan Kuic, intro by Russell Hittinger. New York: Fordham University Press, 1992 reprint, p. 23. Simon explains the role of prudence in *Practical Knowledge*, ed. Robert J. Mulvaney. New York: Fordham University Press, 1991, pp. 1–40. See Hittinger, Russell, "Natural Law and Catholic Moral Theology," op. cit.

31. National Conference of Catholic Bishops, *The Challenge of Peace: God's Promise and Our Response*. Washington, D.C.: USCC, 1983, #9. See also "Vatican Synthesis," *Origins*. 9 August 1984.

32. Johnson, James Turner, *Just War Tradition and the Restraint of War*. Princeton: Princeton University Press, 1981, pp. 120–21.

33. For a natural law critique of Machiavellian realism, see Maritain, Jacques, *Man and the State*. Chicago: Univ. of Chicago, 1951; and *The Range of Reason*. New York: Scribner's, 1952.

34. Lincoln, Abraham, "Address before the Springfield Temperance League," 1842; found in *The Political Thought of Abraham Lincoln*; Richard N. Current, ed. Indianapolis: Bobbs-Merrill, 1967, p. 33.

35. Augustine, *Contra Faust*, xxii. 74; cited by Thomas Aquinas in ST II-II q. 40 a. 1; see *Augustine: Political Writings*, translated by Michael W. Tkacz and Douglas Kries (Indianapolis: Hackett Press, 1994), p. 221

36. Aquinas, Thomas, *Summa Theologia* I–II, q. 40, a. 4: "There is much more reason for guarding the common weal (whereby many are saved from being slain, and innumerable evils both temporal and spiritual prevented), than the bodily safety of an individual."

37. *Viz.*, right authority, just cause, last resort, proportionality, right intention, reasonable chance of success, aim of peace, proportionality of means, and noncombatant immunity from direct attack.

38. See Simon, Yves R., *Philosophy of Democratic Government*. Notre

Dame: Univ. of Notre Dame Press, 1990, ch. 1 on authority; see Hittinger, John P., "Jacques Maritain and Yves R. Simon's Use of Thomas Aquinas in Their Defense of Liberal Democracy," in David M. Gallagher, ed., *Thomas Aquinas and His Legacy*. Washington, D.C.: Catholic University of America Press, 1994.

39. Ramsey, *Just War*, ch. 1.

40. A similar point is made by C. S. Lewis in "Why I am not a pacifist," in *The Weight of Glory and Other Addresses*, revised and expanded edition, Walter Hooper, ed. New York: Macmillan, 1980.

41. See Maritain, Jacques, "The Immortality of Man," in *A Maritain Reader*, Donald and Idella Gallagher, eds. Garden City: Doubleday, 1966, pp. 212–13.

42. See Coll, Alberto, "Normative Prudence as a Tradition of Statecraft," in *Ethics and International Affairs*, Joel H. Rosenthal, ed. Washington, D.C.: Georgetown University Press, 1995, pp. 58–77.

43. Ryan, John K., "The Thomistic Concept of Peace," in *Modern War and Basic Ethics*. Milwaukee: Bruce, 1940, pp. 5–15.

44. Augustine, *Contra Faust*. xxii. 74; cited in Aquinas, op cit.

45. Finnis, John, "The Ethics of War and Peace in the Catholic Natural Law Tradition," in Nardin, *The Ethics of War and Peace*, p. 25.

46. II-II 64, a. 6; see Ramsey, Paul, *War and the Christian Conscience*. Durham: Duke Univ. Press, 1960, pp. 34–59.

47. Ramsey, Paul, *The Just War*, p. 153.

48. Howard, Michael, "Temperamenta Belli," in Michael Howard, *Restraints on War*. Oxford: Oxford University Press, 1979, pp. 7–8; see also Ryan, John K., "The Character of Modern War," in *Modern War and Basic Ethics*.

49. Howard, Ibid., p. 9.

50. Douhet, Giulio, *The Command of the Air*, trans. Dino Ferrari. New York: Coward–McCann, 1941; see Paret, Peter, ed. *Makers of Modern Strategy: from Machiavelli to the Nuclear Age*. Princeton: Princeton University Press, 1986, pp. 629–35.

51. *International Law–The Conduct of Armed Conflict and Air Operations*, Department of the Air Force Pamphlet 51–710, 19 November 1976, pp. 1-5–1-6.

52. *International Law—The Conduct of Armed Conflict and Air Operations*, Department of the Air Force Pamphlet 51–710, 19 November 1976, pp. 1-6–1-7.

53. Tucker, Robert W., *Just War and Vatican Council II: A Critique*. New York: Council on Religion and International Affairs, 1966, p. 21; see response by Paul Ramsey, "Robert W. Tucker's *Bellum Contra Bellum Justum*," in *The Just War*, pp. 391–424.

54. Found in Wakin, Malham, *War, Morality and the Military Profession*, p. 182.

55. Hackett, Lt.-General Sir John Winthrop, *The Profession of Arms: The 1962 Lee Knowles Lectures Given at Trinity College, Cambridge*. London: Times Publishing Company, 1962; reprinted by the United States Air Force Academy, 1974; see "Today and Tomorrow" in lecture three.

56. Howard, Michael, "*Temperamenta Belli*: Can War be Controlled?" in Michael Howard, *Restraints on War*. Oxford: Oxford University Press, 1979, p. 4.

57. Ramsey, Paul, *The Just War*, p. 146.

58. Murray, John Courtney, *Morality and Modern War*. New York: Council on Religion and International Affairs, 1959, p. 19.

59. For a transcript of the exhibit and an account of the events leading to its cancellation, see Philip Nobile's *Judgment at the Smithsonian*. New York: Marlowe and Company, 1995.

60. Kagan, Donald, "Why America Dropped the Bomb," *Commentary* (September 1995): 17–23. Letters in response appeared in the December issue.

61. *Trials of War Criminals Before the Nuremberg Military Tribunals*, Nuernberg October 1946–April 1949 (US Govt Printing Office) vol 4, p. 467. I wish to thank Lt. Col. Patrick Tower USAF for showing this material to me.

62. I have found useful here an unpublished manuscript by USAFA history professor Lt. Col. Peter Faber USAF, "The Ethical–Legal Dimensions of Strategic Bombing During World War II: An Admonition to Current Ethicists," a paper presented at the Joint Services Conference on Professional Ethics, held at Fort McNair, Washington, D.C., January 1996.

63. Dougherty, James E., "Just War, Nuclear Weapons, and Non-combatant Immunity," *Orbis* (Fall 1982): 765–87.

64. "For there is, I think, an insight of secular value in the religious observation that men are the 'children of God.'" Jeffrie G. Murphy, "The Killing of the Innocent," *The Monist* 57, no. 4 (1973).

65. Grant, George, *English Speaking Justice*. Notre Dame: Univ. of Notre Dame Press, 1978.

66. See Hehir, J. Bryan, "Intervention: From Theories to Cases," in *Ethics and International Affairs* Vol. 9 (1995): 1–13; Himes, Kenneth R., "Just War, Pacifism and Humanitarian Intervention," *America* (August 14, 1993): 10–31. See especially Phillips, Robert L., and Duane L. Cady, *Humanitarian Intervention: Just War vs. Pacifism*. Lanham, Md.: Rowman & Littlefield, 1996.

67. Walzer, "The Politics of Rescue," p. 40.

68. See Arkes, *First Things*, pp. 280–82; it is interesting to note that Arkes makes his case for intervention, and explains the qualifications that prudence can make, in a discussion of the Vietnam War. Unlike the new converts to humanitarian intervention, Arkes presents a consistent account.

69. For Himes and Hehir, see note 65.

70. John Finnis' article on the instrumental nature of the political common good raises the issue sharply; presented at APPI conference in 1994; to be published by Oxford Press.

71. I acknowledge here the influence of Clifford Orwin, who recently lectured at the Air Force Academy on this matter.

72. See Dunlap, Charles J., Jr., "The Origins of the Military Coup of 2012," *Parameters* 22.4 (Winter 1992–93): 2–20.

73. For an ethical analysis, see Alasdair MacIntyre's "Is Patriotism a Virtue?" University of Kansas lecture, 1985.

74. Arkes, First Things, p. 281.

75. Johnson, James Turner, "Historical Roots and Sources of the Just War Tradition in Western Culture," p. 26.

Part Six

Doubts and Affirmations

Questions About the Place of Natural Law

KENT GREENAWALT

I offer my perspectives on natural law with some trepidation. Despite a continuing interest in natural law, I have never kept abreast of its scholarship. I doubted that I could fairly appraise the prospects of natural law; and I knew that in presenting my views before a distinguished group of natural law scholars, I was bound to say things that would seem naive or ill-informed. Nevertheless, David Forte's sense that having comments from someone outside the tradition might have value seemed right; and he was more persuasive than I was resistant.

This essay shares thoughts about natural law as informed by the preceding articles and discussions, which altered my views on some subjects. I have focused on more general aspects of natural law theory, not such "local" questions as whether the United States Constitution embodies natural law or whether American judges and legislators are now likely to be drawn to natural law approaches.

I retain some major questions about natural law. These are partly concerns of clarification—how may we understand claims about natural law? But they are partly doubts about those claims as I understand them. I begin with these questions:

1. How culturally relative, if at all, are valid, specific moral conclusions?
2. How universally valid are forms of moral reasoning and, in particular, the categorical approaches of a traditional natural law view?
3. How crucial are religious convictions for (1) belief in something like a natural law and (2) specific conclusions on moral and political issues?
4. How much is a natural law approach a general inquiry about human fulfillment and common good; how much is it a particular tradition with long-standing and settled ways of approaching moral and political problems?

5. What judgments about the place of human law and the roles of actors within legal systems need to be made, if one is to recommend adoption of moral conclusions for official action?

I concentrate on a full, robust, natural law position, a view that has roots in Aristotle and the Stoics and has found its most influential formulation in the writings of St. Thomas Aquinas. I have always perceived a large gap between that position and such partial claims as Lon Fuller's "procedural natural law"[1] and Ronald Dworkin's "naturalism."[2] The modern systematic account of natural law with which I am most familiar is John Finnis's *Natural Law and Natural Rights*.[3] Although his emphasis on self-evident human goods, as contrasted with teleological purposes, represents a controversial reading of Aquinas, I believe that many of his positions are broadly representative.

The Basic Natural Law Position

According to my understanding, which here fits with David Forte's introduction,[4] the standard natural law position rests on a number of premises.

1. Human life is integrally related to all of existence.
2. Human nature is universal.
3. The defining characteristic of human beings is their reason or rationality.
4. Human beings have inherent purposes, or self-evident goods.
5. These purposes, or goods, are discoverable by reason, reason being understood in a broad sense to include the light of experience.
6. Morality is objective, universal, and discoverable by reason.
7. People's moral obligations are consonant with their own true purposes, or their realization of self-evident goods, and with their true happiness.
8. At the deepest levels, there is no conflict between individual good and the common good.
9. Human laws appropriately reflect the natural law (though not every dictate of natural law should be subject to state coercion). Human laws appropriately determine details left open by natural law, such as the precise punishments for various crimes, and they settle matters of indifference.
10. Human laws that are not in accord with natural law are not

> "really" law in some sense. A failure to accord with natural law may occur if a law requires behavior that natural law forbids or forbids behavior that natural law values, or if the burdens and benefits of a law are highly unjust.

I have four brief comments about this list. First, I have not included any connection between natural law and God. Although in our times belief in natural law is strongly correlated to belief in God, *and* opponents of natural law views often mistakenly suppose these views are simply religious, the tradition has consistently been that individuals can discover the natural law, independent of their particular religious beliefs. Finnis certainly claims, further, that one can establish the validity of natural law theory without invoking religious premises. These points are crucial issues about the plausibility of a robust natural law.

My second comment concerns the idea that a human law that violates natural law is really not a law. Finnis and others, going back to Aquinas, have acknowledged that even an unjust law may have a claim to obedience in some circumstances; a citizen should not regard such a law simply as if it does not exist. The law is a law *in some sense* even if it lacks a purpose to promote the common good. Since most people who are not natural lawyers believe that moral reasons may justify disobedience of immoral laws, what distinguishes them from natural lawyers in this respect? Their conceptual apparatus and their exact approach to issues of obligation and obedience may differ subtly,[5] but these differences do not mark some major disagreement. The query whether an unjust law is "really" a law is less significant than it once may have seemed.

My third comment ties closely to my second. Natural law is dominantly a theory about human good and morality. Legal positivism, by itself, is a theory about what makes a human law a law; that theory can be joined with a wide range of theories about moral truth, about how judges should interpret, and about obligation to obey the law. The true opponents of natural law are not legal positivists as such, but proponents of competing theories of morality (many of whom are also legal positivists). If we assess how useful natural law is for the development of human law, we must ask how well natural law serves as an account of moral understanding *and* how much it can contribute to law. For the latter inquiry, we need to develop an account of how moral determinations should affect actors in legal systems. We might conclude, for example, that legislators should take account of the truths of natural law, but that judges interpreting statutes should be guided by standards of original meaning.

My fourth comment concerns natural rights theory, of the sort developed by John Locke, which has been highly influential in our history. That theory may or may not be based on a state of nature analysis of the kind found in Locke. According to natural rights theory, what reason mainly teaches that is relevant for political society is the limits of justified interference with the freedom of individuals. These limits apply to other individuals and to the government. Typically, natural rights theory connects to a social contract explanation of the legitimacy of government. The government has authority because people have created it to protect them from wrongful interferences with liberty. If the government trespasses against protected liberty, it becomes illegitimate and may be overthrown. Much of what I say applies both to traditional natural law theory and to typical natural rights theory; I do pause to work out possible variant implications for natural rights.

Difficulties in Using Natural Law to Develop Human Law

I have always been modestly skeptical about the value of a genuine natural law approach to assist in the determination of human laws. My skepticism has been grounded in: (1) doubts about the appropriateness of some legal actors relying directly and dominantly on natural law; (2) doubts about the practical usefulness of persuasive natural law claims; and (3) doubts about the soundness of other natural law claims. Very roughly, my impression has been that some highly general claims are persuasive but not very useful, and that many specific claims that would be useful, if persuasive, are not persuasive. As I shall explain shortly, my views about this have shifted in light of the articles presented. Before exploring this complicated subject, I shall begin with a few words about my first doubt, covered in such illuminating ways in the articles of Terry Hall[6] and Christopher Wolfe.[7]

Considerations of the Place of Government and Roles of Particular Officials

When officials concern themselves with legal coercion, they must ask what is the appropriate role of government and law, as well as what behavior is moral. Many lies, for example, that may violate natural law should not be the subject of legal redress. Although some passages in Hadley Arkes' powerful essay might be read to suggest that the law should be invoked if a moral wrong is serious,[8] I do not think he denies that *any* decision about law must involve judgment about the proper role of the state. No decision rests solely on a determination that behavior violates important moral norms. Beyond this, the role of particular officials will matter.

I will start with judges. When judges interpret legal materials, they usually do not (and should not) decide simply what they think is the proper role of the state and what is moral behavior in the circumstances. They must consider their responsibilities vis-a-vis other actors: the makers of constitutions, legislatures, executives, higher courts, and earlier judges on their own court. Even if a decision comes down to moral evaluation, a strong argument exists, at least for common-law cases, that judges should be guided substantially by community sentiments, not by their own assessment under the best moral theory. I do not mean direct moral evaluation has *no* proper place; indeed I think it has much more of a place in constitutional adjudication than Professor Wolfe's strict originalist approach allows. But anyone needs to devote substantial thought to the proper role of courts in particular kinds of cases before he or she can conclude that they should adopt principles called for by natural law.

Matters may seem simpler for legislatures and executives, since their task is to adopt and administer good laws; but even here complexities face us. How far should government discourage actions that are immoral, but which most citizens do not regard as such? Professor Hall explores this problem, as does former Governor Cuomo's famous Notre Dame speech defending his support of permitting abortions.[9] In respect to another kind of legal power, what should a governor do if he believes capital punishment violates natural law, but the state authorizes capital punishment and many murderers are sentenced to it? Should the governor commute *every* death sentence, or is this an improper exercise of the power of executive clemency? If natural law theory is sound and useful, natural law should figure in the work of legislators and executives, but concerns about role and about the functions of law preclude any easy assumption that what is called for is unblinking application of natural law to positive law.

Is There a Helpful Universal Natural Law?

We now reach more difficult terrain. I have always thought the plausibility of natural law views has depended substantially on their level of generality, and that as plausibility increases, usefulness for actual choice decreases. My opinion about this shifted in reaction to the articles within this volume.

Some of the papers in this volume start with relatively uncontroversial premises about human good and work through to significant ideas about public policy. George Wright's discussion of welfare[10] is a notable example.

He shows that careful attention to the implications of broad premises can be useful.

Judge Noonan's stirring defense of a commitment to natural law[11] and a number of the papers have brought home to me a different distinction, a distinction between (1) reasoning broadly about public problems from the standpoint of human fulfillment and common good, and (2) using the vocabulary, concepts, and modes of analysis characteristic of the particular natural law tradition, as does William May's paper on bioethics.[12] Perhaps, as Judge Noonan suggests, everyone does natural law as everyone speaks prose. But, if this is so, we are left to ask what the distinctive natural law tradition offers for the resolution of social problems.

Much of the argument in the papers of Professor Wright and others could be cast in terms of widely accepted values, or a Rawlsian starting point. Are the *distinctive* natural law components crucial? I am not sure. Of course, even if much of the argument could be served in a different form, the natural law focus, if sound, could provide conceptual clarity and give guidance on some troublesome issues. In any event, my earlier doubt about the potential usefulness of most general natural law precepts has partially transmuted into a question of whether practical conclusions based on some of these precepts *need* the precepts or could typically be equally well grounded in other approaches.

On some issues, the distinctive natural law tradition adopts approaches and conclusions that are not generally shared. At the conference, as in contemporary public life, abortion, assisted suicide, and homosexual relations loomed large. The general tenor was that permissiveness in law was a baleful commentary on the state of contemporary society, that we are quickly moving toward a culture of narcissism and death that substitutes selfish satisfaction of preference for human good. With reasoning and conclusions about such issues in mind, I want to examine the claims of universality that natural lawyers typically make.

The Challenge of Historicism and Cultural Relativism Three of the vital premises of natural law—that human nature is universal, that human purposes or goods are discoverable by reason, and that moral principles are objective and discoverable by reason—are sharply challenged by varieties of historicism and cultural relativism. Very briefly, we are the people we are because we are members of a particular culture. Our concepts of understanding and what we take as good reasons are the products of that culture, as are our moral beliefs. There is, so the attack goes, no universal human nature, no transcultural reason, no objective moral perspective. The notion of a fundamental human reason that can discern moral principles is a delusion, one of the culturally bound premises of traditional Western society.

This is a stark challenge to what I call traditional natural law theory. I believe that the real issue is not either/or, but more or less.

Is there a universal human nature? Anthropologists tell us how different mainstream modern Americans are from people who have lived in various parts of the globe across the ages of history; but all people want food, a sense of well-being, and companionship. There are some universal human characteristics, but much is culture-dependent. The same is true about human reason; to a substantial degree, our sense of what is reasonable depends on our culture *and* our particular place within it.

If some human goods are universal, the understandings of those goods and their orderings in context are different. Natural lawyers, of course, acknowledge that individuals order goods in many ways in developing the best life for them; but different cultures also have different orderings. If these variations concerned *only* the lives individuals choose for themselves, they might pose no problem for natural law; but the variations also concern what people regard as appropriate interferences with others and as appropriate laws. To some extent, moral principles are relative to culture.

Are Cultural Variations in Social Morality Consonant with Universal, Objective Moral Answers? Where does this leave us? Cultural variations certainly do not rule out the possibility of objectively determinable, universally valid moral judgments; but we must proceed with caution. Cultural variations do preclude the possibility that, as to all significant moral questions, people of ordinary good will in different cultures will take the same view. We should not expect, for example, that people in all cultures will agree about assisted suicide or abortion, to take two perplexing modern issues. No doubt, people in virtually all cultures do believe murder and theft against other full members of the community are wrong, but that will hardly help settle difficult moral and legal questions.

On reflection, we can see that no one could expect universal human reactions directly to settle difficult moral questions, since questions are not regarded as difficult when reactions are uniform. Natural lawyers are well aware that controversial issues divide people. Their arguments for their views do not depend on their views attracting nearly unanimous acceptance.

What difficulties, if any, do cultural variations pose? As more about social morality is seen as culturally dependent, a higher percentage of moral questions will be seen as difficult, at least if one tries to think in cross-cultural terms. For example, one might no longer be so confident that monogamy is best for human beings in general. The presence of difficult moral problems is one difficulty, but by no means the greatest.

Cultural variations cast into some doubt the processes by which natural lawyers move from premises to conclusions. Very roughly, we can think of arguments that begin from premises that have a very strong claim to acceptance, such as that life and friendship are inherent human goods. These premises are usually supported by broad cross-cultural acceptance (though perhaps not in the conceptual formulation given them by natural law theory). From the premises, a careful process of reasoning yields conclusions that are much more controversial.

We should by no means suppose that advocates of natural law think social institutions should be uniform across cultures. Most obviously, matters that might require legal enforcement in some societies may be handled well enough by conscience and social morality in others. Exactly when to use the coercive apparatus of positive law is a question of prudence. Further, as James Stoner points out,[13] the genuine achievement of basic human goods can be accomplished by variant structures of rights and duties, and the best structures may depend partly on stages of economic growth. Thus, to take the topic of Professor Stoner's paper, we should expect the rights and duties connected with the ownership of private property to vary at different periods of economic development.

Finally, there is the point emphasized by Terry Hall. What measures should be embodied in law depends on the moral views of the broad population, as well as on what is morally right. It might be better not to enforce some moral conclusion of natural law if that conclusion has insufficient acceptance. Thus, the natural law approach hardly is rigid and static in its implications for legal orders. Nevertheless, natural lawyers do typically adopt the view that most basic moral conclusions are universally valid. It is that view that I am examining here.

Belief in universal, objective moral answers, discoverable by reason, might be defended on this basis: Starting with premises that have a very powerful appeal to our understanding and are widely accepted, we can reason our way to correct moral answers whose acceptance is much less widespread.

Thus, to take a powerful example, a compelling and widely shared view about human beings might ground a conclusion that slavery is morally wrong, even if slavery has seemed acceptable to many cultures and still may seem acceptable in isolated pockets of societies. How could people have made the moral mistake of accepting slavery? They might somehow not have recognized that certain groups of people are full human beings, a factual mistake about the fundamental characteristics of those people. Or they might mistakenly have supposed that moral respect extends only to an "in group," whereas reason can somehow establish that we owe respect to all people. Or they might have reached a conclusion about what victory in war entails that reason can show to be faulty.

In any event, refined reason might build on basic judgments to reach conclusions that are not universally shared. A different example might be a rejection of homosexual marriage, built on a premise that procreation is the central purpose of marriage.

Many claims about the substantive content of natural law and natural rights contain details that are rejected in some cultures. In principle, conclusions recommended by reason used in this way could have universal force. But a serious problem remains with the claims of reason itself; the reasoning employed may rest on categories and methods of thought that themselves may be culture-dependent.

I want to offer three examples. For the latter two examples, I draw on my personal experience. I do so to suggest a somewhat different way of reasoning about moral issues than one is likely to find in most treatments by proponents of natural law. I then connect this critique to the broader theme of cultural variation.

My first example is the principle that one should not intentionally take life, except in self-defense, etc. Suppose one is given a choice of killing one innocent person and saving nineteen, or watching someone else kill all twenty. According to the standard natural law view, one should not kill. I have no resolution for this acutely painful moral dilemma; but the categorization that so confidently concludes that one should refuse to kill strikes me as rigid and as unconvincing for such extreme circumstances.[14] For the rules of warfare, so ably examined by John Hittinger,[15] a prohibition on intentionally killing innocent civilians may be a healthy restraint on the common excesses of military conflict, but I do not believe a line between intentional and knowing (but not intended) killing can do all the work it has done in traditional natural law morality.

My second example is homosexual relations and gay marriage. In my own life, love in marriage has had a transforming power; it, and the children of my marital union, have been the two greatest blessings of my life. Robert George talks of "the intrinsic good of marriage itself as a two-in-one-flesh communion of persons" that is consummated and actualized by acts of the reproductive type. Only such sexual acts can be "truly unitive."[16] Other sexual acts fail to accomplish this basic good and are immoral. Acknowledging that 2 to 5 percent of the population may be strongly inclined from birth to desire homosexual unions, Professor George says that the moral course of action for them, as for nonmarried heterosexuals, is to remain celibate. George is careful, measured, thoughtful, patient, and respectful of those of opposing opinion. However, my experience of life tells me that to consign to a lifetime of celibacy many persons who are not called to such a life by devotion or inclination is to insist that they should deprive themselves of one of our richest sources of deep affection and understanding. His substantive position, though not his intention, strikes me as harsh, even cruel.

My third example is the problem of assisted suicide. I may begin by saying that I thought *Roe v Wade*[17] was wrongly decided; that I have not expected a constitutional right to commit suicide, much less to be assisted in the effort, in my lifetime; that I do not favor a general legal right to commit suicide; and that I would be troubled if I were a legislator considering a limited right of the terminally ill to have assistance in dying.

I agree with David Novak that fear of lack of control has much to do with the wish of many people to "die with dignity;"[18] indeed, I think that graceful acceptance of dependence is a lesson that many who are dying teach us all. But Professor Novak is strangely silent about the nearly unbearable pain that some persons suffer as they slowly die. He remarks, "Of course, now such a suicidal course of action is only advocated for those who are 'terminal.' But if death is our inevitable lot in the world into which we have been cast, then who is terminal and who is not can only be a matter of inherently imprecise degree, not one of essential kind."[19]

I understand Novak's philosophical point about "degree," but the sentence in which the point is made asks me to deny what life has taught me. The two months between the discovery that my late wife Sanja had incurable cancer and her death was a time of great stress and extreme intensity. Although sadness about her approaching death was never absent from my feelings, our already strong love was deepened yet more as she embraced my support, and I was moved by her incredible spirit and courage. For Sanja, suicide was never an option; she expressed her powerful will to live until she lost consciousness for the last time. For me, this period was unlike any other in my life, and I know that was true for Sanja. If Novak's implication that terminal illness is just a matter of degree is not actually insulting or insensitive, it is at least remote from the lives of people who themselves are terminally ill or who have loved ones in that condition. Perhaps a right to assistance in dying will create pressures, internal and external, for people to die to save money; perhaps a limited right of the terminally ill will evolve into a broader right of people to receive help in dying. But Professor Novak's paper and the comments of some others seemed not to respect the special plight of those who suffer painful terminal illness.

In each example I have chosen, the recommended natural law approach relies on abstract, categorical modes of thought in preference to greater emphasis on qualities of lived experience and contextual distinctions drawn from that experience. In relation to the widely cited and widely attacked thesis that women, in general, and men, in general, adopt different approaches to moral problems,[20] we can easily place the approaches of traditional natural law far on the male side of the spectrum. I have always had a distrust for highly abstract ideas, whether they come from the political left or the political right.

What has my challenge to do with cultural variation? At the most obvious, I am objecting to a certain approach to moral reasoning and proposing an alternative I believe is better. Thus, I assume that there are sounder and less sound ways to reason about moral matters, and I offer an approach I regard as sounder. Moreover, I most certainly am located within the same broad culture as the natural lawyers I dispute, so my claims here have little directly to do with cultural variations.

Here are the connections. Whether people are attracted more to abstract principles or contextual evaluation itself depends significantly on habits of mind and personal psychology. While all we can do is to pay attention to a wide range of positions, and adopt and defend those that seem most persuasive, we should be aware of the possibility that reason itself may not resolve which among certain plausible approaches is the most sound. If such differences exist within single cultural traditions, we can certainly expect even greater differences if the reference point shifts to a broad range of human cultures. If the abstract, categorical approaches of a traditional natural law seem bound to *one particular strand* of the wide culture of Western Europe, they will seem even less universal from a transcultural perspective.

In sum, my theoretical point is this. We do not have an evidently correct, universal form of moral reason that can build an imposing edifice of moral norms on the basis of simple compelling, widely shared judgments about human goods and moral obligations. Our processes of reason about these matters no more escape cultural dependence than do particular moral judgments that are outside some shared universal core.

The Best System Natural lawyers might make a modest retreat at this point. They might acknowledge that, over some range, different cultures make different moral judgments and employ different forms of moral reason; but they might further claim that the system of reason and judgments represented by the natural law tradition is indeed the best. This view might be combined with a belief in a certain kind of moral progress, namely, that thoughtful people of good will can make more accurate moral appraisals as human civilization develops. (I put the view of moral progress in this form so that it can explain the increasing rejection of slavery, without being refuted by horrors like the Holocaust.) It is logically possible that the forms of reason employed by most natural lawyers are both partly culture-dependent and the best of which people are capable, or at least the best yet developed.

Such a retreat saves the crucial claims of universality and objectivity, but carries certain difficulties. Natural lawyers would have to surrender the idea that their norms should seem valid to thoughtful reasonable people in all cultures. Some of the norms would seem valid only if the members of other cultures could be persuaded to exchange their forms of moral reasoning for some of the forms dominant in Western societies. Since we are here supposing that a particular type of Western reasoning about morality is actually superior, perhaps that persuasion could be effective (though it is not inconceivable that people with other cultural backgrounds would be unable to see this superiority). Even if the persuasion could be effective, one could not expect it to work comfortably, since people of other cultures might have to drop deeply ingrained characteristics of reasoning, not an easy task for moral and social evaluation. (Scientific reasoning may be different, scientific successes giving some approaches a strong appeal across cultures.) Many people of good will in other cultures would remain unpersuaded by natural law reasoning leading to specific moral norms.

Another difficulty, already mentioned, is more fundamental. If forms of moral reasoning differ in some crucial ways, how can natural lawyers be confident their forms are best? They might be confident if they could rely on crucial standards of evaluation that transcend cultures. They might claim, for example, that natural law reasoning and conclusions, if followed, yield lives that are recognized by all as more fulfilling than lives lived under other approaches. Unfortunately, it seems more likely that forms of reasoning within cultures fit fairly well the ideas of human fulfillment within those cultures.

Observance of natural law norms may lead to fulfilling lives, as proponents of natural law see them; observance of other approaches may lead to fulfilling lives, as people of other cultures see them. None of this rules out the possibility that some forms of life may really be most fulfilling and some disputed moral norms really best; but establishing this by reason will be difficult, to the extent that reason is culture-bound.

Intracultural Evaluation One might believe in a kind of natural law for a particular culture, claiming that from a location within the premises of one's own culture, a single answer to any moral question will be correct. What counted as a single culture would be troublesome; but for some issues of international commercial practice and human rights, the relevant culture might be the modern international community. For the United States, at least, it could be argued that correct moral answers are salient not only for legislation but also for interpreting a Constitution adopted in the midst of wide acknowledgement of natural law.

If natural lawyers lowered their sights to this degree, they would still have to face the worry that internal conflicts or contradictions in values might preclude uniquely correct moral answers. They would also have to face troublesome constitutional issues for which the implications of a Lockean natural rights outlook might differ from those of a Thomistic natural law. The main problem with this idea of intracultural natural law is that it surrenders a central aspect of natural law and natural rights theories, their claim to universality.

Religious Premises Natural lawyers may invoke religious premises to support their claim to universality and to deflect the argument that practical reason is culture-dependent. That argument, if valid, does not preclude the possibility that a Higher Spirit exists who loves us and establishes true moral standards. Without attempting to discuss the bases for such a belief, I shall simply say here that I hold it.

Some natural lawyers may suppose that their attachment to valid religious belief establishes that objective moral standards do exist and that their views reflect these standards. David Novak argues forcefully in his paper that ideas of natural law are much more deeply rooted in religion than has commonly been recognized. A natural lawyer who relies significantly on religious premises can retain the claim to universal objective moral standards, but cannot expect all reasonable people of good will to accept them (unless his or her religious belief includes the idea that God gives everyone the reasoning power to ascertain their validity).

An approach that relies on religious conviction faces another obstacle. Why should we suppose that religious perceptions are any less culture-dependent than moral understandings? If one began without any religious commitment, one would probably conclude that religious perspectives are at least as culture-dependent as moral perspectives, to which they are intimately tied. Nevertheless, the believer may suppose, based on faith or on overwhelming evidence of some kind, that the core of his convictions is reliably true. Once this is granted, he may think that moral understandings tied to the convictions in various ways either are true to a high degree of certainty or are at least more likely to be true than moral understandings otherwise developed.

A Christian believer in natural law may think that detailed moral norms that have been developed in the Christian natural law tradition (especially the Roman Catholic tradition) are reliable partly because they, and the forms of reasoning that lead to them, have the authority of the tradition. Religious believers who are more skeptical about the unique validity of their own tradition might conclude that some religious truth helps to support universal moral truths, but have less confidence that their own religious tradition yields privileged insights.

Norms That Vary by Culture I want now to reprise possible natural law groundings on a rather different assumption about basic premises and detailed conclusions. Suppose that one thought that certain minimum basic moral premises could be established, but that their proper application might vary widely among cultures. One might think, for example, that human beings should count equally and should care for each other's welfare. In some cultural settings this might properly yield a "rights"-focused morality; in others informal mutual care might predominate. This account would assert a universal, objective standard for morality, but one whose best application could vary significantly. (One might compare within a single culture the differences between family morality and the morality that governs relations among strangers.) One would acknowledge that many detailed moral norms would be valid only for some times and some places. To return to one of our examples, gay marriage might be appropriate for some cultures but not all.

As with more detailed norms, such a flexible system might be grounded on (1) compelling, widely shared moral judgments about human good plus reasoned development; (2) the best reasoned understanding among culturally variant forms of reason; or (3) religious convictions. Because this system would be more modest in its universal claims, it might seem somewhat easier to support. The problem of how to support the basic premises would remain, but the more limited the premises are, the more reasonable it will be to assert their transcultural truth.

Assume, for example, these premises of equality and caring are at the core of the moral understanding of many religions and are more *indisputably* enjoined by particular religions than highly specific norms (as the injunction to care is more indisputably an aspect of Christianity than the principle of double effect). One could move more confidently from a belief in religious truth to a belief in the validity of these basic premises than one could move to disputable, specific norms.

With what confidence could one move from the fundamental premises to specific norms for particular cultures? My first observation is that one could have more confidence assessing one's own culture than other cultures. This is because of one's greater familiarity with its social conditions and because the forms of reasoning dominant in a culture are more likely to reflect how broad principles can best be worked out in that culture than in other cultures.

This does not mean all assessment of other cultures is foreclosed. One can sometimes see plainly that other cultures do not treat people equally or even care about some of their members. Nor could one adopt without examination the dominant forms of reasoning in one's own culture. Feminists and critical race theorists, for example, have argued that forms of reason in our culture tend to thwart genuine equality. Any assessment of how well fundamental moral premises are achieved in context would need to approach our own cultural reasoning, as well as specific cultural norms, with a critical eye.

Conclusion

My own views lie along the lines of belief in certain fundamental moral perspectives that are universally valid, with appropriately different manifestations in different cultures. My belief in the truth of these views rests substantially on religious conviction. Insofar as religious conviction plays a direct role in our moral evaluations, further questions arise about its appropriate place in the political decisions of liberal democracies. These complex questions I put aside here.[21]

Many of the difficulties I have raised about the relation between natural law approaches and different approaches in other cultures apply when one focuses on disagreements between natural lawyers and proponents of different views within our own culture. I have illustrated this point with my own dissent from analyses of moral issues that strike me as too categorical and detached from human experience. I have focused on other cultures because, as to them, the claim that disagreements can ultimately be resolved (at least in theory) on the basis of a common reason seems most vulnerable.

I should emphasize that natural law reasoning and conclusions have an important place, even if skepticism about assertions of universality, reason, and unique correctness are well-placed. If judges must often make moral assessments, natural law approaches, at a minimum, are one fruitful source of moral evaluation with a rich tradition in our culture and, arguably, with some embodiment in our Constitution. As such, they can be recommended for judicial consideration. But natural lawyers want to claim much more than this; it is these more ambitions claims to which I have responded.

It remains to supply tentative answers to the questions I posed at the beginning of this chapter.

- Complex judgments about the place of human law and the roles of particular officials need to be made before one proposes adoption of moral conclusions for official legal action (Question 5).
- "Natural law" connotes a general inquiry about human fulfillment and common good, and also a particular tradition with distinctive approaches to moral and political problems; conflation of these two senses is bound to yield confusion (Question 4).
- Some specific moral conclusions are culturally relative, valid for some cultures but not others. The number of relative moral conclusions is greater than most writers in the natural law tradition have recognized (Question 1).
- Forms of moral reasoning themselves, including categorical approaches of traditional natural law, are relative to a degree that natural lawyers have not acknowledged (Question 2).
- Reason can establish a kind of minimum natural law, including such precepts as that people should refrain from willfull killing of members of their own communities. However, religious convictions are a crucial condition for justified belief in a robust natural law that asserts universal values and uniquely correct moral answers (which themselves may vary somewhat by culture). Religious convictions also bear on specific conclusions about moral and political issues (Question 3).

I have called these answers "tentative." They represent my present thinking about problems of immense difficulty. My own perspectives were enriched greatly at the conference, and I realized that natural law approaches could be more useful in resolving controversial practical social problems than I had previously recognized. I hope this essay, like the conference, will promote dialogue with those many scholars who will think I grant too much to the natural law tradition and most especially with those from within the tradition who find my doubts about universal moral norms derivable from reason to be ill-conceived and unpersuasive.

NOTES

1. *See* LON FULLER, THE MORALITY OF LAW (1969).
2. *See especially* RONALD DWORKIN, LAW'S EMPIRE (1986).
3. JOHN FINNIS, NATURAL LAW AND NATURAL RIGHTS (1980).
4. *D. Forte, The Natural Law Moment*, in DAVID FORTE, ED., NATURAL LAW AND CONTEMPORARY PUBLIC POLICY 3–9 (1998).
5. I discuss these differences in KENT GREENAWALT, CONFLICTS OF LAW AND MORALITY (1987).
6. *T. Hall, Natural Law and Legislation*, in DAVID FORTE, ed., *supra* note 4, at 135–156.
7. *C. Wolfe, Natural Law and Judicial Review*, in DAVID FORTE, ed., *supra* note 4, at 157–189.
8. *H. Arkes, Axioms and Accidents*, in DAVID FORTE, ed., *supra* note 4, at 109–134.
9. *M. Cuomo, Religious Belief and Public Morality: A Catholic Governor's Perspective*, 1 NOTRE DAME JOURNAL OF LAW, ETHICS, AND PUBLIC POLICY 13 (1984).
10. *G. Wright, Natural Law and Welfare*, in DAVID FORTE, ed., *supra* note 4, at 280–297.
11. *J. Noonan, The Natural Law Banner*, in DAVID FORTE, ed., *supra* note 4, a 380–383.
12. *W. May, Natural Law and Bioethics*, in DAVID FORTE, ed., *supra* note 1, at 41–54.
13. *J. Stoner, Natural Law and Property*, in DAVID FORTE, ed., *supra* note 4, at 193–218.
14. *See K. Greenawalt, Natural Law and Political Choice: The General Justification Defense; Criteria for Political Action; and the Duty to Obey the Law*, 36 CATHOLIC UNIVERSITY L. REV. 1 (1986).
15. *J. Hittinger, Natural Law and the Use of Military Force*, in DAVID FORTE, *supra* note 4, at 333–360.
16. *R. George, Nature, Morality and Homosexuality*. in DAVID FORTE, *supra* note 4, at 29–40, 36.
17. 410 U.S. 113 (1973).
18. *D. Novak, Natural Law and Privacy*, in DAVID FORTE, ed., *supra* note 4, at 13–28.
19. *Id.* at 24.
20. *See generally* CAROL GILLIGAN, IN A DIFFERENT VOICE, (1982).
21. I develop my views in RELIGIOUS CONVICTIONS AND POLITICAL CHOICE (1988) and PRIVATE CONSCIENCE AND PUBLIC REASONS (1995).

The Natural Law Banner

JOHN T. NOONAN, JR.

When I was the editor of the *Natural Law Forum*, Calvert Magruder, then chief judge of the United States Court of Appeals for the First Circuit, asked me in not unkindly fashion, "Why are you Catholics so interested in natural law?" I was surprised by the question. Natural law was supposed to be what was common to all, an ecumenical way to morality, not the province of a particular denomination. I am afraid that I also caught the prejudice in the question. A speaker who addresses "you people" has distanced himself by more than six degrees of separation from those he is addressing. I could have answered, "We have particularly pondered the fates of Germany and Russia, where the natural law was derided." Instead, I smiled ecumenically.

During the course of my editorship, I received various letters from correspondents unfamiliar with, or incredulous about, natural law. One correspondent simply addressed "The National Law Forum," eliminating the problem. Another wrote to "The Natural Law Farm," assuming that in Indiana we grew our product like corn. Many would-be contributors entitled their offerings "The Natural Law And __________," as if it were necessary to mutter the right mantra to write about natural law. In the face of bias, ignorance, and ultraconformity, I suggested that the magazine change its name to what it now calls itself, *The American Journal of Jurisprudence*. I did not, however, abandon the substance of natural law.

"Law is not a brooding omnipresence in the sky." Half, at least, of the charm of this famous Holmesian phrase is that it denies an oxymoron. No omnipresence could be confined to the sky. The other attraction of the phrase is its implied truth. Law is something that happens here on earth. It is as natural as the trees or the mountains. Or almost. It is as natural as human creatures.

Human creatures make law the way human creatures produce food and make habitations. They do so because they cannot live without it. My favorite example is the anonymous car pool that has operated for over ten years between Berkeley and San Francisco. The would-be passengers, men and women, line up at a spot where the would-be drivers stop. Two, but no more than two, passengers enter each car; the first always gets in back, the second in the front passenger seat. The car drives off. The passengers read their paper or magazine or, at the driver's initiative, engage in conversation with him or her. The car proceeds into the fast lane, a no-toll lane on the Bay Bridge that is reserved for car pools. The driver drops off the two riders near the bus terminal in the city.

Is this quotidian set of transactions a case of natural law? Of course; it is shot through with natural law: the treatment of other human beings as equals, the respect for the rights of such other persons, and the practice of reciprocity as the key to harmonious cooperation. The details may vary—the make of the automobile, the profession of the driver, the number of the passengers, even whether the protocol on conversation is observed—but in essentials the transactions are governed by unwritten law, and in essentials that law is immutable.

In myriad ways, myriad human laws, infused with natural law, perform their three major functions of channeling human beings in cooperative ventures, of coercing a few evildoers into refraining from harm, and of teaching millions of uncertain or confused human beings what is a good way to conduct a transaction or lead their lives. Law in these functions is a purposeful process engaged in by human beings. It is unintelligible; it would not exist if the persons in the process were not seeking to realize a human good. The process will go better the more those engaged in it are aware of human capacities and attitudes and dynamism, are aware of human nature. In this way, as Bracton observed more than seven centuries ago of English law, law is "a branch of moral philosophy."

That all law derives from a bedrock in humanity, that all law is meant to carry out purposes, and that each purpose incorporates a vision of a human good and therefore incorporates a morality based on human nature, appear to be propositions so indisputable that they do not need stating or restating. Natural law must be part of the enterprise of human law. Q.E.D. Who denies it?

The principal deniers are of two very different kinds: the positivists and the individualists. The positivists identify with written commands of the state. They know no other measure, although in the United States they add written constitutional norms to these commands. It is their banner that Holmes unfurls with his rejection of the nonexistent oxymoronic omnipresence. They flourish now on American courts, even on the highest, and often under the mask of being conservatives. Pilate's "*Quod scripsi, scripsi*" is dear to them; they will alter it only to read, "*Ouod scripserant, scripserant.*" The control of law by its moral purpose, by human nature, makes them uncomfortable, uncertain, and fearful of anarchy. Better, they think, the certain words of the statute. The positivists, for example, continue to celebrate *Erie RR v Tompkins* because it enshrines Holmes's dictum as if the written law of a state were more readily ascertainable than unwritten federal common law.

The individualists or libertarians act from a different impulse—the sense that each rational adult person should decide his or her destiny for him or herself. The notion of nature is not congenial to them. The communal ties that bind us are oppressive to them. Like the heroes of German romanticism, they thrill to the uniqueness of their existence. Every restraint upon it in aid of the weak is an affront. Every check upon its exercise in order to protect those not able to protect themselves is a type of tyranny. Their banner was held aloft in *Casey v Planned Parenthood.*

Each of these camps, of course, is talking a brand of natural law—they can no more avoid it than they can avoid writing prose. The positivists cling to the written script because they implicitly contend that is the way that humans must take to escape subjectivist chaos. The individualists celebrate individual unfettered liberty because, they insinuate, such liberty is the human goal. Without covert reference to human nature, neither position can be maintained. Formally and facially, they do not acknowledge this covert dependence. The explicit defenders of natural law, in the view of the deniers, have a morality. The positivists and the individualists are impartial and are beyond the morality that common human nature invites us to develop.

A hidden bond unites these two very different kinds of opponents of natural law and makes their brands of natural law inauthentic. Either they explicitly reject the existence of a Being transcending humankind or they are what Theodore Parker termed "practical atheists;" they proceed as if no such Being existed. The sting in Holmes's hostile comment on the brooding omnipresence is in its intended reference to the God of New England Congregationalism: hence the attraction of the quotation to other unbelievers.

The *ressentiment* nourished against natural law arises because one who says "nature" says "creatureliness," and creatures require a Creator. Law requires a lawgiver, and one who speaks of a law governing human purposes speaks of a Lawgiver transcending the state and individual desires. The foundations of natural law rest in the Shaper of Nature, the Creator of creatures, the Ordainer of law, a Being whose external purposefulness transcends humankind.

Does natural law have a banner of its own under which to fight? The answer is No and Yes. No, first, because the natural law approach is one hospitable to inquiry. It is a way of exploring human capacities and dynamisms as thoroughly as possible, asking the most challenging questions, examining closely every convention and every assumption, seeking the most satisfying solutions. It need not and should not have a prearranged agenda. The most glorious contribution this approach has ever made was the discovery, after thousands of years of institutionalized slavery, that such slavery was *contra naturam*, an evil to be extirpated.

That discovery once enunciated, natural law became a banner under which it was fought. Appeal to Christian belief had a part as well. But in the century from William Blackstone to Theodore Parker, it was the rational indefensibility of the institution that animated first British law and then the campaign of the American abolitionists. The positivists said constitutional law sanctified it and statutory law should enforce it. The individualists said the slave was their property; no one had the moral right to tell them how to use it.

"An ordinance of nature"—that is, natural law—as Parker declared in attacking the infamous Compromise of 1850, was what forbade the introduction of slavery into California. The demand of nature for equality shines through Lincoln's critique of *Dred Scott,* through his speech at Gettysburg, and through his advocacy of the Thirteenth Amendment. Natural law triumphed in emancipation.

Today we face issues as grave as those facing the nation at the time Parker spoke and at the time Lincoln acted. The issues need to be explored as freely and as fully as slavery was once debated. The issues, like the slavery issue itself, are only incidentally economic, although major economic interests would be glad to have them buried in obscurity. The issues go to the purposes of human beings joined as equals in society, in which some by nature are strong and some are weak and nature creates the bond uniting us.

First the child, secure in the recesses of her mother's womb, was put outside the law. Now it is the child untimely ripped from the womb, and the geriatric grandmother hustled by her heirs, and the member of the HMO cut off from his benefits by his insurer and from his lifeline by his physician, who stand beyond the protection of the law. But not forever. When the natural necessity of cooperative protection of the weak becomes evident, the natural law becomes the barrier, the natural law becomes the cause. Its flag is visible in the storm and in the battle.

Contributors

HADLEY ARKES, Edward Ney Professor of Jurisprudence and American Institutions, Department of Government, Amherst College

JOHN COONS, Professor Emeritus, Boalt Hall, University of California

DAVID F. FORTE, Cleveland–Marshall College of Law, Cleveland State University

ROBERT GEORGE, Department of Politics, Princeton University

KENT GREENAWALT, University Professor, Columbia School of Law, Columbia University

TERRY HALL, Department of Philosophy, Center for Thomistic Studies, University of Saint Thomas

JOHN HITTINGER, Department of Philosophy, United States Air Force Academy

PATRICK J. KELLEY, Southern Illinois University School of Law, Southern Illinois University

WILLIAM MAY, Michael J. McGivney Professor of Moral Theology, John Paul II Institute for Studies on Marriage and the Family

JOHN MUELLER, Senior Vice President and Chief Economist, Lehrman Bell Mueller Cannon, Inc.

HON. JOHN T. NOONAN, JR., United States Court of Appeals for the Ninth Circuit

DAVID NOVAK, University of Toronto

JAMES R. STONER, JR., Department of Political Science, Louisiana State University

CHRISTOPHER WOLFE, Department of Political Science, Marquette University

R. GEORGE WRIGHT, Cumberland School of Law, Samford University

Index